Computer Strategies
1990–9

Computer Strategies 1990–9
Technologies—Costs—Markets

GEORGES ANDERLA

and

ANTHONY DUNNING

JOHN WILEY & SONS
Chichester · New York · Brisbane · Toronto · Singapore

Copyright © 1987 by John Wiley & Sons Ltd.

All rights reserved.

No part of this book may be reproduced by any means, or transmitted, or translated into a machine language without the written permission of the publisher.

Library of Congress Cataloging-in-Publication Data:

Anderla, Georges.
 Computer strategies, 1990–9.

 1. Computer industry—Forecasting. 2. Computer industry—Planning. I. Dunning, Anthony. II. Title.
HD9696.C62A53   1987   338.4'7004   87-8173

ISBN 0 471 91585 8

British Library Cataloguing in Publication Data:

Anderla, Georges
 Computer strategies 1990–9: technologies-costs markets.
 1. Computer industry
 I. Title II. Dunning, Anthony
 004   HD9696.C62

ISBN 0 471 91585 8

Typeset by Acorn Bookwork, Salisbury
Printed and bound in Great Britain by Biddles Ltd., Guildford

Contents

INTRODUCTION vii

Part 1: **ANATOMY OF COSTS** 1

CHAPTER 1   **Cost Trends and Patterns** 3
      1.1   Graphing Made (Almost) Joyful 4
      1.2   Operating under the Umbrella of Predictability 11
      1.3   How Japan's Chip Makers Stole the Show ... 16
      1.4   IBM Did More of It, More Often 22
      1.5   Falling out of Step: Communications Costs .. 26
      1.6   Conclusion and Outlook 28

CHAPTER 2   **Exposure to Fluctuations** 34
      2.1   Developing Differentiated Products 35
      2.2   Coping with the Problem of Lumpiness 39
      2.3   Staggering of Product Cycles 43
      2.4   Piercing the Business Atmospherics 47
      2.5   Conclusion and Outlook 54

CHAPTER 3   **Easing Cost Constraints** 57
      3.1   Bidding up Software against Hardware 58
      3.2   PCs: The Glaring Miscalculations 63
      3.3   R&D Escalation Must Be Reversed 68
      3.4   Cost-Saving Opportunities 75
      3.5   Conclusion and Outlook 80

Part 2: **THE DYNAMICS OF MARKETING** 83

CHAPTER 4   **Gains from New Information Technology** 85
      4.1   Tracking the Benefits of Computing 86
      4.2   A New Justification of Factory Automation .. 90
      4.3   Attractions of New Office Technology 96
      4.4   The Conundrum of Decreasing Returns 100
      4.5   Conclusion and Outlook 106

CHAPTER 5	**The Emerging Buyers' Market**	109
5.1	Going Back to Basics	109
5.2	The Issue of Integration	114
5.3	Patterns of Computing Deployment	121
5.4	Best-Selling Software	126
5.5	Conclusion and Outlook	131
CHAPTER 6	**Revitalized Segmentation of Markets**	134
6.1	The World Framework	134
6.2	The Electronic Imaging Market Explodes	139
6.3	Japanese Views of Media and Markets: A Lesson	146
6.4	In Search of Hot Niches	152
6.5	Conclusion and Outlook	158
Part 3:	**MEGATRENDS IN TECHNOLOGY**	161
CHAPTER 7	**New Exigencies on Hardware Development**	163
7.1	The Confines of Doped Silicon	164
7.2	Limits to Microminiaturization	169
7.3	New Architectures Are Overdue	180
7.4	Could the Optical Computer Be the Answer?	193
7.5	Conclusion and Outlook	199
CHAPTER 8	**Closing the Software Gap and Beyond**	202
8.1	Going It the GM Way	203
8.2	Some Shortcuts Have Been Tried	208
8.3	System Software: The Musical Score	211
8.4	Extending the Musical Metaphor	218
8.5	Intelligent Software: The Final Movement	228
8.6	Conclusion and Outlook	238
CHAPTER 9	**Signposting Rejuvenated and Novel Systems**	241
9.1	Automating Data Gathering and Input	242
9.2	Improving Man/System Interaction	251
9.3	New Storage Technology Impacts	258
9.4	Florescent Societal and Personal IT Services	267
9.5	Conclusion and Outlook	273
GENERAL CONCLUSION		277
INDEX		283

Acknowledgements

The obligations we have incurred in the preparation of this volume are numerous. Writers of any book such as this draw upon a body of knowledge built up through the efforts of many people over many years. It will be clear that they have stimulated the many lines of thought that have developed into the principal messages outlined in this volume. We wish to record our appreciation to all of them.

Specifically, we would mention our good friend and sound judge of IT developments, Brian Blunden, who for several years has been the moving spirit behind many European initiatives in electronic publishing and printing. We thank, too, Ian Shelley, formerly with John Wiley, for his encouragement and many suggestions. To those specialists, particularly in the United States, who aided us with critical counsel and constructive ideas in the early stages, we are deeply grateful.

There are a number of people without whom this book could not have been completed. We wish to thank those authors and publishers who have given permission to cite and reproduce many of the figures and tables. One of us, A.D., is grateful to the Commission of the European Communities for permission to publish his part in this work. We would cite also the many colleagues at the OECD and the Commission of the European Communities who have helped to clarify the ideas set down in the following chapters.

We are also indebted to Diane Taylor, Robert Hambrook, and Tony Carwardine of John Wiley who have been a great source of help particularly during the crucial final stages. Nor can we leave unsaid our gratitude to Beverley Filling, Christiane Hansen, and Martine Vicic for their understanding and equanimity during the preparation of typescript and drawings. Last but not least, we thank our immediate families—Georgette, Wendy, Roger and Fiona for their continuous encouragement and support and ever-ready willingness to fit in with the exigencies inevitable in such a project.

Introduction

Within five years the computer products that are currently the market leaders will be definitely on the way out. By 1995, all computer and information systems being installed now will have become obsolete. Such is the iron law of innovation.

Far from being a prediction, that is a well-established fact of life. Indeed, an almost identical statement could have been proffered at the beginning of this decade or at any time during the previous one.

THE WHY OF THIS BOOK

What makes the present situation fundamentally different from the past is the realization that we are approaching physical confines to miniaturization, despite current efforts to push the process further and further, and that there is therefore a definite limit to the continuous increase in computing power of machines whose basic architecture, due to the genius of Johan von Neumann, has remained unchanged for some forty years. To put it another way: what is the expectancy that some truly revolutionary concepts or designs will prevail and become commercially exploitable within the foreseeable future, e.g. better solid-state materials, superconductor circuits, parallel processing, erasable optical disks, extra-fast laser-operated computers, optical fibres and so on? The question is relevant to thousands of vendors, for each and any of these epoch-making projects might lead to innumerable ramifications and open up new business opportunities, or spell the death of those firms that find themselves at the losing end.

If you were in charge of a small manufacturing company, on what niche would you be prepared to put your money, not in some distant future, but today, next month or next year? If you were on the board of a medium-sized firm, how would you apportion the company's investment in view of the intoxicating potentialities of the newest technologies, yet keeping in mind the need concomitantly to develop the present line of products and the one in between? Finally, assuming you were a departmental manager of a very large corporation, where would you find the moneys to be ploughed into R&D in several key areas at the same time, as might be necessary in order to remain competitive with your rivals, possibly including some powerful new entrants?

'Take your place in the information industry', says a call for membership (Exhibit A) issued by the US Information Industry Association, suggesting the choice between some 80 specialty niches. Likewise, Exhibit B from Harvard University presents the information business according to four characteristics. Unfortunately, these publications offered no practical advice on how to choose and how to proceed.

Thus, the temptation is great to fall back on past experience. This is understandable and partly justified. In retrospect, the computer and information industries can collectively pride themselves upon their overall performance and many remarkable achievements. Their aggregate gross earnings exceeded $250 billion in 1985 worldwide (outside the Communist countries) and amounted to $485 billion when all electronics goods are included, with the US holding a 44 per cent share

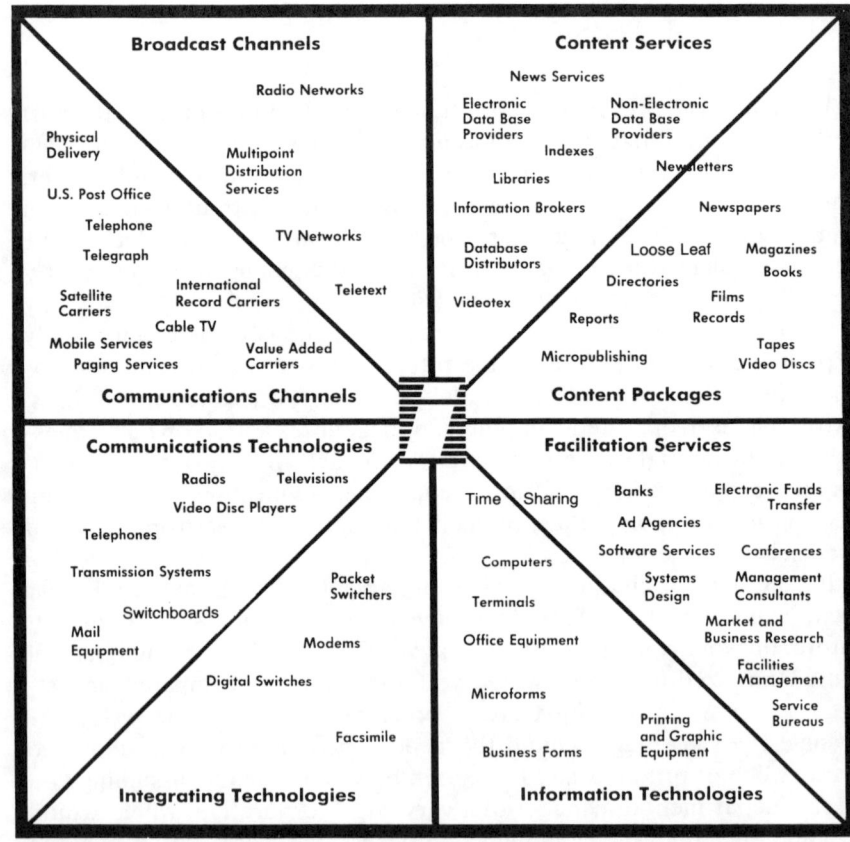

EXHIBIT A   *Take your place in the information industry. (Reproduced by permission of Information Industry Association)*

xi

	FORM												SUBSTANCE
SERVICES													
GOVT MAIL	MAILGRAM	INTERNATL TEL SVCS		VANs	BROADCAST NETWORKS		DATABASES AND						PROFESSIONAL SVCS
PARCEL SVCS	TELEX	LONG DIST TEL SVCS		DBS	BROADCAST STATIONS		VIDEOTEX						
COURIER SVCS	EMS	LOCAL TEL SVCS			CABLE NETWORKS		NEWS SVCS						FINANCIAL SVCS
OTHER DELIVERY SVCS					CABLE OPERATORS								ADVERTISING SVCS
		MULTIPOINT DISTRIBUTION SVCS				TELETEXT							
		DIGITAL TERMINATION SVCS											
		MOBILE SVCS		FM SUBCARRIERS									
PRINTING COS		PAGING SVCS	BILLING AND METERING SVCS			TIME-SHARING	SERVICE BUREAUS						
LIBRARIES			MULTIPLEXING SVCS				ON-LINE DIRECTORIES						
RETAILERS		BULK TRANSMISSION SVCS					SOFTWARE SVCS						
NEWSSTANDS			INDUSTRY NETWORKS				SYNDICATORS AND PROGRAM PACKAGERS						
			DEFENSE TELECOM SYSTEMS										LOOSE-LEAF SVCS
			SECURITY SVCS										
				CSS SVCS									
					COMPUTERS								
				PABXs									
					TELEPHONE SWITCHING EQUIP		SOFTWARE PACKAGES						DIRECTORIES
			MODEMS	CONCENTRATORS									NEWSPAPERS
				MULTIPLEXERS									NEWSLETTERS
													MAGAZINES
			RADIOS										
			TV SETS										SHOPPERS
PRINTING AND			TELEPHONES										
GRAPHICS EQUIP			TERMINALS										AUDIO RECORDS
COPIERS			PRINTERS										AND TAPES
			FACSIMILE										
			ATMs										FILMS AND
CASH REGISTERS			POS EQUIP										VIDEO PROGRAMS
			BROADCAST AND										
INSTRUMENTS			TRANSMISSION EQUIP										
TYPEWRITERS			WORD PROCESSORS										
DICTATION EQUIP			VIDEO TAPE RECORDERS										
BLANK TAPE AND FILM			PHONOS, VIDEO DISC PLAYERS										
			CALCULATORS										
			MICROFILM, MICROFICHE										
FILE CABINETS			BUSINESS FORMS		GREETING CARDS								BOOKS
PAPER													
PRODUCTS													

ATM - Automatic teller machine
COS - Companies
CSS - Carrier "smart" switch
DBS - Direct broadcast satellite
EMS - Electronic message service
PABX - Private automatic branch exchange
POS - Point-of-sale
SVCS - Services
VAN - Value-added network

© 1986 Program on Information Resources Policy, Harvard University

EXHIBIT B *The information business. (Reproduced with permission from John F. McLaughlin with Ann Louise Antonoff,* Mapping the Information Business, *Program on Information Resources Policy, Harvard University, Cambridge, Mass., 1986)*

of all these markets combined. In other words, the complex of electronics industries contributed close to 5 per cent to the aggregate GNP of the free world, and it is anticipated that this figure will rise to 8 per cent by the year 2000.

This glamorous record was not without its problems, which have become really troublesome and widespread since the early 1980s. The software gap, a term which refers to the general inadequacy of computer languages and programs relative to hardware, is as yawning as ever. Manufacturers of mainframes and those of minicomputers have not really recovered, with the exception of IBM, from the onslaught of personal computers. The Japanese now control 70 per cent of the world market for silicon chips and low-grade circuitry. British, American and German videotex projects all ended in fiasco. So also did electronic games for home computers, after a short-lived illusion, and so did literally thousands of promising products, packages and services.

In 1984, Stephen T. McClellan, a vice-president and chief computer industry analyst for Salomon Brothers, published a well-documented study under an eloquent title: *The Coming Computer Industry Shakeout. Winners, Losers, and Survivors* (published by John Wiley and Sons). The book is in reality three stories in one. The first is about the overall champion, International Business Machines; it contains a comprehensive explanation of the spectacular rise to preeminence of the company, but it also shows that IBM had been through at least one major crisis owing to errors of judgement at the top in critical areas at a critical time, the 1970s. Second, there is a vivid gallery of portraits of Gene Amdahl, Adam Osborne, Andrew S. Grove, Kenneth H. Olsen, An Wang, Steve Jobs and Steve Wozniak, John Cullinane and perhaps a dozen other exceptional technical talents, men of vision not always endowed with business acumen, but whose sheer brilliance had masked the weakness of the rest of the pack.

Major portions of the book were given to a dispassionate, almost clinical examination, one by one, of dozens of US computer and service companies and to discussion of the reasons for their disappointing performance, if not straightforward failure. By and large, the author's diagnosis boiled down to three points: bad product policy, no sense of timing, compounded by poor marketing.

To put it plainly, IBM's overall strength may not be due essentially to its mammoth size and quasi-monopolistic practices, as most people assert. IBM's dominance of the market is at least as much the consequence of its competitors' chronic inability to define and implement a winning strategy—even in those areas to which IBM is a relative newcomer.

IBM is not, however, the only case in point. In 1980, Texas Instruments, Motorola and National Semiconductors led the world in semiconductors, whilst NEC, the largest chip maker in Japan, had just about half the sales of Texas Instruments. In 1985, NEC overtook TI for the first place, Hitachi jumped to the third place, relegating Motorola to the fourth place, with National trailing behind Toshiba, Fujitsu and Intel, in that order. The only European contender, Philips, was last out of the top ten semiconductor companies. Can the virtual surrender to the Japanese of the US chip makers be explained by wage differentials and Japanese aggressive price cutting? Is it legitimate to use the same excuses to convince the good people in America and Europe that, because the Japanese exports of video recorders, television sets and other consumer electronics are now 15 times those of either the United States or Europe, our deficient domestic producers are entitled to permanent government protection?

A totally unexpected support for the McClellan thesis is to be found in a relatively recent best-seller, *In Search of Excellence* (published by Harper and Row), whose two authors, Thomas J. Peters and Robert H. Waterman Jr, had initially meant to work out a new theory of successful management on the basis of in-depth interviews with the top brass of a number of high-tech firms, and among them IBM, Texas Instruments, Xerox, Hewlett-Packard, Digital Equipment, Schlumberger, Wang, Data General, National Semiconductor. The project misfired. No sooner had the book been published (1982) than the income statements of a good half of the companies labelled 'excellent' started turning into the red, whilst others, with only a handful of exceptions, were running into deep difficulties.

Surveying the entire field, the failures—and there are likely to be more to come, e.g. in optronics, facsimile transmission, in digital audio tapes—share too many common features to be wholly unrelated. Time and again, managements of computer manufacturing firms and information providers have failed to grasp the deeper significance of emerging new technologies, underestimated the development costs of alternative products and systems, misjudged the mood and growing exigency of their customers. Whether the root cause is managerial incompetence or complacency, a remedial action is urgenty needed.

TO WHOM IT MAY CONCERN

Inasmuch as the primary purpose of this book is to assist in laying down company policies and formulating strategic guidelines, it is intended for all those in the computer supply firms and related trades who participate in, or contribute to, this complex, never-ending, yet fundamental business. This includes, in the first place, all general managers, chief executives, managing directors and key decision makers whose responsibility in this respect may under no circumstances be delegated. Obviously, it should also include the rising generation of junior assistant managers and young, bright heads of department from whose ranks the future top echelons will be chosen. Exhibits A and B, which have already been commented upon, give an idea of the breadth and variety of the firms concerned, although they could be further extended by taking into account many additional manufacturing specialities and the distributive trades and outfits.

Second, the subject matter of the book is pertinent to another category of people, made up of all those who either are involved in the preparation of strategy and policy decisions or are in charge of control of implementation, auditing, evaluation and review. We can readily think of planners, higher-level engineers, designers and developers of new products, key systems analysts and chief programmers, heads of marketing units and a few other company officials whose job is to coordinate different activities, typically the chairmen of *ad hoc* groups.

If there be one sort of person for whom our general survey is definitely not intended, it is the narrow specialists. Every single topic and issue we discuss, when taken separately, is better known to these experts, who are generally unconcerned with concepts, patterns, relationships and the underlying principles.

Third, additional readership of the book can logically be expected to come from selected outside consultancies, specialized market research organizations, industry federations and also the company bankers, financial advisors, holding companies and venture capitalists active in this field.

Last but not least, in composing this book, its authors never lost sight of the special needs of students of information technology, students of technology management and students of management generally. Traditionally, a manager was expected to know a few products or one industry. Owing to the rapid obsolescence of every new wave of innovation in computing, this skill can no longer be expected from a future manager. Instead, the manager of tomorrow must have acquired the ability to relate the firm's products and the industry to the global environment, to identify and create new markets for the products derived from the ever-changing technology and to integrate worldwide trends into the strategic and key policy decisions.

To sum up, the book has a definite slant towards the supplier/vendor companies. As such, it is not directly relevant to computer and information system users. However, some developments that are included could be of interest to managers of the computing department in the customer corporations and their planners. Thus, Chapters 7, 8 and 9, dealing with megatrends in information technology, or again the discussion in Chapter 4 of the benefits from office and factory automation, which are typical selling arguments, could provide the buyers, too, with useful information and new vistas.

Like in other business activities, strategic decision-making by computer manufacturers and other information suppliers is today less than ever based on hunch or intuition. The management's first and foremost responsibility is to organize the decision-making process in an orderly fashion. Indeed, strategic decision-making can be broken down into several phases. The very first step must, of course, be to identify what the problem is. This sounds simple and easy, yet it is probably one of the most difficult tasks that managements must discharge. Once this is done, the next step is the analysis of the problem. The third phase consists of defining alternative solutions, or strategies. Then and then only come the final two stages: making the final choice between the alternatives and implementing the strategy decided upon.

In any structured organization, managements rely on their key collaborators and sometimes outside consultants in the two middle stages: analysing the problem and developing alternative solutions. It is also during these two phases that modern decision-making aids come into their own. The battery of tools to help in strategic decision-making in the computer industry is being constantly extended and refined. These tools partake as much of operational research, business games and simulation, statistics and sampling, market analysis and motivational research, accountancy and corporate finance, as of several hard sciences, especially physics, chemistry, electronics, optics, mathematical theory of information, telecommunications and engineering. They are tools of systematic, logical and quantitative analysis and synthesis, with the significant adjunct of techniques of technological assessment and forecasting.

The technical people who contribute to the elaboration of strategy must, of course, be able to work with these tools personally, whereas the managers need not—even though their use in most instances does not require greater mathematical skill or higher competence in physics than is needed for reading sales charts or for extrapolating the future capacity of memory chips. It has also been alleged that some managers are little interested in, and have anyhow little time for, such matters. We sought a compromise. While dispensing with unnecessary technicalities, we decided to provide the reader with enough introductory or explanatory material to make him aware of what tools and methods of inquiry are available, and of their more general validity, leaving it to him or her to figure out how they could be applied to specific problems. Furthermore, even when managers have the benefit of competent technical advisors, inside or outside the firm, it is essential for them to be able to tell these specialists what is wanted from them, in what context and for what purpose, and against what pitfalls they should guard themselves.

STIMULATING CREATIVE METHODOLOGIES

However powerful and valuable the quantitative tools of strategic decision-making may be, they have their inherent limitations. They cannot by themselves identify what the central problem is; nor can they determine the right question to be asked. They are of little help in deciding upon the best solution and in setting objectives for that solution. Yet, referring again to the five-phase model sketched out previously, these two phases, the first and the fourth, are crucial in the elaboration of business strategy.

When misapplied or when stretched out too far, these tools can become potent means for making the wrong strategic choices. In the words of a great management practitioner, 'precisely because they make possible concrete and specific analysis of problems which hitherto could only be roughly defined or sensed, the new tools can be abused to "solve" the problems of one small area or of one function at the expense of other areas or functions or of the entire business'.[1]

One of the ambitions of the present book is to show how these methodological gaps in strategic decision-making could be filled, or at least narrowed. The principles of systems analysis provide us with a convenient starting point. Having chosen to consider strategy in its global dynamic environment, our first job is to organize and structure the problem at hand and to assure completeness of factors to be included and the comprehensiveness of all conceivable outcomes.

In Chapter 7, for example, we show how a systematic exploration of Mendeleyev's periodic table, which had permitted the prediction of the properties of elements, including gallium, unknown at that time (circa 1869), could now assist in the active search for new semiconducting materials capable of competing successfully with doped silicon. More generally, the advantage of these methods is that they result in the generation of additional, otherwise unsuspected, alternatives, including new strategic options, some of which may be superior to those currently pursued. In the same style, in Chapter 5 we apply a simple square matrix technique to the issue of how best to deploy/redeploy computing resources within user companies, on the basis of a systematic comparison between centralized, decentralized and distributed patterns—although the primary aim here is to alert computer system designers and suppliers to the problems experienced by, and the preferences of, the buyers/users.

The systematic approach conceals, however, risks of error often due to misjudgement in defining what the problem at hand is and/or to the lack of care in specifying the objective, the area of application and the

---

[1] Peter F. Drucker, *The Practice of Management* (first published in 1955).

inherent limitations. In Chapter 8 we show how counterproductive and costly it can be trying to 'close the software gap' by making inconsiderate demands on program designers and writers. For instance, raising the level of performance of distributed systems has little to do with the programmers' skill, but is contingent upon discovering the principles that govern the behaviour of complex systems universally. Equally, no software package will ensure by itself error-free machine translation or voice recognition, unless we first improve substantially our understanding of the nervous system and the mechanism, and the underlying rules, of human speech.

The problem of selection of specific topics for more detailed discussion, in a book such as the present, is very difficult. Should local area networks or the current controversy over the future of artificial intelligence be treated at any great length? Is machine-aided translation or electronic music of sufficient general interest to be included? Without specifics, a book becomes jejune and tedious; with detail, it is in danger of becoming intolerably pedestrian or local. Whenever possible, we have selected examples that are illustrative of a general principle.

Using a loose analogy, just as portable software can run on different computers, so general principles can be applied to various situations. For example, the simple tradeoff principle involved in the design of RISC machines (Chapters 5 and 7) is just as relevant to choosing alternatives between stand-alone systems and networks or between packaged and customized software, and we have therefore given the matter the airing it deserves.

Our choice of a fifteen-year reference period, looking both forward and backward, is easy to justify provided this time span is not interpreted too rigidly. As we shall see, the life cycle of a new information technology product is seven to eight years on the average. Doubling that length of time by linking, whenever possible, two successive cycles often permits us to uncover meaningful changes in the rate of progression (or retrogression) or, alternatively, to identify critical turning points. When looking forward, the sharper view of the next seven or eight years stands in contrast to the blurred visualization of the more distant future, say, beyond 1995, which is, however, not as far off as it sounds at first. Moreover, basic discoveries and inventions in information technology laboratories currently take about fifteen years to reach commercial production, and therefore our consideration of megatrends in this field have kept this horizon in view to a great extent. Finally, we strongly believe that new insights can be gained by linking future prospects to past performance, and vice versa.

All this may sound somewhat academic. Let us therefore illustrate the general approach followed in this book by a couple of concrete examples.

One of the conclusions of this book is that there is shortly going to be a great deal of market-driven, innovative activity in image processing and the use of visual information in combination with textual and numerical data, and that these developments are likely to lead to a series of innovations spreading over perhaps the next fifteen years, with rapid acceleration in the second half of that period.

For some time now, there was a growing feeling among observers that the dominant market influence was gradually swaying in favour of customers away from vendors. This impression could however be documented only in a number of isolated cases. In order to gather corroborative evidence, we decided to broaden the approach and concentrate on a number of critical, apparently unrelated issues, and in particular on the much-heralded idea of integration (Chapter 5). On closer examination it turned out that, far from being a panacea, as some enthusiasts profess, maximal integration remains impractical on account of prohibitive costs or, in other words, for lack of market support. The investigation also confirmed that it is possible to merge images with alphanumeric data, script or numbers, on a PC at a price affordable right now by quite a few eager users. Thus, if we accept that integration is not an absolute but a series of shifting responses to clearly specified needs, the problem becomes one of identifying the categories of solvent users, estimating the size of that market and, if necessary, suitably adjusting the characteristics of the products being designed to the real needs of the subcategories of would-be buyers. Without, at this stage, going into details, an impressive list of applications could be drafted pointing to no fewer than five or six key market segments, i.e. manufacturing industries, transport systems, publishing, medicine, television and advertising, and the military, all of which can rightfully be called global markets. No wonder that these bright prospects are attracting the attention of Texas Instruments, Inmos in Britain and several other leading chip makers, and thus giving a strong and probably long-lasting impetus to R&D in electronic imaging.

Ideally, the (often-complex) analysis of the interlocking aspects, as this example suggests, should conclude with the identification of new, valuable opportunities or the demonstrable lack of them. However, the actual positioning of this or that supply firm for action, which is the obvious next step, is beyond the scope of this book, as it must be decided by the management.

Our second example is of a different kind. The appearance of a new or a substitute product has always been a major concern for manufacturers and vendors of similar and complementary products. The announcement usually provokes a frantic scrutiny of technical and trade journals and often leads to quick decisions as to what moves the makers of the established brands should take, e.g. speed up the development of a promising new design or cancel the project altogether, scrap an existing production line or disband a team of programmers, and so on. What is frequently lost sight of, in this rush, is the deeper understanding of the causal relationship between the new technology and changes in the relative costs of ingredients (Chapter 1) that have made the new technology feasible and, just as importantly, the delicate tradeoff between economic factors and technical features (Chapter 5) that makes the new product or system commercially viable.

The supreme irony occurs when improvisation in defining a new product policy entails throwing away the results of a long, painstaking monitoring of slowly changing cost trends, and with them perhaps also the opportunity of working out one's own, more effective, strategy.

THE LAYOUT

The material in the book is divided into three parts, devoted respectively, but not exclusively, to the anatomy of costs, the dynamics of marketing and megatrends in information technology and, of course, their interactions. By costs, we mean all outlays and other items of expense, including overheads and amortization charges, incurred by manufacturers/vendors in connection with design, production, assembly and marketing of their hardware and systems.

Like any other goods and services, computers and information systems serve little purpose unless they are made available to the buyer/user in the configuration, at the time, within the environment he or she is prepared to pay for. In practice, marketing is taken to include, among other functions, market analysis, advertising, promoting, merchandizing and servicing, either addressing directly the end-user or acting through intermediaries.

As for the third subject, rather than putting together words of our own, we adopt here a conception presented by Professor C. Freeman, Sussex University, and L. Soette, Stanford University, at a recent, IBM-sponsored symposium:

> ...we define 'information technology' as a new technological system for the storage, processing, communication and dissemination of information, based on an inter-connected set of technical and organisational innovations in computers, software engineering, control systems, integrated circuits and telecommunications.

The three-way division—costs, markets, technology—departs somewhat from the traditional model containing two sets of players, respectively the producers/vendors and the buyers/users, linked together by a flow of goods and services supplied by the former to the latter and the reverse flow of financial settlements for the purchases made. For a long time, the manufacturers/vendors, with the support of their product designers and their financial backers, did most of the running. Those were the heydays of the sellers' market, a time when almost any new product, any new system, any new technology, however primitive by today's standards, found eager buyers. The only serious constraint came from upstart companies and, of course, from competition growing keener among the established suppliers.

As the computer industry matures, signs multiply, pointing to the emergence of a buyers' market, as a result of the observable widening of consumer choice. How can we be certain that our reading of the symptoms is correct? How can we know that this trend will continue and possibly gather momentum? What implications will there be, in particular in terms of new and old markets? The crucial importance of these questions provides the main justification for the general layout of the book and for assigning the central place to the dynamics of marketing.

However, a prior consideration must be given to the underlying economics of the computer industry and related trades. Revisiting this much neglected area, as is done in Part 1, pays dividends. It turns out that changing cost relations, e.g. between hardware and software, between manpower and materials, etc., have of late played a key role in the belated, yet now increasingly forceful, assertion of consumer sovereignty in the new information technology arena. The fact is generally unacknowledged, or underestimated, probably because the impact of changes in relative costs on users' buying patterns and producers' plans is seldom direct and immediately discernible, but most of the time is roundabout and cumulative, though real and lasting.

Witness the absence of a convincing explanation for the apparent paradox of rising costs of software relative to hardware at a time when the so-called software gap, which underlines the inadequacy of ever-more-expensive software, keeps widening. Similarly, how many people, besides the professional accountants, realize that the main drain on computer makers' resources is due to excessive financial charges and consistently heavy spending on R&D? The survey of pertinent cost trends and their interaction, undertaken in Part 1, helps to explain the flow of substitute products, to understand product diversification and product differentiation, and also to evaluate the impact of business cycles and other outside interferences.

Part 2, which deals with markets and marketing, opens with Chapter 4, entirely given to tracking the benefits from computing and computerization, looked at from the corporate customer's point of view. Also included is a discussion of whether successive waves or doses of computing respectively into offices and factories lead to decreasing or increasing returns. Our user-friendly approach should come as no surprise; all manufacturers/vendors ought to be in the same frame of mind all the time, for their own sakes.

Although technical aspects of the business have necessarily been raised in relation to costs and markets, Part 3 of the book has been fully given to megatrends in new information technology, that provide the indispensible frame of reference for individual manufacturer's planning. Two qualifications are here in order. Whenever possible, discussion focuses on market-driven development of hardware, new materials as well as new designs, on software bottlenecks and ways of breaking them, on the basic building blocks from which systems and products capable of handling all of the various types of information are built, paying special attention to new approaches to the man/machine interface. Part 3 is, however, not intended to be an exercise in technological forecasting; the estimates included are based on ongoing laboratory research, prototype testing and other corroborative evidence.

The synthesis of all the major issues involved in strategy formulation is to be found in a separate section, in which an attempt is made to show how strategic decisions by separate manufacturers and vendors relate to the state of the art and the prospects of the supply industry as a whole. While there is obviously no simple recipe for success, a winning strategy is always associated with a good understanding of the technology push, a correct reading of the market pull, a solid experience in mastering the ever-changing cost equations and, as if that were not enough, the admixture of creative thinking and opportune timing. For readers' convenience, this section is presented as a General Conclusion.

The narrative is frequently illustrated and sometimes supplemented by statistical tables, simple charts and diagrams, numbered serially for each chapter. The understanding of these visual aids and presentations requires no special skills except a reasonable familiarity with elementary arithmetic and statistics, including logarithmic graphs. All technical terms and methods of analysis are briefly explained in simple terms, as and when they occur.

Finally, there is the usual problem of variations in terminology and semantics. Thus, new office technology, office automation, office of the future and bureautics are synonyms or quasi-synonyms. Yet again, in a book that does not profess to treat philosophical questions, no particular distinction is made between 'data' and 'information'; they are used equivalently, whereas in some contexts 'data' is used in counterpoint to 'text' in order to distinguish aggregates of characters in general from those which have the particular layout and rules normally associated with linguistic works. In numerous other instances, the terms computer industry, computing business, information industry and new information-based industry are used interchangeably, either for the sake of style or because these terms express genuine nuances, and their exact significance is closely tied to the immediate context.

Part 1
Anatomy of Costs

People who currently do business in computing and who do it successfully, often under trying conditions, are very different from both the early pioneers and the brilliant improvisors of the 1970s. The solo performer has definitely been replaced by committees and task forces. Inventiveness has yielded to organized R&D. The world around us, too, suddenly seems alien. First-hand knowledge of the communication and meeting facilities offered at the two hundred or so international airports is at a premium, and familiarity with forward dollar, sterling and yen rates can bring huge rewards.

A parallel, near-revolutionary change is needed—who can deny it?—in vendors' approach to the marketing of new information technology. In Part 2, we set the tone and define the main lines of attack.

Prior attention, however, must be given to the often overlooked and much neglected issue of cost assessment and control. What is the use of having enlarged your market share in one specialty, or even of having created a new market for a new product, if your company's management miscalculates production costs or the price to be charged, misjudges the length of the product cycle or proves helpless when faced with discontinuities in demand and is unable to foresee swings in market trends and moods?

The several problems which we discuss—whether they be related to changing technology, to production or marketing—are quantifiable and can be appraised in terms of monetary values: costs and prices, gain or loss, saving versus extra spending. With money being the only universal measuring rod, it is useful to put these various topics into that perspective and to deal with them under the generic title: anatomy of costs.

The purist might claim that to use the words cost and price almost interchangeably could be confusing. We assume nevertheless the risk and we have good reasons for doing that. Under competitive conditions such as those prevailing in the computer business prices approximate costs quite closely. Second, there are many intermediate products that enter a computer system, e.g. components, circuit boards, operating software, etc.; prices charged by their makers are costs to computer manufacturers. Third, since our outlook is vendor oriented, stressing the cost aspects is quite natural. Last but not least, owing to a dearth of reliable data, we were frequently faced with Hobson's choice.

The layout adopted for Part 1 is as follows. In Chapter 1, emphasis is on medium- and long-term trends in costs and on appropriate cost–performance ratios. The primary aim is to identify significant cost patterns and to test their regularity and predictability. In Chapter 2, we consider the broad range of outside disturbances, which can often be identified as deviations from the underlying trends. These departures from 'normalcy' have a negative and, generally, costly impact on the vendors' business. We endeavour to show that clever vendors have, or can acquire, the ability to cope and occasionally even find the means of turning the challenge to their advantage. Chapter 3 offers an overview of cost-saving opportunities—some traditional, some perhaps unsuspected, yet potentially just as efficacious.

Chapter 1

Cost Trends and Patterns

The interpretation of a statistical table or a column of raw numbers—e.g. the yearly value of sales, increase in computing power over time, declining unit costs in relation to storage capacity—may be a daunting task. Presented in graphic form, the same data may convey a simple picture and tell an easily understood story.

As cost matters and constraints provide the leitmotiv of this and the two following chapters, it seems appropriate to give some consideration, in a brief introductory section, to the types of charts and diagrams best adapted to our purposes. The section is especially intended for those who need a refresher on the basic notions and tools involved in graphic presentation of time series and other elementary functions including the principles of logarithmic plotting. The reader conversant with these techniques may skip the first few pages and move on directly to Section 1.2, although he or she, too, might be pleasantly surprised by gaining new insight into functional relationships in design and production that only a proper cost analysis can reveal.

Even the most sanguine vendor cannot stay in business unless, as a minimum, he or she breaks even and makes enough profit to invest in innovation. This is easy to say but is more difficult by all odds to achieve. One of the essential prerequisites for bringing under control a vendor company's costing problems is to be knowledgeable about relevant cost tendencies within the computer industry and aware of the prevailing winds.

Section 1.2 begins, therefore, with a simple, yet reasonably comprehensive model, capable of explaining the declining trend in the cost of computer equipment and systems under different circumstances or as a result of different vendor strategies. A few examples, recent and ancient, are cited in support of the widely held belief, especially popular in the early 1980s, that the prior rapid slide in costs and prices would soon peter out and the industry would be heading towards calmer waters.

A fuller treatment is given, in Sections 1.3 and 1.4, to the opposite case of accelerated decline in costs, a situation that is seldom without precedent, yet always seems to take the competition by surprise. The penalty for failure to identify early enough the new trend, and the rival's new anticipative strategy based thereupon, is usually harsh and the time to react successfully, alarmingly short.

Just about the only exception to this rule of thumb is provided by the growing discrepancy between the evolution of cost–efficiency ratios respectively in telecommunications and computing, which is briefly commented upon in Section 1.5. As long as the two media and the two technologies were complementary to each other, the situation was tolerable or had to be tolerated. However, as the two industries now increasingly tend to offer substitute services for each other, a serious bone of contention might soon emerge in this area, too.

1.1 GRAPHING MADE (ALMOST) JOYFUL

Just as the pocket calculator has rendered the slide rule and tables of logarithms obsolete for most mundane calculations, too great a familiarity with binary numbers and boolean logic can blur the principles on which decimal arithmetic is based.

Suppose you were asked point-blank to explain the term order of magnitude. Would you immediately and without hesitation define it as the range that extends from some given value, say 5, to ten times that value, or 50? By the same token, number 500 is two orders of magnitude bigger than 5 and the number that is six orders of magnitude greater than number 1 is necessarily 1,000,000.

The capacity of a random access memory chip, for example, has been raised from 1 Kbit in 1970 to 64 Kbits in 1977 and to 1 Mbit in 1986, or by three orders of magnitude altogether. By comparison, the density of data stored on magnetic tapes has increased relatively much less, going from 200 bits/inch in the 1950s to ×12000 bits/inch at the present time[1]—in other words, by more than one but less than two orders of magnitude, or ×60 times. The same approach is applicable to downward trends. Thus, the cost per kilobit of fast semiconductor memory, which stood at $10 in 1975, declined to $0.50 in 1985 and is expected to drop to a mere $0.10 by 1995—an overall decrease by two orders of magnitude.

Whereas the concept is childishly simple, the implications may not always be fully appreciated. Let there be a vendor selling 100 mainframes at $2 million a piece in a given year; assuming that the profit is 1.5 per cent, the net earnings come up to $30 million. Let us now assume that a minicomputer endowed with comparable computing power is marketed a few years later at one-tenth of the price of the old mainframe. In order to attain the same level of earnings, our vendor would now have to sell 1,000 machines. Similarly, a drop in costs by two orders of magnitude implies that the vendor must work harder to increase the

---

[1] For further examples, see Chapter 7.

sales by a factor of 100. The figures just quoted are imaginary, but they are not out of line with some well-documented performances of the computer industry in the not too distant past.

A layman may possibly be thrown off by an obvious lack of symmetry between counting orders of magnitude and our ingrained habit of converting absolute values into percentages, as we often do for comparison purposes. Going from $100 to $1,000 is a jump by one order of magnitude that is equivalent to an increase by 900 per cent. The apparent confusion disappears as soon as we remember that 100 per cent increase means doubling the previous number or volume (e.g. of shipments, of computer speed, etc.); a 200 per cent increase is equivalent to thrice the previous figure; and so on. The reverse is also true: a 90 per cent drop, say in costs, is exactly the same thing as a decrease by one order of magnitude.

Selecting the appropriate scale

A real difficulty is connected with graphic presentation of markedly different quantities, or that of large swings in the variable, or again that of long-term trends. Here, using a natural scale, as is done for plotting monthly sales charts or short-run fluctuations, would be most unhelpful. Either we simply cannot represent all the widely dispersed values within a single diagram or we include the totality of the data, but in that case all low values are so close to each other that that part of the chart becomes meaningless, which of course defeats the purpose.

There are fundamentally only two alternatives, i.e. the semi-logarithmic scale or the log-log scale. It is beyond the scope of this book to give any detailed account of logarithms and logarithmic functions and, indeed, other mathematical functions. The basic principles of logarithmic graphing may be briefly recalled, however, and some of its advantages pointed out.

We have noticed at the outset that the number that is six orders of magnitude greater than 1 is the number 1 million, which can also be written as 10^6. Here, 6 is the common logarithm[2] or power to which 10 must be raised to obtain 1,000,000. In fact any positive number can be expressed as a power to the base 10. For example:

$\log 100 = 2$ $\qquad$ $\log 147 = 2.1673$
$\log 10,000 = 4$ $\qquad$ $\log 42,886 = 4.6323$

---

[2] Here we use logarithms to the base 10. However, there is nothing constraining about which base we choose. In science and engineering, the base used is frequently an irrational number e, which is approximately 2.718; such logarithms are called natural logarithms, but need not concern us here.

It is easy to show, with the help of some numerical examples, how the properties of logarithms can be used to construct a logarithmic scale, also called a ratio chart. Let us, first, consider the following sequence of ordinary numbers, together with their logarithms:

log of   7.3   = 0.8633
log of   73   = 1.8633
log of   730   = 2.8633
log of   7,300   = 3.8633
log of   73,000   = 4.8633, etc.

In the logarithmic series the mantissa (0.8633) remains the same whereas the characteristic, or integer part, increases regularly by a single unit—in contrast to the progression in the natural numbers which increase by multiples of 10. Similarly, a logarithmic scale is constructed in such a way as to make actual distances from the base line proportional to the logarithms of the natural numbers to which they correspond.

Let there be two sequences of numbers:

Sequence A	100	150	200	250	300	etc.
Sequence B	100	150	225	337.5	506.25	etc.

of which the first displays a regular increase of 50 units and the second a regular increase of 50 per cent from one number to the next. We can readily think of two aggressive vendor companies of roughly comparable size following, however, different market strategies. On a natural scale (Figure 1.1a), the points corresponding to the first series appear at equal distances from each other and those representing the second series at increasing distances along the vertical axis. Let us now consider the sequences A′ and B′ of the corresponding logarithms:

Sequence A′	2	2.1761	2.3010	2.3979	2.4771	etc.
Sequence B′	2	2.1761	2.3522	2.5283	2.7044	etc.

Hence, on a logarithmic scale (Figure 1.1b), it is the second series that gives points at equal distances from each other, whereas the first sequence shows points at distances which decrease along the vertical axis.

To generalize, equal distances between points on a natural scale indicate equal *absolute* changes in the variable and equal distances between points on a logarithmic scale indicate equal *proportional* changes in the variable. Similarly, the two decreasing sequences of numbers,

Sequence C	100	80	60	40	20	etc.
Sequence D	100	80	64	51.2	40.96	etc.

are marked by decreases of 20 units and of 20 per cent respectively. Graphically, sequence C would be represented by points located at

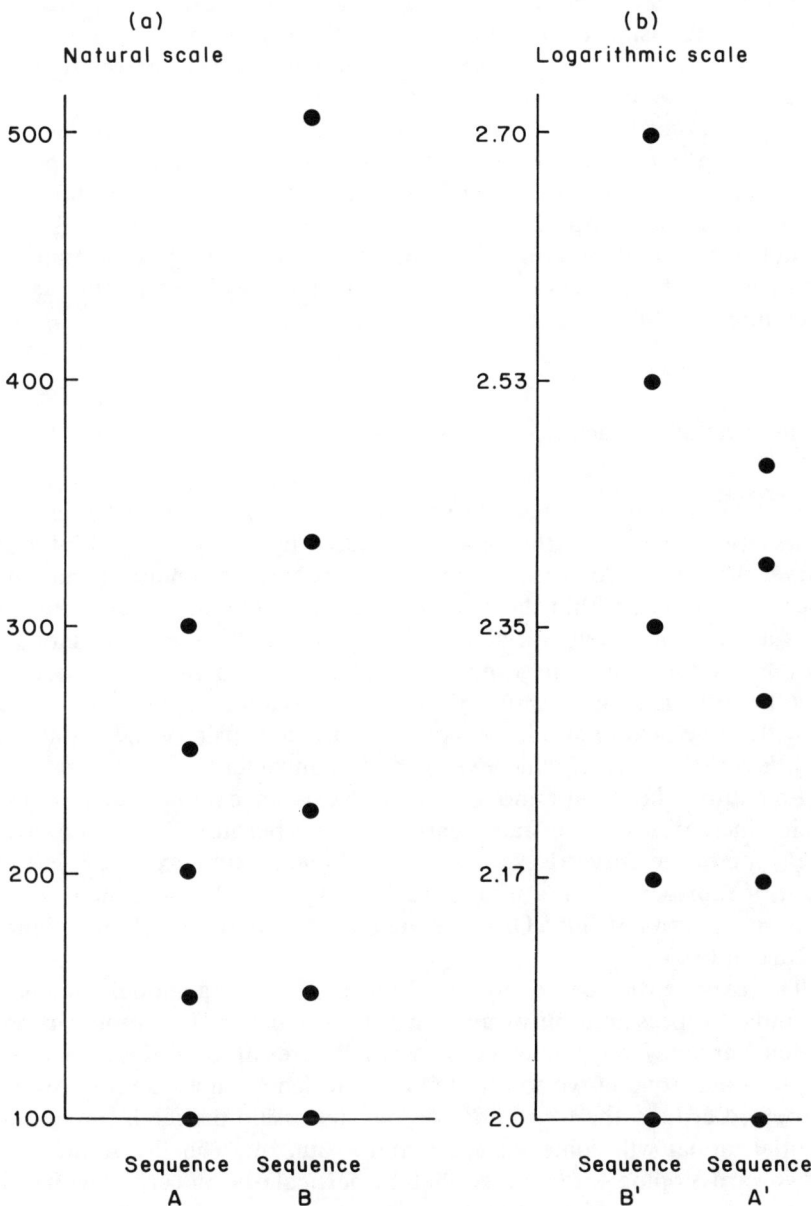

FIGURE 1.1 *Contrasting the natural and the logarithmic scales*

equal distances on a natural (downward) scale and at increasing distances on a logarithmic scale (also downward-sloping). Sequence D would correspond to points at equal distances on a logarithmic scale and at decreasing distances on a natural scale (also pointing downwards).

As we have referred earlier to percentage changes in relation to order(s) of magnitude, it is interesting to notice that sequence B and sequence D are both examples of so-called geometric series, or geometric progressions, in which each successive number is a multiple of the immediately preceding number by a factor which is constant. In sequence B, the multiplier is 1.5; in sequence D it is 0.8. No doubt the reader will have figured out that sequences A and C are both arithmetic series in which the progression is by constant absolute increments or decrements.

Time series at a glance

One small step only is needed to move on to graphic presentations of a time series, which is perhaps best illustrated by the compound interest curve. The main departure from the preceding argument is that the successive values within the sequences are now dated. A time series is thus a function in two variables. Time as the independent variable is plotted horizontally on a natural scale; the dependent variable—whether it be the capital value of investment as a function of time or the growth curve of annual sales—is plotted vertically, using either a natural or a logarithmic scale, whichever is more convenient.

In reality, the compound growth curve is an exponential function which increases at a constant yearly rate, but because it is cumulative, the slope of the curve rises as we move along the time axis from left to right, if represented on a natural scale. On a semi-logarithmic chart it becomes a straight line. Using sequences A and B, we obtain Figure 1.2(a) and (b).

The exponential curve may be looked upon as a model that is a simplified representation of an abstract (or idealized) relationship between variables or it may be seen as the result of fitting the most appropriate trend curve to real-life data, which are always more or less dispersed around the trend line. As our discussion proceeds, the exponential model will come up again and again, often in the shape of a downward-sloping curve for we shall be particularly concerned with cost trends and with changes in cost–performance ratios. Two other models should, however, be mentioned in this connection.

It is a truism that, however marked and persistent a growth pattern may have been in the past, this escalation cannot follow indefinitely a compound–interest curve. Many believe that the inevitable slowdown

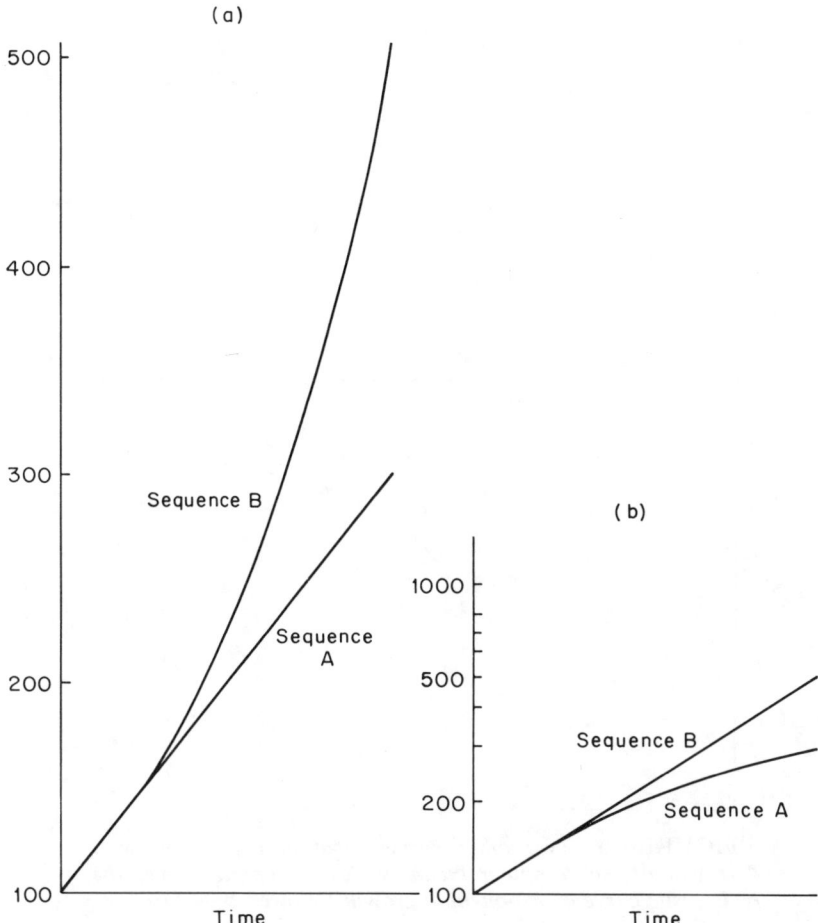

FIGURE 1.2 *Plotting a compound interest curve on natural and semi-logarithmic scale*

could take the form of a logistic curve, as in Figure 1.3(b), which initially grows at an exponential rate but then flattens off, the point of inflexion being located halfway between the base representing the beginnings of an industry or production line and the upper asymptote representing a kind of absolute limit. Since the curve by definition is symmetric, the steep growth at the start would be matched by an increasingly slower growth in the later stages. The relatively saturated markets for both the all-purpose mainframes as well as the minicomputers could very well be characterized by a set of logistic functions.

The so-called Gompertz curve (Figure 1.3a) provides an interesting variation. The curve has the shape of an elongated S inasmuch as it portrays a process of cumulative expansion to a maximum value; this

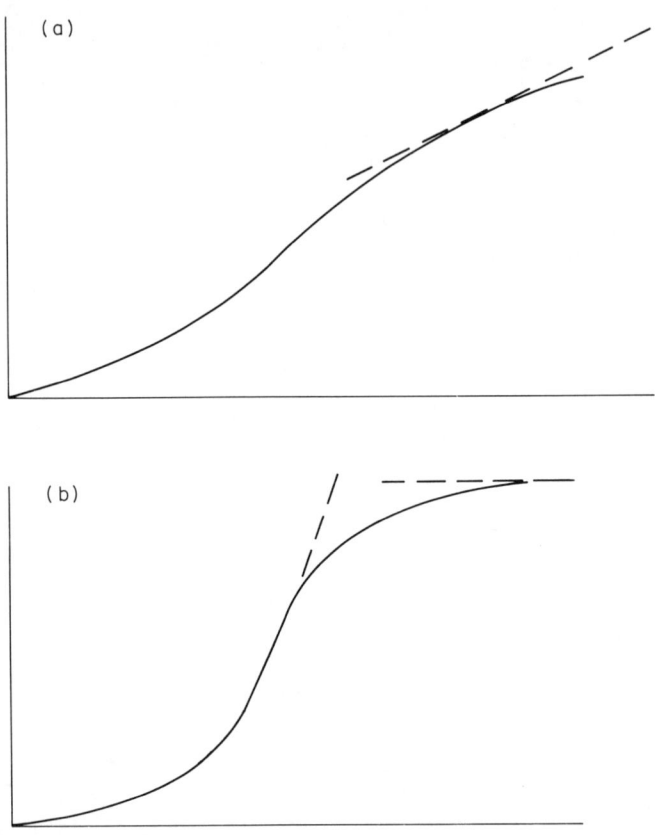

FIGURE 1.3 *Two other curves cited in connection with growth of the computer business: (a) Gompertz curve; (b) Logistic curve or exponential growth followed by saturation*

expansion proceeds by decreasing relative amounts in the later stages, but continues to the end without retrogression. In other words, whereas a logistic has a horizontal asymptote, the Gompertz curve has an oblique asymptote inclined to the horizontal.

Two final remarks are in order. In studying a time series the essential object is to interpret the chronological variations in the value of the variable—be it output, productivity, performance, etc., or be it declining costs, lower prices and the like. Somewhat different are the problems arising in the analysis of data not ordered in time or for which the time order is not relevant, e.g. frequency distributions. Each such function will be described briefly at the appropriate place.

Only exceptionally shall we make use of log-log paper, on which both axes are on a logarithmic scale. One example is to be found in Section 1.5 (viz. Figure 1.12); it is intended to facilitate the analysis of transmission costs in relation to carrying capacity of different telecommunications technologies. A few more illustrations of this type will be found in Part 3, dealing with technological megatrends.

1.2 OPERATING UNDER THE UMBRELLA OF PREDICTABILITY

The image of the computer industry is associated with innovation, growth and declining production costs. Despite some disappointing results of late, the industry's future prospects are still generally rated from good to excellent.

The purpose of this and the subsequent sections is threefold:

1. To suggest a model that would prima facie accommodate all the main known patterns of rapidly changing cost functions, assuming that technological progress entails continuous cost reductions;
2. To use this conceptual framework in order to identify real-life trends in the computer–telecommunications business and to point out significant discontinuities or reversals;
3. To throw fresh light on a number of current issues, e.g. the why of the Japanese sudden thrust forward in electronics, the rationale behind IBM's rise to power and its subsequent woes, the increased competition between computing and communication, etc.

The comforts of the exponential function

Various types of curves may be employed to represent the declining trend in the cost of computer equipment and systems over time, but unfortunately there are no general principles on which the selection could be made. Our choice has been greatly influenced by two considerations. The curve selected must fit reasonably well the data reflecting past and current performances and it must also assure comprehensiveness, so that notable or recurring deviations from the trend, either way, are not overlooked.

The freehand diagram in Figure 1.4, drawn on a ratio chart, comprises a family of curves corresponding to three types of evolutionary process. The straight line A is in fact an exponential function, diminishing at a constant rate of decrease throughout, the actual rate being indicated by the slope of the curve. Curve B follows the same shape and slope up to point I, beyond which there is a marked deceleration. In other words,

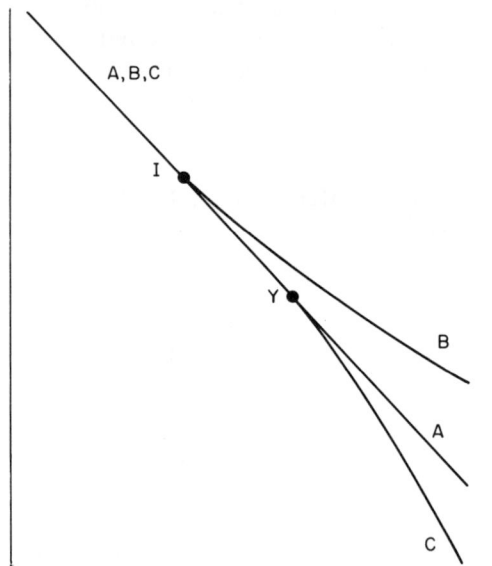

FIGURE 1.4 *Three models of decreasing computer costs*

after declining by a constant percentage during the initial phase, the downward slide in the costs is gradually damped during the next phase.

Curve C is also regularly downward sloping during the initial period up to point Y, beyond which the corresponding costs go on dropping faster and faster, playing havoc (as we shall see in Sections 1.3 and 1.4) with well-established patterns and confronting many traditional vendors with very serious problems. To appreciate the full implications of the C alternative, it is useful, first, to restate briefly the case for exponential decline in computer costs. Fortunately, most of the recapitulation can be done in visual form, for it is the broad tendencies that matter rather than the exact numbers.

Figure 1.5, originally compiled for an OECD report, reproduces in graphic form some ten independent estimates of changes in storage and/or processing costs, prior to 1972 or 1975. All the curves, with the sole exception of old-fashioned typewriters, exhibit a very steep downward slope, with costs falling at 30 per cent per year cumulatively, or more. In just about 20 years, they declined by three orders of magnitude, which was equivalent to being halved every two years.

Whereas Figure 1.5 portrays smooth, idealized functions, the two broken-line curves in Figure 1.6 refer to actual measurements in cost–performance ratios of, respectively, large- and medium-sized mainframes at ten-year intervals between 1950 and 1983. In both instances, the basic measure is provided by MIPS (millions of instructions executed per second) divided by standard outlays on the equipment used respectively in units of $1 million. No violence would be done to the original data in MIPS, as reported from industry sources, by fitting a couple of exponential curves sloping upwards. In Figure 1.6, however, the two curves are downward sloping, inasmuch as we have used the MIPS reciprocals in order to bring out changes in the inverse ratio of cost to performance. If any readers are perturbed by this simple arithmetic, they might think of the analogy with viewing the Eiffel Tower from the ground, as the Parisians do, against looking down from the top, as most visiting Americans do.

A slowdown seemed inevitable

Common sense suggests that the exponential law cannot prevail unabated for too long a period. This was, and still is, generally taken to mean that the rate of decrease itself would eventually begin decreasing and would decline further over time. The resulting cost curve would thus gradually flatten out—viz. function B in Figure 1.4. As we assumed from the start that technological progress brings about savings in costs, the first explanation that comes to mind is that the vigour of cost slashing fades as a result of the flow of innovation running out of steam. Conversely, the sharpest decreases in costs could often be traced to a radical improvement in a specific technology, e.g. chip making, disk drives, etc., or to the bunching of innovations giving birth to radically new, complex products, such as the appearance of minicomputers and microprocessors, the advent of digital switching in telecommunications, and so on.

The tendency to subsequent deceleration has been abundantly documented. Here we include a single illustrative diagram, intended primarily to contrast it with the opposite trend towards accelerated cost reductions, to be dealt with in the next two sections. Figure 1.7 covers a span of 20 years and includes cost projections for the period 1975–95. Going from top to bottom, the four broken-line curves refer to the median cost ranges respectively of CRT terminals, 16-bit and 8-bit microprocessors and 20,000 characters (=10 pages) of disk memory. The inflection which corresponds to the slowing down in the rate of decrease can easily be dated: it is supposed to have occurred in all the four cases between 1980 and 1985.

In the most general case, the flattening of the relevant curves was taken to mean that, as the technology was maturing, the vendors would eventually be able to bring under control the earlier practice of repeated cost-cutting and the parallel squeeze on their profits. As the world entered the 1980s, the vendor community was swept by a wave of

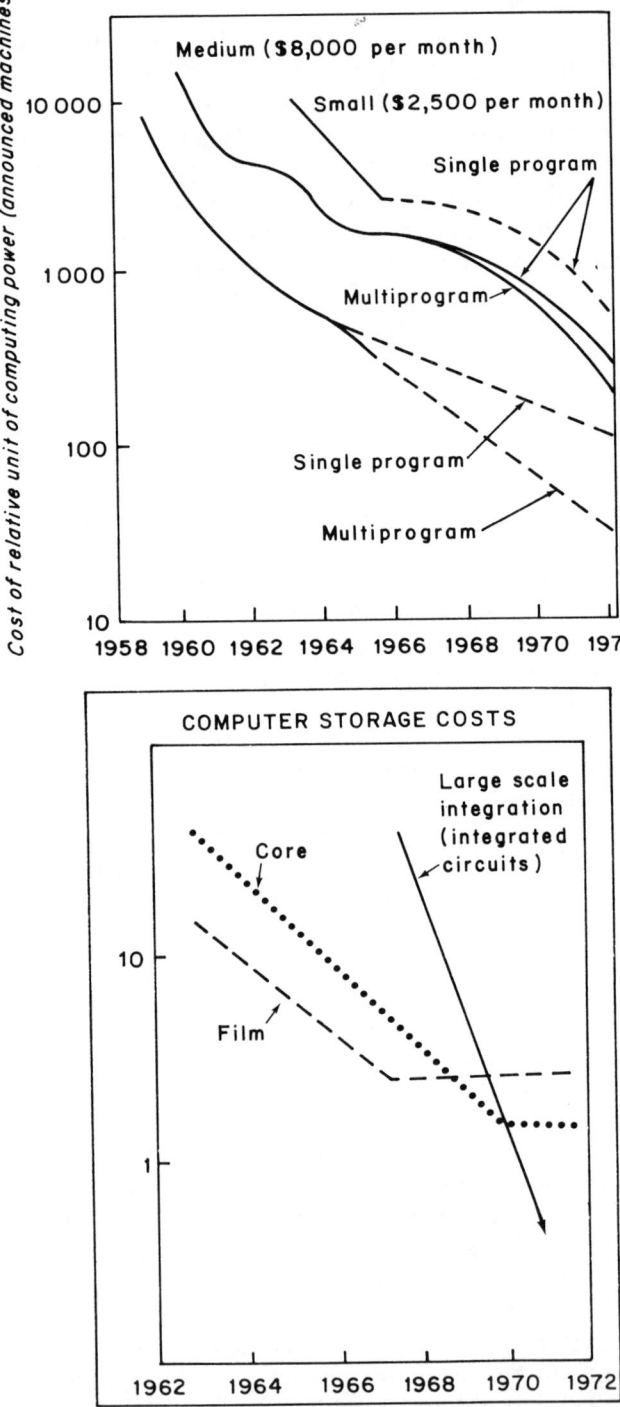

FIGURE 1.5 *Decrease in unit costs of automatic information processing. Various evaluations and extrapola-*

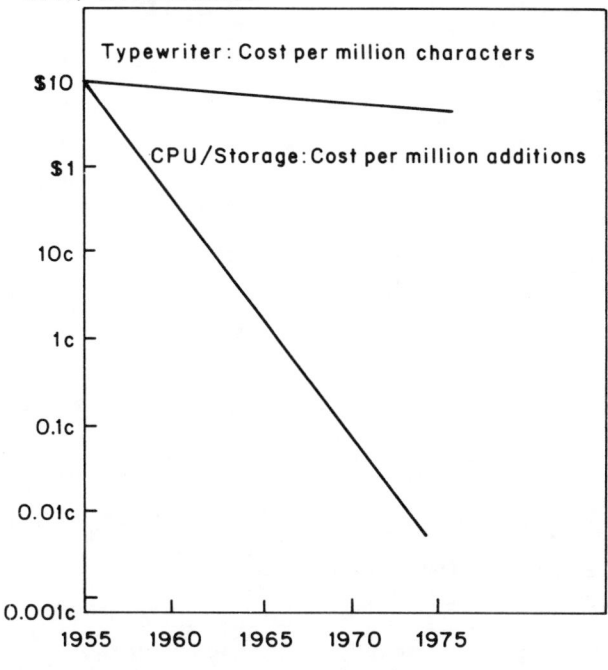

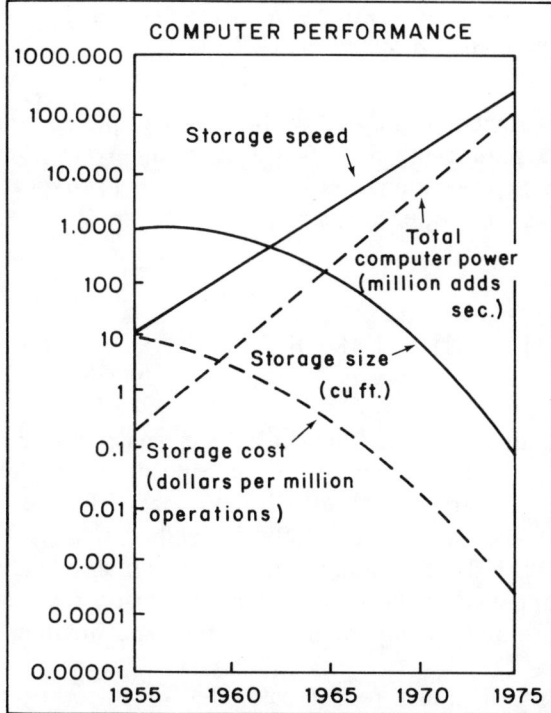

tions. *(Reproduced with permission from Georges Anderla,* Information in 1985. *OECD, Paris, 1973)*

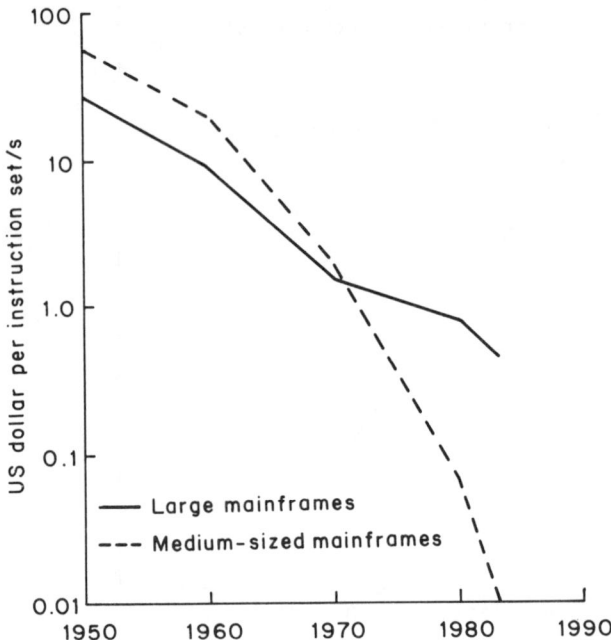

FIGURE 1.6 *Comparing cost–performance of large and medium-sized computers, 1950–83*

optimism, which was further prompted by the just-completed conversion of IBM from a mainframe manufacturing company to a multiproduct, multinational corporation, boasting once again a provocatively robust growth in sales and net earnings.

1.3 HOW JAPAN'S CHIP MAKERS STOLE THE SHOW

The awakening to reality three or four years later was rude for many vendors. However, it is only now that we are in a position rationally to diagnose this reversal of fortunes, by using our model of Figure 1.4 in the previous section and, more specifically, by elaborating upon the compound curve C. With this aim in mind, it is worth while to analyse in some detail what happened in the semiconductor industry respectively in the United States and in Japan and the relevant medium-term projections.

Table 1.1 contains the most recent estimates of prices of mass-produced memory chips for different RAM (random access memory) capacities, all expressed in US cents/kilobit and thus directly com-

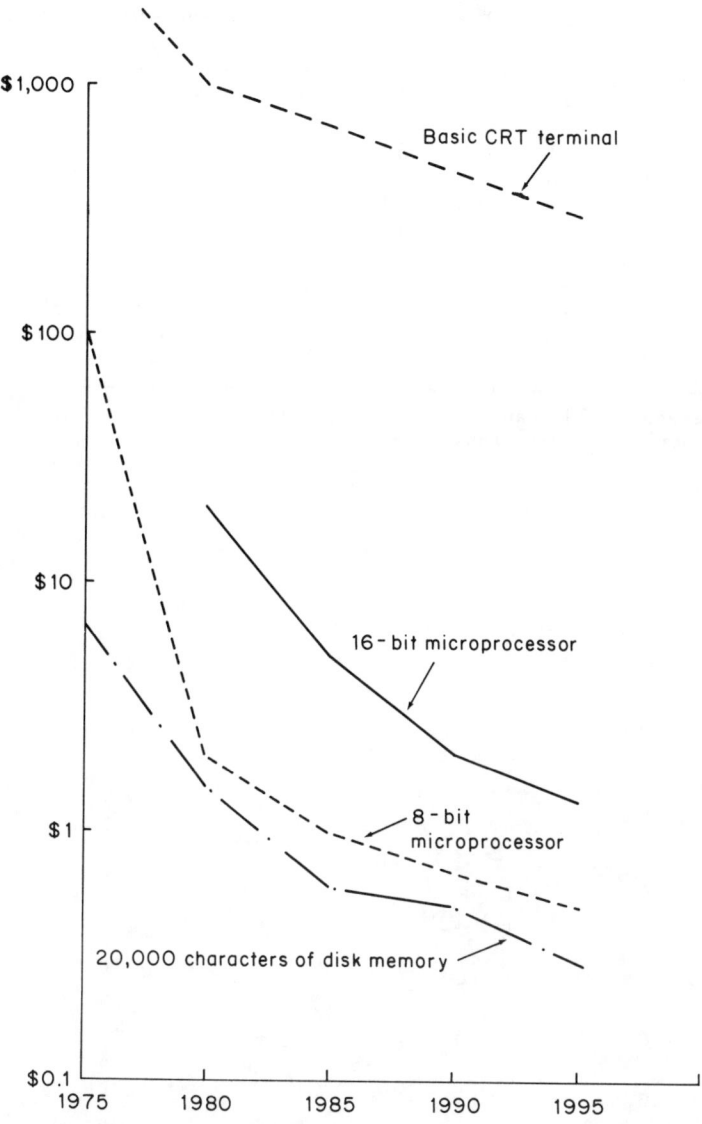

FIGURE 1.7 *Computer technology cost projections, 1975–95. (Adapted with permission from data compiled by Arthur D. Little, Inc.)*

parable among themselves, for the years 1983 to 1991. Also included are the 4-megabit chip unveiled by IBM and the futuristic 16-megabit chip described by Nippon Telegraph & Telephone, at the 'Solid State Circuits Conference', held in New York in February 1987. The same data is presented in graphic form in Figure 1.8.

Table 1.1 Average world prices of RAM chips, 1983–91 (in US cents/kilobit)

Capacity	1983	1984	1985	1986	1987	1988	1989	1990	1991
32K	11.0	11.0	6.0	5.5	5.5	—	—	—	—
64K	10.5	8.6	3.5	3.1	2.8	2.7	2.5	2.1	2.0
128K	—	—	2.8	1.9	1.4	1.3	1.2	—	—
256K	—	—	2.1	1.2	1.0	0.8	0.6	0.5	0.4
512K	—	—	—	1.95	1.35	0.75	0.45	0.40	0.35
1M	—	—	—	—	—	1.00	0.55	0.35	0.20
4M	—	—	—	—	—	—	—	0.40	0.20
16M	—	—	—	—	—	—	—	—	0.30

Estimates and projections are medians for the projected price ranges.
RAM = Random Access Memory.

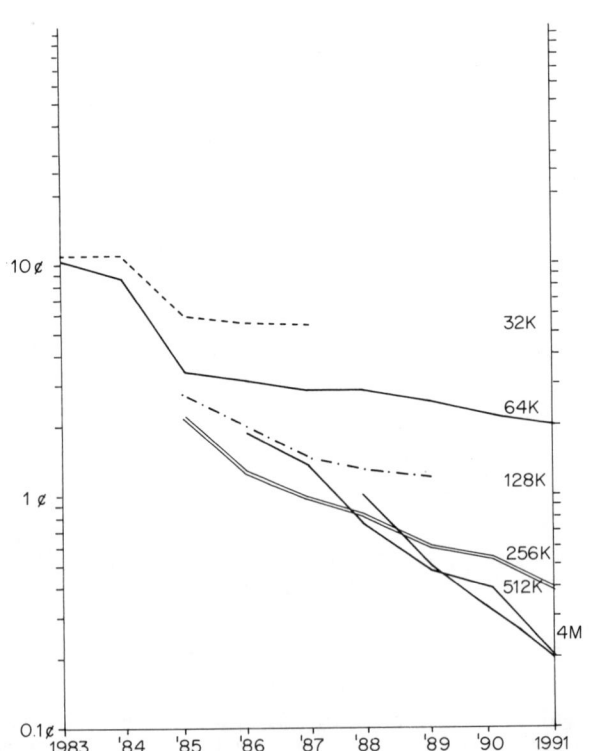

FIGURE 1.8 *Cost projections of RAM chips 1983–91 (in US cents/kilobit). Based on Table 1.1*

Even a superficial inspection of the diagram reveals several interesting features. The 32K and 64K memory chips are definitely on the way out, as they have ceased to be competitive. The middle-weights, the 256K and 512K chips, will dominate the field for the remainder of the 1980s; but the future clearly belongs to the top, megabit class.

The bigger the capacity, the steeper is the slope of the corresponding curve and therefore the faster is the rate of decrease in unit costs. Should an exponential be fitted, it would display a 19 per cent decrease in cost per annum for the 128K memory chip, a 24 per cent decrease for the 256K, a 30 per cent decrease for the 512K, a drop in excess of 40 per cent for the 1-megabit, and a dazzling 50 per cent for the 4-megabit chip, also per annum and cumulatively.

A dangerous self-deception

To put it in a simple way: falling costs and declining prices are nothing new; however, the fact that this trend may not stop, and may even gather momentum, is worth emphasizing. In the first place, this finding invalidates the earlier theories about the inevitable slowdown in cost reductions and price-cutting.

The delusion, to which many have fallen victims, including at one time the authors of this book, is made manifest by comparing the previous diagram with Figure 1.9, based on data supplied by the Bureau of Industrial Economics in 1985, two years earlier. The graph comprised a family of five downward-sloping curves relating to the phased development of ever more powerful RAMs. The pattern repeated itself, as all the five curves displayed an inflection point halfway through, prior to which their shape was exponential (i.e. their slope was constant); beyond the inflection point, the curves tended to flatten out. It is worth noting that this change in the rate of decreasing costs coincided with the launching of a yet larger random access memory. Given this repetitive pattern, it was easy to fit an envelop curve E having the same overall shape as the five constituent cost curves.

This seemed to confirm the starting assumption that deceleration in the downward cost trends is ultimately inescapable. The deception resided not in the initial hypothesis, which is in fact unimpeachable, but rather in the additional, tacit assumption that the turning point had already been passed or, alternatively, that the break in the earlier trend was just about to occur—hence the final, misleading 'inference' and hence also the false sense of security it may have conveyed to some vendors only too eager to listen to soothing arguments and theories.

To put it plainly, whilst American chip makers were still moving along

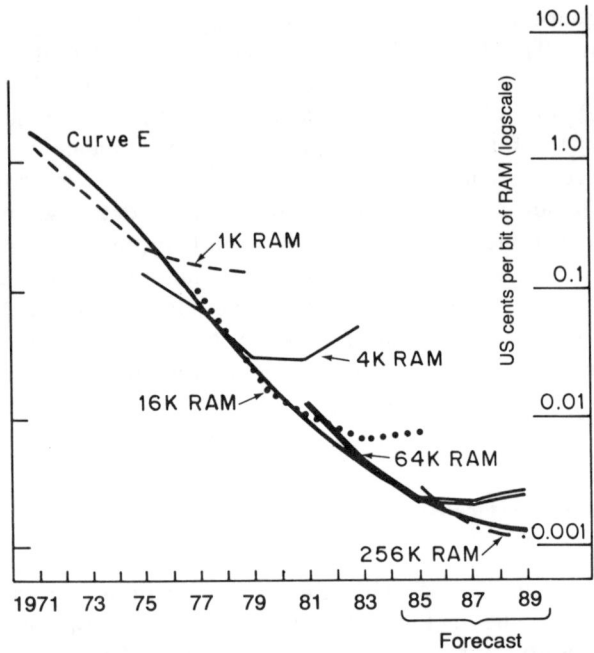

FIGURE 1.9 *Electronic memory prices. Estimates 1971–84 and forecasts 1985–89 (in US cents/bits). (From the Bureau of Industrial Economics. Adapted from* The Economist *(London), 6 July 1985. Reproduced by permission of* The Economist*)*

the B curve in our model (Figure 1.4), which portrays staggered cost reductions, their Japanese counterparts were already following the explosive curve C and were ruthlessly cutting, by a kind of anticipation, their prices by as much as 30 and even 40 per cent per year, thus mercilessly undercutting their American competitors, who for a long time seemed unable to grasp what was happening. (As for the European semiconductor firms, they were never really in the race and were more than ever reduced to the role of bystanders.)

The consequences of such a serious misjudgement, on the part of the US semiconductor industry, are there for everybody to see. By 1985, Texas Instruments, Motorola, National Semiconductors and Intel had lost the world leadership, which had looked unassailable only five years earlier, to NEC, Hitachi, Toshiba and Fujitsu, in that order. By Spring 1986, at least six American semiconductor plants and production lines had been shut down and the employment in the industry had dropped by 20 per cent. To top it all, most US vendors had left the RAM market, with the sole exception of Texas Instruments and Micron Technology in Idaho.

Aping the style of one another

The story of mass-produced memory chips and low-grade semiconductors is neither unique nor an entirely new phenomenon. For instance, the photocopying market, once the preserve of Xerox and a handful of other vendors, has for all practical purposes fallen—for the very same reasons—into the hands of Canon, Mita, Ricoh, Toshiba and a few smaller makers, with Japanese exports in 1985 totalling 2.1 million machines. Some 40 per cent of that number, or 900,000 photocopiers, were shipped to Europe alone, as against 600,000 two years earlier and just over 300,000 in 1981. The massive Japanese thrust forward in electronics took place between 1980 and 1985.

The reader should be reassured: there is no anti-Nippon bias in our analysis. Whether by design or by intuition, IBM has in fact followed very similar policies in the area of disk and disk drive technology as early as the 1960s. By the mid 1950s, the random access drum and disk storage devices had superseded the magnetic tape. IBM's RAMAC 350,

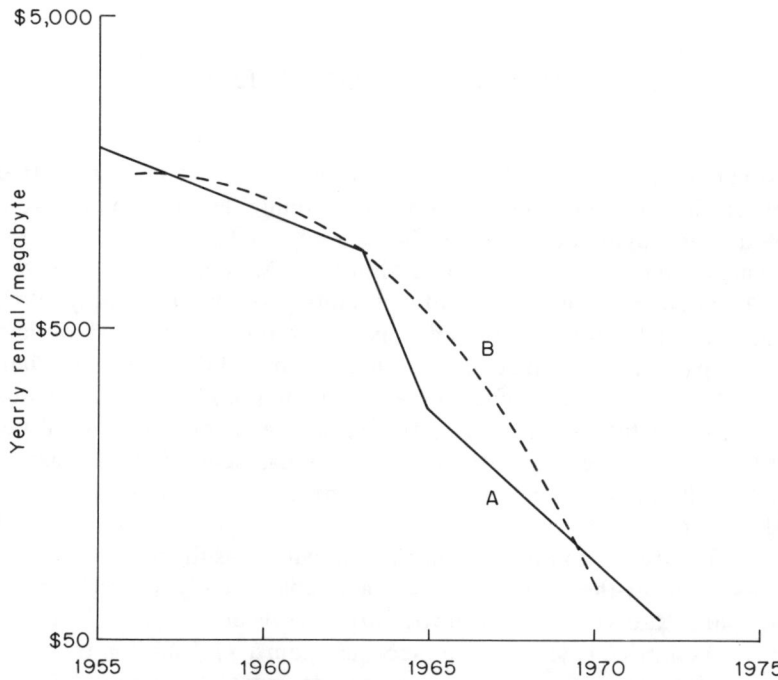

FIGURE 1.10 *Storage cost related to progress in disk technology, 1955–72. The solid line (A) is based on the original data with a doubly exponential trend line fitted (curve B)*

launched in 1956, had a capacity of 5 million characters, an access time of one second and cost a yearly rental of over $1,800 per megabyte. By 1963, IBM 2311 provided a stack of half-a-dozen disks in an exchangeable pack with a capacity in excess of 7M bytes—costing $900 in annual rental. With the advent of the minicomputer, the same firm started marketing small-size disk drives having a capacity of over 29M bytes, at a price of $276 per megabyte. In the early 1970s, the double density 3330 offered a capacity of 200M bytes per spindle, for a yearly charge of $58. The sixteen-year span story, which saw the doubling of storage capacity every two years eight times over, is summarized in Figure 1.10.

However, the story is not yet over. In addition to the current high-capacity floppy disk, the cartridge drives, the Winchester disk, etc., thin film technology is being developed for both disk media and heads, and the expectation is that exponential decline in the respective costs will gather momentum. In the long run, optical disk technology could produce yet another quantum jump. Thus, the cheapening of the storage media might start all over again, but with a slight difference, for we know now that policy-making in the area of costs and prices can be fully supplemented with, or corrected in the light of, rational economic analysis of environmental and industrywide trends.

1.4 IBM DID MORE OF IT, MORE OFTEN

However important, cost is not the only variable that matters. Other considerations influence production and planning decisions on the vendor side and buying decisions on the user side.

Whatever the future of the Space Shuttle, IBM is under contract with NASA to deliver the first bunch of new shuttle computers by May 1987. As before, each orbiter is to carry six mainframes—five working and one as a spare. The new machines are half the size of the older ones, half the weight at 64 pounds each and their main memory has been extended to 256K of 32-bit words from 104K previously. They consume 20 per cent less energy, their operational reliability has been increased sixfold to 6,000 hours and they run nearly three times faster than their predecessors.

There is, however, nothing radically innovative, as the new computers are based on off-the-shelf technology available already in 1984; that is what makes the comparison particularly significant for our purposes. The contract price is $500,000 a piece, as against $1.5 million ten years ago, which corresponds to an exponential decrease at a constant annual rate of 10.4 per cent. Using the familiar MIPS formula, which takes into account the 'improvement' in performance, the corresponding ratio would be 25-30 per cent per annum, always assuming that the pattern is a downward-sloping compound interest curve.

Whenever new technology was involved, IBM had usually gone much further. After its introduction of the highly successful 4300 series and several successive reductions in the posted prices, the company claimed that the new machines were offering a cost-performance ratio seven to eight times more favourable than that corresponding to the outgoing family of computers.

Precise, weighted figures are not available, as IBM follows a policy of volume discounts—reportedly up to 30-35 per cent—for very large quantities and it also bids lower prices when dealing with a prestige customer or with a university. Overall, it is clear that IBM has consistently depended mainly on deep and repetitive price-cutting, astute salesmanship and dedicated customer support to drive its business and sustain its growth. It was as if IBM management had always correctly guessed the pattern of achievable savings in their overall costs and had systematically passed the major part of the anticipated benefit on to their customers.

Figuring out the damages inflicted

How effective such a policy can be and, reciprocally, how devastating can be its effects on the competitor, who is either unaware of these cost trends, incapable of prognostication or too slow to react, is made plain by inspecting Table 1.2 and Figure 1.11, based thereupon. Imagine that during an initial period of ten years, all vendors in the same branch or specialty—peripherals, screen displays, simple word processors—

Table 1.2 Cost differentials resulting from departure from a constant exponential decrease

Function and assumed constant rate of decrease	Initial year	After 10 years	After 15 years	After 20 years
25% p.a. throughout	$10,000	$563	$134	$32
25% p.a. during 10 years and 20% thereafter	$10,000	$563	$185	$60
25% p.a. during 10 years and 30% thereafter	$10,000	$563	$ 95	$16

24

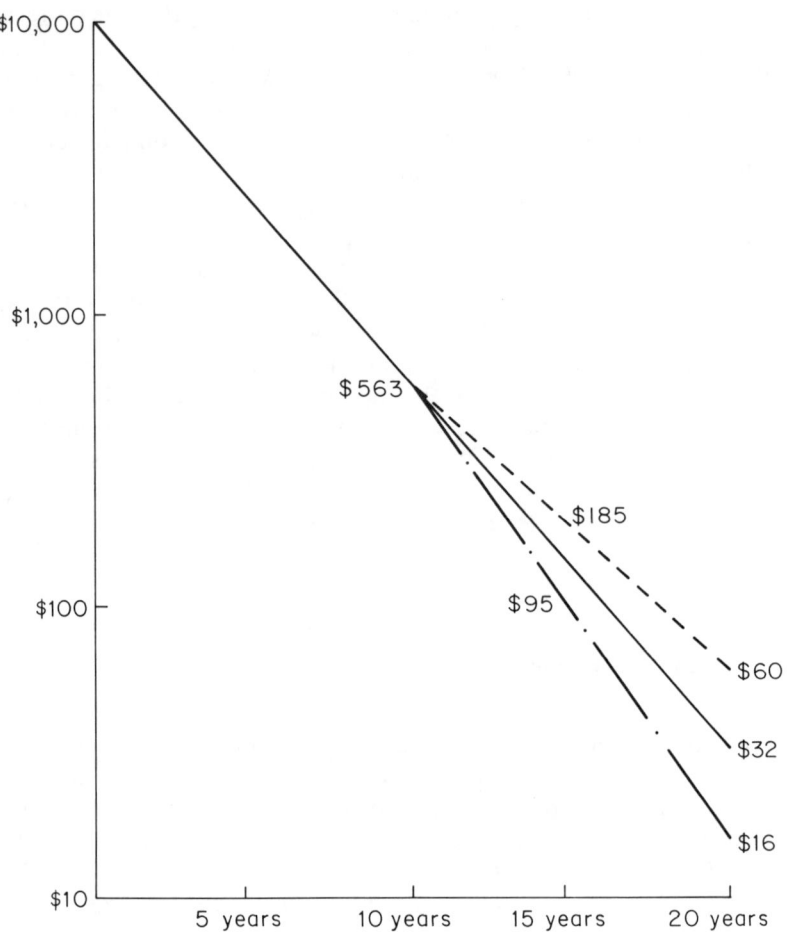

FIGURE 1.11 *Departing from a constant exponential decrease and the resultant cost spreads*

operate on the basis of an identical cost function, assumed to be an exponential curve, sloping downward, at a constant 25 per cent cost saving per year, and also follow similar pricing policies. At the end of the decade, an item that used to cost $10,000 is now down to $563.

Let us now assume that most vendors continue in the same way during the next decade, whilst a few aggressive manufacturers see the opportunity to improve on the cost-cutting, raising the yearly rate to 30 per cent from the previous 25 per cent. A few others may be unable to follow and in fact they choose to retreat to a 20 per cent discount p.a.

Five years later, the traditional-minded vendors post a price tag of $134, the aggressive vendors, $95 only, and the ultra-conservative vendors, $185. The numbers cited, whilst imaginary, are probably not out of line with the cost differential that arose between the US and Japanese leading chip makers, in the period 1980–5, as we have noticed in an earlier section.

If five years is not enough to knock out all opposition, we may pursue the hypothesis for another five years. The respective cost differentials, for identical products, would in the end reach extraordinary (dis)proportions—from single to double to quadruple, as can be seen in Table 1.2.

It can be objected, of course, that the overall time scale of 20 years is far too long, and the objection is perfectly valid. However, continuous uniform and simultaneous cost slashing by 25 per cent per year by all vendors would bring down the posted price from $10,000 to $2,373 after five years. At the end of another three years, during which the yearly rates of decrease might be, say, 20, 25 and 30 per cent respectively—as before—the new spread would still be unsustainable. With $1,000 being the median, the range would go from $814 to $1,215, or an unbeatable 50 per cent.

The message is clear: when even a small initial cost differential is compounded over a few years, the price-leader's pressure simply becomes unbearable. This, more than the customary wordy digressions, helps us to understand, especially, the discomfiture of the so-called plug-compatible companies ever since the 4300 series appeared in the marketplace. Itel went into bankruptcy and so did Magnuson; National Advanced Systems gave up the manufacturing of mainframes altogether; Amdahl has still not recovered from the shock.

We must not overlook the other side of the coin. 'No country is permanently strong, nor is it permanently weak' was the preferred saying of the Chinese philosopher, Han Fei. Meting out apparently evenhanded justice, IBM, after capturing 46 per cent of the US business market for personal computers in 1985, found itself six months later engaged in an uphill battle with a number of the IBM PC clone makers, offering at half the market price personal computers running faster or offering additional features, or both. We shall have more to say on this subject in the context of Section 3.2.

There are, obviously, many situations and many areas to which we could apply the type of analysis based on the compound interest law, which we have used to disentangle the long-term cost and cost–performance trends in the computer field. The methodology has served us well. Of course, it would be foolish to attribute to it more than it can achieve. However powerful, it is just a kit of tools to be used alongside, or in combination with, other methods.

1.5 FALLING OUT OF STEP: COMMUNICATIONS COSTS

It is beyond our framework to analyse telecommunications costs and their evolution in any depth. In view of the increasing technological and operational interdependence between computing and networking, it is appropriate to give a few general indications in order, as a minimum, to dispel some dangerous misconceptions.

A case of fallacy of composition

Figure 1.12 is an interesting attempt to demonstrate visually that a close correlation exists between carrying capacity of modern telecommunications systems and unit costs of transmission of voice or data. The fact that the diagram is plotted on a log-log scale should not worry us in the least; nor should we be concerned with the exact shape and slope of some 20 minicurves included. Two observations are important, however.

First, as the capacity grows exponentially, the cost per circuit over a given distance decreases, also exponentially, but not at the same rate. More specifically, to an escalation of three orders of magnitude in capacity corresponds a decrease in relative costs by two orders of magnitude only. Second, this relation seems to hold irrespective of the technology actually used, i.e. cable and waveguide systems on the one hand and radio systems on the other.

The trouble is that an unimpeachable demonstration such as this is conducive to drawing a wrong inference. It is all too easy to confuse transmission costs with telecommunications costs, which include many other cost items, e.g. switching, terminal equipment, etc.[3] To assume, even though tacitly, that what is true of each item in a class or part of a whole will be true of all taken together is plainly fallacious and deceptive. Worse still, nobody will ever know what prejudice future extrapolations made on such doubtful premises may have caused to overcredulous vendors of computer systems and, possibly, to other sectors of the economy as well.

'... even before the end of this century telecommunication may become virtually costless, and should certainly be in no way dependent on distance for its price', wrote the London *Economist* in 1972 under the signature of its assistant chief editor; in fact, Norman Macrae was

---

[3] See also Section 2.2 dealing with the problem of discontinuities in telecommunications gear.

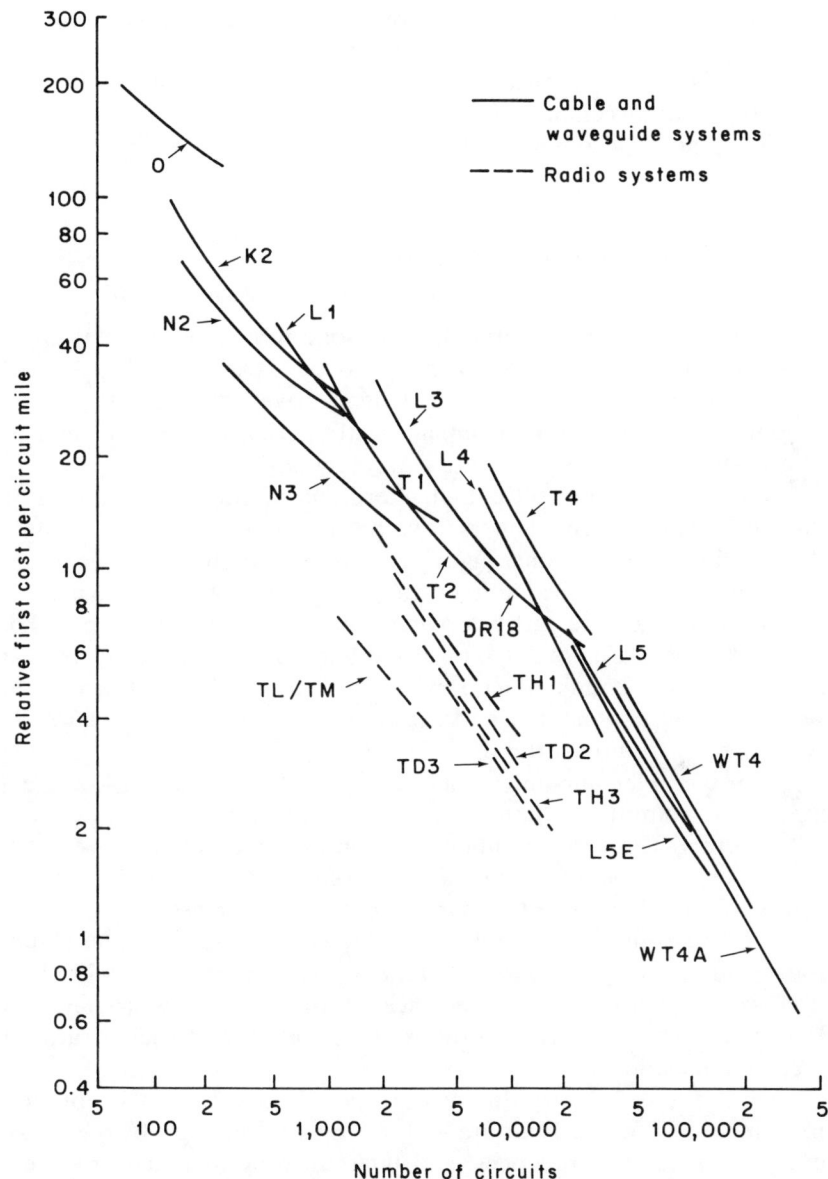

FIGURE 1.12 *Transmission cost trends related to carrying capacity. (From Eugene F. O'Neill, 'Radio and Long-Haul Transmission',* Bell Laboratories Record, *January 1975. Copyright 1975,* Bell Telephone Laboratories, Inc. *Reprinted by permission)*

merely echoing earlier statements by US analysts and anticipating identical forecasts made repeatedly by a number of European 'experts'. The argument has been hammered down in the popular book *Computerization of Society*, by Nora and Minc,[4] originally a study commissioned by the President of France, and it became the cornerstone of the—notoriously unsuccessful—French government policy in the area of computing and telecommunications.

The laggards must catch up or suffer

It was never easy to interpret shifts in long-term telecommunications costs and to relate them convincingly to the tariffs actually charged. Since the breakup of AT&T and the demi-privatization of the telecom business in Britain and in Japan—with perhaps more changes to follow—the exercise has become extremely hazardous.

The prevailing view still is that telecommunications costs are dropping, but more slowly than processing and/or storage costs. This is illustrated by two diagrams. Figure 1.13 relates to an American system with computer and telecommunications requirements that are fixed or vary little; the data are partly derived from past records, partly based on future estimates. Figure 1.14, on the other hand, is extracted from an extensive survey commissioned by the collective PTTs in Europe;[5] all the curves are exponential and are based on estimates arrived at by extrapolation from past trends.

In Europe, telecommunications costs have been declining—and are expected to continue declining—at a very moderate 5 per cent per year, in real terms. The corresponding figure in the United States is close to 13 per cent, in nominal terms. When discounted for inflation, the US rate is still nearly double the European rate of decrease.

On the other hand, the curves related to computer costs in the United States and in Europe, as shown here, are pretty much in line with those discussed previously. In both instances, computer cost–efficiency went down much more rapidly than the concomitant cost–efficiency ratios in telecommunications.

Several different interpretations are possible. Indeed, it is not clear how much such comparisons are influenced by technology, by regulation and other restrictive practices, and how much by market factors, e.g. competition, pricing policies, etc. The question is of utmost importance, for what is at stake is how much data processing will be done in the

---

[4] Original title: *L'informatisation de la société*, Documentation Française, Paris, 1978.
[5] Eurodata Foundation and Logica Ltd, *Data Communications in Western Europe in the 1980s*, Eurodata Foundation, London, 1980.

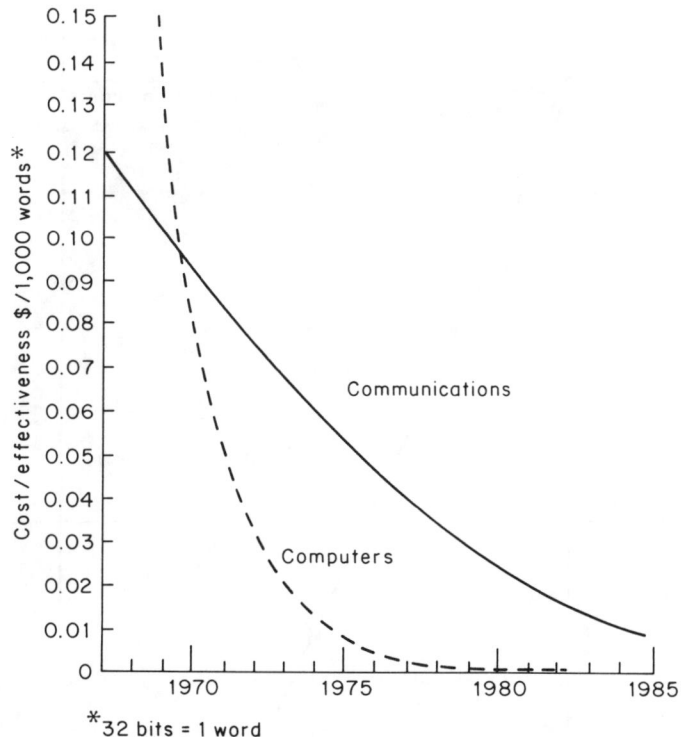

FIGURE 1.13 *Comparing computing and telecommunications costs. (Reproduced by permission of The Diebold Group, Inc.)*

longer term via networks and how much carried out through stand-alone computer systems, supplemented, if and when required, by an alternative data distribution channel. The matter properly belongs to Chapter 4, where it will be taken up in the more general context of consumer choice in a marketplace that is increasingly dominated by the buyers, and especially corporate buyers of services and complete systems.

1.6 CONCLUSION AND OUTLOOK

In this brief concluding section, the broad assumptions about cost trends and patterns, discussed in this first chapter, are put into perspective. Implied is the suggestion that models based on comparative or differen-

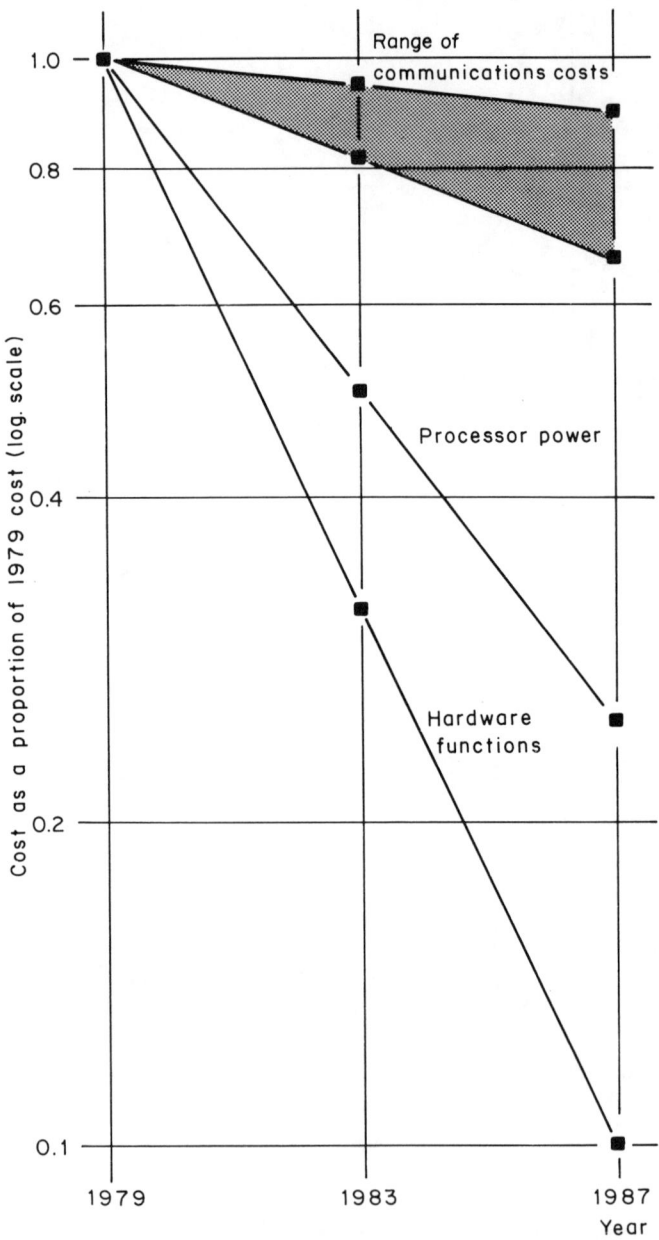

FIGURE 1.14 *Expected trends in computer hardware and communications costs. (From Eurodata Foundation and Logica, Ltd.,* Data Communications in Western Europe in the 1980s. *Reproduced by permission of Eurodata Foundation)*

tial cost analysis could greatly improve strategic decision-making and planning.

1. Until recently, few vendors of new information technology have bothered about developing exact curves of cost and relating them to the stream of revenues. This neglect was due partly to lack of incentive inherent in the cozy growth environment and partly to the fact that, operating under imperfect competition, firms may have anyhow to make all sorts of rough guesses on the basis of incomplete information. Hence their traditional reliance on such rules of thumb as the rather hazy concept of break-even point; markup pricing in good times; repeat price cutting under tense competition; setting up prices at less than full costs when times are hard; or just mimicking Big Blue in marketing new products.
2. For a long time, including the agitated 1970s, these rough indicators of business changes have served well most computer and system vendors who, additionally, drew comfort from the assumed permanence of an exponential (constant-rate) trend towards more powerful computers at lower unit costs. In retrospect, major business failures were surprisingly few and they have nearly always been attributed to conspicuous recklessness and seldom, if ever, to lack of managerial insight. Take, for instance, the BUNCH group[6] of mainframe makers: should we be more impressed by their stubborness in following misguided strategies ever since the microprocessor revolution in the early 1970s or rather by their resilience under the onslaught? Having survived in the past through thick and thin, some by the skin of their teeth, managements of hundreds of large- and medium-sized firms quite naturally tended to underrate, or dismiss altogether, the more recent prophecies about the computer industry's shakeout as inevitable. Now, however, all are in for a shock—for reasons that many of them do not even suspect yet.
3. Here, indeed, comes the catch. The conventional array of business indicators used by most vendors as a matter of routine concealed from their view the sudden accelerated erosion of the fundamental cost assumptions on which their operations have been—and continue to be—based. When falling profits, the piling up of inventories and thinning order books were reported in the early 1980s, and then became commonplace, managements were quick to ascribe their shortcomings to depression of the economy and put the blame on government policies, foreign competition, IBM's aggressiveness, Japanese (unproved) dumping practices, and what have you, dismissing out of hand the idea that, perhaps, they themselves were not

---

[6] BUNCH = Burroughs, Sperry (UNIVAC), NCR, Control Data Corporation (CDC), Honeywell.

blameless. In reality, by 1983 for some and by 1985 for most, US and European computer vendors had priced themselves out of several key electronics markets. Ironically, IBM itself of late has fallen victim to the excess cost syndrome, which Big Blue has so adroitly exploited against its rivals in the past.

4. In order to fully appreciate the practical value of comparative cost analysis expounded in this chapter, it is necessary to remind ourselves of the hitherto common practices. There was nothing intrinsically wrong with applying the compound interest law to their business operations, as some computer vendors used to do, often with the help of professional accountants. What definitely proved fatal, however, was the absence of an appropriate conceptual framework that would have permitted the integration of alternative patterns (of growth, of declining costs), even though as remote possibilities, and would have provoked useful in-house brainstormings along the 'what ... if ... ?' lines and thus alerted the top brass to potential dangers. Finding itself suddenly beleaguered, IBM demonstrates vividly in its present disarray that Big Blue's executives, too, have made, by omission, the same unfortunate mistake in not taking into account the hypothesis of a significant reduction in their competitors' production costs.

5. Strangely enough, a wave of optimism swept the computer and software industries in the early 1980s, at the very moment when the seeds of rot—as we now realize in retrospect—were already at work. Both in 1980 and 1981, income statements of many US vendors were highly encouraging and the future looked rosy. In that ambiance, the difficulties experienced by some vendors were seen as symptoms of yet another short-term crisis. For some time yet, all warning signals of a forthcoming gale, by the more lucid observers, fell on deaf ears. In all fairness to the vendors, however, it must be acknowledged that these pessimistic analyses and dire predictions were hardly credible because they, too, lacked a conceptual base, a theory which alone could explain and relate the widely scattered and isolated discomfitures.

6. However crude, the differential cost analysis, based on the assumption of variable exponential growth rates, helps to fill this crucial gap. Of course, the method could, and should, be refined and supplemented with other techniques. Using this newer approach has now become a matter of urgency, inasmuch as a reversal of fortunes induced by changes in the vendors' respective cost patterns can result in a consumptive phtisis of the losers within a short time. The US supremacy in semiconductor design and manufacturing has been surrendered to Japan's chip makers in four years, over 1981–5. It took just about that long for the Japanese to capture the lion's share of the world markets for electronic typewriters and facsimile

machines, and soon, presumably, for optronics as well. Previously, IBM had squeezed out of the market a number of rival vendors, saddled with higher costs and thus unable to match IBM's fully justified price slashing. More recently, IBM itself was caught on the wrong foot by Asian clone makers in a matter of a couple of years, between 1985 and 1986.

7. The comparative cost analysis approach is relevant, with slight modifications, to a number of current issues, for instance, the emerging competition between dumb/smart terminals and PC systems. The differential that existed between base costs of these potential substitutes has of late narrowed down and, judging by current trends, will soon disappear. Consequently, according to a recent survey,[7] it is only a matter of time before vendors of multiuser systems start to discard conventional terminals that can only use a single central processor and to replace them with disk-based PC systems that can integrate with many host operating systems. Terminal manufacturers should be made to realize that, in order to survive, they will have to offer extra features at no extra cost to users, e.g. greater throughput rate, higher graphics resolution, etc.

8. Looking further ahead, the differential approach may well be of assistance in determining, especially on cost grounds, how much computing will eventually be done via networks and how much carried out on stand-alone equipment supplemented by independent data distribution systems.

---

[7] 'Multifunctional terminal survey', *Systems International*, October **1986**, 37–42.

Chapter 2

Exposure to Fluctuations

Business conditions never stand still, and the smoothed-out, idealized curves we used for the purpose of demonstrating the existence of long-term trends, e.g. in unit costs and in improved cost efficiency as a result of innovation, are obviously only approximations to real-life evolutions, as computer vendors know only too well. Trend lines, however, are useful not only as signposts, as we saw, but also as embodiments of 'normalcy' in operating a business. Thus, they provide the best frame of reference for the identification of all kinds of significant fluctuations, which can most of the time be interpreted as deviations from the trend line, or central tendency, and as such quantified by comparison with the relevant value of the trend.

Inasmuch as these outside interferences cause a series of disturbances in the business of the vendor, they are from the vendor's standpoint equivalent to extra costs. The loss of revenue may be only temporary, but it may endure, it can be occasional or recurring and it may be tolerable or highly detrimental. However, just as every cloud has its silver lining, an astute vendor eventually learns how to cope and possibly even succeeds in turning the momentary headache to an ultimate advantage.

Keeping in mind that there are always two sides to a coin, we undertake in Chapter 2 to provide a systematic review of the main types of fluctuations to which the computer industry is exposed. The rapidly increasing diversification of products and markets justifies not only a strategy of narrow specialization but also alternatively that of sharp product differentiation, depending on the size of the vendor company (Section 2.1). The critical problem of lumpiness (Section 2.2) is never fully soluble, but it may be by-passed, opening up new vistas and creating new business prospects in the longer run.

As several examples cited show, failure to adopt preventive or corrective policies in good time may cause painful losses. This is particularly the case when a vendor company—even Big Blue itself—loses control over its product cycle periodicity and must close down production lines only partly amortized (Section 2.3). Heavy penalties are especially in store for those vendors who close their eyes to the writings on the wall provided by unimpeachable business surveys clearly pointing to an impending, industry wide depression (Section 2.4). Few sectors of the computer industry remain immune to business cycles, with the main exception of the supercomputer makers (Section 2.5).

2.1 DEVELOPING DIFFERENTIATED PRODUCTS

Established beliefs often die hard; long after their validity has been disproved, or severely restricted by fresh research or new evidence, the torso of the old model lingers on in some people's mind. Our argument begins with just a case in point, namely the need for a complete overhaul of the old Grosch's law about the optimum relation between computer power and operating costs. The conclusions of the just-completed reassessment imply, as we shall see, major changes in product strategies of the largest vendors of computer systems.

The best computer value that money can buy

The first published formulation of Grosch's law appeared in 1953, although the discovery of the principle by Herbert A. Grosch is said to predate the printed version by several years. The costs (c) of computer systems, states the law, increase as a function of the square root of their power (w). Thus

$$c = f(w^{\frac{1}{2}}).$$

In other words, the average cost of computing (c/w) decreases as the square root of the power of the machine, as can be shown by dividing both sides of the previous equation by w. Therefore:

$$c/w = f(w^{-\frac{1}{2}}).$$

Thus, by doubling all inputs, output would be quadrupled. Conversely, in order to double the output, it is sufficient to increase all inputs by about 40 per cent only.

To put it the other way round, Grosch's law posits that the cost of a given job will decrease with more powerful computers. This may of course be translated into the following practical recommendation: the most economical and expedient solution is to procure the largest computer compatible with the user's particular needs. Also, one large computer system is to be preferred to several small ones. It follows that as long as Grosch's law holds, no convincing argument could be made in defense of distributed computing power.

It has been found independently that MIPS (millions of instructions executed per second), as described earlier, is closely correlated in a competitive market with the price of central processors.

Information science and industry are indebted to Phillip Ein-Dor of

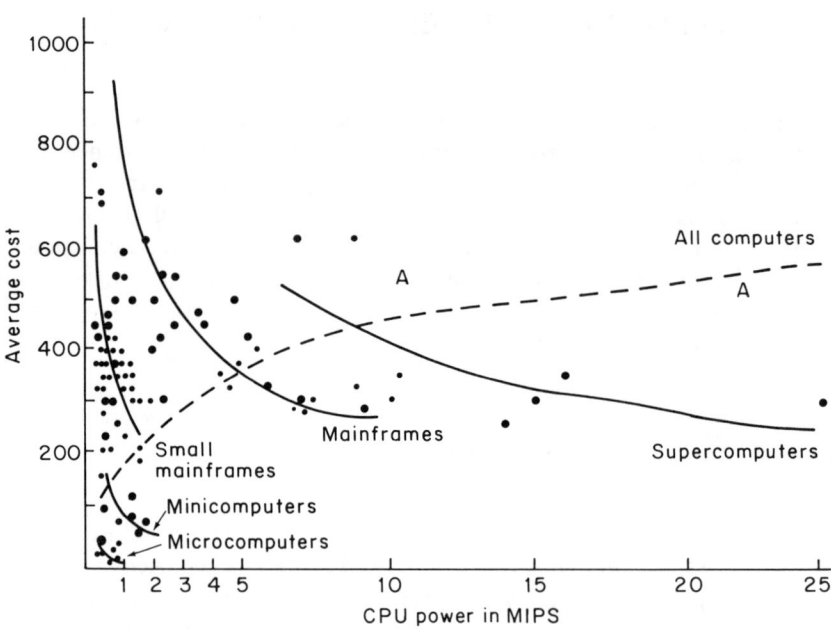

FIGURE 2.1 *Relationship between power and average cost for five categories of computers.* Copyright 1985, Association for Computing Machinery, Inc. Reprinted by permission

the School of Management at the University of Tel-Aviv[1] for carrying out a thorough re-examination of Grosch's law. Ein-Dor started from the self-evident statement that 'computers can no longer be regarded as one homogeneous product and that they should be divided into categories for analytical purposes'. He distinguished five categories: microcomputers, minicomputers, small mainframes[2], large mainframes and supercomputers, using their price as the main discriminant, and applied this classification to recent data for 106 systems obtained from *Computerworld* and other reliable sources.

The results of this analysis presented in graphic form in Figure 2.1 amount in reality to a new theory. This is condensed below in five propositions:

1. Contrary to Grosch's expectations, the average cost of computing did not diminish with increased power. It actually increased at a rate equal to the cube root of that power (curve A).

[1] Phillip Ein-Dor, 'Grosch's law re-revisited: CPU power and the cost of computation', *Comm. ACM*, No. 2, February 1985.
[2] Alternatively labelled small business machines or superminis.

2. This finding, however, does not invalidate Grosch's law altogether. The old law seems to hold good within each of the five categories of computers as defined, but not between the different categories (viz. all other curves in Figure 2.1).
3. The optimal solution, especially for a corporate user, is to procure the most powerful computer within the appropriate category. Thus, one powerful minicomputer will perform the given job more cheaply and efficiently than a pair of less powerful minis.
4. Returning to the average cost curve A, it is easy to see that 'the most economically efficient computing is being done on microcomputers; average costs rise through the minicomputer-small-mainframe-and-large-mainframe range and then fall somewhat for supercomputers'. Within large organizations, mixed solutions are likely to prevail, requiring a high degree of compatibility.
5. Ein-Dor demonstrated that other parameters of power which he initially took into account did not affect the results in a significant way, with the only exception being communications expenses involved with distributed systems. This factor may, of course, run counter to the tendency to decentralize via networking. This is another subject altogether and will be discussed in greater detail in Section 5.3.
6. Ein-Dor's analysis of cost–performance ratios has stimulated further research. A recent paper[3] suggests that for minicomputers Grosch's law is not valid, but that, other things being equal, there seems still to be some economic force in favour of using very powerful computers.

Product differentiation—a must for large vendors

The Ein-Dor model, which we presented in a highly condensed form, helps in an understanding of the disasters that have befallen the US mainframe manufacturers, including IBM, but also ICL, Siemens and CII in the 1970s. Their excessive concentration on building ever more powerful processors was, so it seemed, fully consistent with Grosch's teachings. Furthermore, the Ein-Dor discovery of the true nature of the law provides a rational explanation of the initial success, first, of the minis, then of the microprocessors and also of the more recent revival of interest in supercomputers.

The relatively recent yet dramatic shift to the smaller machines away from the large mainframes that took place in the United States is illustrated in Figure 2.2. The market share of the large mainframes,

---

[3] Y. M. Kang, R. B. Miller and R. A. Pick, *Comm. ACM*, **29**, No. 8, 779 (August 1986).

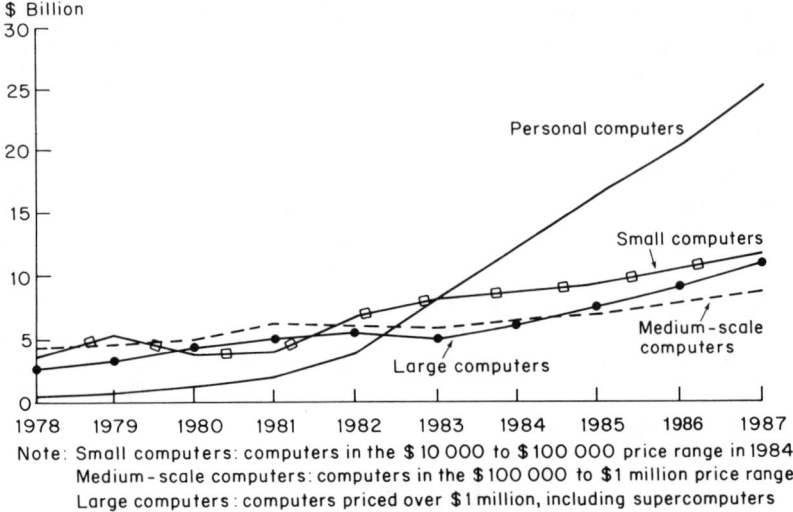

FIGURE 2.2 *Composition of US computer shipment value, 1978–87. (From OECD,* Software: An Emerging Industry. *Based on data provided by International Data Corporation (IDC). Reproduced by permission of OECD)*

measured by the value of shipments in 1979, represented 62 per cent of the total, whilst small business computers, the minis and microprocessors together accounted for the remaining 38 per cent. By 1985, the value of shipments of microprocessors alone had reached some 40 per cent of a much wider market, or just about double that of large mainframes, which regressed in relative terms.

Will computer makers take the clue from Ein-Dor? For specialty vendors the question does not arise, for their products by definition are distinct in performance or in appearance. As for the large vendors, it is obviously too early to give a definite answer—the results of Ein-Dor's investigation were first made public only in February 1985. Of course, nobody expects that IBM, Hewlett-Packard or Xerox will ever issue an official statement saying that they approve of the new theory and promising that they will live up to it.

There are, however, symptoms of their direct interest in the matter. In February 1986, IBM announced two smaller models of its most powerful mainframe, the 3090, nicknamed 'Sierra', doubled the optional extra storage capacity of existing 3090 machines and promised upgrades for its smaller mainframe line, the 4381. In June of the same year, the company announced three new models of its System 36 and three additional models of System 38, and offered a new program, called 'Advanced Peer-to-Peer Networking', which allows the Systems 36 and 38 to communicate directly with each other. The System 36 and System

38 are often spoken of as 'intermediate' computers, as they are smaller than mainframes but bigger than personal computers.

At the same time, Big Blue spelled out publicly its new overall strategy, which calls for:

1. Phasing out a number of incompatible office products selling in the $100,000 to $1 million range, but in fact selling rather poorly;
2. Concentrating on three basic systems: the IBM PC line, at the low end; the System 36 and System 38 in the middle; extensions of and upgrades for the huge 'Sierra' and the 4381 lines;
3. Counting on its future PCs to act as the engine that drives uphill long-term demand for medium processors and large mainframes;
4. Linking all future IBM computers via Systems Application Architecture, the new programming standards released in March 1987.

The new IBM product policy, to say the least, is clearly reminiscent of the Ein-Dor recommendations, although it can be argued that the change of strategy was prompted by market share losses since 1985. In the meanwhile, Digital Equipment has staged, partly at the expense of IBM, a remarkable comeback, which its rivals did not expect. Yet the surge of DEC was perfectly predictable by Ein-Dor's canons. The revival of DEC fortunes came with the launching of the new line of VAX 32-bit computers, stretching from the tiny microprocessors to powerful sophisticated minis, to high-speed mainframes, all crowded with high-density circuitry and all compatible with each other.

The new VAX 32-bit series was greeted by immediate success and appeared in the market at the very time when IBM was still offering too many undifferentiated products, thus confusing potential customers, and at least two years before the new IBM strategy will have been implemented—even if we assume that it will work, which is far from certain.

2.2 COPING WITH THE PROBLEM OF LUMPINESS

The unceasing escalation in processing power and storage capacity, especially in the category of mainframes and supercomputers but also in telecommunications media, raises the puzzling question of discontinuities and their influence on costs and prices, or tariffs. That this troublesome aspect has generally been overlooked by most industrial analysts and tackled with insufficient vigour by some vendors may be due partly to the dearth of reliable data and partly to the lack of awareness of the user predicaments.

The reader will have noticed the difficulty, semantic as well as operational, involved in defining the five classes of computing machines used by Ein-Dor in his reassessment of Grosch's law. However, the problem could be minimized without serious consequences as long as both the sellers and the buyers were dealing with directly comparable products and homogeneous market. This, obviously, is no longer the case, and the issue must be given appropriate consideration.

Whenever possible, distinction should be made between technical discontinuities and jumps, on the one hand, and discontinuities in demand, on the other. Consequently, also, CPU power, or capacity, or throughput rate (in communications) ought not to be confused with the degree of actual utilization, which may vary a great deal between (corporate) users and over time.

The best illustration of the problem is to be found in the area of data communications. In addition to short- and long-haul transmission costs, which decrease smoothly with scale, outlays on line termination, switching and staff are among the elements that enter the total cost of operating a complete telecommunications system. For the sake of simplicity, it is assumed that the latter cost items are held constant, so that multiplexing,[4] which introduces lumps, is isolated as the only cause of disturbance. This is shown graphically in Figure 2.3, in which curve 4, relating to multiplexing investment, proceeds by jerks and jumps. For instance, a tenfold increase in multiplexing capacity (see points A and B) results in a 50 per cent saving per channel. However, if multiplexing capacity is increased by a factor of 15 (see points A and C), the unit saving per channel vanishes altogether in relation to the starting position. On the other hand, the smooth, regularly downward-sloping curve 3 refers to the investment required for transmission capacity alone. The impact of multiplexing on aggregate costs is reflected in curves 1 and 4, neither of which is smooth.

It is easy to find examples of similar technical discontinuities in the field of computer design. From 8-bit, to 16-bit, to 32-bit processors, the progression has been geometric, by doubling and doubling again. The jump was fourfold from 1K to 4K bit RAMs (dynamic access memory), then to 16K, to 64K, to 256K and now again from 1-megabit, to 4-megabit, to 16-megabit RAMs.

The problem is immensely complicated by lumpiness in demand. As a general rule, all the comparisons over time that have been made are by definition fallacious inasmuch as they are based on calculations that assume either full load or a load factor supposed to increase proportionately with storage capacity or processing power. Since such drastic assumptions are totally unrealistic, they are occasionally replaced, espe-

---

[4] Multiplexing is a technique that permits multiple channels to be carved out of a single facility.

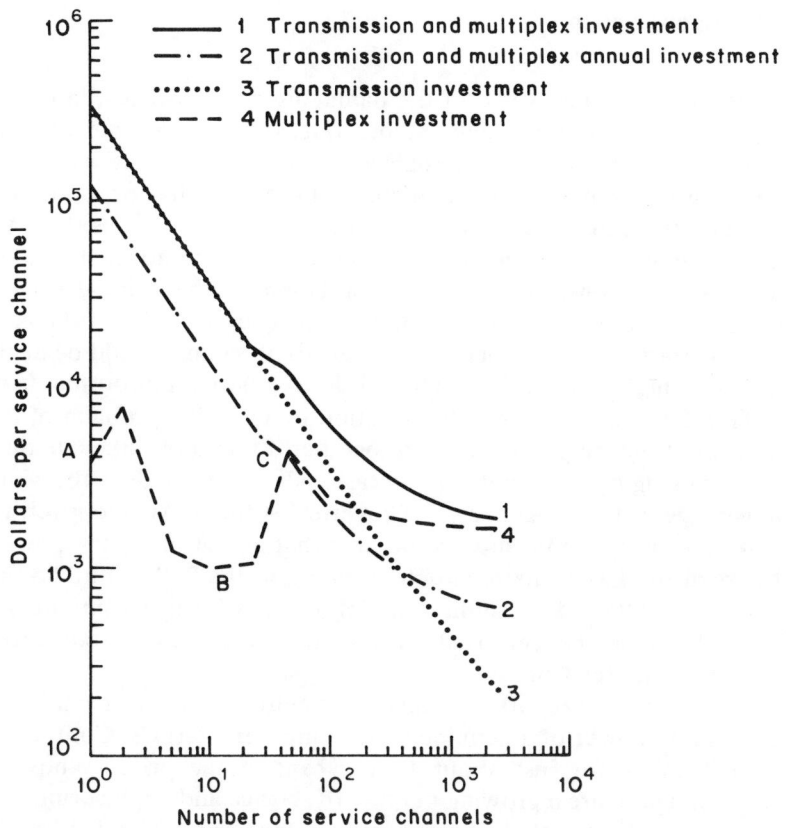

FIGURE 2.3 *Relationship between carrying capacity and average cost per telephone channel. (From Mandanis et al., The Domestic Telecommunications industry: Economic Behavior, Competition, and Public Policy, R73-40. Reproduced by permission of Systems Applications, Inc.)*

cially for planning purposes, by a fixed set of assumptions about startup demand, its rate of growth, its seasonal patterns, peak and off-peak models, etc., and this may be no better.

All these variables, together with other parameters, directly affect short-term and medium-term costs and, consequently also, the return on investment. Furthermore, it is not unusual to come across patches of inelastic demand, with sales remaining low in spite of theoretically lower user costs, coupled with occasional huge discontinuities of demand.[5]

---

[5] See Paul A. Samuelson, *Economics*, 5th ed., McGraw-Hill, 1961, p. 581.

Filling power gaps

In order to alleviate some of the damaging consequences, most manufacturers offer not a single model but a family of intercompatible products having the same design and comparable functions, but with differing performance characteristics. This allows the corporate user to upgrade the computer installation in several smaller steps, but it does not eliminate the trouble entirely. This is due partly to the fact that the processing power of the machines that belong to the same series usually increases by doubling, trebling or even quadrupling. Since no computer ever operates at full capacity, however, some savings could be achieved by procuring slower and, therefore, less expensive input/output devices.[6]

Trying to find an acceptable solution to a specific problem of lumpiness, or attempting to bypass it altogether if that looks like a better bet, is a challenging task, but may occasionally be turned to the vendor's advantage in the longer term. 'Crayettes' is the nickname given to the several prototype minisupercomputers that aim at filling the power gap between the Cray supercomputers selling in the $10–20 million range and the standard $1–2 million mainframes. Minisupercomputers must not, of course, be confused with superminicomputers, pioneered by Prime Computer Corp.

'Crayettes' are reportedly capable of delivering over one-third of the computing power of a genuine supercomputer—Cray's, Control Data's or Hitachi's—for just about 10 per cent of the price. Who are the buyers? There are a growing number of science and engineering firms or research institutes that either cannot afford the real thing or have a supercomputer that is already overloaded. The market is estimated to grow to $1 billion by 1990 in the United States alone.

The main reason for including this particular example is that, having started from a concrete problem of technological and economic hiatus, Floating Point Systems, Convex Computer Corp., Scientific Computer System, Inc. and a handful of other firms active in the field have in fact positioned themselves to exploit whatever breakthroughs they might be able to achieve, for example, in the use of new materials, such as gallium arsenide, new software languages, new computer architectures and other innovations in the making, which will be discussed in greater detail in Part 3 of this book.

---

[6]This raises the general question of inventory costs of carrying unutilized—or grossly underused—'lumpy' plant or equipment, which, however, must still be maintained under any circumstances. The cumulative effects may be such as to cancel any anticipated economies of scale.

2.3 STAGGERING OF PRODUCT CYCLES

This section deals with product-related cycles, their impact on costs and prices and how some adverse effects can be mitigated. For the sake of clarity, discussion of the computer industry's sensitivity to changes in the business environment and, in particular, to business cycles is deferred to the next section.

Obsolescence adjudged by business acumen

A good starting point is to put in contrast the 'length of life' of a product and the notion of 'life cycle'. Length of life usually refers to plant and hardware wearing out after a certain period and therefore needing replacement. Obviously, two different, though at first sight similar, products seldom have the same length of life. It is thus a measure of durability, especially relevant to the user, but it is also of some interest to the vendor. True, the period of actual utilization of the installation may be somewhat shortened or extended by a discretionary decision of the user company in response to its momentary needs or to changes in the business environment. Thus, there is a link of a kind to business cycles, which by definition affect more than one industry.

The connotations of 'life cycle' of the product are quite different. This implies obsolescence as distinct from wear and tear. The actual period is determined primarily by the maker–supplier, especially when acting under competitive conditions. It has been said over and over again that in the computing and networking business, life cycles are relatively short; furthermore, that they tend to get shorter and shorter; and, moreover, that these trends are related to the rate of innovation and to increased competition. However, no conclusive, generalizable evidence, either way, has been produced so far. Of course, industrial lobbies are prone to quoting a few, at first sight, impressive examples, but they are isolated and may be untypical. In all such comparisons, perhaps the greatest difficulty is where to draw the dividing line between mere upgradings and the quantitative jump that the launching of a new, higher-performance system, product or component implies.

A few examples will illustrate this point. During the decade 1963–73, Control Data put on the market no fewer than five large mainframe models, whose computing power went up from under 1 MIPS to well over 100 MIPS, or an increase by more than two orders of magnitude.[7]

---

[7] The models were the CDC 3600, CDC 6600, CDC 7600, CDC Star-100 and CDC STAR-X. Source: Harold Sackman and Harold Borko (Eds), *Computers and the Problems of Society*, Afips Press, Montvale, New Jersey, 1972, p. 91. MIPS = million instructions per second.

Was that a case of staggered upgradings or an instance of excessively short life cycles of distinct products? Moreover, does two- or three-year-old gear and *a fortiori* any recent computer installation become obsolete simply because your competitor has in the meanwhile 'beefed up' a specific function or a piece of hardware?

The life cycle of each successive 'generation' of optical fibres for telecommunications usage has been some five to six years, a period which is not particularly short, and the next cycle is predicted as lasting another five years. In Section 1.3, above, it has been shown that the period needed to design, develop, mass produce, sell and eventually withdraw from a market a new class of dynamic random access memory chips (RAMs) covered almost exactly eight years each, and the figure remained stable for five life cycles in succession.

Calculation of life cycles runs into additional difficulties brought about by loose usage of the words 'new generation' that many manufacturing firms see as a good selling point, irrespective of whether it corresponds to real, substantial innovation. Echoing noisy announcements by leading vendors, McClellan, in an otherwise well-documented book,[8] wrote: 'Mainframes, which once could be counted to have a viable life span of 5 years, now last no more than 3. The standard 4-year cycle of minicomputers has been cut in half. Microcomputers, terminals, and word processing products are made obsolete annually.'

In reality, McClellan was not referring to obsolescence, in the common sense of the word, but rather to the syndrome of frantic competition, with vendors ready to blow up even the tiniest innovation for advertising purposes. The ruling on the obsolescence of product X or Y implies two elements: a broad consensus among several vendors concerned, backed by their determination to act accordingly, and a certain concurrence by a significant segment of the market. The second condition is a truism but the first is also pretty obvious. Whereas scientific discoveries and inventions occur independently of business fluctuations, the subject of our next section, their economic introduction on any appreciable scale most certainly depends on the general business environment and the vendor's own situation and policy.

When IBM borrows from its future

The theory of the shortening life cycle of computer products definitely runs counter to the traditional practice of IBM, which for some time

---

[8] Stephen T. McClellan, *The Coming Computer Industry Shakeout*, John Wiley & Sons, 1984, p. 29.

now has accounted for some 65 per cent of total mainframe sales worldwide and was therefore supposed to be the pace-setter. Estimates of IBM product life cycles stretch from five or six years to a somewhat longer duration. By our way of reckoning, ever since IBM introduced the epoch-making System 360, followed eight years later by System 370, IBM has never seriously departed from the eight-year periodicity, proceeding in orderly succession until the present time—counting new lines of products but excluding additional models within each family of machines or systems.

Another insight into this intricate notion of length of life and life cycle may be obtained by recalling the pre-1979 practice of IBM of renting its equipment, thus saving its customers the necessity of having to lay out the full amount required for an outright purchase. In those days, the average rental period was four years, and the 45–55 monthly instalments were equivalent to the list price. The extra cost incurred by the buying company—in the opinion of its own board—was, however, fully compensated by the assurance that the company could rely on speedy and compatible replacement, whenever needed, even before the equipment had become obsolete, and would thus be spared the trouble and high cost of conversion.

Seen from the supplier's side, IBM realized higher profits. It also kept its customers captive. More importantly still, IBM was able to control the rate of innovation by introducing new products only at the optimum point of the life-cycle curve after full amortization of its previous line of products (inasmuch as IBM, too, had to take into account its own cost of periodic replacement and retooling in its own plants).

By establishing and maintaining a direct linkage between product cycles and the length of life cycles on the customers' side, IBM attained a seemingly unassailable position. All of IBM's innovations, introduced with optimal periodicity, proved to be highly lucrative. It also conferred undisguised benefits upon all information technology users. Clearly, IBM's own customers could replace their aging equipment by new, more powerful models at lower unit prices. However, the chain of price repercussions did not end there, for all of IBM's competitors had no choice but to follow suit.

In keeping with its well-established product-cycle policy, IBM was planning to introduce its new top end 3090 mainframe, codenamed 'Sierra', just a few weeks before Christmas 1985. The company caused quite a stir when it announced that it would bring forward the delivery dates for the first two models, the 200 and 400, of the Sierra series by several months and also in February 1986 when it added two further, smaller models, the 150 and 180, again ahead of schedule. Simultaneously, IBM offered a 10 per cent markdown on all the 3090 mainframes.

Analysts immediately concluded that IBM's hand must have been forced by poor trading, and this was confirmed by several quarterly statements in succession ever since Summer 1985. The company officials explained later that the imminence of the Sierra was preventing customers from buying current mainframes. Clearly, IBM expected that the early launching of the new machine would boost business in 1986. Apparently, this did not happen. Lost sales of the older mainframes are, in all likelihood, lost forever. The worst part is that IBM, for the first time ever, lost control over the life cycles of its key products and, with it, lost its aura of invincibility, as a shrewd commentator has put it.

Can software outlast generations of computers?

To what extent is the concept of the life cycle of a product applicable to software? The question is not as incongruous as it may seem at first, granted that thousands of new software packages are put on the market every year, especially designed for the micro- and minicomputers, and granted also that many of these offerings have an ephemeral existence. On the other hand, the dozen or so best-known computer languages, notably those of the more sophisticated type, have been on the whole astonishingly enduring.

Database search and retrieval strategies and the related software is another case in point. As is well known, the business of online interrogation of hundreds of databanks and databases could be developed—say, by DIALOG or SDC—by simply adapting the tools originally created for the military and for aircraft manufacturers in the United States, such as for Lockheed. Of course, DIALOG and SDC kept improving their search techniques and software (using the retrieval language STAIRS); it still remains true that the basic philosophy has not changed much in over 25 years—a kind of record in the rapidly moving world of computing. However, it is also a fact that all the 'information supermarkets' specializing in bibliographic references were unable in the last five or six years to find additional customers and consequently their profit ratios suffered. To what extent the obsolescence of their retrieval software has contributed to their troubles is anybody's guess. Similarly, Siemens' database management system GOLEM has now been in existence for well over a decade.

Perhaps the most extreme case of software obsolescence is found in the area of basic operating systems. The pioneering effort put by IBM analysts into designing, testing and debugging the 360 series in the early 1960s had neither precedent nor comparable follow-up. Univac, Sperry, Control Data, Burroughs, Honeywell and the other mainframe makers in the United States, Europe and Japan were forced to do likewise and maintain their own brands of basic operating systems—all of which are at present in an advanced stage of aging.

IBM itself was faced with a serious dilemma every eight years or so, when a decision had to be made regarding each successive basic mainframe model. Would it be appropriate to design a completely new, up-to-date operating system, thus causing disruption among its thousands of corporate customers? Would it be worth spending enormous amounts of money on R&D without a guarantee of commercial success and with the related risk of upsetting its shareholders? The ultimate outcome was not difficult to predict; upgrade, upgrade, improve yet once more! In very much the same way, Control Data's Cyber 170 is still based on an operating system designed some fifteen years ago.

As with the database retrieval software, the growing obsolescence of the basic operating system has been detrimental to the user. The basic system had to be increasingly supplemented by application-oriented, often tailor-made software or software packages, which added to the cost.

The situation began to change only when the Pentagon launched its project ADA in 1975–9 with the aim of unifying most of the 400 languages used by the American military. Then AT&T increased its pressure for the adoption of a basic set of computer instructions, UNIX, originally developed by Bell Laboratories. This led to several spin-off versions, in direct competition with IBM's DOS, OS and MVS. Eventually, in early 1965, NSC, Intel and Motorola agreed to put the UNIX system on their products.

These threats were taken very seriously by IBM. In 1983 the company created the 'event of the year' by unveiling a new computer architecture supplemented by a new basic operating system, MVS/XA. IBM seems now set actively to prepare the overdue migration to its flexible, forward-looking design and software concepts. Inevitably, the competition between IBM and AT&T in this crucial area will soon heat up. However, the future developments of ADA should not be underrated. There is more than a glimpse of hope that the users will in the end reap tangible benefits, in terms of substantially better software whose cost, in the longer run, will go down.

2.4 PIERCING THE BUSINESS ATMOSPHERICS

Business cycle is a generic term, susceptible to conveying several meanings. Different cyclical phenomena may combine giving rise to an acceleration process. Furthermore, an internal cyclical mechanism necessarily interacts with other, often external, factors. The effects of business cycles may be immediate or delayed, short lived or enduring, wrenching or diffused and, in most instances, multifarious. According to the generally accepted terminology, the successive periods of prosperity and depression, also called expansion and contraction, are neatly separated by peaks and troughs. In Western industrial nations, and especially in the United States, major cycles are said to last about seven to nine years.

Minor cycles, typified by 'inventory recessions', with a duration of two to four years, may usually be fitted into a complete major cycle. This is neatly illustrated by IBM's performance over the last 25 years. During that period, which started just before IBM launched the S-360, Big Blue's gross earnings increased consistently from year to year, rising from $2.2 billion in 1961 to $50 billion (in current prices) in 1985, although the net earnings have been cyclical. On the basis of IBM's yearly income statements, there have been six full earnings cycles in 24 years, giving an average duration of four years, as can be seen from Figure 2.4.

The developments that follow are, however, primarily concerned with recurring business cycles lasting some eight years on the average. The purpose is to assess the sensitivity to general economic conditions of the information industry, with due regard to its specificity and unique features, and, in addition, to evaluate the impact on information technology, production, overhead costs and profit margins.

Where a bit of modelling can help

For the sake of simplicity, we shall consider all information processing machinery and equipment, together with its indispensible complement of software, peripherals and telecommunications installations, and also all automated office and automated production equipment, tools and devices—collectively called IT—as durable goods subject to wear and tear.

Imagine a medium-sized firm specialized in small domestic appliances or a textile-manufacturing company whose capital equipment is kept equal to about four times the value of its annual sales and is written off and actually replaced after ten years, using the straight-line depreciation method. Suppose, further, that IT items represent 20 per cent of the firm's capital stock.

Equipped with these simple rules, it is easy to follow the scenario in Table 2.1, in which all figures are in real terms, i.e. inflation free. In year 1, sales amounted to $100 million and the stock of capital stood at $400 million. Replacement just balanced depreciation and there was no additional investment and therefore no extra purchases of information-related products either. Let us now suppose that, in the third year, sales

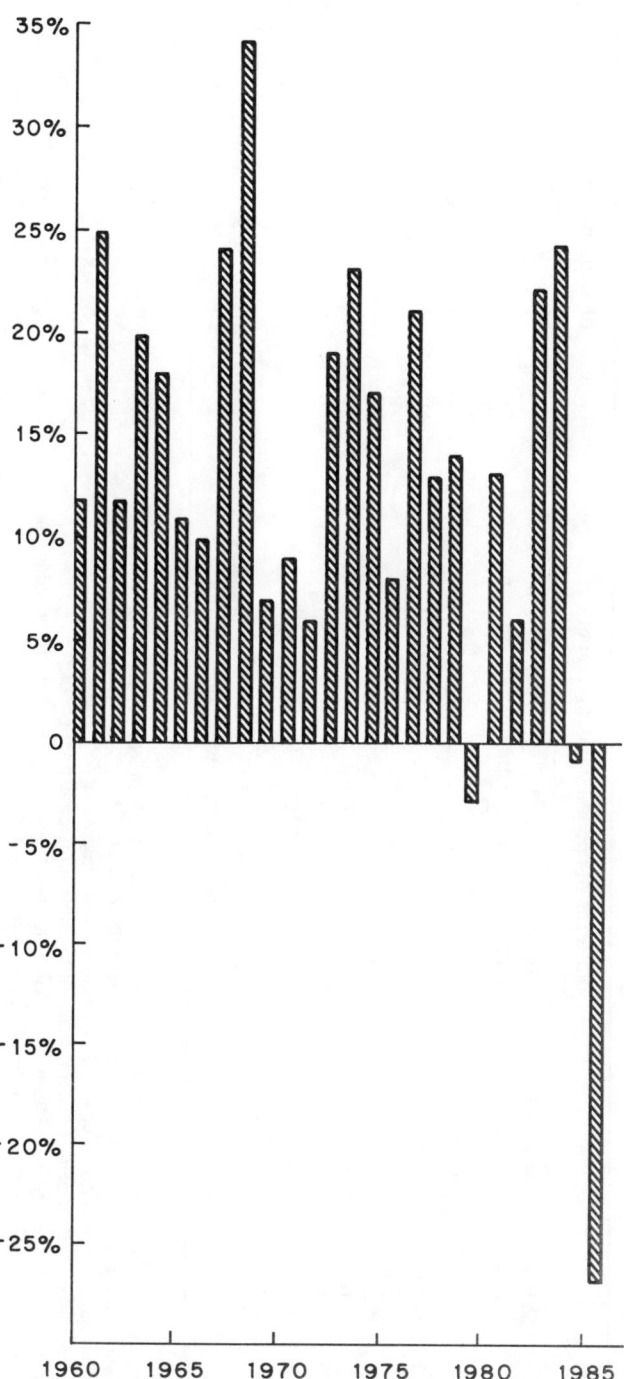

FIGURE 2.4 *IBM net earnings cycles, 1960–86, measured by annual percentage changes*

Table 2.1 Investment patterns induced by the acceleration principle (in $ million)

Time (1)	Yearly sales (2)	Total stock of capital (3)	Patterns of spending on capital goods			Patterns of spending on IT equipment		
			Replace-ment (4)	Net investment (5)	Gross investment (6)	Low (7)	Medium (8)	High (9)
Year 1	100	400	40	0	40	8	18	36
Year 2	100	400	40	0	40	8	18	36
Year 3	105	420	40	20	60	12	22	40
Year 4	110	440	40	20	60	12	22	40
Year 5	120	480	40	40	80	16	26	44
Year 6	135	540	40	100	140	28	38	52
Year 7	135	540	40	0	40	8	18	36
Year 8	125	500	0	0	Disinvestment under consideration	0	0	0

Assumptions:
Length of life of stock of capital: 10 years, except for last column ('high' spending on IT equipment), where it is reduced to 5 years.
Amortization: straight-line depreciation method used throughout.
Three different *patterns of spending on IT equipment* are distinguished:
Low: assumes a 20 per cent, constant, share in total spending on capital goods;
Medium: further assumes that replacement of worn-out plant and equipment results in additional demand for IT equipment, incorporated into new (replacement) equipment, in the extra proportion of 25 per cent;
High: also assumes, in addition to the 'medium' assumptions, that depreciation period is reduced to 5 years (instead of the previously posited 10 years).

increased by 5 per cent. Then the capital stock, too, must have risen by 5 per cent. However, total gross investment (= replacement + new investment) jumped by 50 per cent. This investment pattern was unchanged the following year, despite another modest increase in the volume of sales.

In year 6, sales rose to $135 million and remained at that level in year 7. This led, at first, to an impressive 75 per cent jump in the company's total orders of new equipment and, consequently, to a parallel increase in purchases of IT items. This, however, was quickly followed by a complete turnaround: in year 8 sales levelled off but remained high, with the result that the company curtailed all investment and started considering whether to disinvest, e.g. by selling some of its partly used equipment.

Several caveats are in order. The scenario of Table 2.1 is oversimplified, for it ignores the degree of utilization of capacity. It also ignores productivity gains based on new equipment and it glosses over variations in interest rates and other relevant parameters.

Despite its obvious limitations, our imaginary example brings out some interesting relationships and illustrates the disturbing effects of the acceleration principle. At the beginning of the eight-year cycle, both consumption sales and investment spending were stagnating. During the next phase, a modest increase in sales of consumer goods led to sharply increased purchases of durables, including IT items. However, the acceleration mechanism can work in the opposite direction as well. If, in any given year, sales of finished products should drop—or just level off—gross investment would drop away to nothing. Furthermore, whilst swings in replacement demand may occasionally be large, swings in new demand for IT and other capital goods are always incomparably larger.

Anticipating market swings and moods

Some of the initial assumptions may now be relaxed. So far, we have treated all IT items like ordinary durable goods, which indeed they are not. Slight modifications in our arithmetic example allow us to probe the assertion that computer business is fundamentally a growth industry, little, if at all, affected by changes in other production sectors.

According to several authoritative surveys of the US economy, the share of computers in total spending on capital equipment in the United States jumped to 15 per cent in 1984 from 10 per cent in 1980, or an increase of 50 per cent. Picking up the clue, we have revised upward the figures in column (7) by now assuming that every piece of equipment bought in replacement of old machinery incorporates more of the new information technology, in the proportion of a more modest 25 per cent.

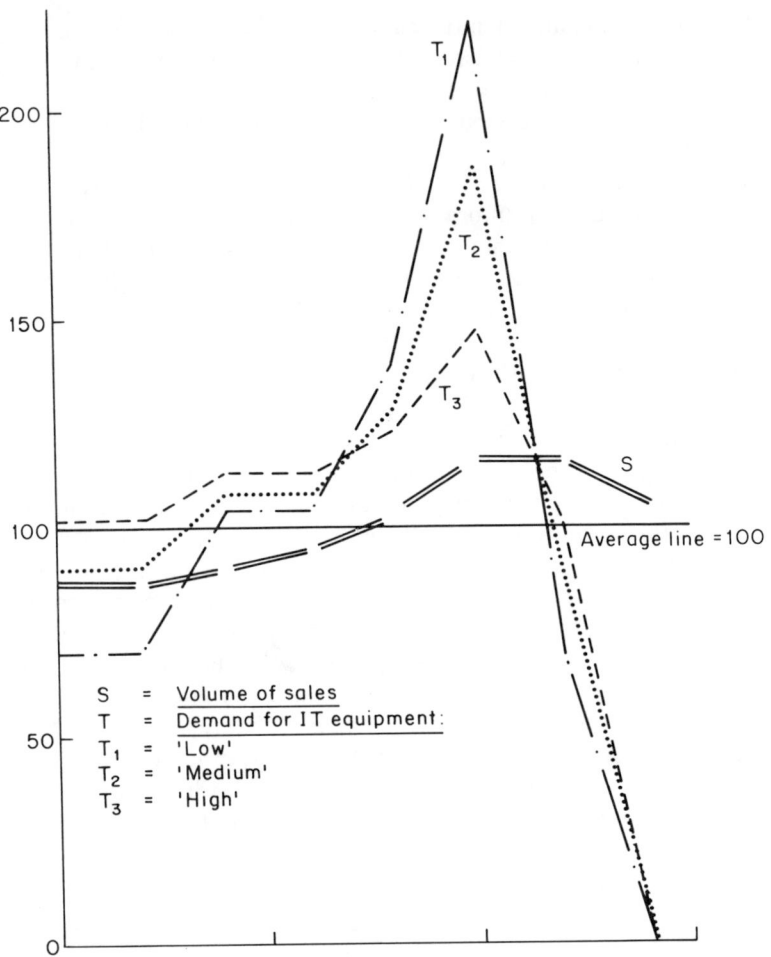

FIGURE 2.5 *Variations in demand for information technology equipment induced by the acceleration principle (index numbers: average of 8 years = 100)*

This correction (viz. column 8) naturally increases the volume of IT equipment purchases, whilst reducing the amplitude of cyclical swings. These are portrayed respectively by curves T_1 and T_2 in Figure 2.5, with the first curve corresponding to the uncorrected cycles whereas T_2 is based on the revised numbers.

One more step is needed to complete the analysis. Let us now assume that the length of life of the company's plant and assets is five years, instead of the previously posited ten years. The new set of figures is to be found in column (9) and the results can be more easily visualized by looking[9] at curve T_3 in Figure 2.5. The fluctuations in IT orders are now markedly less violent.

The model may be extended in several directions in order to approximate still further real-life industry swings. Sales and investment variations, as portrayed in Figure 2.5, evolve around a horizontal trend line; in reality, sales have increased independently of business cycles and consequently the trend line should be made upward sloping. Also, a second eight-year cycle could be added, thus consolidating (or correcting) the previous findings.

None of these refinements, however, would substantially modify the essential lessons of the previous exercise. As a general rule, the new IT-based industry is perhaps affected by general business conditions to a lesser extent than are most other industries producing capital durable goods. However, it is not, if it ever was, immune to them altogether. Commented the London *Economist*:[10] 'The (computer) industry's size now leaves it more exposed to shifts in capital spending. . . . So the industry is hurt when buyers cut capital investment.'

Furthermore, as the size of the industry increases, so does the risk of miscalculation. According to John F. Akers, the chairman, IBM's current problems, which became highly visible in Spring–Summer 1985, are directly related to the downturn in capital spending in the United States. Unless the trend is suddenly reversed—and we do not see why it should—Big Blue will undoubtedly post further declines in yearly profits, certainly through all of 1987 and probably well into 1988, as the cyclical pattern of IBM's net earnings portrayed in Figure 2.4 above suggests most convincingly.

In retrospect, it is clear that IBM top managers seriously misread a number of business surveys and forecasts when they first decided on a five-year, $20 billion investment in new plant and equipment, and even more so when they refused to scale down their plans, which it would have been easy for them to do, in the light of pessimistic business reports. True, their stubbornness may yet pay dividends in the long run. However, in the short run, with industrial demand for IBM products unusually low, the cost of that overhead is being spread over too small a volume of sales, thus further depressing IBM's profit margins. The acceleration processs operating in reverse, now works against Big Blue after working in its favour for many, many years.

The IBM current malaise—and dozens of smaller fry share in that predicament—contributes to the growing consensus that the computer

---

[9] The zero bottom line in the eighth year has little significance, for when we aggregate data related to several buyer/user companies, the extreme fluctuations in individual firms' schedules partly offset each other and the interindustry troughs are never as sharp as Figure 2.5 might suggest.
[10] *The Economist*, 22 June 1985.

industry may no longer be operating under the privileged condition of an undersupplied market, dominated by vendors, as it was for the better part of the last three decades. In many product lines, including telecommunications, overall supply tends to exceed solvent needs.

2.5 CONCLUSION AND OUTLOOK

It now remains to bring together the different arguments and show how the several causes of disturbance, discussed separately, interact and affect the cost trends in information technology and industry. The consolidated findings are tested with the help of a number of concrete business experiences.

1. Enough has been said to shatter the comfortable image of long-term growth industry, shielded from outside winds and gales. True, overall, its growth has been impressive, but not entirely without precedent or without parallel, viz. space activities, laser technology, bioengineering, health and medicine, etc. Nor is this the first time that the industry is faced with a serious crisis causing it to undergo a vast reorganization. Likewise, the smooth cost curves of the previous chapter in fact conceal recurring, substantial deviations from the underlying trends.
2. In retrospect, the period 1951–86 may be conveniently subdivided into four phases of some eight years each. At the beginning, there was Remington Rand's UNIVAC 1. IBM countered with its models 704 and 705. Other mainframe manufacturers entered the field. For several years, the race remained undecided, with IBM in the lead for most of the time. The second cycle period, which opened with the launching of System 360, saw the undisputed domination of IBM. Sperry-Rand, after their merger, continued the UNIVAC line, but gradually lost ground to IBM, and so did Burroughs, NCR, RCA and Honeywell. So also did CDC, which succeeded, however, in establishing itself as a serious contender in peripherals.
3. Throughout the 1960s, IBM called the tune. It maintained firmly its price leadership based, as we have seen, on sound economics, introducing each new model only after the life cycle of the older one was coming to an end. This strategy forced the competitors to be constantly on the defensive and, by limiting their shares of the market and their earnings, acted as a deterrent to entry of other firms into the small club of mainframe manufacturers. Being thus in a position to control the rate of technological progress, IBM management was free to pass onto its customers, at regular intervals, some of the savings on production costs.

4. There was only one flaw in the strategy pursued by IBM and, by imitation, all other mainframe makers. Their ceaseless endeavour to upgrade the power of their machines seemed fully justified by the then popular Grosch's law, according to which, as we saw earlier, every increase in computing power should procure greater savings on costs. They therefore stood aloof from minicomputers whose development, based on the rapid progress in integrated circuits and large-scale integration, was contemporary with the triumph of the IBM 360 series. All mainframe manufacturers were equally blind but IBM, as the then unchallenged leader, should be blamed for misleading the others, including several European and Japanese companies active in the field at that time.

5. The appearance of minicomputers many times cheaper than mainframes of roughly comparable capacity signalled the end of a previously homogeneous market. However, it was only the first step, soon to be followed by the advent of microprocessors—in 1971, to be precise—and then the portables, personal computers, desktop computers, home computers, superminicomputers, fail-safe computers, and so on. Specialization prevailed also in several related areas, including storage devices, printers and other peripherals, local networks, text processors, etc. This product diversification went hand in hand with the fragmentation of the market, opening the way to a slowdown: it now grows by a mere 5 or 6 per cent per year as against 15 to 20 per cent in the 1960s and 1970s.

6. The misreading of the trends, on which Grosch has built his theory, and ignorance of the problem of discontinuities were thus at the origin of the strategic errors repeatedly committed by the managements of a good dozen mainframe manufacturers worldwide. Their difficulties were compounded by cyclical variations, both internal and external, over which of course they had no control, with the exception, prior to 1985, of IBM, better able to tune the timing of the unveiling of its new models. In turn, the minicomputer companies, by their failure to capitalize on microcomputers, have shown that they learned nothing from the unhappy experiences of the mainframe companies.

7. The 1970–86 period also comprised two distinct phases. During approximately the first half of that period, thousands of new firms made their entry, offering mostly specialty products, in response to new, previously unperceived needs. They contributed significantly to the widening of the market for IT equipment and systems. Soon the new products began siphoning off demand from the older types, thus pushing down their prices or accelerating an ongoing downward slide. This conferred a clear benefit upon the users. To those who continued buying the old models there accrued a direct additional enhancement in their real income arising out of the lower prices,

while the others derived an indirect benefit on account of increased adequacy of the new products or models relatively to their specific needs—as evidenced by their buying preferences.

8. During the late 1970s, old-established vendors began fighting back, varying the nature of their products and abandoning some of their former position in the commodity belt. IBM itself was forced to reconsider entirely its product philosophy and strategy as its share of an otherwise expanding world market fell to 40 per cent in 1980 from over 60 per cent in 1967. By 1984–5, IBM had established itself as Number One in personal computers, office automation and software sales, and attained a strong position in factory automation, telecommunications (through its acquisition of Rolm) and in local networks, in addition to its traditional mainframe business. These moves were completed by a thorough internal reorganization and its new policy of outright selling, instead of renting, inaugurated in 1979. Intoxicated by success, IBM top management failed to see that the company's latest net earnings cycle, which started from a low in 1981, had reached its peak in 1984, to be followed by a new trough in 1986.

9. Had the Ein-Dor reinterpretation of Grosch's law, pointing out the cost–performance advantage of the supercomputer, been undertaken a few years earlier, Control Data surely would not have given up its activity in this field only to reenter later with Cyber 205. In the meantime, Cray Research forged ahead, followed by Amdahl. Hitachi in 1982 put in a claim to a faster machine, but was outdistanced by a Fujitsu supercomputer boasting over 1,000 megaflops (floating-point operations/sec.). In Spring 1987, a NEC SX-2, which can reportedly manage flat-out 2–3 gigaflops, set a new world record for number crunching. However, the SX-2 has only a single processor, whereas the Cray-2 has four, working in parallel, and vastly superior software. Worldwide, the number of complete installations sold, each costing up to $20 million, jumped to 75 in 1986, from 55 a year earlier and a mere 21 in 1982. Demand should grow 50–60 per cent in 1987. The supercomputer sector is perhaps the last bastion that remains immune to fluctuations in the general economy— although Japanese competition, non-existant in 1980, is now set to take its toll of the market.

Chapter 3

Easing Cost Constraints

The regular practice of cost analysis and auditing does not come naturally to managements of computer makers and other vendors, accustomed as they were until recently to function in a growth environment. For a very long time, the marketplace has remained seller-dominated and most business enjoyed exceptionally fat profit margins.

Since the early 1980s, however, the truth dawned on the industry leaders at last. The impetus from technological progress may no longer be sufficient to sustain by itself the earlier momentum of the computer industry, and hence the newly discovered need to control certain key cost elements. As the title suggests, the purpose of this chapter is to review a number of critical factors and to indicate the means of getting the vendors' cost equations right.

The idea that the well-documented downward movement in hardware costs is somehow offset by rising expenditure on software is one that has been accepted for some time. However, the mechanism through which the process of compensation operates has never been fully elucidated. An attempt to throw some new light upon it will be made from the outset (Section 3.1).

The analysis is carried forward in Section 3.2 by including additional items of cost. The complexity of cost relationships, under dynamic conditions, is illustrated with reference to convulsions of the personal computer industry and dramatized by the current predicament of IBM whose great expectations, raised by the IBM PC's initial triumph, may very well end in discomfiture.

The matter of escalating costs of research and development in computing and telecommunications is taken up in Section 3.3. It is suggested that for the individual vendor the correlative financial burden could be made more bearable by fostering cooperative research and especially by drawing on spin-offs from publicly financed R&D. More fundamentally, however, the present highly duplicative pattern, which is proving increasingly ruinous to the industry, must be somehow brought under control.

Other cost-saving opportunities are investigated briefly in Section 3.4. As a general rule, classical retrenchment policies aim at reducing overheads and/or trimming the wage bill, but streamlining the financial structure of the vendor company, automating its factory operations or again cutting the often-prohibitive costs of carrying idle inventory may be potentially more rewarding and produce longer-lasting effects.

58

Finally, the reversal of the once ultra-liberal licencing and patenting practices is rapidly gaining wide acceptance in the United States as a legitimate means of holding off cheap Asian imports.

3.1 BIDDING UP SOFTWARE AGAINST HARDWARE

Probably the best-known figure in computer literature is the S-shaped curve showing changes over time in the relative costs of hardware and

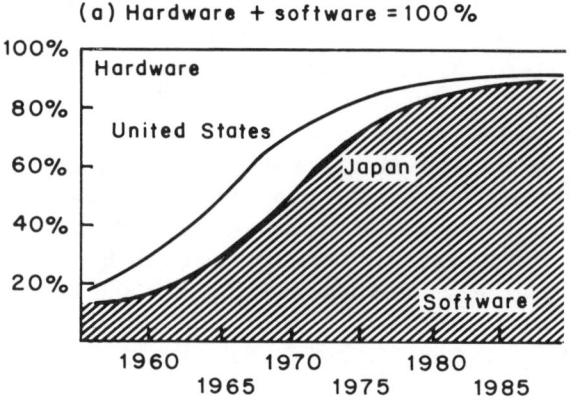

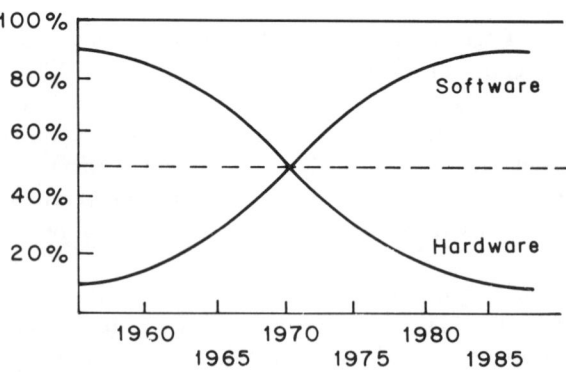

FIGURE 3.1 *Hardware/software cost ratios, 1955–85. (From OECD,* Software: An Emerging Industry. *Reproduced by permission of OECD)*

software, as in Figure 3.1(a). Since its appearance in *Datamation* in June 1968, it has been cited in *Electronic Design*, *Dun's Review*, *Science*, *Computer* and innumerable other journals and books. In a report published in 1985, OECD included a composite diagram consisting of fifteen 'versions' under the heading: 'History of a curve: hardware/ software cost ratios'.[1]

After 20 years, the message is still the same: the dramatic decline in the cost of hardware components has been accompanied by a parallel increase in the cost of software design and production. Put in this way, the statement is a mere tautology, a fact that, strangely enough, generally went unrecognized. The pleonasm is inherent in the concept inasmuch as the sum total of hardware and software costs is always equal to 100 per cent—whereas overall costs in absolute numbers have declined over the last two decades, as we saw in Chapter 1 above.

Robbing Peter to pay Paul

The figure lends itself to yet another presentation, as in Figure 3.1(b), in which both the hardware and software cost relatives are displayed vertically from bottom up, whereas in Figure 3.1(a) the shaded area is at all times proportional to the value of the hardware/software ratio. Actually, the two diagrams are fully equivalent.

By its construction, the figure carries a deeper significance. It is generally taken to mean that as information systems become more powerful, or more versatile, or sophisticated, the amount of grey matter required to design them rises rapidly both in absolute terms and relatively to the price of hardware. This relationship has traditionally been portrayed by a smooth, freehand curve, but it has seldom, if ever, resulted from fitting the curve to a set of real-life data.

The relation implies continuous substitution. Eventually, this process must come up against the incompressible minimum of either hardware or software, as indicated by the two asymptotes. In the immediate vicinity of either asymptote, there is a marked slowdown in the rate of substitution, which is indeed measured by the slope of the curve at any point. Most analysts have settled for a maximum ratio of 80:20; a few others suggested 85:15.

In the earliest formulations, the curve was a perfect 'logistic'[2] showing exponential growth in phase 1 up to an inflexion point located midway

---

[1] OECD, *Software: An Emerging Industry*, 1985, pp. 20 and 184.
[2] Examples of a logistic curve and the so-called Gompertz curve were given in Section 1.1 (Figure 1.3).

between the two asymptotes, followed by deceleration in phase 2, as indicated in Figure 3.1(b) and also by the curve relating to Japan in Figure 3.1(a). Most observers now favour a stretched-out curve having an elongated S-shape, typified by the 'US curve' appearing on the same diagram. There are other conceivable refinements, for instance using a modified functional form, but the result would not be substantially altered.

Parity between hardware and software costs is said to have been reached, especially in the United States, in either 1960 or 1965. The Japanese computer industry is thought to be five years behind. Europe's lag is estimated at five to eight years. The current hardware/software cost ratio in the United States is probably close to 40:60 and might soon reach 35:65. Another feature worth mentioning is that whereas earlier writers did not hesitate to give their long-term predictions, very few contemporary analysts attempt to look beyond 1990. Some observers are beginning to sound a note of caution and a few go as far as predicting the reversal of the seemingly irresistable tendency towards rising costs of software, as we shall see in Section 5.4.

The reader will have noticed that the principal weakness of the foregoing argument lies in its speculative nature. Quite obviously, the credence of the model would be considerably enhanced if the theory could demonstrably apply to other dual phenomena, in computing or, better still, in other areas.

According to the US Federal Communications Commission, transmission costs declined regularly relatively to switching costs over some 30 years, from 1946 to 1974. This is shown in Figure 3.2(a), in which both series are expressed as percentages of total investment in the telecommunications plant in any given year. At the beginning of the period, 40 per cent of outlays on new plant was spent on transmission facilities, as against 30 per cent on switching equipment. By 1974, switching accounted for over 40 per cent (or $35.5 billion) and transmission for 28.5 per cent (or $25.3 billion) of plant value.

Throughout the entire period, all 'other' cost items remained remarkably stable, at around 30 per cent of the total, and they can therefore be treated like a constant. On that basis, the actual split between transmission costs and switching costs respectively is portrayed by curve A in Figure 3.2(b), to which a smoothed-out trend curve B has been fitted.

Glancing simultaneously at Figures 3.1 and 3.2, we are immediately struck by the conspicuous similarity between the evolution in relative costs of hardware and software, on the one hand, and the parallel evolution in transmission costs relatively to the cost of switching equipment, on the other. In this particular instance, however, the argument is fully supported by statistical evidence, coming from a highly reliable source. Also, the 50:50 split is dated with precision: the year 1960.

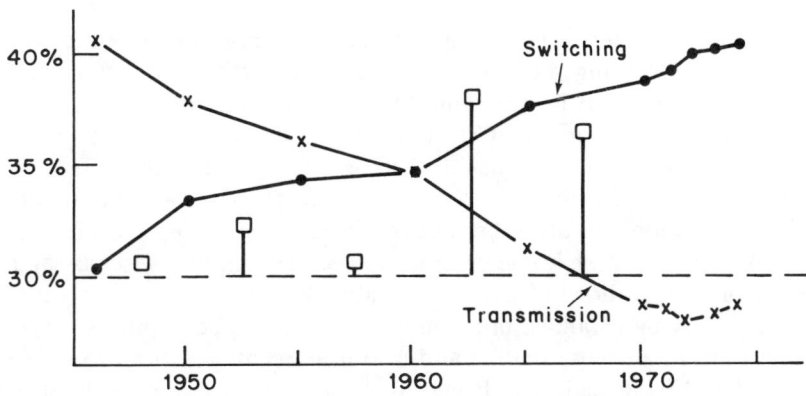

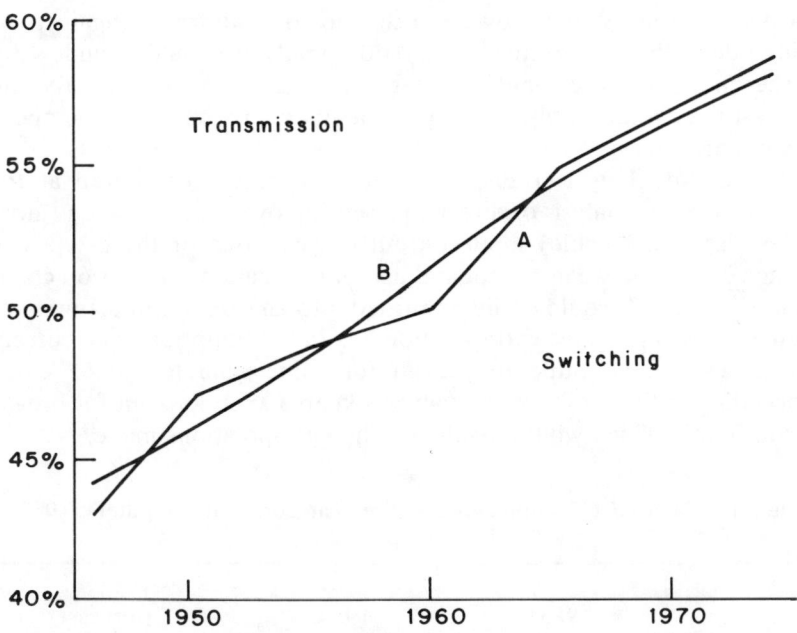

FIGURE 3.2 *Transmission/switching investment ratios in the United States, 1946–74. (From US Federal Communications Commission,* Statistics of Common Carriers, *cited in Anthony G. Oettinger, Paul J. Berman and William H. Read,* High and Low Politics: Information Resources for the 80s, *Ballinger Publishing Co., Cambridge, Mass., 1977. Reproduced by permission of Program on Information Resources, Harvard University)*

Digression on constant-sum models

The model with which we have been working is applicable to a variety of problems confronting the computer industry, but it is also of value to individual vendors. It is by definition a constant-sum model, for all the pertinent numbers represent relative values, or percentages, and their sum total is necessarily equal to 100 per cent at all times. The best results are normally obtained when the number of variables is small.

This condition can often be met by suitably modifying the raw data, using a piece of simple boolean logic, and proceeding stepwise, as can be seen from the following example. Table 3.1 gives estimates of US shipments of mainframes, minicomputers and microcomputers respectively, both in absolute figures and also in percentages, for 1983, 1984 and 1985. In particular, it brings out the spectacular growth of the personal computer market from some $6 billion in 1983 to $11 billion two years later.

Furthermore, when the numbers relating to the minis and microprocessors are amalgamated, the two dominant market trends stand out sharply, i.e. the relative slowdown in sales of mainframes against the rising tide of the smaller machines. Additionally, we could exclude sales of the minis, which are anyway stagnating, and compare directly and contrast the evolution respectively of the microcomputer and the mainframe markets.

The methodology is transposable to problems encountered at the firm's level, e.g. analysis of direct competition over time between (more or less interchangeable) input–output devices, two or three types of storage media, between broadband and narrowband transmission channels, and so on. It could easily be turned into an exercise in planning or even in forecasting by extrapolation on the assumption that current tendencies will continue to prevail for some time to come. When proceeding in this way, we must always keep a keen lookout for breaks in continuity, which would invalidate the extrapolations made.

Table 3.1 Value of US shipments for three categories of computers, 1983–5
($ billion and percentages)

	1983		1984		1985 (forecast)	
Mainframes	21.6	*51.0%*	23.2	*45.8%*	24.4	*44.7%*
Minicomputers	14.8 ⎱	*49.0%*	18.3 ⎱	*54.2%*	19.2 ⎱	*55.3%*
Microcomputers	5.9 ⎰		9.2 ⎰		11.0 ⎰	
Total	42.3	*100%*	50.7	*100%*	54.6	*100%*

Source: Gartner Group, quoted in *The Economist*, 22 June 1985.

The ongoing reorientation of IBM's overall strategy provides us with a near-perfect illustration. According to IBM officials, Big Blue is shifting its revenue mix away from hardware products to software and services. These areas have been growing at a compound yearly rate of 21 per cent of late and attained $11.5 billion in gross revenues in 1985, or 23 per cent of IBM's total sales. The company expects this trend to continue into the future, whilst hardware sales may keep growing at a moderate 12 per cent per annum. By 1990 or shortly thereafter, IBM management calculates that software and services could amount to a third of IBM's total turnover, while its mainframe business drops to a mere 15 per cent from 25 per cent at the present time. That this is no sheer speculation is substantiated by the fact that IBM is directing nearly 50 per cent of its R&D spending into software.

3.2 PCs: THE GLARING MISCALCULATIONS

The short, tormented history of the personal computer business partakes as much of a genuine saga as of a cloak-and-dagger tale. Whatever the future holds in store, the next episode features a contest pitting Taiwanese and Singaporean dwarfs, first, against IBM and, next, against all the other contenders, and it promises to be just as nerve-racking.

Overdoing the fireworks

The common ancestor was a 4-bit microprocessor, the 4004, created by Intel in 1971. The first 8-bit processor was unveiled by Apple Computer, Inc. in 1977. Commodore undercut Apple offering its own personal computer at just under $600; it was also the first manufacturer to penetrate the European market. The portable Osborn 1 made its debut in 1980 and it, too, had its days of glory. In the meanwhile, Atari (Warner Communications), Tandy, Texas Instruments, Xerox and other companies, including the British Sinclair Research Ltd. and Acorn Computer, as well as the relative latecomer, Compaq Computer Corp., had made their mark.

Booming sales and phenomenal growth prospects attracted dozens of startup companies, but also enticed IBM into the marketplace. The IBM PC was introduced in Autumn 1981. By the end of 1986, there were over 8 million IBM PCs in use around the world. Despite its late start, by 1985 the company was able to claim that over 45 per cent of all microcomputers sold to businesses were made by IBM.

That same year, Apple's share of the market plummeted to 15 per cent, Tandy's share was down to 6 per cent, Commodore, AT&T and Compaq sold no more than 4 to 5 per cent each, followed by a dozen smaller computer makers with 1–2 per cent each. The receding tide played havoc with profit-and-loss accounts of such highflyers as Texas Instruments, Osborn, Victor Technologies, Atari, together with some of the smaller fry. It wiped out most of the profits of Apple, the principal remaining contender and direct competitor to IBM.

In retrospect, it is clear that manufacturers of microprocessors have initially speculated on larger-than-actual sales, hoping wrongly to recoup later their large investments and current outlays on material. Acting in a hurry, they paid insufficient attention to product design and organization, and failed to streamline their factory operations. Thus, several vendors have for all practical purposes priced themselves out of the market.

According to Future Computing, Inc., a market research organization, most of the 1983 and 1984 models were far too expensive owing to high cost of semi-integrated circuits and some hardware items (and that included all of Atari, Commodore, Compaq and Italy's Olivetti PCs), whilst a few others were overpriced in relation to their performance (e.g. Apple's workstation Lisa,[3] Apple's IIc and IBM's PC Jr). Apple's Macintosh, a neat looking computer, offering high resolution graphics and equipped with a 'mouse', turned out to be too costly (at $2,500) as a home computer, without being really adequate for sophisticated business users. Realistically, IBM withdrew its overpublicized PC Jr.

None of these criticisms applied to Apple IIe, among the low-priced machines, nor did it concern the high performance IBM PC XT and PC AT, the latter connectable to IBM 370 and 4300 mainframes. It was thus mainly on cost grounds that IBM won its fight, at that stage, with the clone makers and finally also with the few vendors who for some time continued marketing personal computers of their own which were non-compatible with IBM's.

Clones unbeatable at half the cost

Short-lived was to be IBM's triumph and record earnings. After retreating in 1984, with the notable exception of Compaq, many of the earlier cloners staged a spectacular comeback in 1985 and they were rejoined in 1986 by dozens of newcomers, including especially a strong, aggres-

---

[3] In Chapter 9, Lisa will be further discussed as an example of a machine that offers too many, seldom-used functions, for which people are unwilling to pay the premium.

sive group of Taiwanese, South Korean and Singaporean vendors–importers.

The turn of the tide was sudden and the flooding seemed irresistible. In 1986, Apple and Tandy each accounted for 25 per cent of the 2.7 million personal computers sold at Computerland, Radio Shack and other retail outlets, as against 17 per cent for IBM. These numbers do not include direct sales to large corporations, a huge market dominated by IBM, but difficult to measure. Other winners were Japan's Epson Corp. and Leading Edge Computer Products, which distributes South Korean Clones, with each climbing from 1 to 5 per cent of total US shipments of PCs. Even smaller players, e.g. Atari, Commodore, Kaypro and UK's Amstrad were whooping it up. Conversely, IBM's share of an otherwise expanding market fell dramatically, as Compaq, Apple and Tandy seized the initiative with new products and as lower-cost clones were eating away market share at the low end.

Once again, the key battle has been fought and lost on economic grounds. Clones are now sold for hundreds of dollars less than the original IBM PC, XT and AT computers. They closely mimic the same hardware options, use the same software; some of them are faster and a few claim to be even more reliable.

By redesigning the basic PC with fewer parts and purchasing cheaper disk drives and more versatile chips, Far Eastern clone makers were able to cut their costs down to the $360–450 range, and even less by procuring components in large quantities; they could therefore sell their models for as much as 60–70 per cent below the IBM price. In a certain sense, IBM itself has made copying easy by designing the original PC as an 'open system' and furthermore by keeping the technology of all its subsequent PCs basically unchanged for some six years.

What will happen now is obviously the $64,000 question. The drive for cheaper clones will, no doubt, go on for some time. Figure 3.3 which contains short-term cost projections arrived at through several more or less independent approaches, including recent estimates by *Business Week* and the French daily *Le Figaro*, strongly suggests that there is considerable elbowroom for further savings. For instance, the expensive metallic chassis could be replaced by a plastic one. We saw previously that prices of memory chips and consequently also those of microprocessors are, once again, being halved every two years; it is thus safe to anticipate a parallel saving on some of the more expensive parts: the mother board, controller cards and ROM chips. All told, the *minimum* total costs ex-works could very well drop to $175, and even less if a way could be found to cut down on keyboard and video screen. Even more dramatic is the anticipated downward slide in *average* costs. The time is not far off when stripped-down PC clones will be retailed in the United States at between $250 and $300.

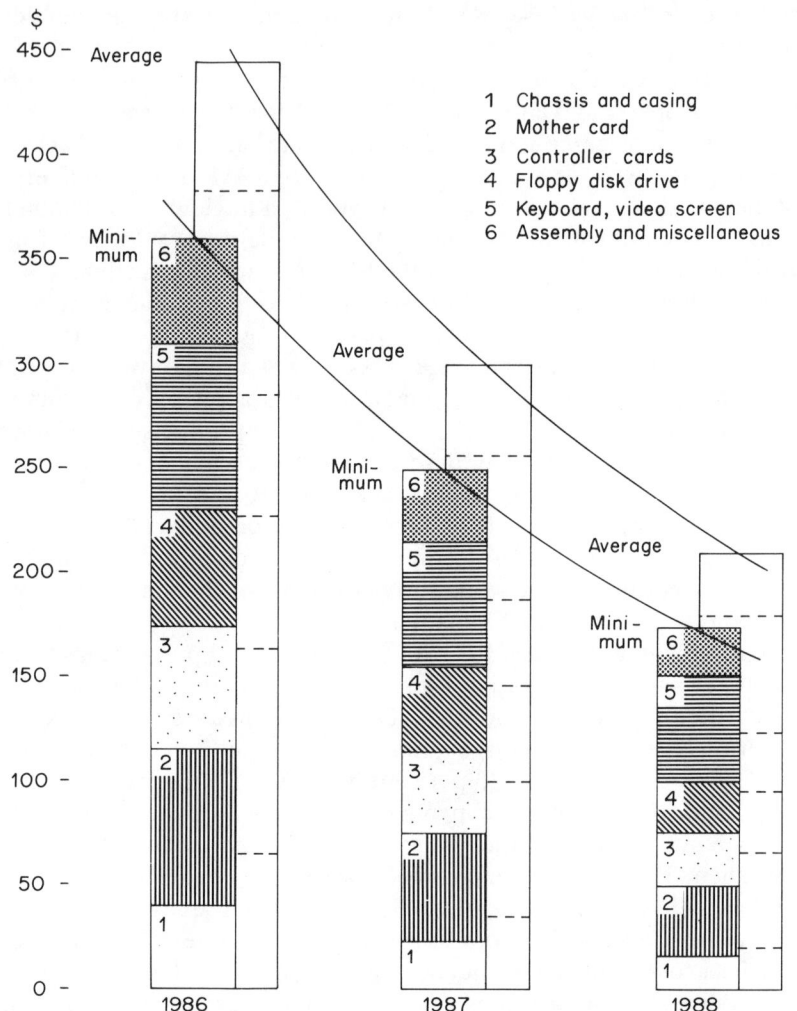

FIGURE 3.3 *Itemized cost of PC clones, 1986–88: Minimum and average ex-factory price projections*

At that price level, the PC would sell as a near commodity, a disposable item, cheaper to replace than to maintain and repair. When that happens, IBM 'will probably depart from that part of the industry', said its chairman, John F. Akers, in June 1986.

Besides withdrawing from the low-end, 'commodity' market and concentrating on more sophisticated and presumably also more profitable models for corporate users, what other strategic options are there left for IBM management? Design a low-cost PC using some revolutionary, inexpensive technology? Alter the current PC and use custom chips in order to make copying more difficult? Launch several new models in rapid succession while slashing prices on older models?

IBM executives, no doubt, realize that clone makers can copy whatever IBM does, without violating any copyrights. Therefore, just about the only logical way for IBM to escape from the current vicious circle would be to introduce a proprietary operating system for its entire PC line. In other words, the 'best'—or least damageable—strategy for IBM would be to close its PC architecture, thus departing from the initial open-system concept, and to functionally differentiate its personal computers from clones and other imitations.

After much soul-searching, Big Blue executives eventually settled for an ill-assorted compromise. The newly-designed PCs, announced in April 1987 and renamed PSs ('personal systems'), may be technically impressive; they are not, however, as 'clone-proof' or as aggressively priced as some had predicted. None of the four models unveiled will be delivered until 1988, which gives rivals time to adjust.

Wall Street's immediate reaction was unmerciful. Whilst IBM's stock fell, Digital Equipment, Apple, Wang and Compaq were up, and so were also Texas Instruments, Motorola and National Semiconductors. Big Blue's downward drift is likely to continue for some time yet; ultimately, however, the company will have to go through a 'cultural revolution' of its own.

Walking on a tightrope

With the IBM PC as we know it doomed, the outlook for the other established personal computer vendors is far from bright. In the short-term, as we saw, several were able to rebound—at the expense of Big Blue. However, few vendors so far have developed defensive strategies that would give them a fighting chance to resist the threatening invasion of cheaper and cheaper Asian imports. So much for the low end of the market. Apple Computer in mid-1986 announced a new, spectacular reversal of policy, stressing once again the advantages of Macintosh's incompatibility with the IBM PC. Tandy and Kaypro may manage for a while to hold their own. Tandon, whose disk-drive business has been losing money in recent years, announced its plan to reposition itself as a maker of personal computers.

The Houston-based Compaq Computer Corp. has confounded analysts who time and again predicted the company's early collapse. Compaq, too, had rushed in 1982 into the market for IBM-compatible PCs. However, unlike the other makers, Compaq was still prospering in the shadow of IBM in 1985. Commented Rod Canion, the company's president, formerly with Texas Instruments: 'For years, we have been hearing that when you elect to follow the IBM standard, you have essentially written off building anything innovative. We are living proof that, if you do it right, you can have it both ways.'[4] A year later, Canion dismissed the threat of low-end clones, insisted as before on constant improvement and innovation and sped up development of a new machine based on Intel's latest, powerful 80386, reportedly placing Compaq ahead of IBM, but still remaining close to Big Blue's basic philosophy.

The once-successful British makers, Sinclair Research, Acorn Computers and Apricot Computers (formerly Applied Computer Techniques), fell on hard times and they too had to undergo a thorough reorganization, accompanied by a radical shift in strategy in the direction of narrower specialization. In Europe, only Italy's Olivetti is really prospering through its association with AT&T, which distributes Olivetti's PCs and other products in the United States. Since 1985, Olivetti is the largest PC producer in Europe, with a market share of close to 12 per cent; Olivetti also overtook Apple Computer as the world's second largest manufacturer of personal computers, after IBM.

The microcomputer software developers—who reportedly numbered 5000 in the United States and turned out some 27,000 software packages by early 1985—live on dangerously moving sands. Digital Research, founded by Gary Kildall, dominated basic software for 8-bit microcomputers with its CP/M operating system, but when it came to the 16-bit generation Bill Gates' Microsoft stole a march on Digital Research. Microsoft's connection with IBM, which began in 1980 and led to the development of its MS/DOS operating system for the IBM PC, had propelled the company to the leadership in microcomputer software. The contract ensures Microsoft royalties on every personal computer sold by IBM; in practice MS/DOS has become an industry standard.

Despite these advantages, Microsoft was eventually overtaken in the overall turnover stakes for software houses by its direct competitor, Lotus, the designer and successful promoter of the 1-2-3 integrated software package and, more recently, with its Symphony software, which combines text processing, communication and record-keeping functions. Ashton Tate was a close third in 1985, with gross revenues of $130 million, compared with $175 million and $155 million respectively for Lotus Development and Microsoft. Digital Research now has plans to bounce back with two new operating systems for IBM machines and GEM (Graphics Environment Manager). The market is fluid and the competition intense. The packages are expensive to produce, maintain and develop, but cost very little to duplicate; thus success or failure hinges on marketing as much as on product quality. Clearly, single-product companies are particularly vulnerable.

[4] *The International Herald Tribune*, 17–18 August 1985.

3.3 R&D ESCALATION MUST BE REVERSED

Year in year out billions of dollars are channelled into research and development with the aim of improving information and communication technologies and inventing new ones. The industry is intrinsically innovation oriented; however, it is also exposed to outside pressures, which operate in the same direction.

Three contributing factors should be stressed in this connection. The computer business is highly competitive and open to new entrants. Competition is also fierce among the dozen or so large manufacturers of telecommunications equipment, despite limitations due to nationalistic procurement policies of most Western countries and Japan. Finally, the development of the computer-cum-telecommunications complex is vitally important from the standpoint of the military. However influential these outside factors may be in fostering innovative efforts, it is primarily from the point of view of the vendor companies that spending on R&D will be discussed here.

How much is too much?

Let us consider, first, the thousands of upstart firms that sprang up in Silicon Valley and in Texas in the late 1960s and early 1970s, and a few years later in Scotland's Silicon Glen, around Cambridge in England, near Munich in Bavaria and in a number of other locations, especially in the United States. Unremunerated research by young, enthusiastic engineers and some self-made men was often the thing that started the ball rolling. There is of course no way of calculating the money equivalent that would have to be expended to achieve comparable results within the framework of established, incorporated companies—assuming that such a parallel could be drawn. Incidently, we are even less able to estimate the social costs involved in thousands of small projects, which have failed to develop into marketable products or saleable software packages.

Incorporated companies have developed three, somewhat different, approaches to R&D spending and budgeting. In the first place, it is perfectly legitimate for a computer manufacturer or software house or again for a telecommunications equipment supplier to regard spending on R&D as investment, to be depreciated over several years, together with other assets. This approach is thus closely related to the concept of product cycles, discussed in the previous chapter. Consequently, and unless the company practises accelerated depreciation, an overestimation of the lifetime of a product, or family of products, can turn out to be a costly mistake.

Second, a vendor is equally justified to consider the cost of R&D as an expense, i.e. an item of outlay incurred in the operation of the business and therefore chargeable against its revenue for a specified period, usually the current year. In practice, expenditures on research and development are evaluated in relation to revenue or gross earnings, or as percentages of total value of shipments.

The industry-wide rule of thumb is said to lie within the range of 6–8 per cent. AT&T, IBM (prior to 1984), Motorola—to mention just a few examples—fall within that bracket, but so do Canada's Northern Telecom, France's Alcatel Thomson, Sweden's Ericsson, the Netherlands' Philips, etc.

Due to differences in accounting procedures, the relevant numbers for different vendors are not always strictly comparable. It remains, nevertheless, that IBM's R&D appropriation is seven times the amount expended by Xerox and nearly four times the sum total of R&D spending by Digital Equipment, Hewlett-Packard and Xerox together. At a cost of $3.6 billion (in 1984) IBM research centres and laboratories 'delivered' over 600 new or significantly upgraded products, systems and packages in a single year.

Other vendors have occasionally reported relatively higher expenditures on development. France's Bull claims that its R&D appropriation amounted of late to 10 per cent of its revenue, but much of it has come from government subsidies. Computer Vision's development expenses amount to 11 per cent, with the corresponding figure for Intergraph reaching 13 per cent.

The dominant tendency was a steady upward climb both in dollars and in relation to vendor revenues. As in so many other areas, here, too, Big Blue was setting the tune for the entire computer industry. In 1984, IBM's R&D appropriation jumped to $3.6 billion, from $2.2. billion a year earlier, and in 1985 it reached the truly staggering amount of $4.7 billion, just a shade under the benchmark of $1 out of every $10 sale. Clearly, not everybody could follow IBM's lead. When faced with serious financial difficulties, ITT, Sperry, Burroughs and many others slashed—for a time—their developmental efforts, only to resume the forward dash in R&D spending at the earliest opportunity.

The US semiconductor industry channels as much as 10 per cent of its gross earnings into R&D, yet finds itself trapped in the well-known vicious circle. Heavy outlays on R&D nourish a constant stream of innovations, which make current designs obsolete and depress prices. The trap reinforces the need for further innovation and whips up competition, with the circular action and reaction starting all over again.

Some vendor companies favour yet a third approach to product/system development. They set aside, or earmark, development funds for a specific project, e.g. designing a new machine, streamlining an existing line of production, creating a user-friendlier interface, etc. The method seems to offer a better opportunity for keeping expenses under control.

Unfortunately, the best-documented cases refer to excessive outlays and unplanned overspending. Mr Gene M. Amdahl left International Business Machines in 1970 and started a company of his own, which eventually became a pioneer in making IBM plug-compatible machines. In order to compete with the highly successful 308X computers, Amdahl betted heavily on developing the 5860/70 mainframe line at a cost that overtaxed the company's resources, siphoning off 18 per cent of total revenue.

Finally, management attitudes towards R&D matter as much as the amount of financial resources allotted. A few years ago, in Xerox's books R&D spending was just another corporate overhead and laboratory work was completely divorced from manufacturing. Without a clear product development strategy, it was not surprising that Xerox should tumble from its peak performance back in 1974, never to recover again. The company muddled through until its thorough reorganization in 1984: at long last, R&D appropriation was restored at $500 million, or over 6 per cent of total sales, and, more importantly, the costs of research and development are now charged to the budgets of the specialized divisions that stand to benefit.

Poker games at the summit

All told, aggregate spending on R&D by industry alone in the area of hardware, software and related services amounts to approximately $20–22 billion p.a. worldwide, excluding the Communist countries. If, however, we consider the whole range of electronics (including especially electronic components and consumer electronics), the bill rises to the astronomical amount of some $35–40 billion.

The geographical breakdown follows pretty closely the production and trading patterns analysed in Section 6.1. The United States alone accounts for 55–60 per cent of the total, Western Europe and Japan for some 15–20 per cent each. These apparently huge discrepancies are due to heavy reliance on government funding of both fundamental and applied research in Europe and to massive purchases of mostly US patents by large Japanese vendors. The subject is discussed in greater detail in the next section. In both instances, the burden of industry-financed, proprietary research is thus considerably lightened.

However impressive the outlays on R&D may look, they conceal from view two rather unpleasant aspects, the cost of R&D projects that fail and the further waste due to duplication. While failures are not uncommon, sometimes they set into motion a chain reaction which may affect several partners in a venture. Trilogy Systems, founded by Mr Amdahl in 1980, was forced to announce in 1984 cancellation of its programme for building an extremely fast computer based on large-scale silicon wafers that could hold far more circuitry than the conventional microchips used by IBM's Sierra. The defeat for Trilogy was also a setback for Sperry Corp., Digital Equipment and the French Bull (formerly CII–Honeywell–Bull), which invested[5] heavily in Trilogy Systems in return for access to technology that did not materialize.

It is not for us to belittle the vital role that R&D plays in the advancement of computer technology and applications, and that necessarily involves painful losses, but there are limits not to be trespassed. Northern Telecom, AT&T Technologies, ITT, GTE and Rolm have spent some $3 billion so far designing and developing advanced digital switching gear, the computerized nerve centre of a modern telephone system. The system analyses several thousands of 'phone calls simultaneously, makes the connections, calculates the rates to be applied and prepares the bills for customers. Designing essentially similar equipment has cost Japan's NEC, Fujitsu and Hitachi about $2 billion. However, Europe's Siemens, Ericsson, CIT Alcatel, CGE, Philips, Plessey-Stromberg disbursed so far over $7 billion to do the same job, whilst the European market is just about the size of the US market. It is therefore not surprising that actual sales of digital switching equipment by these three groups of producers are inversely proportional to their respective R&D spending, with an estimated total of $9.6 billion for the North American suppliers, $2.2 billion for the Japanese and only $3.7 billion for the half dozen European producers in 1986.[6]

R&D expenses in telecommunications display a particularly sharp, rising trend. Before the advent of the microchip, the average central office switch cost $50 million to develop and it had a useful life of at least 20 years. According to a reliable German estimate, based on 1985 prices, a new digital switch requires an R&D investment of $500–1,000 million, which must be recouped within ten years. The figures must be doubled to allow for adaptation to different standards in export markets and for software support. When capital cost is added, the total bill comes to $1.5–2 billion.

Symptoms of a climb-down

As the cost of developing a major piece of telecommunications gear, a supercomputer, a new line of mainframes or a complex operating system reaches levels accessible only to a handful of industrial giants, there is clearly a need to look for alternative solutions. Short of amalgamating—

---

[5] Respectively $40 million, $24 million and $13 million, giving Sperry, Digital and Bull respectively 15 per cent, 9 per cent and 7 per cent of the equity.
[6] Computed from estimates for some 20 producers, as published in *Datamation*, 1 July 1986.

viz. the recent Burroughs–Sperry merger (Unisys)—the second-league players are increasingly obliged to pool R&D resources with some of their (often keenest) competitors. The second approach is to look out for spin-offs from government procurements and government-financed R&D programmes.

In the United States, collaborative ventures have been rare and restricted in their object inasmuch as American companies are barred by antitrust law from pooling research for product development. Consequently, when the Semiconductor Industry Association in December 1981 announced the creation of the Semiconductor Research Cooperative, with a membership of some 50 firms,[7] it had to limit itself to raising funds for university basic research. Its counterpart, the Japanese Semiconductor Industry, is not only unhindered by legislation but its research activities are government subsidized.

Six Japanese computer makers and two manufacturers of electrical goods in April 1982 founded with government blessing ICOT, the Institute for New Generation Computer Technology. Miti, Japan's all-powerful ministry of international trade and industry, underwrote one-third of development costs of very large-scale integrated circuits (VLSI), of fibre optics and of factory automation, including advanced robots and flexible manufacturing systems. This highly publicized initiative has given an impulse to collaborative efforts in the United States and in Europe, e.g.:

1. The Microelectronics and Computer Technology Corp. ('MCC'), a research consortium[8] that began operating in 1982, concentrates on: microchip packaging; VLSI computer-aided design; parallel processing; artificial intelligence and knowledge-based systems.
2. Since 1984 the Pentagon encouraged a dozen major military contractors[9] to set up a consortium for software research.
3. The German government has pushed through Parliament a five-year programme backed by $1 billion of public money. Britain has its own five-year Alvey programme, worth £200 million, most of which is to go to precommercial R&D undertaken jointly by some 50 high-tech firms and 40 universities, especially in semiconductor technology, man–machine interfacing, software engineering and intelligent knowledge-based systems.

---

[7] Including IBM, Burroughs, Control Data, Digital Equipment, Intel, Hewlett-Packard, Monolithic Memories, Motorola, National Semiconductors, Rockwell International, Advanced Micro Devices, etc., and also Signetics (a subsidiary of the Dutch Philips) and Fairchild Camera and Instrument (controlled by Schlumberger and later renamed Fairchild Semiconductor).
[8] Made up of Control Data, Honeywell, Digital Equipment, National Semiconductors, along with such innovative smaller companies as Advanced Micro-Devices and Mostek.
[9] Boeing, TRW, General Electric, Lockheed, etc.

4. The European Community had co-funded the first international data network Euronet/DIANE (since 1980) and is currently underwriting 50 per cent of the cost of some 200 pre-R&D projects aiming at intra-European collaboration between dozens of firms and universities, within the framework of a ten-year programme, ESPRIT. A somewhat similar approach may yet prevail in R&D in telecommunications (project 'RACE').
5. Over a hundred European high-tech companies have come up with pre-R&D projects under the new pan-European scheme, Eurêka, whose main trusts seem to lie in advanced computer architecture, improved network design, software engineering and knowledge processing.

Potentially profitable spin-offs from government involvement in the promotion of high technology provide alternative means of easing the burden of in-house, duplicative research for a growing number of vendors, although the actual benefits are often difficult to track. Some $100 billion of federal funds may have been expended over 1945–70 to subsidize the technological development of the high-speed computer. Command and control systems commissioned by the Pentagon ran into several extra billions. The manned spaceflight programme launched by President Kennedy gave further impetus, especially to real-time computing. To boost the man to the moon had cost $2 billion of computing power. The SDI project will, no doubt, follow the same pattern on a grand scale.

Government involvement may of course take many forms in addition to its direct contribution to R&D, and it varies somewhat between the major nations. The biggest and most enduring impact is usually created by the following *modi operandi*:

1. The Federal government in Washington was and still is both the largest user and developer of computers in military, scientific and administrative applications. The British, German, French, Italian and Japanese governments provide similar backing to their national computer and telecommunications manufacturers.
2. Perhaps the biggest slice of public funding is channelled via military procurements. The Pentagon spent more than $30 billion on defense electronics, including communications, in 1984. Defense chips accounted for 12 per cent of the total semiconductor sales in the United States. Furthermore, when a foreign company wins a major contract, e.g. the RITA battle area network, known in the United States as Mobile Subscriber Equipment, the (French) supplier is expected to share the market with an American firm.

3.4 COST-SAVING OPPORTUNITIES

In the electronics bazaars of Taipei and Hong Kong anybody can buy everything needed to duplicate any model of the IBM PC: off-brand main circuit cards, densely packed semiconductor chips, floppy-disk drives, etc., at less than half the world market prices. Cunning entrepreneurs can be found everywhere. In the United States, 'milspec', or military specifications, require computer and telecommunications chips to perform to very high standards and the shipments are subject to strict quality-control tests; consequently they cost 5 to 20 times as much as standard commercial semiconductors. In connection with the quality-control problems experienced by Texas Instruments on deliveries of batches of chips to the US army in 1984, it has been reported that an undisclosed number of 'deficient' chips, after being rejected by the Pentagon, ended up in personal computers, medical instruments and other consumer electronic products.

It is beyond the scope of this book to present any detailed account of the multiplicity of cost-saving devices employed by respectable vendors and countless backyard peddlars. The more classical methods fall, broadly speaking, into the main categories of saving on personnel and lightening financial costs, to which we must add the current trend to an upwards re-valuation of electronics patents.

Trimming wages and overheads

Overhead expenses loom large in the accounts of many big corporations. After divestiture, AT&T was still left with 373,000 employees and overheads amounting to a full 43 per cent of total revenue. Despite its geographical spread and an incomparably more diversified product mix, IBM's selling, general and administrative expenses, also in 1984 and calculated on the same basis, did not exceed 25 per cent of revenue generated by a labour force of comparable size, or 395,000. Also AT&T was saddled with an average cost of $61 an hour to install and maintain products and equipment, compared with $49 per hour for the old Western Union, but only $33 per hour for IBM and $28 for MCI Communications. To appreciate the longer-term effect of these discrepancies, it is necessary to keep in mind that wages were rising by 7 per cent per year.

As anticipated, AT&T announced that it would reduce its workforce by 24,000 and freeze its management salary structure, and even that proved to be too little. Burroughs closed down 25 plants worldwide and dismissed 4,000 employees in 1985 alone. Like most of its Silicon Valley neighbours, Hewlett-Packard has adopted an austerity programme, which included shutting down its factories several days a month, reducing paychecks of most of its 84,000 employees and severely restricting the hiring of new staff.

Substantial layoffs have been carried out in all branches of computer and telecommunications manufacturing in the United States at, quoting at random, Control Data, Data General, Wang Laboratories, Apple Computer and many other vendors. Staff reductions have been particularly severe in the semiconductor business (one of the worst hit, Fairchild Semiconductor reduced its workforce from 28,000 in 1979 to 11,500 in 1986) and among the mini- and superminicomputer makers. The movement spread to Europe in 1985 and reached Japan the following year.

In order to curtail operating staff, many vendors began contracting out the costlier parts of production or assembly to small, specialty companies, at first in the United States and of late to South Korean, Singaporean, Taiwanese, etc., upstart companies, in a massive way. Large European vendors now proceed in very much the same fashion and claim that they are thus able to achieve considerable savings on their operating expenses.

The principal weakness of retrenchment policies aiming at work force reductions is the difficulty of defining realistic targets in the absence of a commonly accepted yardstick against which the desirable level of economies could be measured. AT&T provides a case in point. Having elimited more than 50,000 jobs, i.e. twice as many as originally intended, mostly among blue-collar workers, an AT&T spokesman in September 1986 freely admitted that senior executives were still searching for ways to trim their management staffs as part of a 'new hard look' at the company's overall costs.

This serves to underline the need to develop statistical indicators to be used as signposts to guide managements of vendor companies in their rationalization drives. Table 3.2, which is intended as an example, contains two different productivity indices for a dozen selected vendors classified by the performance of their work force in comparison, first, with IBM average sales per employee (some $120,000), second, with the weighted average for all the vendors combined ($87,500). Except for IBM, there was a remarkable degree of consistency, irrespective of the product mix of each vendor.

IBM's gross earnings per employee were 37 per cent higher than the industrywide average, and 45 to 55 per cent above those of its nearest competitors, CDC, Wang, Digital and Burroughs. However, the apparent productivity gap in money terms between Japanese/European and American vendors has disappeared as a result of the depreciation of the US dollar since 1985, as indicated by the retrospectively 'adjusted' values in the last column.

Table 3.2 Sales per employee as an indicator of productivity: selected computer vendors, 1985

	Index-numbers		
Vendor (& Country)	Basis IBM = 1.0 x)	Basis: Weighted average = 1.0 xx)	Adjusted for depreciation of US dollar xxx)
IBM	1.00	1.37	
Control Data	0.69	0.95	
Wang Laboratories	0.65	0.89	
Digital Equipment	0.64	0.88	
Burroughs	0.64	0.88	
Sperry	0.59	0.81	
NCR	0.58	0.80	
Bull (France)	0.57	0.78	1.12
Fujitsu (Japan)	0.48	0.66	0.94
Nixdorf (W. Germany)	0.48	0.66	0.94
Olivetti (Italy)	0.43	0.59	0.84
Hewlett-Packard	0.37	0.50	

x) IBM sales per employee: $120,000
xx) Industry average sales per employee: $87,500
xxx) Assuming a 30 per cent depreciation of the US dollar relatively to the DM and the yen.

Lightening financial costs

In a matter of five to six years, since approximately 1980, the computer trade has become one of the riskiest businesses. In view of this trend, it would have been natural to expect vendors to give serious consideration to ways of reducing financial risk and, more generally, alleviating the burden of financial costs. Unfortunately, no corroborative evidence could be found. In fact, few vendors, if any, have attempted to modify their traditional capitalization structures or change their financial canons of their own volition. Table 3.3, which has been compiled by Stephen T. McClellan, a foremost financial analyst specializing in computers, of Salomon Brothers, drives this point home. The classification adopted is self-explanatory and so is the message.

Equity financing and a generally low level of indebtedness are the two outstanding features of the best-managed US computer companies. That was the situation already in the 1970s and it remains so well into the 1980s. *A contrario*, the turmoil that has afflicted the once-prosperous Rank Xerox, Honeywell, Storage Technology and Wang Laboratories was not unconnected with excessive fixed costs resulting from earlier, repeat borrowings. Thus the lessons went virtually unheeded.

Table 3.3 Level of indebtedness of selected US firms (total debt as a percentage of capitalization)

Little or no debt	Under 30% debt	Over 30% debt
IBM	Burroughs	AT&T
Digital Equipment	Control Data	Honeywell
Hewlett-Packard	NCR	Wang Laboratories
Automatic Data Processing	Sperry	Xerox
Computervision	Data General	Storage Technology
Diebold	Computer Sciences	AM International
Electronic Data Systems	Harris	

Reproduced with permission from Stephen T. McClellan, *The Coming Computer Industry Shakeout*, John Wiley & Sons, 1984, p. 48 and Errata Sheet.

No comparable figures are available as regards European vendors. It is public knowledge, however, that with the exception of Britain's GEC, the larger companies and conglomerates in Europe are burdened with high financial charges and consequently have little elbowroom for charting independent strategies of their own. The financial structure of Japanese giant firms is generally so complex that no valid comparisons could be made.

It is appreciated that changing the financial structure of an established vendor, whether it be a publicly held or privately owned company, is necessarily a slow, painstaking process. Just about the only exception is a thorough reorganization, usually carried out under duress and resulting in a clean sweep. Applying such a radical remedy, however, does not guarantee that the new financial arrangements will prove more enduring. Britain's Acorn Computer is still famous in people's minds for going broke twice in the same year, rather than for its earlier breakthrough into the educational market, with its celebrated BBC Master Series.

It is not surprising, therefore, that most vendors concentrate, instead, on improving control of their inventories, which is yet another way of curtailing financial costs. Experience shows that paying insufficient attention to the cost of carrying idle inventories can lead directly to bankruptcy. Prior to selling off his name and rights to all existing products and designs to Amstrad in April 1986, Sir Clive Sinclair, of Sinclair Research Ltd, has been through an atrocious six months with virtually no sales, while inventories and debts kept piling up. This, more than anything else, broke the back of the once-flourishing personal computer inventor and maker.

On the other hand, nothing should ever be taken for granted in an area particularly exposed to business fluctuations. For several years running, Big Blue boasted with some justification that the company assets were the best managed. At one point IBM's entire inventory turned over every 5 to 6 weeks. Recent performance is unknown, but is certainly down ever since the marked slowdown in mainframe sales which started in mid-1985, but also as a result of the sudden slump that occurred in PC sales in the last quarter of 1985. All things being equal, the revival of Digital Equipment's fortunes in the second and third quarters of 1986 is just as much traceable to sharply improved control of its inventory, which now turns four times a year and possibly even more of late, as it is due to the growing popularity of its new VAX series.

The giveaway of patents must stop

The review of cost-saving opportunities would be grossly deficient without at least a brief discussion of patenting and licensing practices by US vendors and the penalties inflicted upon them as a result of a long-standing tradition of liberal granting of patents for nominal fees. Naturally, it is the financial/economic aspects that will be considered here, rather than the legal principles involved.

The fierce battle pitching US firms against Japanese and South Korean interests, which is currently gaining in intensity, is likely to decide whether American computer and electronics companies will eventually be relegated to the role of mere designers (of components, intermediary products, computer systems) or whether a better overall equilibrium can be achieved between the two industrial giants.

Having discovered the transistor in 1948, Bell Laboratories decided to stimulate the development of semiconductors by licensing its patent for a token royalty of about 2 per cent of the net selling price. By so doing, AT&T set the style for licensing electronics patents; it went even further and actively promoted cross-licensing arrangements on the basis of a reciprocal exchange of patents, including especially the many Japanese-held patents relating to very-large-scale integrated (VLSI) circuits. Since 1968, Texas Instruments and other US chip makers swopped patent rights with Japanese vendors. For example, Texas Instruments had negotiated three five-year licensing agreements and in 1983 initiated discussion with its Japanese counterparts on yet another long-term accord. Then, in late 1985 it suddenly pulled out of the negotiations and in January 1986 introduced lawsuits for alleged infringement of patents by eight Japanese and one South Korean semiconductor manufacturers.

Whether this change of mind was prompted by the outcome of IBM's action alleging infringements of patents against Hitachi and Fujitsu in 1982 is debatable. Eventually, the lawsuits were dropped, only to be replaced by a costly out-of-court settlement against the two Japanese computer manufacturers, putting temporarily an end to a serious threat to IBM's technological supremacy.

Be it as it may, TI is now demanding substantially higher royalties—reportedly some 13 per cent extra—for its patents on dynamic random-access memory (DRAM) chips. According to Japanese observers, Texas Instruments either seeks to redirect major financial resources to the US electronics industries, by reversing the royalty payment flows, or to prevent cheap Asian and particularly DRAM chips from entering the United States altogether. NEC Corp., Japan's largest semiconductor company, promptly filed a countersuit against Texas Instruments Japan, claiming infringement of its own patents on 256K DRAM chips.

The issue transcends the bilateral US–Nippon wranglings over how to split patent rights revenues and who in the future will be paying what to whom. While the legal battle was being fought in the courts, IBM quietly raised prices on its mainframe/software licences by 12 per cent in mid-Summer 1986 and the increases partly offset the company's hardware price cuts. Consequently, IBM's price per unit of computing power has stopped falling as rapidly as it used to, and we are thus left wondering whether IBM mainframe buyers will not end up paying double for IBM proprietary software, say, by 1990 or 1992.

This brings us back to the very first question with which we opened this chapter. Are we not witnessing the beginnings of real bidding up of software against hardware—this time, however, to the customer's detriment?

3.5 CONCLUSION AND OUTLOOK

We have been very much occupied in this chapter with the evolution of cost relations in information-based industries and with *ad hoc* remedies used to correct short-term disequilibria. Before we leave the subject of costs altogether, we ought to make an attempt to sum up the key findings, taking especially into account second- and third-round impacts and adjustments. Our foregoing analyses yielded results that go beyond the mainstream of current ideas.

1. The seemingly irresistible tendency to rising costs of software has been identified long ago and accepted by the manufacturers as a consequence of sophisticated information systems and escalating wage rates. Concomitantly, of late, R&D spending and financial costs have also shot up and the upward movement appears to be accelerating, thus throwing into turmoil the prior, relatively stable, chemistry of cost relations across the industry.
2. Increased outlays on R&D are due partly to higher costs of skilled labour and partly to skyrocketing prices of laboratory equipment.

The problem of financial costs has been compounded by inflation and high interest rates, in addition to the often-unbearable burden of unsold inventory, extra borrowing and the ensuing weakening of the capitalization structure of many companies in the United States and even more so in Europe. No wonder that, when faced with disappointing trading results or a sudden drop in demand, management reacts, first, by resorting to such expedients as shorter working hours and layoffs.

3. In the medium run, the squeeze is on the makers of such intermediate products as printed circuit boards, on the suppliers of components, e.g. microprocessor chips, memory chips, etc., and—by a chain reaction—on the manufacturers of polysilicon,[10] whose price has fluctuated in recent years from $20 to $100 a pound. The pressure is somewhat less compelling as concerns peripherals, floppy disks and other devices sold separately. Cut-throat competition, dumping practices and the real dominance of the world market by low-wage oriental producers must be attributed, in the first place, to the inner troubles of the computer and telecommunications industries in the Western nations, rather than to a somewhat mythical conspiracy by Japan. Corrective policies to redress the present imbalance could only backfire should they be misapplied or misdirected.

4. To fight creeping wage rates and avoid rising wage bills, computer manufacturers are making a determined effort to automate their factories, offices and laboratories. By mid-1984, Digital Equipment Corp. had installed an internal network linking their 2,300 computers and 40,000 workstations implemented in 32 factories in 11 countries and 600 offices in 44 countries, employing altogether a staff of 73,000. In order to achieve regular productivity gains, IBM has been investing in new plant and facilities between $2.5 and $3.5 billion per year.

5. Cost compressions having long-lasting effects are being sought and successfully implemented, especially at AT&T,[11] by way of flexible, robotized production lines, on the one hand, and via a new approach to quality control, on the other. Since traditional manufacturing of an integrated circuit necessitates up to 200 steps, the control has become an unwieldy task. The new offline quality control implies that all quality engineering activities be carried out before a product goes into full-scale production, that the prototype be designed for ease of manufacturing, that it be insensible to variability on the factory floor and that only a light final verification be required.

---

[10] From which silicon chips, as well as high-quality wafers are made. The German Wacker Chemitronic GmbH and the London-based Monsanto Electronic Materials Co. are the leading suppliers.
[11] *The Wall Street Journal*, 6 November 1984.

6. Let us now revert to the farming out of specific production processes by cost-conscious manufacturers and the contracting for software development or a specialized research project, a practice currently used in the United States, but now also increasingly popular in Europe. Cumulatively, these methods tend to erode the vertical integration pattern within the large corporations. Pulling in the same direction, centrifugal forces unleashed as a result of divestiture of AT&T and of privatization of telecommunications in Britain and Japan are also at work. The resultant trend is towards mission-oriented industrial groupings, e.g. avionics, automobile electronics, aircraft manufacturing and space vehicles, teleinformatics, which are likely to lead to novel, permanent, horizontal integration, e.g. IBM/Rolm, AT&T/EDS[12] with extensions to Philips and Olivetti, etc. Europe and Japan offer several examples of horizontal, electronic conglomerates, such as Philips, Siemens, Ericsson, Hitachi.
7. The slicing of the production process into discrete phases should give, so it seems, a lasting boost to specialized, low-cost suppliers as subcontractors. More generally, niche markets, a high degree of specialization and small size are hailed as positive hallmarks. The longer-term prospects are far less certain. As the niche markets tend to fragment further, the specialized company may sooner or later be faced with the dilemma: either concentrate on an ever-narrowing market segment, with the risks this course entails, or diversify and thus *ipso facto* start expanding in size. Either way, smallness is seldom a durable configuration.
8. Balancing short-term advantages against longer-run anticipations is one of the duties of management. Today, however, the general climate which provides the backdrop for decision-making is being altered in several ways. The breakup of AT&T put an end to internal cross-subsidization—between products, services, markets. Increased indebtedness creates a first lien on future earnings. Prior to offering British Telecom shares for sale, it was thought necessary to advertise immediate juicy profits and neglect long-term needs: whilst the American, German, Japanese and French telecommunications agencies invested in their plants $14,750 per employee on the average[13] in 1983, British Telecom reduced their investment to a mere $9,700—presumably in view of the coming privatization. Overall, short-term itemized profit is gradually becoming the overriding criterion.

---

[12] Electronic Data Systems Corp. The AT&T/EDS agreement was announced in January 1985.

[13] The number $14,750 is a weighted average, to be compared with $23,000 for NTT (Japan), $20,000 for the German Bundespost and $19,000 for the French Telecom. IBM's investment per employee in 1983 amounted to $14,000.

Part 2

The Dynamics of Marketing

Part 2 of this book deals with the challenging problem of marketing the new information technology. The issue is examined in its three main aspects: the rationale of computerization; widening the customer choice through tradeoff; and the identification of the most promising market prospects.

The focus is on the buyers and the users, in contrast with Part 1 in which the producers and the suppliers occupied the centre of the stage. The emphasis also shifts from the computer to computing, from computer networks to wholesale computerization, from hardware and software to systems and applications.

The subject of marketing takes on added importance in view of the growing pains of an industry just coming of age. As the analyses in Part 1 suggested, the computing business and the related trades may have, indeed, reached a plateau.

On the one side, computer-aided diagnosis, computer-controlled air safety and computer-directed space flights bear witness to the exceptionally high degree of dependability of the new technology. Computers are found everywhere, in every size, configuration and employment. They are now sufficiently low priced to be affordable for millions of individual and, especially, corporate and professional users. Yet at the same time, oversupply, slackness of demand, inventories running high, cut-throat competition, layoffs and factory closings, industrial amalgamations, the winding up of once-prosperous companies and abysmal losses on the stock exchange have created an atmosphere of gloom on the suppliers' side and dimmed the earlier enthusiasm on the buyers' side.

Just as troublesome is the realization that even the most powerful supercomputers and integrated systems of today are unable to translate accurately, are too slow to satisfy the needs of advanced research in many scientific disciplines and would, no doubt, lose any star war should one be fought this week or next. The personal computer may have triumphed in business applications, but the home computer and videotex have both failed to attain the status of standard household goods. The feeling is growing that, despite a brilliant record of achievements, the new information technology falls short of its potentialities. It is as if the godfathers were suddenly holding their breath in the hope of discovering—by trial and error or through black magic—what the future has in store that would enable the boards of vendor companies, their financial backers and their top-class engineers to devise particular paths that would lead to a renewed period of success and prosperity. May they find food for thought and discover new vistas whilst going through the next three chapters of this book.

Chapter 4 is an elaboration on a fundamental question. On what grounds do business corporations and service industries decide to proceed with automating production processes and office operations? It also deals with the many different answers to that single query. It is a truism that the strongest selling argument that a vendor can make is pointing out the benefit the buyer would derive from the acquisition of, say, a more advanced computer configuration, network or system. The difficulty is that the demonstration may not be easy to carry through and the proof of the cause-to-effect relationship is often elusive. It is thus doubly important for all vendors and intermediaries alike to understand how managements of the buyer companies approach this issue and, equally, to be familiar with the tools used by the buyers/users for evaluating their gains from computing and also potential incremental gains from further computerization.

Another much neglected area is explored in Chapter 5, which reviews the growing body of recent evidence pointing to the changing relationship in the marketplace, where the dominant influence is gradually switching from vendors to corporate buyers. The buying public has of late reacted strongly against the complexity syndrome and costly, stretched-out integration, and it exercises strong pressure in favour of streamlined design, simplified algorithms and procedures, portable and easily adaptable software packages, more efficient deployment of computer resources, and so on. System designers and vendors thus find themselves under compulsion to redefine, or modify as the case may be, the technical/economic tradeoffs, or sets of assumptions, on which their traditional lines of products/systems used to be based. There is every reason to believe that the buyers' market is here to stay. It is to be hoped that, faced with sophisticated, self-assertive buyers, the vendors will realize thay they had better start pushing 'the new frontier' of computerization farther afield and look seriously and strenuously for new openings.

Revitalized market research is, indeed, construed in Chapter 6 as a systematic search for new business opportunities on behalf of firms active in the new information technology industry and possible new entrants. The discussion opens with an overview of the global market for electronics and of the relevant market shares, to be used as a backdrop against which each vendor can project his own technological choices and marketing plans. After this short prelude, the balance of the chapter is an attempt to identify a number of future growth sectors and to provide pointers to promising, uncrowded market niches.

Chapter 4

Gains from New Information Technology

Choosing between investment alternatives is one of the thorniest problems that modern managements must tackle. The task is particularly intricate when the choice concerns rapidly changing information technology. Should the company automate additional production processes and/or computerize some office functions? Should it upgrade an existing configuration or replace it by a new installation, or should it wait for the 'next generation' of machines or systems? Should it proceed stepwise or rather make a clean sweep?

Ideally, the decision makers ought to have at their disposal a set of quantitative aids towards the planning of investment in the new information technology. Assembling such a kit of tools and evaluating the different methodologies that have been proposed are prominent among the aims of the present chapter.

Experienced managers know, of course, that numerical criteria and the quantitative measurements that they yield are, in the majority of cases, insufficient—at best partial, at worst misleading. Hence the continuous quest through the next four sections for better, more comprehensive or more reliable estimates of the benefits derivable from contemplated purchases of capital goods based on new information technology.

Two symmetrical dangers are involved. Cost/benefit techniques and other quantitative models, as we shall see, are frequently associated with an upward bias, which leads to overoptimistic estimates of future gains from a given computerization program. On the other hand, assessments that stress the indirect and intangible gains often have a distinct downward bias, conducive to the abandonment of some sound modernization schemes.

Several related aspects are explored in Section 4.1, which also contains an overview of the criteria used in evaluating the gains from computerization in general, irrespective of the area of application. Section 4.2 is concerned with tracking the benefits of computer-controlled automation of industrial production. The beneficial impacts of introducing new office technology are identified and analysed in Section 4.3.

There follows, in Section 4.4, a discussion of the truly intriguing, yet seldom-asked, question as to whether the successive rounds of computerization bring about increasing or diminishing returns. Another feature of Section 4.4 resides in the macroeconomic approach, whereas microeconomic analytical tools are used in the three prior sections.

As usual, a summary of findings is appended.

4.1 TRACKING THE BENEFITS OF COMPUTING

It is generally accepted that computerization of the Western world and of Japan has made extraordinary strides, partly because it was bringing about demonstrable gains and partly because many companies, public bodies and other organized entities believed that the benefits were there. Whereas this opinion is, on the whole, reasonable and widespread, the evidence available is not as unquestionable as we would wish and the actual proof of the causal relationship is in fact very difficult to establish. Our discussion may conveniently begin with the most favourable case, illustrated by three examples of the profitable use of computer systems in the office, laboratory and factory.

Demonstrable gains

In 1981, the price of a personal computer for business use was equivalent to 18 per cent of the cost of employing an office worker. By 1985, that ratio had dropped to less than 12 per cent, and it is now thought likely that it will be less than 5 per cent in 1990. By inference, it is currently anticipated that every second American white-collar worker will have at his or her disposal a microprocessor in 1990, whereas today there is one such device for every four or five staff members.

In the days of time-sharing, computer efficiency was of critical importance, with computer time selling for upwards of $100 per hour, compared with $10 per hour for the average employee's time. Since then, the situation has been turned upside down. Computer time costs essentially nothing, whereas the user's time is expensive—as the cost of skilled labour keeps rising by some 6 to 8 per cent per year.

Second, gains from an intensive utilization of computers can be particularly striking in product design and planning. CATIA is the code name for one of the most versatile and successful CAD systems, marketed by IBM since 1981. Created by Dassault-Systèmes, a subsidiary of the French aircraft manufacturer of the same name, it can be used indifferently to design a new airplane wing, the future European Spacelab, a self-levelling rear suspension for an automobile or a dental prothesis. The time required to complete the job has reportedly been cut by from 70 up to 90 per cent in comparison with traditional design methods.

Impressive gains from computerization have been reported by several manufacturing companies. According to a French source,[1] in such industries as steel, machine tools, automobiles and electronics, overall labour saving from the use of industrial robots amounts to between 15 and 20 per cent; computerized manufacturing might reduce the wage bill by 20 to 30 per cent; and flexible assembly systems should permit economies up to 40 per cent on manpower. Furthermore, it has been reported that robots employed for industrial paint spraying save between 10 and 30 per cent of the paint ordinarily applied by the workers. In other instances, computer-controlled machines reduce waste in steelmaking by generating less scrap metal than workers.

In the early 1970s, the Japanese industry was producing 2.5–3 million cars a year and employing some 450,000 people, including subcontractors.[2] By 1980, production had quadrupled to between 10 and 11 million, whereas the work force remained unchanged. At first view, average output per worker had risen by 300 per cent over less than a decade, or some 15 to 20 per cent per annum.

A few general remarks are in order:

1. In all the examples cited, the advantage is overwhelmingly on the side of computerized operations—in office, product development, manufacturing. Under the circumstances, no additional evidence is needed to convince the managements concerned that they should proceed with the contemplated computerization on a case-by-case basis. However, instances of this kind are the exceptions rather than the rule.
2. In a rational world, it is the rate of return on investment achieved or achievable under different technologies that should, on the whole, determine which way the decision goes. In practice, the theoretically unequivocal notion of rate of return on investment is approximated by the use of such ambivalent terms as gain, advantage, benefit, beneficial impact, differential, extra profit, and the like.
3. There are, also, several methods of ascertaining this increment. It is usually 'calculated' on the basis of a straightforward comparison between two periods, using whatever fragmentary data are available. Examples include: (a) a higher speed of operations, from which a time-saving formula may be deduced; (b) some measure of cost-saving, such as labour-saving, or economising on raw materials or on

---

[1] 'De la mécanique traditionnelle à la production', Cahier du Groupe de Stratégie Industrielle, Number 11 (an official report prepared for the French Government).
[2] Statement by Mr Ohmae, the managing director of Kinsey & Co. in Tokyo, as reported by the *International Herald Tribune* in 1981.

certain production processes; (c) a demonstrable reduction of waste through improved quality control or via simplified administrative procedures.
4. These pragmatic methods might occasionally be carried beyond what is reasonable or ethical. Thus, it is necessary to reject any suggestion that a meaningful parallel could be drawn between labour-saving induced by the purchase of a mainframe, as against non-computerized operations, on the one hand, and the savings on staff flowing from use of personal computers for identical applications, on the other. This kind of 'sin' against professional deontology is committed quite often, perhaps unwittingly. A careful reader has probably spotted the slant implied in the first two examples cited at the outset. Worse still is the tacit assumption that a given trend will prevail again and again, provided only that the earlier interplay of forces be resumed later on.
5. The foregoing example of the Japanese automobile industry, which had quadrupled its output while keeping its work force constant, suggests that other contributing factors, e.g. a superior organization, a well-disciplined labour force and an abundance of cheap capital, were at work, amplifying the productivity gains derived from comprehensive automation of the Japanese factories and the utilization of flexible manufacturing systems. Quite generally, benefits from advanced or complex applications are more difficult to identify and even more difficult to apportion.

From the pitfalls of narrow-based evaluations, there is only a short step to bias and another step to systematic bias, or, to put it plainly, 'convenient evidence'. The risk of getting biased advice is particularly acute during the planning phase. In support of a formal recommendation to introduce new information technology, management is usually provided with a fine impact analysis of one or two specific computerizable applications. In most cases, the choice of applications is somewhat arbitrary, justified as it is by the dearth of comparable statistics of performance.

As no two firms are alike in every respect, management should be aware that duplication of a beneficial implementation of new information technology in company A is unlikely to yield identical results in company B or C. The risk of error is further increased when the predicted performance of computerized operations is based on experiences of a small number of companies that belong to different industrial sectors. All assumptive arguments relying on far-fetched extrapolations or hasty generalizations should be closely scrutinized.

It is also well to remember that the benefits actually realized may fall short of what is attainable experimentally. Whilst the introduction of a wordprocessor reduces the typing time per page by a certain coefficient, the actual daily output of the average secretary using the machine will invariably be inferior to that norm. Elsewhere, the gains may perhaps be as large as forecasted, but they may not be as lasting as predicted. In other cases, the hoped-for gains may not be forthcoming according to plan, being delayed by unforeseen impediments.

At any rate, management should resolve that the decision to introduce new or additional information technology be preceded by extensive, technical and cost/benefit analyses, supplemented by a realistic evaluation of the underlying assumptions. It is often wise to engage outside consultants in order to get an unbiased assessment and implementation plan—provided, however, that the study is carried out in full cooperation with the company's own technicians and provided also that both teams of experts are in a position to resist the usual pressure from competing salesmen.

Intangible benefits

Too much can be made of this sort of argument. Witness the thousands of fully conclusive computerization ventures in office operations, particularly in the United States, and of factories, especially in Japan and Sweden. It is in the (insufficient) use of new information technology that Europe is losing out, as can be seen from the fact that spending by European companies on computerizing their operations does not even come up to 50 per cent of the corresponding figure for comparable American firms. Such huge differences cannot be explained away by pointing out the traditional conservatism of European industrialists, in contrast with the bright image of dynamic entrepreneurship in the United States and Japan.

What is at issue is the readiness (or the reluctance) to acknowledge that there may be other kinds of benefits, of a qualitative nature, and that in the final decision to go ahead with the computerization programme, the weight attached to these indirect gains ought to be upgraded. The second point, of equal import, is the ability of management (or the lack of it) to turn the benefits into new opportunities. These general propositions must be elaborated upon.

Observation shows that tangible benefits from computerization, such as cost reductions or staff reductions, are seldom 'cashed in' by American and Japanese employers, but rather ploughed back into streamlined operations, improved capabilities, additional lines of production or, at the very least, utilized to avoid further costs, e.g. startup costs of diversification. The possibilities are countless and widespread, and it is left to the reader to think of practical examples.

The handling of labour-saving innovations obeys, by and large, the same principle. Common sense suggests that higher output per worker, as a result of computerization, should lead to staff reductions and thus result in cost savings. In reality, it does generally avoid the need to hire additional staff, as illustrated by the earlier example of the Japanese automobile industry. It is a matter of record that most US and Japanese firms and industries have avoided—except in deep or lasting depressions—laying off redundant workers by assigning them to other jobs, factories and offices, by providing retraining facilities and by diversifying their lines of business.

When interviewed, executives of a number of buyer companies have cited the following qualitative improvements: reduction in error rates and/or failure rates; increased accuracy for some tasks; more efficient, and therefore cheaper, quality control; substantial reduction in rejects; better control of inventory; as well as certain intangible gains arising out of improvements in information flows and communications. They amount to what some analysts call 'value-added benefits'.

Recent research suggests that in the United States some decision-support systems, planning systems, flexible-production scheduling and other advanced applications are yielding overall benefits that exceed the initial expectations. Just as important, these indirect gains, by their synergetic effects, create a degree of flexibility unimaginable even ten years ago and this, in turn, increases the capabilities for performing structural, but more complex, tasks alongside standard operations.

4.2 A NEW JUSTIFICATION OF FACTORY AUTOMATION

Under the aegis of the Institute for Economic Analysis of New York University, a team of prominent economists working under Nobel prize winner, Wassily Leontief, has been developing over the past four or five years a fresh approach as an alternative to the traditional cost/benefit analysis which suffers, as we saw, from serious limitations. Ex-Harvard Professor Leontief acquired his title to fame 50 years ago when he perfected a technique called input–output analysis. The model had many extensions and it still provides one of the solid foundations for computing net national product and its cousin, gross national product, or GNP.[3] Broadly speaking, both concepts measure in money terms the overall, yearly flow of goods and services in an economy.

The Leontief table comes in the form of an enormous two-dimensional

---

[3] The only difference between GNP and NNP is depreciation.

matrix, containing nowadays up to 600 sectors and industries. Each industry is listed twice: in a row as an output and in a column as a required input. In practice, the computer is fed with a vast array of simultaneous equations and is thus able to calculate the gross amounts of each good and service needed as intermediary inputs and for final consumption. The matrix is more than a record of past performance. For instance, it has been used to forecast the effects of changing consumption patterns.

What and when to automate

In 1983, Wassily Leontief, together with Professor Faye Duchin and other colleagues, compiled a mass of data in order to apply the input–output technique to the current prospects for new information technology in and across the American industry, divided for that purpose into 89 input–output sectors. The goal was to help rationalize the decisions to introduce the new technology by taking into account interactions between industrial sectors.

There is no need to assimilate the rather heavy statistical apparatus involved. On the other hand, the essential premises and the working of the Leontief model are easily understood. Let there be no mistake: the method is not an exercise in futurology, nor does it consist in making projections about future technological trends. The new information technology whose impact is being assessed is the current one, proven, although not yet in widespread use.

The underlying, highly plausible, assumption is this. The ripple of the new information technology is going to give rise to effects that are not predictable by examining each industry or firm in isolation. Unlike in the previously discussed attempts, no effort is made here to ascertain directly the economic gains from computerization in a given industry, then in another, and so on. Indeed, we are reminded that the effects of every economic sector propagate to every other sector in a roundabout fashion by means of the price system. This well-known truism has provided Professor Leontief with the second pillar for building his model.

Consequently, all input–output relations are expressed in monetary units or, more specifically, in terms of prices, real wages (as rewards of labour) and the rate of return on investment (as the reward of capital). Calculations are performed assuming, first, the continuous utilization of the traditional technology and then repeated for the new technology, as defined above. The two sets of relevant technical coefficients, which are a kind of 'cooking recipe', are derived independently, being based in both instances on expert judgements, mostly by engineers and practitioners, supplemented by records of newly built, automated and semi-automated plants.

Once established, the complex system of simultaneous equations permits any number of permutations. In practice, Leontief and his colleagues simulated four different scenarios, or sets of assumptions, about the rate at which computer-controlled automation is introduced in the US economy. In the following demonstration, which centres on Figure 4.1, two scenarios only are considered.

The straight line (labelled 'Old technology') shows the relationship between real wages, equated with the index number 100, and the rate of return of some 12.5 per cent prevailing in the US economy in 1979, when operating predominantly under the so-called old technology. 1979 has been selected as the base year for which the data used throughout were derived from US Department of Commerce statistics. The slope of the line reflects the assumption that should the rate of return rise to 20 per cent, the real wages would fall to about index 80; conversely, if the rate of return were to fall to 5 per cent, the real-wage index would jump to over 120.

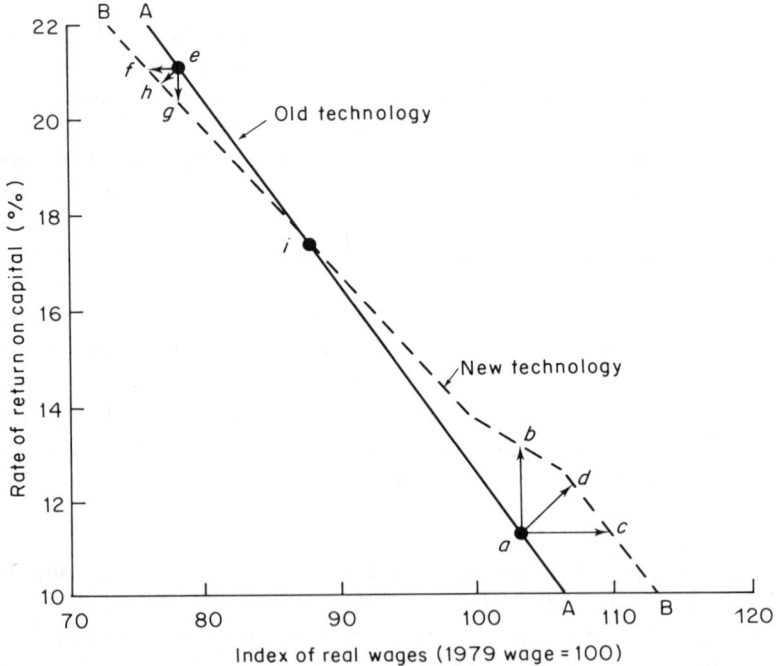

FIGURE 4.1 *Illustrating the switch from old to new information technology across the US economy, 1980–2000. (From Wassily Leontief, 'The choice of technology',* Scientific American, **252**, *No. 6, June 1985. Copyright © 1985 by Scientific American, Inc. All rights reserved)*

In fact, the straight line summarizes the Leontief scenario 1, which presupposes that final demand for goods and services will continue to grow until the year 2000 as it has in the 1970s, and that no automation or any other technological changes will be adopted after 1980. However unrealistic, the go-as-before scenario provides the base line against which all comparisons can be made.

The other line (labelled 'New technology') in Figure 4.1 portrays scenario 2, as it displays the results of the same calculations, now however based on the assumption that investment in computer-controlled automation will grow at increasingly rapid rates, i.e. by an extra 15 per cent in the 1980s and by about 30 per cent in the 1990s. The stage is now set for testing various hypotheses:

> For example, if the rate of return were 11 per cent under the old technology (a), the introduction of the new technology would enable it to increase to about 13 per cent (b). If one were content with the 11 per cent rate of return on capital, real wages would increase from 103 to almost 110 ... under the new technology (c). Both owners and wage-earners could also share in the benefits of the new technology (d). On the other hand, if the rate of return were as high as 21 per cent under the old technology, real wages would be about 78 ... (e) and the costs of changeover to the new technology would lead to a drop in the real wages (f), a drop in the rate of return (g) or both (h). There is neither incentive nor disincentive to switch from the old to the new technology if the rate of return at the time of the switch were about 17.5 per cent (i).[4]

At this point, it is important not to lose sight of the purpose of the exercise, which is to provide management with more reliable assessments of the benefits from automating. Previously, when contemplating investment in the new technology, the company's executives had to base their decision on the current spot prices. As a general rule, these prices reflected, as they do most of the time, the dominance of the old technology, inasmuch as the prices of the new technology-based equipment have not yet been (sufficiently) lowered. Given such constraints, the board of the company, specializing in products X, Y and Z, might have legitimately concluded that the then-going high price of a computer-controlled machine, which would modernize the factory operations, would in all likelihood reduce, rather than increase, the overall return on the company's total capital investment. Consequently, the decision would be to drop the plan for switching to the new technology.

---

[4] Quoted from Wassily Leontief, 'The choice of technology', *Scientific American*, **252**, No. 6 (June 1985).

The chief merit of the input–output analysis is to show that in most instances such a conservative decision would be detrimental. Moreover, this technique permits us to define the essential prerequisites for making rational choices, one way or the other. Using the same set of data as before, Leontief convincingly demonstrated that, as long as the rate of return lies between 14 and 17.5 per cent, the firm making products X, Y and Z would rule against computer-oriented modernization, even though a more comprehensive assessment leads to the conclusion that both employees and shareholders of the company would benefit from the changeover.

Automatizable industries: from A to Z

The technique is susceptible to many applications and extensions. Thus, a computer rerun of the relevant array of equations could provide a more systematic, quantitative explanation for the failure of some industries to adopt the new information technology on any appreciable scale. Again, further calculus performed on the same data basis yielded a plausible answer to the question: what combination of the two technologies, old in some activities, new in others, would optimize the wages for a given return on capital, and vice versa?

The New York University economists were able to assign the 89 industrial branches initially taken into account to homogeneous sets of candidates for switching to the new technology as the prevailing cost of capital varies. Should the rate of return exceed 20 per cent, 7 sectors only would qualify: manufacturing of mainframes, manufacturing of semiconductors, petroleum refining, government enterprises, lumber products, wood containers, plus real estate. If the rate drops to 18.5 per cent, 26 other industries ought to switch to the new technology. However, a more comprehensive automation of printing and publishing would require a further drop in the rate of return to 15 per cent. At the other end of the spectrum, health and education services should continue operating under the old technology no matter how low the cost of capital—unless the computerization is decided on political rather than business grounds.

Incidentally, this intersectoral analysis explodes the myth of a 'paperless society', which has fired public imagination but haunted the boards of directors of the pulp and paper industry for a long time. True, the introduction of new office technology had the effect of reducing the demand for a handful of special products, e.g. carbon paper and copy paper, but this was more than compensated by a new, strong demand for all shades of photocopying paper, printout paper and the like, and this overall upward trend seems set to continue until at least the year 2000.

Finally, the Leontief study explains why the Japanese industry is far more computerized than the American. Japan has traditionally followed a policy of low interest and low rates on invested capital. This, more than anything else, opened the door to a massive introduction of new information technology. In due course, the rapid computerization contributed to raising Japanese wage levels and, more recently, to a moderate increase in the rate of return on capital, as well. On the other hand, the policy of high interest rates pursued consistently, for whatever reasons, by the Republican administration in Washington slowed down or delayed corporate investment programmes and eventually put a freeze on their purchases of computers and related equipment.

A somewhat similar comparison can be made, with the help of the Leontief theory, between Western Germany, a country with low inflation and low cost of capital, and the United Kingdom which kept luring foreign bank deposits and capital by very high rewards. Using the index of semiconductor penetration into different sectors of industry as a rough indicator of the level of industrial computerization, we can say that by 1984 the German corporations had been winning the race over their British counterparts in the proportion of two to one.

However impressive in its scope and applicability, the input–output technique has its own built-in limitations. Whereas the model consists of a vast array of equations, the selection of the key variables of prices, wages, the rate of return, plus sets of technical coefficients, is very restrictive and thus open to challenge. Surely there must be other forces at work and additional mechanisms through which synergy effects propagate. Furthermore, there is no evidence that the reciprocal relationship between the rewards of labour and those of capital is as rigid as Leontief says. There are many known instances in which both the wages and the rate of return on capital have risen at the same time.

Next, by emphasizing the quantitative relations, the theory implies that qualitative factors are either (relatively) unimportant or can be assumed to play a neutral role. This is, of course, contradicted by our findings in Section 4.1 of this chapter. A less obvious, yet real, weakness is the timelessness, or the absence of dating, implied in the model, which does not specify, even approximately, how long it will take for the presumably beneficial impact of computerization in one area to be felt in other sectors. Professor Leontief has spoken enthusiastically about the General Motors' scheme for the fastest and most comprehensive computer-driven automation ever undertaken, with the aim of making GM the lowest-cost auto producer. Since 1983, the giant corporation spent billions of dollars on new plant, new transfer presses, a factory of the future, software development and the acquisition of Electronic Data

Systems Corp. and the high-technology Hughes Aircraft Co. Two years later, the results still did not come up to expectations. Whether in terms of vehicle output per employee, fixed costs per vehicle or pretax profit per vehicle, GM in 1985 was trailing behind both Chrysler and Ford. Top GM managers now claim that the huge investment in new information technology will be repaid by handsome dividends by 1990. If that proves to be true, it will be a major triumph for Professor Leontief and his colleagues as well.

4.3 ATTRACTIONS OF NEW OFFICE TECHNOLOGY

The most popular rationale of the decision to invest in new office technology is that the introduction of computer-based information systems, simulation models, workstations, local area networks and other automated aids tends to raise the white-collar worker's productivity. In this view, higher productivity is the end, the office technology, the means.

The root out of which sprang this conception lies in the historical fact that average productivity in the service sector changed very little over the past two centuries, whereas average output per blue-collar worker rose continuously since industrialization got underway in the eighteenth century. The quasi-stagnation of office workers' productivity, so went the argument, was due to the blatant lack of investment. Indeed, not so long ago, the average capital per worker amounted to $20,000 in the US industry, $30,000 in agriculture, yet less than $3,000 in the services. Presumably, the *causa causae* was the high cost of sophisticated office tools which, designed for individual usage, could not be amortized by sharing. The whole tertiary sector was thus caught in a kind of circular psychosis.

A first opportunity to escape from the vicious circle came with applications of operational research to such mundane tasks as stock control by computer, computerized pay, customer billings, and the like. Here was the proof that speed and accuracy of routine office functions could be increased, but also that an average operator was capable of performing better.

The argument of higher productivity of the staff was later invoked in support of wordprocessing, on the one hand, and of networking, on the other. Moreover, computer time-sharing set the pattern for other forms of joint use, e.g. of high-quality photocopying, semi-industrial reprography, programmable dissemination, semi-automatic filing systems and other facilities. As the prices went down, the sales climbed—so much so that today the average capital invested per white-collar worker in the United States and Western Europe has caught up with average fixed capital per blue-collar worker.

The concept of productivity discussed

The foregoing recapitulation of what went on in the offices since the early 1970s brings us back to the yardstick of productivity as the major justification for repeat upgradings of automated equipment. Productivity, or the productivity index, is a simple yet somewhat ambiguous concept. Strictly speaking, it is the quotient of output divided by input. Changes in this ratio define changes in average output per unit of factor input. The meaning of the ratio depends, obviously, on what is included in the output measure in the numerator and in the input measure in the denominator. Output is usually expressed either in physical units or in money value equivalents. As to the factor input measure, many alternatives are open. The denominator might be a composite measure of all productive resources—labour, capital, management. It might also be any one factor or an element of some one factor. Thus, we might measure productivity of land per acre or calculate the net productivity of capital in a given industry or firm, which is yet another name for our old friend, the rate of return on capital invested.

Here we are particularly interested in variations in labour productivity or, in other words, in changes in output per man-day or man-week of work done under different conditions. The input data may be restricted to the clerical staff working directly with the new technology, or they might be enlarged to include all forms of human effort, supervisory and managerial, as well as direct.

While it is convenient and useful to measure changes in office output with reference to changes in the labour component of the factor composite, it would be a serious mistake to assume that this factor operates alone in bringing about a gain. The final result depends not only on the skill and intensity of the human factor but also on the nature of office organization and several other features, last but not least being the number and quality of the new technological tools employed.

However, not everybody accepts the convention of equating labour productivity with faster or cheaper per capita performance—far from it. Another view gives prominence to efficiency, or the effectiveness in utilizing labour, capital equipment, organizational talent and knowhow and other factors of production in such a way as to enable the staff to do better work, rather than the same work better. This conception seems to be gaining ground. However, many proponents of this alternative approach argue that when human and organizational components of productivity are taken into account, they too, ought to be quantified whenever possible, or at least evaluated with the help of indirect indicators.

Multifarious effects of new technology

In order to pursue this line of attack, the obvious first step must be to define a methodology for carrying out overall, balanced assessments, allowing for the great variety of equipment and applications, while minimizing the weight of subjective factors inherent in value judgements. Two remarks, one related to office technology, the other concerned with office functions, will bring this point home.

The new technology is versatile and increasingly flexible. A workstation, for example, can be programmed to perform a great many different tasks, and the order in which these operations are executed can be changed at will. Likewise, a wordprocessor will have different effects depending on the conditions and environment in which it is utilized—whether as a stand-alone facility or linked to a network, whether it is used continuously in a pool of typists or only occasionally by a supervisor or head of department, and so on.

The earlier image of data processing and management information systems, which were both concerned basically with structured information and formalized procedures, are too readily—and often wrongly—applied to present-day office operations. In reality, most office functions are unstructured—the tasks are seldom randomly distributed and are therefore less predictable. Totally unforeseen problems crop up that require *ad hoc* handling and may call for frequent reorganizations. The uses of new information technology cannot therefore be identified by a simple listing of the devices, on the one side, and of the associated applications, on the other side.

A more realistic categorization of the basic approaches to the applications and also the impacts of new office technology is to be found in Table 4.1. The table, with some slight modifications, is reproduced here by courtesy of its Italian coauthors, Federico Butera, the founder and director of the Milan-based Institute of Action Research Organization, and Professor Bartezzaghi, of Milan Polytechnic.

The introduction of new office technology often starts with a piecemeal mechanization of small routine tasks, e.g. typing, electronic mail, filing and information retrieval, and is prompted by the anticipation of improved productivity, of speeding up information handling and of savings, as indicated in the second column in Table 4.1. On the other hand, service industries, bureaux, professional outfits with previous experience with formal data retrieval systems are often inclined simply

Table 4.1 Type and impact of new office technology

	Mechanization of office work	Office information systems	Computer aids	Decision-support systems
Examples	Wordprocessors, facsimile, teletex, enhanced telephony, printers, phototypesetting	Automation of office procedures, order recording, accounting, integration of data and text processing	Electronic mail, viewdata, multifunction workstation, information retrieval and storage	Financial planning models, databases, expert systems, simulation models, project developments
Organization elements affected	Tasks, jobs, formal organization structures, formal communication, conditions of employment, skills and qualifications	Control and coordination procedures, job roles, boundaries between activities and units	Tasks, career development, training, job roles, communications (mainly for managers, professionals)	As for office information systems, with an emphasis on the decision-making process
Main performance factors affected	Clerical and secretarial productivity, staff turnover, absenteeism, staff motivation, product quality	Effectiveness and efficiency of units, systems flexibility, readiness to respond and adapt to changing needs	Productivity and effectiveness of managers and professionals, product quality	Productivity of managers and professional staff and of the groups and units as a whole

Reproduced with permission from Federico Butera and Emilio Bartezzaghi, 'Creating the Right Organizational Environment', in *New Office Technology* (edited by Harry J. Otway & Malcolm Peltu), Frances Pinter (Publishers), London, 1983, for the Commission of the European Communities.

to extend their existing configuration in order to include those office routines that the new technology permits to automate. Here, the incentive comes from the desire to streamline administrative functions and/or improve control and coordination. As we have already pointed out, this system buildup often proves too rigid and inimical to the need to adapt quickly to environmental and functional changes.

These two examples should suffice to illustrate the several ways of putting to good use the Butera–Bartezzaghi matrix which is, of course, much more than a simple structuring device. Reading Table 4.1 vertically helps to identify the different effects, according to the four main types of the new technology, on the organization and operations of the office being impacted upon and to evaluate the key, both quantitative and qualitative, indicators of overall performance. For instance, office information systems aim at automating some decision-making processes, whereas the so-called decision support systems help those in charge to make the final decisions themselves. Thus, a financial planning system can be programmed to suggest what might happen under different assumed rates of inflation and/or rates of interest. More generally, decision support systems are designed to answer the 'What if?' type of questions.

In concluding, the model provides a pragmatically based technique of wide applicability. It is a flexible tool, easy to use and adaptable to a whole spectrum of particular office setups, provided that both the analysts and the managers are aware of the methodological limitations involved.

4.4 THE CONUNDRUM OF DECREASING RETURNS

The problems reviewed so far have dealt primarily with the identification and measurement of gains from the introduction of new information technology on an *ad hoc* basis, using mostly data supplied by separate companies. We must now broaden the terms of reference in two directions: first, by considering the stream of benefits to be reaped over time as computerization in offices and factories proceeds further and further; second, by looking at the issues from the standpoint of macroeconomics, which seldom coincides with the narrower point of view of separate production units.

Impacts of further computerization

The overriding question is whether the successive gains tend to increase, or to decrease, concomitantly with application of additional doses of the new technology. In other words, we want to know whether, under what circumstances, in what areas it is the law of diminishing returns[5] that prevails, and vice versa, when and where ongoing computerization brings about increasing returns.

Clearly, these questions are of more than academic interest, yet they have so far received little attention in the computer literature, probably for lack of historical perspective. As long as the price of mainframes remained high, it was difficult to conceive of computerization within a given organization as a stepwise process. The appearance of smaller, less expensive computers has changed all that. The minicomputer from the middle 1970s and the microcomputer from the late 1970s onwards could do—locally and more cheaply—many of the smaller jobs previously done on a large, centrally located mainframe. This in turn provided alternative ways of assembling a viable computer system within a company via incremental purchases, spread over several budget years.

For technical as well as organizational reasons, a piecemeal approach would be unsuitable for automating manufacturing, mining and raw materials processing. Historically, in most steel mills, glass works, timber works, etc., automation was introduced by chunks and on a large scale, and was most of the time accompanied by reorganization. We are thus once again forced to discriminate between office and factory automation patterns. This two-way split is of course arbitrary, as most corporations combine the activities of white-collar and blue-collar workers under one roof.

Other combinations must be considered. At initially low levels of production, increasing returns have often been observed, only to be superseded by a tendency to decreasing windfalls at later stages. The opposite sequence is also plausible, since a given production curve may have more than one 'peak'. Thus, by trial and error, managements are usually able to approach the 'best combination' by gradually substituting increasing doses of new information technology for labour in specific production lines—without necessarily laying off redundant workers at company level.

A further complication arises from the frequent failure to separate two quite different 'laws'—the law of diminishing/increasing returns, based, as already indicated, on the assumption that one of the factor inputs is kept *constant*, and the law of returns to scale, which involves a marked change in the size of the firm or operation. It is indeed tempting to try to figure out what will happen if the work force, technology, capital and other factor inputs are *increased* in identical proportions. Will the

---

[5] The law of diminishing returns, which reflects the often-observed technical and economic regularity, refers *stricto sensu* to successively lower incremental outputs gained from adding extra doses of a given input (e.g. capital), whilst all other factors of production (e.g. labour, technology, etc.) are kept constant. Alternatively, in a controlled experiment, it is possible to keep output constant whilst injecting extra doses of new technology, and thus obtain successive yet gradually diminishing savings on manpower.

resulting output, too, increase in the same proportion or will it increase more than, or less than, proportionately?

These questions have a ring familiar to anyone who has ever opened a textbook on elementary economics. Let the reader be reassured at once. There is no intention to proceed on a long journey through the clumsy geometry of marginal product, marginal revenue and other related notions which occupy such a large, indeed central, position in economic analysis.

Fortunately, we can dispense with technicalities and get to the business at hand by adapting for our needs a method developed thirty years ago by MIT's Robert Solow.[6] This was later supplemented with extensive investigations by the non-profit National Bureau of Economic Research into the aggregate production function for the whole of American manufacturing. The studies have demonstrated that automation together with the relevant knowhow was directly instrumental in raising the productivity of both labour and capital at least two-and-a-half times between 1900 and the early 1960s, or by a yearly average of 1.5 per cent. Investment per worker had risen even faster and the real wages increased by more than 1.5 per cent ascribable to technological progress alone. Thus, far from downgrading the value of human work, as some had feared, the new technology had the effect of enhancing it.

Evidence is, however, accumulating that shows that, since the late 1960s, these—on the whole gratifying—trends no longer apply. To put it in a nutshell:

1. All through the 1970s and early 1980s, technological innovation made further strides, the new information technology found many new applications and the penetration of computer-based systems and devices into factories and offices accelerated.
2. There has been, as already reported, massive investment in office equipment. In parallel, enormous and increasing amounts of capital were sunk in factory automation, private and public networks, databases, value-added services, simulation models, etc. If there had been any slowdown in the flow of capital to industry, it became noticeable only recently, especially in the United States.
3. In view of the drop in unit costs of computing by two orders of magnitude over the last 15–20 years[7] and considering that total shipments of computing equipment, devices and systems increased approximately one-hundredfold during the period under review, the aggregate installed computing capacity must have increased 10,000 times—or somewhat less if allowance is made for wear and tear and

---

[6] R. M. Solow, 'Technical change and the aggregate production function', *Review of Economics and Statistics*, **39**, 312–18 (1957).
[7] See Chapter 1 above.

obsolescence. The figure is corroborated by an IBM estimate according to which user demand for MIPS has been growing at a compound 60 per cent per annum (multiplication factor: 12,000 in 20 years).
4. Since the early 1970s, labour productivity in America and throughout the industrial world from Japan to Western Europe began slipping and declined sharply in recent years. In the whole of private business in the United States, outside agriculture, the average gain in productivity was zero in 1985. It rose 2.6 per cent in manufacturing, but in the service industries it actually fell. In agriculture, productivity jumped by an extraordinary 11.5 per cent, as a result of thousands of farmers leaving the land.
5. In the last decade, manufacturing employment declined in America as well as in Europe, as manufacturing jobs migrated overseas where cheap labour was in large supply. On the other hand, the US economy was able to create 20 million new jobs, mostly in service-related areas, which have generated over 6 million extra jobs in Japan—as against a 2 million net loss in Europe. Altogether, there were in 1986 some 15 million unemployed in Europe, or 10–14 per cent of the total active population, and little hope of reversing the trend. By contrast, joblessness in the United States dropped to under 7 per cent, one of its lowest levels ever.

'Who stole productivity?' asked dramatically a *Washington Post* (2 February, 1986) headline, adding: 'It remains a mystery and, in terms of its importance to the way people live, probably the most important mystery in current economics.' The present conundrum is made up of crosscurrents that seem to go against traditional wisdom. In an attempt to reconcile the apparent inconsistencies, three propositions are put forth:

1. The overall cost of operating and maintaining up-to-date computer systems impounds the financial resources of many companies more seriously than is generally admitted, thus offsetting in large part earlier productivity gains.
2. The cost of marshalling pertinent information is skyrocketing in relation to other factor inputs, thus siphoning off an appreciable slice of gains from computerization.
3. It is, in the end, the net productivity gains that matter, rather than the gross benefits which make no allowance for mounting wage bills and for expensive improvements in the working conditions.

What holds these axioms together is, indeed, the flexible law of diminishing returns. The three elements of the puzzle must now be briefly expounded.

Expenditures on computing are up

Our first point is corroborated by an unusually candid statement extracted from an extensive study sponsored by the American Association for Computing Machinery. The author, Professor John Leslie King[8] of the University of California, wrote: '... computing is a very expensive business.... In very few cases does a computing installation, centralized or decentralized, get smaller and cheaper over time.'

In fact, the overall expenditure on computing is continually mounting, as computer systems become more powerful and sophisticated, as the costs of maintenance, debugging, learning, security and other hidden items increase, as previously stand-alone equipment and systems are integrated in supernets and as obsolescent subsystems are being rebuilt. The never-ending expansion and technical upgradings entail frequent and expensive reorganizations. As the size and coverage of the existing installation grows, problems related to discontinuities[9] are usually compounded. Last but not least, funds set aside for depreciation are often underestimated and the actual outlays on new information tools and systems must in part be paid out of companies' current earnings.

The second critical feature, frequently overlooked, is the rapidly swelling expenditure on data acquisition and distribution. As a general rule, the volume of messages exchanged between staff members within an organization grows twice as fast as the work force itself. The modern office photocopier has further increased the velocity and also the volume of paper being shuttled around. Information flows may have improved, but, almost as a corollary, information pollution grew worse. However crude, the following estimate illustrates this tendency: in Japan, only 8 per cent of total information generated was 'sold' and used in 1982, as against 11 per cent ten years earlier.

John Diebold, writing in 1965, complained about 'the high cost of input of data ... which currently [ran] from 20 to 40 per cent of the total systems cost'. In the meanwhile, as databases expanded and multiplied, the price tags for gathering, validating, analysing and abstracting information have failed to come down. A great deal of this work is now contracted out to specialized outfits in Hong Kong and Taiwan. Public databases accessible online, especially in sciences and technology, are grossly underutilized and can recoup only by overcharging. According to a survey by LINK, Inc. of online information users in Europe in 1982, elasticity of demand[10] is low, inasmuch as a 15 per cent drop in the rates

---

[8] John Leslie King, 'Centralized versus decentralized computing: organizational considerations and management options', *Computing Surveys*, **15**, No. 4, 320–49 (December 1983).
[9] See Section 2.2 above.
[10] Broadly speaking, price elasticity measures relative changes in the quantities demanded as a result of relative changes in price. By definition, a unit elasticity corresponds to a situation in which a 1 per cent increase (decrease) in price leads to a 1 per cent drop (increase) in the demand for that service.

charged would induce existing users to increase their usage by only 6 per cent, whereas a 30 per cent increase in price would reduce demand by 13 per cent. However, commercially available databases provide the industrial and business users with a minute fraction of the information they need, and must therefore be supplemented with in-house data systems.

Taking all these elements into account, a French expert[11] has calculated that aggregate spending by American corporations on information, including sources external to the firms, grew at twice the average rate of growth of labour productivity during most of this century. Inescapably, these extra expenses on information must in due course outstrip the incremental productivity gains from computerization. Thus it should have been evident, according to the French analyst, that the average annual increase in productivity per worker would drop from the 3 per cent level in the early 1960s to approximately 1.5 per cent in 1965–73, and finally to zero.

Our third and last contention is that factory automation in the early 1970s proceeded more or less in accordance with the law of increasing returns, leading at that stage to economically justified improvements in real wages. Soon after the mid 1970s, net productivity gains began declining, leading to the disappearance of a great many jobs in steelmaking, shipbuilding, automobile and textile manufacturing, etc. In a recent study, 'The plight of manufacturing',[12] Richard M. Cyert, president of Carnegie Mellon University, warned that many more workers would suffer declining incomes as they will be forced to give up better-paid jobs in factories and take up low-paid service jobs, whilst the shareholders of the more fully automated companies will increase their share of the national income.

The implication is that the continuing diffusion of new office technology must have been bringing about diminishing returns in terms of productivity, even assuming that the initial introduction of that technology may have resulted in somewhat more tangible benefits. Most of these early gains were spent on improving working conditions and the office environment. The relatively low level of remuneration of office workers stimulated creation of new service firms in the United States, whilst the relatively high level of wages of office workers in Europe, in combination with lack of entrepreneurship, acted as a drag on European service industries, which hardly expanded their payrolls at all.

---

[11] Jean Voge, president of the Institute for the Development and Redeployment of Telecommunications and the Economy, writing in *Le Figaro*, 19–20 October 1985.
[12] Published by the National Academy of Sciences in early 1986.

4.5 CONCLUSION AND OUTLOOK

It is just as well to open this new summary of findings with a couple of universal lessons to be learnt from the immediately preceding discussion of the law of diminishing returns.

1. The model sketched out in Section 4.4 takes into account the historical fact that labour productivity began declining, and eventually came to a near standstill, concomitantly with, or shortly after, the massive introduction of computerization into offices and factories. Being a macromodel, it admits of many exceptions at the microeconomic level—and therefore the makers/suppliers of specialized computing devices and aids need not be unduly worried that the inexorable reality of diminishing returns in the aggregate might catch up with them, too. The model provides a plausible explanation for the divergent impacts of office and factory automation. Finally, it helps us understand the job surge in the United States, in contrast with the inertia in most of Europe.
2. Despite all the supporting evidence cited, our set of axioms does not, by any way of reckoning, amount to formal proof of validity. On the other hand, both the law of diminishing returns and the law of returns to scale, if handled with caution, are precious tools relevant to such problems as: defining the critical size (of a company, of market share, etc.), adding new products to an existing product line, determining whether a dangerous acceleration has not further affected already declining sales, and so on.
3. It is irritating that the harder we try to show that the model fits real-life, dominant trends, however unstable these may be (e.g. labour productivity), the more our suspicions are aroused that the internal consistency of the theory is formal, rather than real. Pushing the reasoning *ad absurdum*, how meaningful could be the concept of labour productivity in a fully automated, manless plant? As productivity becomes an empty shell, should we not also challenge marginal product and marginal cost, the very foundations of our system of prices, wages and rates of interest? Modern economics is indeed in deep trouble.
4. A related matter likely to become a major concern to managements across the entire computer business, including the suppliers and the business users alike, is the new pattern of split between fixed and variable costs. In Chapter 3, we have discussed the irresistible progression of R&D spending and the ever-rising costs of feasibility studies, system design and custom-made software. What remains to stress is that these sunk costs, plus heavy overheads, are literally dwarfing the variable costs made up chiefly of raw materials, compo-

nent parts, semi-manufactured products, etc. Thus, the concept of 'deepening of capital',[13] which refers to accelerated capital formation as interest rates decline and as credit becomes more easily available, is likely to find its ultimate expression in intensively computerized societies. Today, only a handful of very large corporations and few multinationals have the resources to stay in the race. Hence there is the present trend to industrial mergers, the setting up of international conglomerates and the search for flexible forms of partnerships.

5. As the experience of many disappointed users of computer-based systems indicates, the potential benefits too often fail to materialize owing to inadequate consideration being given, in the first place, to the broad impact of the new technology on all aspects of the user environment. Whilst it is not possible to suggest a single approach to the organizational design to be associated with the new information technology, the first and foremost requirement is for manufacturers and suppliers to enlist the interest of their customers in a joint, *a posteriori* investigation of the problem areas and in a collaborative effort at improving *a priori* assessment methodologies. Perhaps the most urgent task is for both sides to work out a common view of ergonomics in computing systems, with the aim of optimizing the interactions between people, the user organization and the new technology.

6. The economic woes and marketing disasters that beset a great many computer manufacturers and dealers can be traced to their disregard for customer needs and wants. 'In too many companies,' complained Lew Young, the chief editor of *Business Week*, 'the customer has become a bloody nuisance whose unpredictable behavior damages carefully made strategic plans, whose activities mess up computer operations, and who stubbornly insists that purchased products should work.' The citation is extracted from the bestselling book *In Search of Excellence* whose authors,[14] after reviewing the performance of two dozen high-tech companies, came to the sad conclusion that only IBM and to a lesser extent Digital Equipment, Hewlett-Packard, Wang, Schlumberger and Rolm deserve reasonably high marks for 'staying close to the customer'. To that short list we venture to add Nixdorf, of Germany, Olivetti, of Italy, and five or six Japanese firms.

7. The pioneering work of Professor Leontief and his younger colleagues should be supported and popularized. Industrial installations based on computer-controlled robots and flexible production tools amount so far to little more than isolated showcases. A new market-

---

[13] First identified and described by the UK Treasury expert, Sir Ralph G. Hawtrey.
[14] Thomas J. Peters and Robert H. Waterman, Jr, *In Search of Excellence*, Harper & Row, New York, 1982, pp. 156–99. See also the Introduction to our book.

ing approach is urgently needed that would ensure that factory automation is purpose driven and that its promotion relies on the right arguments and is directed to the right people. To begin with, the input–output technique ought to be refined for use at the level of industrial branches with narrow specialization and of individual firms. The method could usefully be extended to cover key service industries, e.g. telecommunications and broadcasting, distribution channels, transport systems, banking, libraries and documentation centres, etc.

8. A fresh approach is probably called for in the matter of office technology. Modern office design lacks no glamour, but is wanting, as we have discovered, in overall, sustained performance. Who stole productivity? has become a public cry. Of course, nobody has a ready-made answer. In Chapter 5, we shall reflect on the subject and, to begin with, formulate the issue in operational terms. Could it be that the newly introduced office tools are inadequate or inimical to the staff or unfit for intensive utilization? Is it an iconoclastic question to ask how often the facilities provided through networking and/or integration are needed?

Chapter 5

The Emerging Buyers' Market

To telescope into a single chapter such diverse topics as the complexity syndrome in computing, the burning issue of integration, computer deployment policies and the problem of packaged versus custom-made systems is, no doubt, a rather arbitrary decision. The four themes are so important that each could easily be the subject of a sizeable book. Our approach, on the other hand, offers a valuable vantage point from where we are able to survey not only a vast panorama but, more importantly, some slow changes which may go unnoticed when looked at separately yet which, if correlated, may become fully discernible.

Computer design and development, by its very nature, involves some trade-off, by balancing one quality, characteristic or feature against another, or several others, in order to come up with a new or a better product. For a considerable period of time, the constraints were mostly technical and the ambition lay in the direction of more computing power, more sophistication, more of nearly everything, except size. Today, it is the market constraints that weigh quite heavily. This apparently sharp turnaround could not be explained by a single cause; rather, it is the cumulative result of imperceptible modifications over a number of years.

The general assertion of customer sovereignty may not have yet become part of the conventional wisdom, except perhaps in a vague, inoperative sense. The changeover is only now being detected in a few isolated happenings in some specific areas. However, the trend, if it continues, means that the earlier dominance by some leading manufacturers, their financial backers and a few star designers would begin to recede and perhaps a different computer industry would be built on the premise of the customer's ever-wider choice.

5.1 GOING BACK TO BASICS

Of overdose and overindulgence, the two typical modern diseases, which is the one easier to cure? The case story of the RISC machines suggests that it may be the former. The market's gradual awakening to the attractions of simplicity in computing algorithms militates in favour of the latter. The truth is that both excesses are only now being brought under control.

Reactions against the complexity syndrome

For years, computer makers and designers worked hard to build complex features into their machines. Both mainframes and microcomputers generally contain tiny instructions etched into silicon chips, called microcodes, each amounting to a sequence of commands for the machine to perform a specific function. Over time, the microinstructions have become more numerous and thus also more cumbersome. Conventional microprocessors contain over a hundred microinstructions, more than half of which are seldom, if ever, used. In fact, some 10 per cent of the built-in commands result in poorer performance and thus also in lower overall speed and unnecessary overheads.

The solution of the problem, according to an increasingly influential school of thought, is likely to come from a new breed of machines known as reduced instruction set computers—in short, RISCs. Starting from the fact that most computers most of the time do simple tasks, the RISC designers contend that a computer's overall performance could be much improved by leaving out the complex functions. A typical RISC machine thus offers no more than 40–50 simple instructions. This, however, is much less limiting than it sounds for quite a few fancy instructions can still be provided by cleverly combining a series of simple instructions. The RISC technology promises, in theory at least, to build computers several times faster than the current ones at no extra cost.

The simplicity also confers other advantages. Since less circuitry is needed, the microprocessor should be easier to design and its layout could allow closer packing together of its components to increase speed further. The RISC machines are not without their problems. Thus, executable software developed for older computers will usually not run on a RISC machine. Bridging the gap requires writing additional programs such as compilers, leading to delays and entailing extra costs.

Early pioneering work had been done in IBM laboratories in the 1970s, and this was followed by intensive research at the University of California, at Berkeley and Stanford. A major RISC development program is also under way at Digital Equipment. Several new firms in Silicon Valley are getting into the business, among them Convex Computer, Ridge, Pyramid and especially MIPS Computer Systems.

However, the leading contenders are IBM and Hewlett-Packard. For several years, HP has been racing to come out with a new line of computers, called Spectrum, based on the RISC technology, with the aim of replacing its thirteen-year-old HP-3000 microcomputer. If it proves successful, Spectrum, which was unveiled in February 1986, will determine the company's strategy for years to come. A month earlier, IBM revealed details of a new top-of-the-line personal computer, the

RT, aimed at a highly specialized part of the market, computer-aided designers. RT is a kind of RISC machine in disguise. It is said to be twice as powerful as the PC AT; it is also twice as expensive, but still cheaper than the microcomputers needed previously to do the same sort of computer-aided designing job. Thus, once again, International Business Machines stole the show. By joining the race, IBM also conferred respectability to the RISC approach.

It is relatively unimportant whether IBM, HP, DEC or a bright startup company wins the contest or even whether the RISC technology will be in the end superseded by yet a better one. What is important is to realize that the new concept represents a shift in the philosophy of computer design. The trend is firmly set towards selectivity, based on rational choice:

1. The kernel of the new approach is the construction of a frequency distribution of the actual uses of the various functions. The frequency table may, if needed, be refined by random sampling.
2. This statistic is used as a guideline for determining engineering trade-offs with respect to instruction sets, storage hierarchies, input–output priorities, etc.
3. The inducement to look for an alternative concept arose, in the case under review, out of the pressing need to beat the complexity syndrome, lest the processor die from indigestion. It is clear, however, that other powerful incentives may likewise start the process of going back to basics.
4. The application of statistical methods and tools like these, which argue in favour of RISC, can be used to analyse trade-offs in systems design involving other engineering parameters, e.g. an acceptable level of error rate, display screen resolution, size and weight, density of circuitry, energy consumption, etc. The trade-off process can also allow for non-technical features, e.g. total and unit costs, ease of access, man–machine interface, pictorial representation, and the like.
5. The ultimate outcome of this rekindling is generally favourable to the customer whose freedom of choice, and thus also influence, is enhanced. At a minimum, the user is offered a 'better' product—from his point of view—without any serious *quid pro quo*.

Having discovered that one of the causes of airline accidents was the excess of information the pilots had to assimiliate in split seconds, rather than too little of it, the Federal Aviation Administration in Washington, D.C., decided to replace the old, complicated, hard-to-read charts by newly designed, streamlined graphs for standard landing approaches.

Working of the trade-off mechanism

The much-advertised convergence of the computer and the telecommunications technologies, based on large-scale integrated circuitry, will not be without its own trade-off predicaments. The push-button tone telephone is indeed capable of handling data as well as voice traffic. Enhanced telephone sets are equipped with expandable memory and may thus be used as local computers in their own right, in addition to their initial function as terminals. Vast electronic telephone systems, using all-digital switching, could equally well provide all sorts of value-added services on a public-utility basis as well as for closed user groups. *Prima facie* potentialities of such combinations seem without limit.

In practice, however, '. . . all-electronic phones as yet lack economic appeal', concluded the journal *Electronics* in a special article written on the occasion of the hundredth birthday of the telephone, in its issue of 11 December 1975. Not very much has changed since then. With every advance in the development of the twin technologies, the difficulties seem to increase and the cost of overcoming the obstacles goes up. Since at least 1983, companies started building their own networks in order to get cheaper, high-performance telecommunications than they could get by using public networks. By installing a microwave radio system linking its 22 buildings in and around Pittsburgh, Pennsylvania, in 1983, Westinghouse Electric Corp. reportedly deprived Bell of Pennsylvania of over $1 million per year in transmission revenues and equipment rentals. Boeing Corp.'s microwave system in the Seattle area costs the local telephone company over $2 million in lost revenue. An astute head of the teleprocessing department at Air Liquide Co. has been able to create a network linking 75 different sites throughout France using non-standard equipment from several suppliers, at half the cost of an equivalent turnkey system.

Japan's NEC, among others, is now offering inexpensive, easy-to-operate local bypass networks, called Pasolink. The system transmits simultaneously up to 132 conversations or TV signals, or equivalent computer data, over a minimum of 3 miles (or more on a clear day), and costs some $15,000. After selling more than 1,000 Pasolinks in Japan and some 2,500 in the United States in just one year, NEC started local production of microwave equipment in Portland, Oregon, in the hope of outdistancing its nearest US competitor, Rockwell.

On the user side, the pressure for attractive alternatives is mounting steadily. The remote-service computer bureau had been built on one fundamental assumption—that it was more cost effective to share large processing power and large storage via remote access and time sharing, even though the user had to pay relatively high charges for transmission of data back and forth. The dramatic increase in processing power of the personal computer, in combination with the equally impressive increase in storage capacity, opened up new opportunities. A service bureau is now, for most applications, only an alternative to doing it on the user's own machine. Therefore, the user now has a real choice, with the decision depending on which alternative is the most convenient and/or most economic.[1]

The balance and trade-off among processing, storage and communication is gradually shifting in favour of computing to the detriment of transmission. For instance, demand for communication can be and is actually being reduced by preprocessing in the form of prior data compression, but also by locally storing data from a previous communication. More generally, reductions in processing and storage costs relative to telecommunications charges encourage substitution of 'more' local computing for 'less' transmission of data. This trend, which is already apparent, may very well lead to the creation of alternative distribution channels. For instance, Chemical Abstract Service, Engineering Information and NTIS (National Technical Information Service) are now distributing five of their chemical and engineering databases on CD-ROMs[2] produced by Digital Equipment. Publishers mail subscribers a new disk with updated information periodically, thus enabling users to avoid high charges for connecting to online databases. Another use of CD-ROM would be to distribute software packages.

Other alternatives are under consideration, e.g. massive data unloading via cheap, night broadcasting, coupled with local intelligence for screening the masses of incoming data. Another possibility would be via a direct broadcast satellite teletext network, using microearth stations, developed and first implemented by Equatorial Communications Co. of Mountain View, California.

Summing up, the take-it-or-leave-it dilemma appears to be a thing of the past. Customers are increasingly able to take advantage of technologically sound alternatives and still get the benefit of whatever economic trade-off each of them offers.

Thus, the philosophy which lies behind the RISC machines is spilling over into and invading all aspects of automation and modern telecommunications. By virtue of the Occam's razor, for sheer number-crunching, for all repetitive jobs or just for shuffling data around, the least expensive solution, provided it does not cause undue inconvenience, will be chosen as a general rule. From the point of view of the

---

[1] On the user side, however, the choice is not as straightforward as it seems at first. If too much is on the micro, it becomes sluggish, overburdened and therefore frustrating to use. If too little is done and if other users follow the same pattern, it is the mainframe, in-house or outside, that may become overloaded. The consequences are equally dramatic for the general-purpose bureaus. They, too, will be faced with difficult choices. They will, indeed, have to adapt, diversify, personalize their services and possibly specialize in custom-made software.

[2] See Chapter 9, especially Section 9.2.

manufacturers/suppliers, who cater for this large segment of the market, this rule of thumb translates into such specifications as low-level specialization, robust equipment and mass-produced and standardized models.

When the 'fit' between products/systems currently available and the corporate user needs is less than satisfactory, several different outcomes must be contemplated. The 100 per cent 'online' option may prevail on the grounds of expediency and instant access, which may be worth the extra costs. Suppose, next, that a stand-alone system is chosen; there may still arise an occasional need to gain access to a database connected to a public or specialized network. The charge for this, by definition, seldom-used facility will of course be significantly higher than the standard rate for regular use.

There is rarely, if ever, a universal 'best' solution—although admittedly certain patterns might emerge making it unnecessary to redesign all the minute details of the 'ideal' system. In many instances, a 'mixed' solution is likely to be adopted, in which case the problem may be one of striking a delicate balance between the pros and cons, without forgetting the need to review the situation from time to time.

5.2 THE ISSUE OF INTEGRATION

Integration can mean quite different things to different manufacturers. It most certainly means very different things to different categories of users. The versatile telephone set capable of handling data as well as voice—referred to previously—is an example of integrated twin technologies. Multimedia integration may, or may not, be equated with multipurpose integration, or multifunction integration: it all depends on a number of factors. Such distinctions, which are especially relevant to the customer, reflect differences in approach as well as differing aims.

Four blueprints for extensive integration

The issue provides an ideal ground for studying the nature of technical/economic trade-off and, in particular, for identifying the options and the most likely outcomes. For analytical purposes, we distinguish four types of integrated system:

1. The integrated office workstation;
2. Global mailbox services;
3. Integrated information systems; and
4. Integrated services digital network, or ISDN.

The sophisticated workstation epitomizes the office of the future. It implies more than simply interconnecting previously stand-alone facilities, such as wordprocessing, electronic mail, facsimile, typesetting, micrographics, etc., and encompasses—in theory at least—audio-processing and image processing, in addition to text and data processing, to which we might add telecommunications and sensor technology. 'The real challenge today, and the exciting opportunity,' according to a spokesman for Wang Co., 'is to multiply their effectiveness by integration.'

Models (2) and (3) lend themselves to graphic presentation. The term 'electronic mail' usually suggests a point-to-point connection between the sender and the addressee (e.g. telex, teletex, facsimile). Figure 5.1(a) portrays, however, an alternative way in which a computer-based mailbox or messaging system (CBMS) provides subscribers with simulated pigeon-holes accessible at the time of their choosing. This type of system, particularly suitable for multi-site organizations can replace telephone calls, telex messages, written memoranda, etc. Potential drawbacks include the reliability of the CBMS and its confidentiality; witness the recent furore when the PROFS system of IBM used by the U.S. National Security Council churned out crucial evidence over 'Irangate' to the consternation of staff members who had assumed their messages had been erased.

Figure 5.1(b), on the other hand, is a visualization of the integrated information environment as seen from the user standpoint. The diagram is based on the results of research communicated by CDC in 1982; however, the underlying concepts were shared by and large by Wang, IBM and other computer makers. At some future date, so went the argument, most offices and working sites will be linked to a broadband network carrying masses of digital signals, which local intelligent devices will split, at will, into data, text, image and voice. No attempt was made to demonstrate the need for an omnibus network, whose coming into being was simply postulated. From this assumption, it was then inferred that R&D should be directed—or redirected—towards parallel processing, standard interfaces and revolutionary peripheral devices, which was of course fully consistent with Control Data's forte.

Figures 5.2 and 5.3 should be studied together. The former offers a bird's-eye view of telecommunications services currently available in Western Germany via three distinct channels, i.e. an analogue telephone network; an integrated text and data network; and broadband TV and broadcast networks. Figure 5.3 portrays the narrowband ISDN, based on OSI, or open-system interconnections, now being built by the Bundespost in accordance with the recommendations of CCITT.[3] Using

---

[3] CCITT, or International Telegraph and Telephone Consultative Committee, is an organ of the Geneva-based International Telecommunications Union. The CCITT study of ISDN started in 1976, the concept was defined in some detail in 1980 and the recommendations referred to above were worked out in 1980–4.

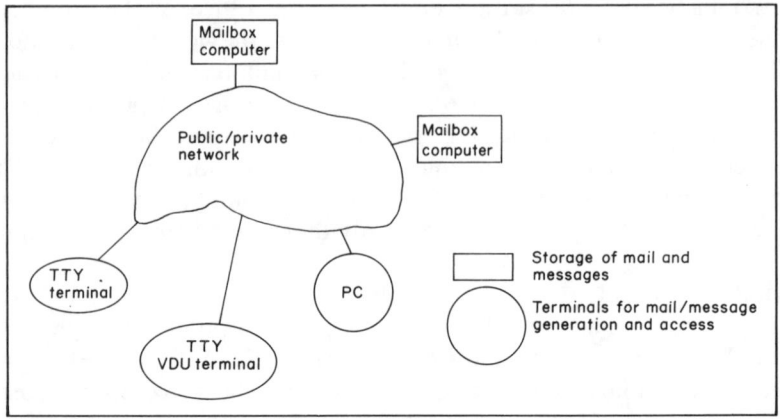

FIGURE 5.1(a) *Global mailbox services. The key to worldwide usability will be conformance with Message Handling System standards (CCITT X 400 series)*

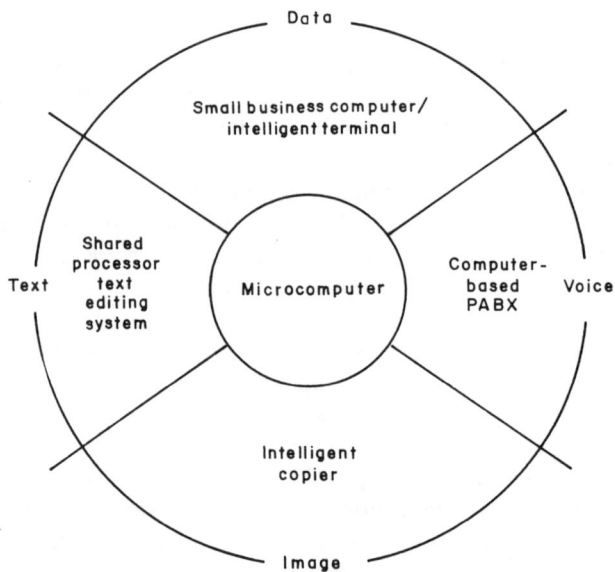

FIGURE 5.1(b) *Integrated information systems. (From 'Distributed Intelligence', in* Systems International, *July 1982. Reproduced by permission of* Systems International*)*

a standard basic bit rate of 64 Kbit/s, all voice, text, data and still-image services known today will be offered, starting in 1988, through a single subscriber line, with the sole but important exception of moving pictures. Consequently, a multifunctional terminal could replace the several separate terminal units corresponding to the existing different telecommunications services. This implies that the present triad of

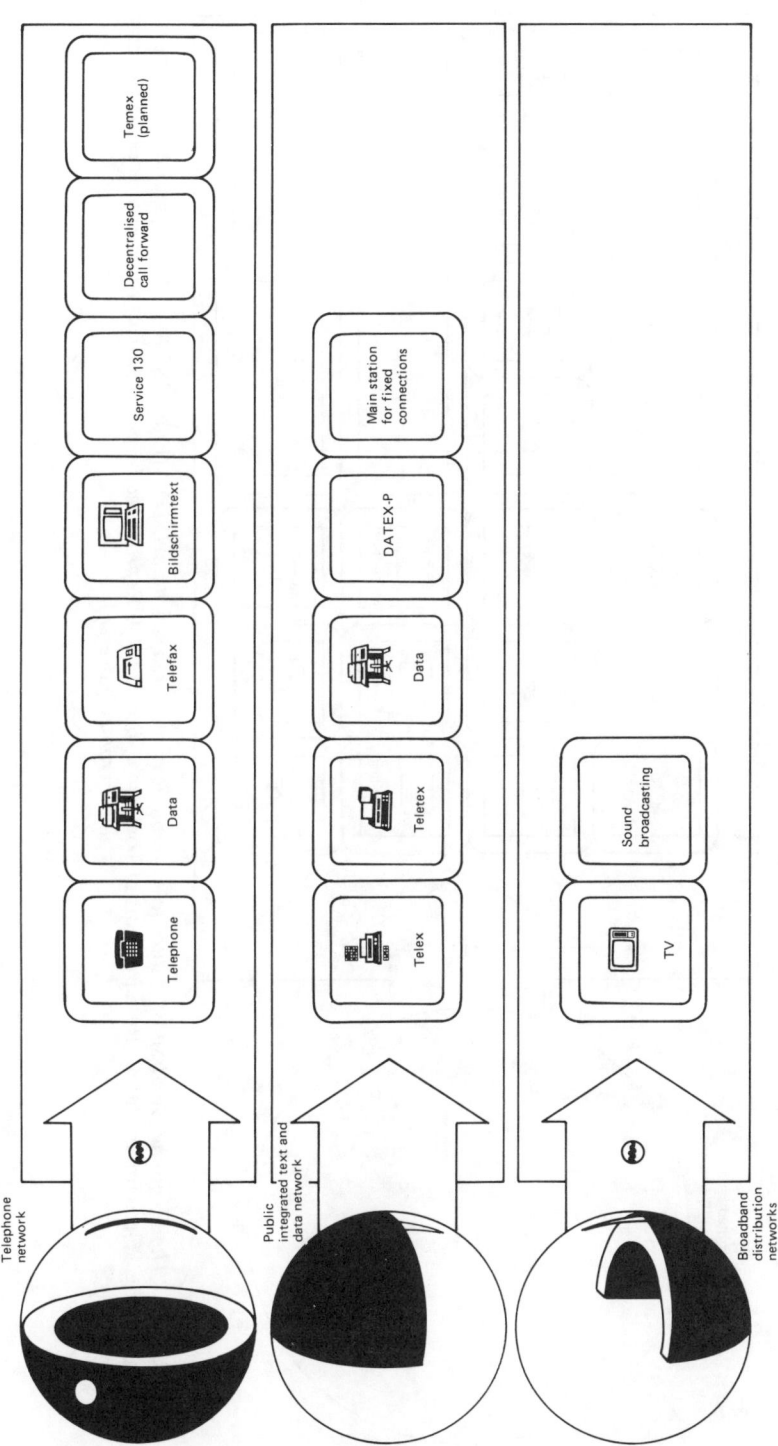

FIGURE 5.2 *The Deutsche Bundespost's telecommunication services today. (From ISDN—The Deutsche Bundespost's Response to the Telecommunications Requirements of Tomorrow, Bonn, 1984. Reproduced by permission of Bundesminister für das Post- und Fernmeldenwesen)*

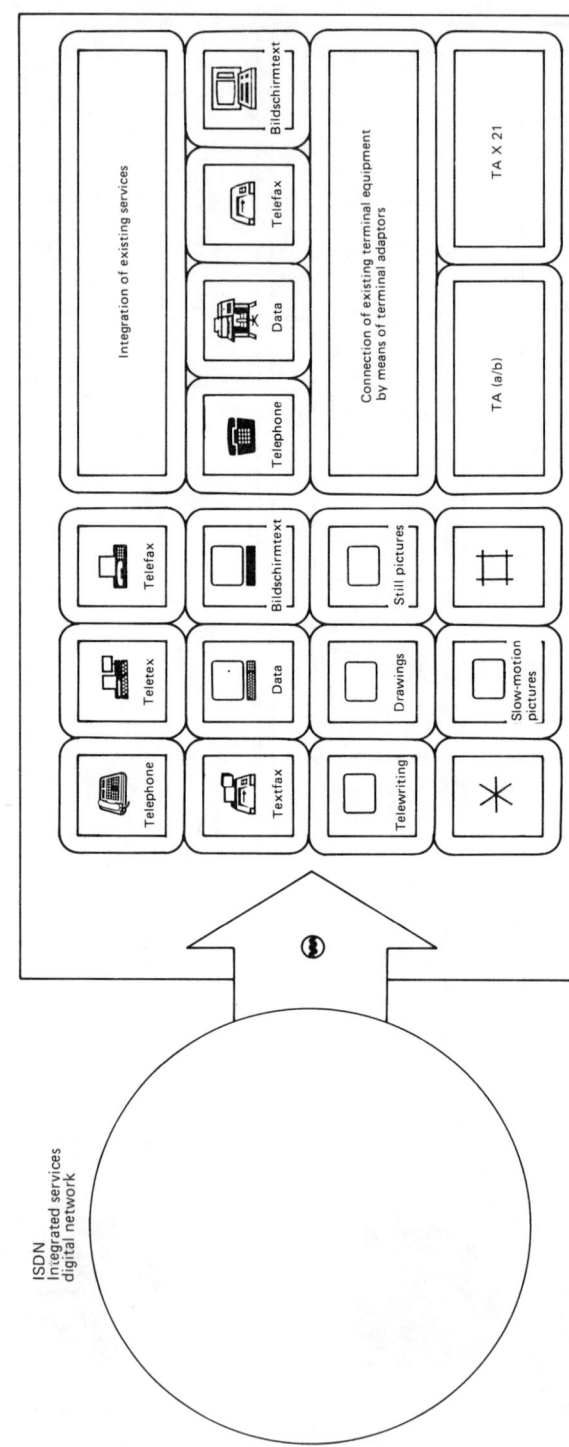

FIGURE 5.3 *The Deutsche Bundespost' future telecommunications services within ISDN. (From* ISDN—The Deutsche Bundespost's Response to the Telecommunications Requirements of Tomorrow, *Bonn, 1984. Reproduced by permission of Bundesminister für das Post- und Fernmeldenwesen)*

PABXs[4] respectively for telephony, telex and data communications, will be gradually merged within a single ISDN interconnection system.

Weighing the pros and cons

Together, the four foregoing blueprints—which is indeed what they are—are fairly representative of the opportunities and the drawbacks of extensive integration. In theory, it is of course difficult to disagree with the concept of maximal integration, whether within the office framework or at the telecommunications level or the global information system level. Since the telephone, the mainframe and the microcomputer work basically in the same way, most manufacturers believed that everyone would naturally prefer to have most of the functions concentrated in one handy unit. Likewise, it was widely assumed that it would be to everybody's advantage to have voice, text, graphs and other pictures combined in a single electronic message, the so-called compound document, transmitted back and forth, with updates at will, via an integrated electronic system.

Against integration, and especially against far-reaching integration, several weighty arguments have been put forth. According to Philip T. F. Kelly, formerly with British Telecom, integration of dedicated networks into an ISDN is technically feasible and even the knotty problem of interworking is soluble.

The difficulty is that under commercial pressure, existing specialized networks are being constantly modified and upgraded, and therefore the cost of conversion would certainly be well above current estimates. Also, the operating companies have committed considerable resources to the telephone networks and the various data networks, and they would be most reluctant to see their investments written off prematurely. Nor would they want to impose unnecessary overheads on the basic telephony service, which is their bread and butter. Moreover, the outlook on the integration of broadband services for two-way transmission of moving pictures and very high density computer-to-computer communications is clouded, as there is no internationally agreed definition of wideband ISDN services.

Second, a micro-mainframe link of one kind or another is an indispensible element in any integration scheme, but such intercommunication is neither easy nor inexpensive. Microcomputers work and communicate at slower speeds than mainframes and have vastly different storage capacities. The 'beefing up' of the former can cost more than the personal computer itself. Also, the cost of switching data through an

---

[4] PABX stands for private automatic branch exchange.

integrated PABX compares unfavourably with older, simpler switching techniques, with the result that integration of voice and data through digital PABXs remains a theoretical possibility rather than a practice. Equally, an advanced computer-based mailbox system, like the one briefly described at the outset, is more expensive both to install and operate than the much simpler, point-to-point connection—not to mention problems of access rights and confidentiality.

Perhaps the strongest criticism of elaborate integration has been voiced by MIT's Michael Hammer, who did not hesitate to attribute the commercial failure of such diverse systems and products as Apple's Lisa, Xerox's workstation (originally) called Star, microportable workstation Workslate unveiled by Convergent Technologies in 1983 and, indeed, Videotex as well, to a single, yet common and current misconception. According to Hammer, users balk at being charged high prices for functions they never use and they obstinately refuse to buy upgraded and/or cheaper versions as well.

By trial and error, manufacturers are slowly discovering that all this theoretically elegant merging of technologies is not what most customer companies want, at least not at the premium prices currently commanded by, among others, integrated voice-data terminals and sophisticated workstations. Disappointed manufacturers thus turn to their engineers and designers and instruct them to scale down their visionary integration schemes. The original concept of a fully integrated workstation has in the last few years lost most of its supporters, who now favour either a restricted access to certain personnel or differentiation between manager's workstation, secretary's workstation, specialist workstation, and so on, primarily in order to save on costs but indirectly also to enhance performance. Here, the incentives are not very different from the rationale of the RISC computer, discussed earlier.

Whilst it is true that it is now possible to merge drawings and script on a personal computer at a price affordable by business customers and researchers who really need it, systems integrating more than two forms of communication are mostly on the drawing board, although some have started working their way into the commercial market a piece at a time. None has a complete capability and transmission standards remain to be developed.

In the area of telecommunications, many people in the United States and Britain doubt the ultimate usefulness of ISDN and support, instead, limited integration, restricted to the local access and transmission networks with dedicated switching modules serving the particular customer needs. The customer is said to be exclusively concerned at having to rent separate telephone, telex and data exchange lines, whilst being fundamentally unconcerned with what happens in the network itself.

In much the same way, it is now clear that home computers as general-purpose machines used for balancing the family budget, running the burglar alarms, making coffee and performing other mundane tasks was a nonsensical mix right from the inception. Such unnatural combinations turned out to be no more than a passing fancy, and that market judgement has stuck.

Under user pressure, an increasing number of manufacturers are quietly dropping the initial idea of maximal, rigid integration and developing instead more realistic approaches, such as modular integration, the option of integrating some additional functions, at will or temporarily only, conditional access to some facilities and a myriad of other flexible combinations that meet the essential requirements of the many categories of users at greatly reduced prices.

5.3 PATTERNS OF COMPUTING DEPLOYMENT

The key concept of deployment of computer resources within an organization, office or factory is now rapidly making obsolete the older organizational theories associated with past waves of innovation in computing and communication. Initially, the dominant and often the only known pattern was the single processing centre built around the mainframe, functioning as a closed shop run by specialists and reporting to the finance/accounting department, which had direct access to top management. As new technological capabilities such as time-sharing via remote terminals and enquiry-response systems provided some end-users with more direct access to the computing resource, these first encroachments upon the ascendency of the computing unit ignited a long debate about the respective merits and demerits of centralization versus decentralization.

The argument soon became entangled in a number of equally controversial side issues, generally also presented in the form of dilemmas: batch processing versus time-sharing, multiapplication versus dedicated facilities, stand-alone versus networked systems, using public carriers versus leased lines, etc. As no universally appropriate configuration has ever been found, the discussion couched in those terms almost invariably encouraged implementation of compromise solutions, combining elements of two or several alternative models. This pragmatic approach has contributed, in an oblique, yet most effectual way, to the progressive widening of consumer choice.

The advent of inexpensive desktop personal computers has radically changed the dynamics of the debate, inasmuch as their spread resulted in the explosion of atomized computing, which brought in its wake the seeds of disorganization. Each new microcomputer or minicomputer, to be found nowadays in virtually every user department, has the potential of becoming an additional computing centre in its own right. However, these new facilities may equally well be used as terminals providing access to the central mainframe. The pendulum had swung from extreme centralization to excessive decentralization, raising a host of new, difficult problems.

Management options

The purpose of this section is to identify the main management options for deploying/redeploying the internal computer resources with the aim of optimizing the computing setup in relation to the general business of the company or administration. There are, of course, many ways of classifying these configurations—too many, in fact. Table 5.1 is an attempt to present a synoptic view of the most frequent types of arrangement, in the form of a 3 by 3 matrix. Listed vertically are: centralized systems, distributed systems and decentralized systems. The respective column headings correspond to the three main discriminants, i.e. location, tools and functions, and communication links.

The fact that the figure is a square should not be interpreted as an indication of symmetry. Decentralization is not the reverse of centralization, the latter is not an exact reciprocal of the former. Some elements are, indeed, common to both models. Distributed systems should not be seen as intermediate solutions between the two extremes of comprehensive centralization and extensive decentralization. Most distributed systems have originally come into existence not at the initiative of either the manufacturers or systems designers but under the pressure of necessity.

Distributed databases, for example, have evolved because the source of data was not, or could not be, centralized and because there was real local need for access to both locally generated information and the consolidated databases. Hence, some processing power had to be placed at the several dispersed sites for collecting and preprocessing data, as well as for accessing the files. However, as soon as data and processing are, even partially, distributed, it becomes necessary to provide communication links between the different locations, together with appropriate gateways and interfaces. As demand grew, distributed systems multiplied and diversified.

A detailed study of Table 5.1 brings rewarding insight. It provides a useful way of exploring the chemistry of trading off managerial, organizational, technical and cost/efficiency requirements, which may all be desirable separately but which are never fully compatible.

The synoptic approach has its limitations, of which two especially need pointing out. Technological aspects are necessarily treated in a cursory fashion; they are, however, developed more fully in Chapters 7 and 8, devoted respectively to megatrends in hardware and the anticipated closing of the software gap. More importantly, all existing and planned distributed systems are pragmatically designed and are therefore subject to unforeseen and (so far) unforeseeable failings. Managements which choose the distributed processing solution should be alerted to the inherent risks. The Defense Advanced Research Projects Agency of the US Department of Defense threw new light on this matter when it authorized the publication, in November 1985, of a summary report on a special investigation into distributed systems. One of the conclusions was that we are still short of an overall theory of distributed systems, as we have been unable so far to discover the basic principles which govern their performance and behaviour.

The other objection to the methodology employed in the construction of Table 5.1 is the apparently limited number of options offered. Here, the answer is twofold. Reading the matrix horizontally, then vertically and proceeding iteratively brings to mind almost automatically a great many additional, more subtle combinations. Second, the matrix is not intended as a listing of ready-made answers to all company problems, but rather as a recipe for working out the 'best' solution—the one which is the most appropriate in each given situation.

Nor is this the place to go to great length rediscussing the issue of the locus of decision making and ultimate control over the deployment of the company's computing resources. Top management usually strives to retain, or regain, as the case may be, control over the growth of the information technology and its priority uses. In larger companies, we nearly always find a separate data processing unit whose supervisory responsibility varies from company to company and also over time. However, the central processing unit, if and when backed by the company's top management, has usually a significant coordinating role to play in an otherwise decentralized framework. This rule of thumb applies even more to distributed systems in which planning, design and day-to-day interworking are essential.

On the other hand, the immediate effect of the ubiquity of computing in modern organizations is to strengthen the claim of the user department to a share in decisions regarding the utilization of the computing facilities and ultimately also the company's computing policies. User consultative boards, evaluation committees, steering committees and numerous working parties are now systematically associated with preparatory work prior to, and occasionally also with, decision taking itself.

Leading vendors have adjusted

It is not easy to ascertain the impact of the growing influence of the end-users on the final choice of configuration and the selection of equipment and software to be purchased. Each user department, or group, has, of course, its own requirements, but also its idiosyncracies. By exercising the indispensible arbitrage between the different points of view, top management usually succeeds in asserting, or reasserting, its authority in matters of strategic choice and in subsequent commercial

Table 5.1 Typology of computing deployment: a set of management options

	Location	Tools	Links
Centralized systems	Concentration of all major computing resources and services, including processing, storage, major peripherals and modems in one place. This type of organization is usually justified by demonstrable cost savings due to economies of scale. Whenever user departments are allowed to create their own facilities to satisfy local needs, the centre acts as supervisor of user operations, keeps a lid on their scope and ensures against inconsistency and excessive duplication.	Consolidation of all major tools and functions, and especially hardware design and operation, operational systems, database management, library of application software, overall management systems, documentation, maintenance, quality control, as well as planning, are all vested in the single centre. However, as the scope of operations grows, user opinion is often sought through consultative boards or committees.	User departments may be given access to central computing facilities through remote terminals, using standard protocols. Multiple data entry is possible only under uniform procedures. All telecommunications networks, including links between central and user facilities (e.g. to allow transfer of data and files) are consolidated, managed and operated centrally.
Distributed systems	Placing some processing power at the several distributed sites for collecting, preprocessing and accessing data. These multiple processors cooperate loosely and carry out separate jobs. Work continues on blueprints for centrally controlled, decentrally operated factory floor	At the global level, the performance and behaviour or distributed algorithms is not fully understood. Subsequent failures may lead to temporary partitioning of the system into isolated subsystems. It is therefore necessary to introduce detection and recovery mechanisms. Whilst a	Links between distributed files and distributed processing units are provided by packet-switched networks, circuit-switched networks, satellite networks, cellular and packet radio networks, metropolitan area networks, etc., using such gateways as PABXs and LANs (see below).

	automation and office automation systems. Whether preplanned or implemented in response to growing demand, complex distributed systems are expensive, yet their performance cannot be guaranteed beforehand.	single microprocessor serving a single master is easy to use and highly reliable, operating systems for multiuser microcomputers (mostly derivatives of AT&T's UNIX system) are still in their infancy; they generally require well qualified operators.	In all distributed systems, careful attention must be given to three crucial interfaces, i.e. man–machine, internetwork and interdepartment.
Decentralized systems	Explicit or tacit devolution to user departments of the right to create, develop, maintain and operate their separate/autonomous computing facilities, subject only to the obligation to utilize central computing resources when this is required by global needs of the organization. Recent efforts by large corporations tend to impose order on the chaos wrought by the microcomputer explosion, by limiting the choice of equipment to a few preselected brands.	Stand-alone decentralization based on small, independent computing activities in user departments has its drawbacks, as fantastic computing power lies idle most of the time and yet does not dispense with central computing facilities. Remedy to excessive centralization has been sought via 'pool arrangements' for coordinated use of systems programming and application software, through enforcement of strict guidelines for systems planning and management and, in large corporations through creation of 'in-house shops', from which user departments may buy compatible wares and software packages at discount prices.	The need to ensure interworking between several desktop computers, nearby printers and other local equipment has led to LANs, e.g. ETHERNET, 'token passing ring'. Local area networks designed for fast machine-to-machine communications could, in theory, permit both decentralized and distributed processing by sharing some functions. The main obstacles include: 'flow control'; the lack of standards for communications protocols, operating systems and database structures; the incompatibility of different workstations. At present, partial solutions only are obtainable by contracting with a single manufacturer or on a custom-built basis.

negotiations with the suppliers. In fact, the composite nature of the user requirements often enables management to bring considerable leverage to bear upon all would-be suppliers of the computing system and its further extension, including a certain degree of integration, if and when appropriate.

Manufacturers with business acumen lost no time in adjusting their stance to the new situation in which the corporate consumer usually has the upper hand. By 1983–4, several major computer makers were emphatically denying that they were in the computer business any more. Instead, IBM, Digital Equipment, Xerox and Wang were purporting to be the leaders in the 'systems business', and forcefully advocating, if not fully compatible, at least 'harmonized system solutions'.

In reality, most of these claims could not be sustained and some are still open to challenge. In particular, none of the local area network systems, starting with Ethernet, launched by Xerox with the support of Intel and Digital Equipment, followed by the broad-band Wang-Net, the British 'Cambridge ring', the French 'Kayak', and including IBM's 'token ring' unveiled with some delay in 1985, have not lived up to the high expectations of their originators. For instance, a few thousand Ethernets have reportedly been installed, but then demand started to drop as the system could not be extended beyond 1 mile of wiring and users found several other shortcomings. Despite the direct involvement in further LAN research by Carnegie-Mellon University, by MIT and by such fine companies as Cullinet and Informatics General, the much hoped-for breakthrough is not yet in sight.

A final lesson in modesty constitutes a fitting ending to this part of our story. When IBM in February 1984 introduced its low-cost, slow 'cluster system' capable of linking up to 64 IBM PCs, but excluding even IBM's own printers and other peripherals, the company's spokesman avoided calling it a 'local network'. More recently, an ITT full-page advertisement featuring a broadly based range of hardware and software under the 'Office 2000' slogan took issue specifically with the stereotyped advice: 'All your company needs is a Local Area Network', saying plainly: 'Not necessarily. There are no simple answers. . . . We have been dealing with this problem long enough to realize that proper integration, real interworking, will take time.'

5.4 BEST-SELLING SOFTWARE

One of the most persistent of controversies within the user community is over the choice between custom software and packaged software.[5] In

---

[5] The different types of software and their technical merits and demerits are discussed in Chapter 8.

order to put the issue in perspective, it is necessary to remind ourselves of some hard facts and stress the huge differences that exist between countries.

In the United States, over 60 per cent of all software is sold as packages, which users adapt to run on their computer systems. In Europe, 40 per cent of software is packaged. In Japan, the ratio drops to 10 per cent. Thus, whilst business customers in America and, by and large, also in Europe can choose whatever alternative suits them best, a Japanese corporation still depends heavily on its mainframe vendor or otherwise must develop its own programs.

According to a report entitled 'Competitive assessment of the US Software Industry', issued by the Department of Commerce, American companies held a 70 per cent share (worth $13 billion) of the $18 billion global market in 1983, making the industry nine to ten times larger than its nearest French or Japanese competitors. Offering both a wide range of packaged products and expertise in personalized system development, the US software houses dominate the rest of the world. In Europe, seven out of eight independent companies selling mainframe software are American. Whatever software packages there are in use in Japan, over 80 per cent of them are marketed by IBM.

American companies do even better in the market for personal computer software. For instance, they supply some 85 per cent of all business software packages for desktop computers in France, a country which was a late starter in the personal computer business and applications. Lotus 1-2-3 and Symphony, dBase III (Ashton Tate), Multiplan (Microsoft), Visio 2 (IBM), Wordstar (Micropro) and half a dozen other packages have so far met with virtually no local competition.

The American and European users' preference for software packages is, of course, closely related to the trade-off between relative costs, convenience, expediency and other factors. The cost advantage is overwhelmingly on the side of packaged software, in the proportion of at least 1 to 10 and more often 1 to 20 or even 50. According to other estimates, a software package is likely to be available for one-tenth of the price of hardware on which it will run, while a custom-built system may add up to ten times the price of hardware.

Package versus custom-made

For routine transactions, packaged software is unbeatable and the range of products offered is now so wide that minor modifications will usually take care of the specific needs of even the most exigent customer. On the other hand, custom-made software is time consuming to write and often quite expensive in terms of the management time and the data processing resource it demands. Then there is the difficulty of finding competent people to do the job, either in-house or under contract with a software company, and of getting an accurate estimate of production costs and a firm delivery date. The problem of subsequent debugging of customized software and of maintenance also looms large.

There still is, and there will always be, a market for custom software and specially designed systems. Firms and service industries with narrow specialization may be either totally unserved by packages or they may find it too costly, or inefficient, to adapt existing packages to meet their very special requirements. Since these special markets are small, whatever packaged software is commercially available necessarily commands a rather high price; consequently, the option of custom software looks relatively more attractive.

As a general rule, very large corporations, banking syndicates, industrial conglomerates, holding companies and multinational corporations, with varied interests and diversified lines of production, often choose to develop their own custom system, neatly tailored to their unique, extensive needs. In fact, it has been found that a close correlation exists between the company size and custom software.

User pressure is building up

It is clear that software has become—except in Japan—far more market oriented than it was a decade ago and also that software companies are much more responsive to market trends than the manufacturers of either hardware or telecommunications equipment. Virtually all major software companies, including Lotus Development Corp., Microsoft Corp. and Ashton-Tate, now go to great lengths to woo their corporate customers, offering large volume discounts and more convenient purchasing arrangements, even selling directly to corporate buyers, thus reversing their earlier marketing policies of active, and often exclusive, collaboration with the computer stores, as their major outlets. Their most recent concession, the so-called site licensing, confers to the corporate customer the right, for a fee, to copy and distribute copies of a program within the corporation.

Other companies have developed systems—known as rapid prototyping—that allow their business customers to try a mockup before the complete software is written. Prototyping techniques had been pioneered by TRW in the late 1970s and their applications now include such jobs as remote maintenance monitoring, ocean surveillance and a proposed space station, as well as dozens of engineering applications. More recently, Martin Marietta Corp., a data systems and aerospace company, has created an entirely new program based on artificial intelligence[6] to help users establish their specific requirements.

Also, several major software companies, instead of coming up with

---

[6] The concept and applications of artificial intelligence are discussed in Section 8.5.

new packages, are now concentrating on making programs easier to use and on integrating different applications, say word processing and accounting. A user may want to retrieve statistical information from an in-house database, plug the figures into a marketing forecast, prepare a pie chart from the computed data, compare the results with budget forecasts and insert the chart, together with appropriate comments, into a written report using a word processing program.

There are two basic alternatives. One is to combine several tasks into a single multifunction package, such as Lotus 1-2-3, which comes with a spreadsheet capable of juggling with rows and columns of numbers, a graph-designing program and a database management system, including automatic filing—but it has no word processing facilities. The drawback is that any multifunction program based on the principle of trade-off necessarily performs less well than any of the constituent specialized programs. The alternative approach is to supply separate programs but allow the user to combine programs from different vendors. For this purpose, the display is divided into separate areas, or 'windows', where the different programs available appear; the user indicates a selection by actioning a sliding pointer, called the 'mouse'.[7]

That customer sovereignty should assert itself most markedly in the area of software is doubly significant. By definition, nearly all software has some degree of basic compromise, e.g. between brilliance of design and transparency to the user, between comprehensiveness and expediency, etc. This is obvious enough in the case of packaged software, but it is also substantially true of custom software inasmuch as all software companies have extensive libraries of routines and utilities in which experienced programmers can always find bits and pieces that can be incorporated or adapted—adding compromise to compromise. In either case, from compromise there is only a short step to trade-off, and the increasingly discerning customer experiences little difficulty in seeing this through.

This lesson has not escaped the notice of some early developers of commercial applications of expert systems. Complex computer programs designed to mimic the process of deductive/inductive reasoning of a human specialist—which is, broadly speaking, what expert systems are all about—take three to four years to write and may cost anything between $1 and $5 million apiece. These custom-made expert systems could, obviously, command only a very limited market and their future therefore remained highly uncertain.

The situation changed fundamentally when a young company, Intelli-Corp, founded in Silicon Valley in 1980, decided to tackle the problem in market terms, and soon other upstart companies, Teknowledge, the Carnegie Group, Inference Corp., followed suit. Without going into technicalities, an expert system can be broken into two parts.

---

[7] The technology of these newer man–machine interfaces is discussed in Chapter 9.

On the one hand, there is a database containing recorded and categorized knowledge about a specific field of expertise, e.g. medical, industrial, etc., in a narrow specialty. Then there is a set of rules for making inferences, plus a kind of *vade mecum* for interpreting the deductive reasonings and the findings. By standardizing this second part, IntelliCorp. achieved a major breakthrough for it could now sell 'shells', called Kee's (or 'Knowledge Engineering Environments'), consisting of the rules-cum-reasoning part, very much as off-the-shelf software packages are marketed. The company has reportedly licensed over 250 Kee systems, with a price tag of $60,000 apiece. With the help of the 'shells', the customer's own analysts are able to write the application program ten times faster and achieve an 80–90 per cent savings on costs.

Outline of a market model for software

There remains one last, albeit important, question. From particulars, such as those discussed previously, is it possible to induce a general conception and derive a market model showing the interactions between the producers, i.e. the software companies and their designers, and the consumer firms as users? Australian professors Frank Milne, of the Australian National University, and Ron Weber, who specializes in business economics, were the first to answer in the affirmative.

The Milne–Weber model aims at a partial formalization of the process of designing software packages generally by choosing the attributes to be incorporated by reference to such global characteristics of the packages to be marketed as the functional capabilities that the packages will provide, their syntactic structure, the user classes they will accommodate, etc. The demand and supply sides are first examined separately; then they are examined jointly on the assumption that both the buyers and the sellers are motivated essentially by profit maximization and, therefore, that they both make, on the whole, rational choices.

> 'In summary, then,' state Milne and Weber, 'successful designers are those who can find a profitable opening. The availability of a profitable opening depends on the demand for a package and the costs of producing a package. In turn, demand for a package depends upon the availability of substitute (or perhaps complementary) packages. Costs depend upon the designer's skill at minimizing the design costs and the variable costs of using the package.'[8]

---

[8] Frank Milne and Ron Weber, 'The economics of designing generalized software', *Communications of the ACM*, **26**, No. 8 (August 1983).

If this sounds like a formal statement of an intuitive conclusion, it must be pointed out in all fairness that Milne and Weber have marshalled an impressive set of mathematical equations, suggested some extensions and discussed the limitations of their model. However, they undoubtedly deserve high praise for opening up new vistas and for providing packaged software designers with new, original analytical tools.

Realizing the great potentialities of the Australian conception, we are led to wonder: Had the model been known earlier, would Intergraph have focused on 'integrated graphics design software' and on database management software or would Intergraph have picked up other 'ideas'? Would Cullinet's choice for priority development have been the same, concentrating on database management programs for IBM mainframes, then application software, later on graphics software and, eventually, a relational database system? Would MSA have found in the Milne–Weber theory convincing justification for its integrated software packages?

A contrario, it can be argued that to follow the Australian approach could prevent software companies from making the wrong choice and thus from going broke altogether. In the words of the originators of the model, '... given the intensely competitive market for software, basic economic theory tells us one thing for certain: software prices will drop and all but the efficient designers and vendors will be forced from the marketplace. Continued reliance on conventional "wisdom" will be a risky affair; formalized design approaches are needed.'

5.5 CONCLUSION AND OUTLOOK

Intentionally, the several vast subjects included in Chapter 5 have been treated very briefly. When taken together, the successive discussions devoted to these topics contribute to the drawing of a relatively coherent picture of the changing relationship between the information industry and its customers.

1. The growing sophistication of the buyers/users is a reality to be reckoned with. Personal computing and word processing are part and parcel of any high school curriculum. The majority of today's managers and professional staff have been exposed to computing and also to a number of related disciplines, e.g. operational research, economics, statistics, modern accounting, planning and forecasting, technology assessment, computer-aided decision making, and so on. Clearly, the white-collar personnel at every level has a better understanding of computerization than the previous generation had. Con-

sequently, corporate boards and end-users alike are more cost-conscious, efficiency minded, choosy and also better equipped to form personal judgement.
2. On the other side of the fence, the manufacturers' body of knowledge about their customers' needs and preferences has for a long time remained essentially impressionistic and superficial. The successful launching of a new product, often unopposed in the marketplace by alternative models, was seen by the suppliers and the designers as sufficient evidence of endorsement by apparently satisfied buyers. Furthermore, the sustained high rate of growth of sales was interpreted as additional proof of users' continued support. As everybody knows, this fairy tale became a shambles in the early 1980s.
3. It is a question for debate whether the customers' decisive influence manifested itself, first and foremost, in the area of hardware through massive purchases of personal computers of all kinds to the relative detriment of mainframes and minicomputers, or rather in the area of software. Now, the louder customers' say in all matters pertaining to software tends to impact upon system design and, by a chain reaction, upon hardware architecture, as well as upon the deployment of all the computer resources within the user company. As software gains ascendancy over hardware, so does the customers' pre-eminence as the dominant market force.
4. The customers on the whole understand better than most manufacturers that integration is not an absolute but a series of shifting responses to perceived needs. Most distributed systems combine features of centralized management and planning with elements of decentralized production and the pertinent data handling. After weighing carefully the pros and cons of respectively packaged and custom software, customer companies often settle for a balanced compromise or, as a minimum, for enhanced, semi-customized programs. In market terms, demand for 'optimal' combinations, on the basis of trade-off, is ten and perhaps twenty times larger than is the demand for maximum speed, the highest performance or extreme complexity.
5. These buying patterns are increasingly impacting upon the attitudes and policies of the vendors. We remarked earlier that IBM and Wang, DEC and Xerox began professing of late to be in the vanguard of the 'systems business', shying away from their traditional image as suppliers of hardware and office equipment. The new industrial strategy is perhaps best epitomized by Nixdorf Computer AG's eloquent slogan: 'We sell solutions', which proved to be very effective. Nixdorf in 1984 became Europe's largest software house, specializing in elaborate software packages tailored to user's needs; furthermore, it developed a talent for finding profitable niches. No

doubt, today's front-runners are about to be imitated by dozens of computer and/or software outfits.
6. The 'systems business' approach could of course be extended in other directions, e.g. remote sensing, telemetry and, most obviously, telecommunications. IBM's investment in Rolm and SBS, and, likewise, AT&T's efforts and its stake in Olivetti, whilst the same Olivetti was teaming up with Hitachi, have been rightly interpreted as strategic choices enabling the consolidated consortia to supply large business customers with virtually everything from workstations to network services, together with recipes for dedicated applications. Whether this mission-oriented strategy will succeed depends also on the acumen of vendor managements, including their readiness to abandon in good time unwanted products and unprofitable ventures. Whilst AT&T closed down its loss-making Net 1000 computer network in early 1986, which had started ten years earlier and had cost the company $1 billion, IBM's losses on SBS continued unabashed.
7. Under the circumstances, the upstart companies with one or two narrow specialities found themselves in danger of being pushed out of the market altogether. Their only viable, long-term defence was to be and to remain compatible at all costs with the big boys' range of products and systems. Many of them joined the bandwagon at an early stage, others resisted for some time—and a few still do, displaying a great deal of stamina and achieving remarkable success here and there—but in the end the vast majority have bowed in. Nearly all makes of personal computers are now advertised as IBM PC compatible. When the pressure for adopting a fundamental standard becomes irresistible, even International Business Machines eventually gives in; e.g. after resisting for two or three years, IBM did adopt the X-25 protocol for connection to packet-switched networks and later on the rival OSI (open system interconnections) concept.
8. Taking a broader view, those firms active in the computer business which have, in one way or another, responded to recent consumer requirements and positioned themselves for future competition represent some 70 per cent of the business. This still leaves out in the cold thousands of companies, small and large, veterans and newcomers in equal proportions, struggling with the problem of defining a winning strategy whilst retaining their *raison d'être*; in sheer numbers more than half the vendors belong to this group.

Chapter 6

Revitalized Segmentation of Markets

The task of the five following sections is to re-orient market analyses in recognition of dynamic phenomena, two of which are particularly relevant. Largely the conversion requires a radical change in the vendors' entire outlook on their business patronage that is made up of a clientele which, however disparate, is now generally price-conscious and knowledgeable about what it can legitimately expect from computerized operations. This message, which has come out strongly from Chapter 4, was carried further in Chapter 5, in which we reviewed the growing body of evidence pointing to the emergence of a buyers' market.

The vendors are thus increasingly faced with a dynamic, lively marketplace in which the would-be customers, whether managements or end-users, are no longer willing to play a passive role. In the circumstances, it was inevitable that our approach, especially to market segmentation, should depart markedly from the older views, according to which the profile and the numbers of potential buyers of a given product/system were invariably defined by a set of parameters such as income, occupation, social ranking, business speciality and background, company pedigree, etc.

As a matter of fact, our successive evaluations in Sections 6.2, 6.3 and 6.4 of key market prospects, based on different criteria and techniques, form altogether a bright, and in some respects, exciting picture. An introductory review (Section 6.1) of the global market shares is intended to provide a useful backdrop against which specific market estimates can be relativized and assessed.

6.1 THE WORLD FRAMEWORK

Taking the global view, total sales of the electronics industries in 1985 amounted to \$485 billion worldwide, excluding the Communist countries. This figure had been compiled mostly from customs statistics, supplemented by independently made estimates by the newly established, Paris-based, Electronics International Corporation.

As can be seen from the pie diagram in Figure 6.1, slightly over one-third of this number, or some \$165 billion, went to hardware, software and related services. When office automation, factory automa-

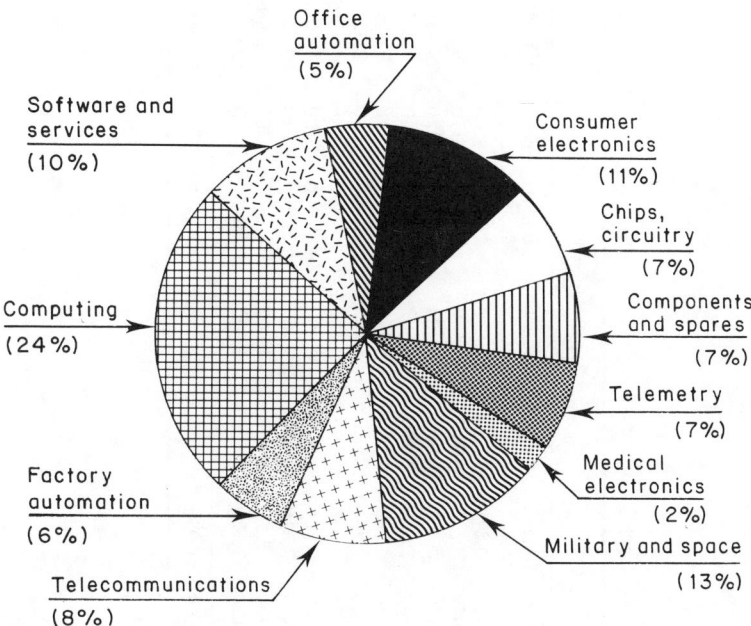

FIGURE 6.1 *Total sales by electronics industries, 1985. Global market shares in percentages. (From: Electronics International Corporation,* L'électronique dans me monde, *Paris, 1986. Reproduced by permission of M. Abel Farnoux, President, Electronics International Corp.)*

tion and telecommunications are added, the global market for teleinformatics in 1985 stood at some $218 billion, or 53 per cent of the grand total. In comparison, military and space electronics, with $63 billion, and consumer electronics, with $53 billion, look—somewhat surprisingly—less weighty than the general public as well as most analysts would probably expect. On the other hand, the market for medical electronics, remote sensing and telemetry looms relatively large, as it is of a size comparable to the market for chips and circuitry, or some $34 billion apiece.

Table 6.1, related to electronics industries in the United States, Japan and Europe respectively, provides highly interesting insight into the relationship between production and market, using the simple equation: domestic production *plus* imports *minus* exports *equals* market, or total domestic sales in a given year. Unlisted are the 'other' countries whose combined contribution to world output was estimated at $92 billion and whose market potential amounted to $115–120 billion.

Table 6.1 World trade in electronics, 1984 (in $ millions)

	Europe				United States				Japan			
	Production	Export	Import	Market	Production	Export	Import	Market	Production	Export	Import	Market
Consumer electronics	8,000	1,020	5,130	12,110	8,000	1,010	10,270	17,260	21,850	15,430	220	6,640
Chips, circuitry	4,410	1,905	4,485	6,990	13,330	5,670	8,250	15,910	13,550	5,640	1,310	9,220
Components, spares	6,150	1,510	1,780	6,420	12,600	2,100	4,400	14,900	8,300	4,130	320	4,490
Telemetry	7,200	2,750	2,330	6,780	16,500	4,780	1,670	13,390	3,600	1,020	650	3,230
Medical electronics	2,300	1,230	680	1,750	4,300	1,140	840	4,000	1,440	520	180	1,100
Military and space	13,000	3,720	2,030	11,310	35,000	6,000	1,830	30,830	3,500	1,440	560	2,620
Telecommunications	12,000	1,890	490	10,600	14,000	780	1,830	15,050	6,200	1,650	40	4,590
Factory automation	5,500	400	1,300	6,400	11,000	1,800	800	10,000	6,000	1,000	100	5,100
Computing	22,000	2,780	9,330	28,550	57,000	13,460	8,410	51,950	17,000	5,690	1,330	12,640
Software and services	8,300	300	1,000	9,000	26,500	2,000	50	24,550	4,000	–	300	4,300
Office automation	3,400	970	2,080	4,510	11,000	1,120	2,720	12,600	6,000	4,050	80	2,030
Total	92,260	18,475	30,635	104,420	209,230	39,860	41,070	210,040	91,440	40,570	5,090	55,960

Reproduced by permission of Electronics International Corporation from *L'électronique dans le monde*, Paris, 1986.

Japan versus all

In terms of production, the United States came out first by far, with a total of $209 billion, as against some $90 billion each for Europe and Japan. American dominance was especially strong in hardware, with close to 60 per cent of the United States + Japan + Europe total, and as much as 68 per cent in software. The United States had an appreciable trading surplus in military and space electronics, as well as in telemetry and remote sensing. It came out just about even in office and factory automation, which is a rather poor performance. The United States was seriously deficient, as everybody knows, in circuitry, and particularly in mass-produced memory chips and in all sorts of consumer goods, which constitute a market ever more dominated by Japanese industry.

The Japanese exported 44 per cent of their total output in electronics goods, but their imports covered barely 9 per cent of their overall domestic needs. There is not a single category—not even software—in which their imports exceed exports. The Japanese overall trade balance in electronics yielded a net surplus of over $35 billion, with the bulk, or some 85 per cent, coming from earnings on shipments abroad of consumer electronics, chips and circuitry, computers and office automation equipment. Interestingly, 80 per cent of the Japanese production of robots and automated gear is sold domestically, leaving—supposedly by design—only a modest surplus for exportation.

It is common knowledge that Europe was falling behind. The newly published statistics drive this point home, as they clearly show how wide and how general this gap has become. Europe's only remaining strong points are military and space electronics, telemetry and, to a lesser extent, telecommunications equipment, medical electronics and precision instruments. Europe is heavily, and increasingly, dependent on foreign supplies of such critical items as hardware in general, office and factory automation equipment and, of course, on Japanese, South Korean and Singaporian chips and circuitry. In consumer electronics alone, Europe's trade deficit (mostly with Japan) was in excess of $4 billion in 1984, despite EEC's introduction of a quota system and the enforcement of higher import duties. Nor is it true, as many people believe, that Europe is doing better in software; the record shows that more software is imported than exported.

Europe: the coveted market

Further insight into the relative—and highly variable—importance of foreign markets is provided by the summary in Table 6.2, which refers to computer hardware, software and services, office and factory auto-

Table 6.2 Assessing the significance of export markets for computers and information systems, 1984 (in $ billion) (computed from data in Table 6.1 above)

	United States	Japan	Europe
Exports[a]	18.4	10.8	4.5
Imports	12.0	1.8	13.7
Trading balance	+6.4	+9.0	−9.2
Ratio of exports to imports	1.53	6.00	0.33
Ratio of exports to total domestic production	0.17	0.33	0.11

[a] Computer equipment, software and services, office automation and factory automation systems combined.

mation, but excludes all the other items included in the previous Table 6.1. At glance, it can be seen that in 1984 the US exports represented one-and-a-half times its imports, whilst Japan's overseas sales stood at six times its aggregate purchases abroad.

Thus, Europe found itself in the reverse situation of a net importer as its aggregate purchases of computer items, services and information amounted to three times its total exports combined. Over the past five or six years, Europe has indeed come to be regarded as the juiciest of electronics markets.

It is hardly necessary to belabour the point. Out of every $100 earned by Japanese vendors, $33 came from sales abroad; for European vendors, foreign earnings represented a bare 11 per cent of total shipments. The US vendors stood somewhere in between, but their expectations of holding their share in the world markets remain uncertain.

Telephony and the runners up

Until quite recently, it would have been incongruous to use a pie diagram in order to represent the breakdown between telecommunications systems, as indeed telephony along monopolized 90–95 per cent of the total telecommunications business on a worldwide basis ten years ago.

Figure 6.2 illustrates how things have changed since. In 1985, telephone services still retained their dominant position in terms of global earnings, with 75 per cent of the total. However, it is no exaggeration to

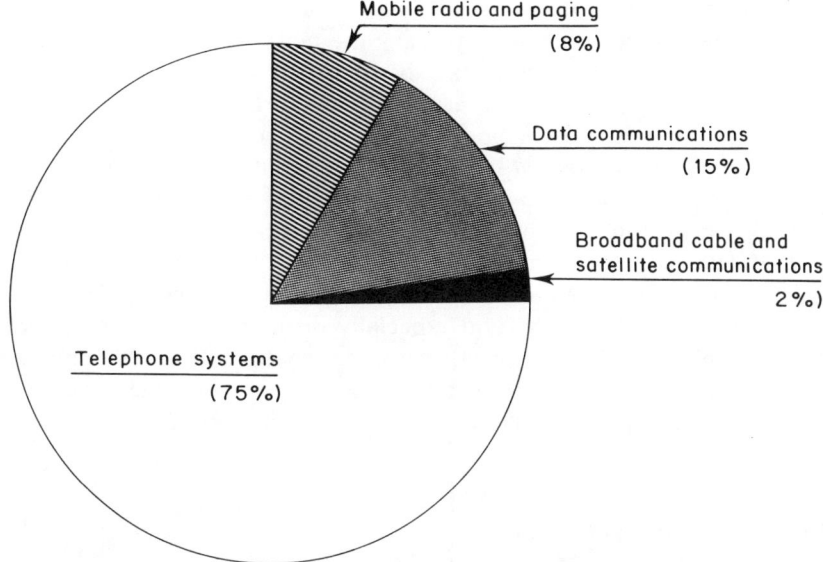

FIGURE 6.2   *Global telecommunications systems. Market shares in percentages, 1985. (Adapted with permission from data compiled by* Arthur D. Little, Inc., *and published in the* International Herald Tribune, *20 May 1986)*

say that, first, data communications and, more recently, mobile radio have both made spectacular inroads on the telecommunications markets. By 1985, their market shares had jumped respectively to 15 and 8 per cent of the total. The significance of the breakthrough, in both instances, is brought out by comparison with satellite communications and broadband cable for which the demand grew substantially less, reaching only 2 per cent of the total by 1985.

6.2   THE ELECTRONIC IMAGING MARKET EXPLODES

The Webster's International Dictionary characterizes synthesis, the antinome of analysis, as 'the combining of often varied and diverse ideas, forces or factors into one coherent or consistent complex'. Consistent with this definition, the emergence of a fabulous market for applications of electronic imaging coincides closely with the fireworks being displayed by this powerful, highly versatile technology. Vice versa, the present clustering of innovations in image processing, display and interpretation matches the rapidly growing, composite demand for all sorts of visual systems and devices. In fact, our synthetic approach brings out immediately the vital issues at stake, which could easily be lost sight of, or grossly underestimated, by using the more traditional analysis of (seemingly) heterogeneous market fractions.

Electronic imaging has been around since the 1970s in various forms under different names: computer graphics, computer-aided design (CAD), navigation control by radar, flight simulation systems, etc. In the interim, each of these application areas has grown into a sizeable specialty market in its own right and evolved its own particular brand of technology.

Until recently, however, electronic capture and manipulation of images on any large scale, and especially of moving scenes, has been possible only on excessively costly computer configurations that only the military, a few research organizations, the biggest aerospace designers and car manufacturers, plus the richest advertisers could afford.

Going interactive is the key

Thus, recent developments have quite naturally all aimed at the same time at better image resolution, faster processing and markedly lower costs. General-purpose computers eventually gave ground to superior, special-purpose processors incorporating semiconductors for processing and analysing images. The new vision processing architecture of hardware was supplemented with sophisticated image processing routines and functions, e.g. edge detection, shape determination, etc. Another crucial step was taken with the advent of mammoth-size, low-cost memories for storing the enormous amounts of data required. In June 1986, Eastman Kodak Co., outdistancing Sony, introduced an advanced electronic imaging sensor, a device placed behind the camera lens to translate images into electronic signals. The Kodak sensor had a capacity of 1.4 million pixels, or picture elements, six times as many as any other commercially available sensor, resulting in impressive gains in resolution and faster processing.

At the lower end of the spectrum, Wang, Apple, IBM, Xerox and a few other vendors have developed office imaging systems costing some $20,000 and upwards, capable of scanning and digitizing an image, displaying it with pre-existing text and/or data, and printing it on a laser printer. Hardly a month passes by without a rich crop of new products coming to market, as the technology makes giant strides.

The crucial question which hundreds of vendors—those already active in the field and those pondering whether to join the race—are asking themselves, is this: can these highly auspicious openings be turned into definite market prospects, and if so, how quickly and in what areas?

The key to unlocking the mass market is the advent of real-time, truly interactive, low-cost processing of still images, synthetic images and moving scenes, fostered by further development of computer aids to vision understanding. Remember that although the swing from batch processing environment to real-time, interactive processing of data did not happen overnight, the migration of customers from the former to the latter was an accomplished fact in less than ten years. At the end of that eventful decade, demand for computing generally had increased by a factor of 15 to 20. A similar scenario is now likely to unfold in electronic imaging, which will undoubtedly also benefit from the superior attraction of image and colour over the relative dullness of data and script as communication media.

Vendors and would-be vendors should also be made aware of the latest trends in electronic imaging R&D. According to Oxford's Michael Brady, formerly with MIT, the evolution has been from theoretical developments to specific practical applications. Consequently, the construction of vast vision systems aiming at maximum integration has been virtually abandoned, and the emphasis is now on mimicking particular modules of the human visual system with a view to putting these man-made replicas to work on concrete problems. Also, whilst the mathematics of image interpretation (properly hidden in black boxes) has become more sophisticated, representations of the visual information processed have been made explicit. Finally, most recent vision algorithms allow for parallel computations involving local interactions, which is fully consistent with the current tendency towards general-purpose parallel processing (see Chapter 7).

Forests made up of trees

A simple listing of the many, diverse applications of electronic imaging could easily fill several pages of this book. We adopt a simple breakdown, building on the findings of Chapter 4, in which gains from computing have been discussed; we also distinguish three broad classes:

1. Vision systems performing extraneous functions, which extend human abilities or performance;
2. Vision systems as substitutes for labour; and
3. Electronic vision aids to efficiency.

Thus, the main criterion used is one of functionality. Whilst there are no sharp demarcation lines between the three categories of applications, the classification is useful in that it brings out the differences in the nature of demand and the underlying motivations, as we shall see shortly.

Despite, or perhaps because of, the successive losses of Challenger and the rockets Titan, Delta and Europe's Ariane in Spring 1986, two companies, Eosat in the United States and Spot Image in France, are racing to exploit the growing demand for images returned to earth by remote-sensing satellites. It is remarkable how quickly the expert opinion had swung from an exceedingly pessimistic assessment of the market prospects for commercial remote sensing (partly due to the flop of Landsat, the earth-resources network) prior to 1984, to very high expectations of profitability two years later. Notice that mining and oil companies already rely heavily on the newest image processing technology for monitoring and filtering the flood of data from oil drill sites and from seismographs.

The domain of remote sensing is immense and is being constantly enlarged. It includes, among others, management of land resources, such as water, soil erosion, forestry and agricultural crops, but also early-warning systems against natural disasters and industrial hazards. However, it also includes digital cartography of high precision and aerial photo interpretation, and its application to flight simulation systems.

Medical electronics, too, leans more and more on sensor technology and visual processing. Screening of medical images such as X-rays, tomography, cancer smears and ultrasound visualization are now performed routinely. Biosensors, which combine biological, chemical and electronic technologies are increasingly used for instantaneous analysis of blood samples of patients undergoing open-heart surgery.

Bunching together remote sensing and medical electronic imaging makes sense in market terms. Indeed, demand for this type of application is relatively inelastic or price-independent. Consequently, the rates of growth of these specialized markets are generally stable and thus predictable, with the help of such variables as health expenditure, space research programmes, etc.

In the second category, however, the pecuniary motive is clearly dominant in corporate buyers' decisions to proceed with, or delay, any large-scale implementation of vision machines and new robotic vision systems in factories and in transport networks.[1] Sales quadrupled between 1983 and 1985 and are expected to exceed $1 billion in the United States alone which is—paradoxically—the slowest growing market, whereas in Japan and more recently in Western Europe a 50 per cent annual growth rate has been reported.

Much of the US industry hesitancy at moving rapidly into robotics has stemmed from the inconclusive evidence as to which overall design will eventually prove superior: either a configuration using a small number

---

[1] See also Section 4.2.

of highly intelligent, flexible robots or the alternative of central computing control over a great many simpler, specialized automated devices performing specific tasks. The outcome of the debate is thus clearly tied to the actual pattern-recognition capabilities of the new breed of vision machines.

Our third category of electronic imaging applications comprises an almost endless variety of vision aids to efficiency, from design aids for architects and mechanical engineers to all kinds of inspection and quality-control vision systems to partial automation of transport networks and vehicles, without forgetting such visual interfaces as icons and mice. In fact, the vast majority of these applications are basically decision support systems, and therefore the interactive displaying of processed visual information is of crucial importance, e.g. in computer graphics, radar data representation, target acquisition, etc.

Another common feature is that the buyers' motivation is never purely economic, dictated as it is by short-term pecuniary advantage. To be sure, the profit incentive is there, but it is subdued. Thus, the growing popularity of three-dimensional CAD, markedly more expensive than the more primitive two-dimensional systems, must be ascribed to sharply improved efficiency and a substantial reduction in error rates resulting from cheaper memory and processing power. Computervision, Intergraph and the Cama division of General Electric are consolidating their dominance of a market growing at 25 and up to 50 per cent per annum.

The big-prize market

All told, electronic imaging applications are of direct, and frequently also of immediate, interest to engineering, manufacturing, transport systems, space and ocean exploration, but also publishing and printing, information dissemination and archiving, television and advertising and, of course, the military. Each one of these sectors is a truly global market. When combined, they probably represent the greatest single challenge—but also the greatest opportunity—for the computer and information-related industries in the closing years of this millenium.

Figure 6.3 synthetizes the evidence available from several sources and sums up our overall assessment of the world market for electronic imaging in quantitative terms. This is supplemented by Table 6.3, which focuses on differentials in growth rates for the three main categories of applications, as discussed previously, the estimates being extended to cover the period 1988–92.

Starting from a relatively low level of $8 billion in 1984, worldwide sales of electronic vision systems and machines are expected to amount

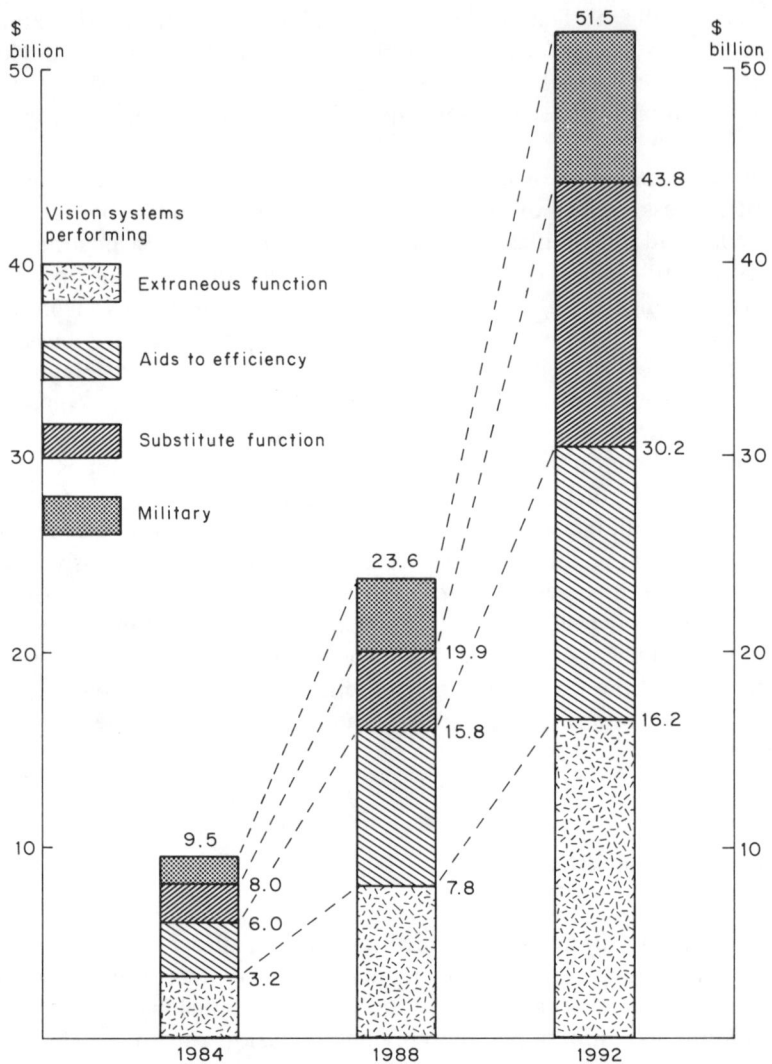

FIGURE 6.3 *Market estimates for vision systems, 1984–1988–1992*

to $20 billion in 1988 and can be estimated at close to $44 billion in 1992. When military procurements are included, the aggregate total is likely to exceed $23 billion and reach some $51.5 billion respectively. In other words, by 1992 the global electronic imaging business will be on a par with total sales of International Business Machines in 1986.

As can be seen from Table 6.3, the current and anticipated rates of growth are far from uniform; they also vary considerably over time.

Table 6.3 Estimating composite markets for vision systems, 1984–1988–1992

Vision systems performing	1984 sales ($ billion)	Growth rate 1984–8 (% p.a.)	1988 sales ($ billion)	Growth rate 1988–92 (% p.a.)	1992 sales ($ billion)
Extraneous function, e.g. remote sensing	3.2	25	7.8	20	16.2
As aids to efficiency, e.g. CAD	2.8	30	8.0	15	14.0
Substitute function, e.g. vision machine	2.0	20	4.1	35	13.6
Total civilian market	8.0	25.6	19.9	21.8	43.8
Military procurements	1.5	25	3.7	20	7.7
Total global market	9.5	25.5	23.6	21.5	51.5

CAD–CAE–CAM (computer-aided design, engineering and manufacturing) display the fastest growth right now, but a substantial slowdown must be expected, owing to relative saturation, before the end of this decade, with a likely drop from a 30 per cent yearly increment to a mere 15 per cent.

Demand for remote-sensing devices, which is, as we already noticed, the most predictable, will grow steadily throughout the eight years under review. As for image processing applications in medicine, we anticipate an early and substantial push forward, possibly followed by slower growth. However, a great deal of uncertainty attaches to this particular forecast.

Purchases of vision engines for (quasi) manless manufacturing progress by some 20 per cent annually at the present time. As the new breed of vision machines comes to market, a jump of 35 per cent, and perhaps even 40 per cent, per annum in 1988 or 1989 and thereafter can be expected.

The different growth rates for the various categories of applications combine to produce an overall increase in demand for vision systems and machines of just about 25 per cent per year during the current phase of expansion. For the 1988–92 period we visualize a stable growth but at a somewhat slower pace—21–22 per cent—with the notable exception of factory vision machines. Both figures are on the conservative side.

6.3 JAPANESE VIEWS OF MEDIA AND MARKETS: A LESSON

'The Netherlands in the information age' was the title of an impressive, 155-page long study prepared jointly by A. D. Little and the local consultancy, Horringa and de Koning, for a group of leading Dutch computer vendors and information suppliers in 1980–1. Whereas most people were still asking when, indeed, will the information age descend upon that small, yet valorous and obstinate nation, the report opened with the bold statement that 'the Netherlands has already shifted to being an information society', inasmuch as the technological, economic and social foundations for such a society were already there. The aim of the exercise was to evaluate the outlook for further computerization of the Dutch economy and society, to assess market opportunities for the Dutch computer, telecommunications and information vendors, and, finally, to point out policy changes that might be called for.

The Dutch situation and the thinking are quite representative of the conditions and attitudes prevailing in most Western countries. We are therefore going to use the survey for the purpose of comparison with the Japanese approach and for bringing out the fundamental differences between the two marketing philosophies.

The unrecognized prophet

Back in 1973, Tetsuro Tomita, a Counsellor at the Ministry of Posts and Telecommunications in Tokyo, submitted to his authorities a slim, 12-page typewritten paper (unpublished), supplemented with tables and diagrams, under the unprepossessing title: 'The volume of information flow and the quantum evaluation of media'. Today, a decade and a half later, hardly anybody in the information community remembers that report, yet the Japanese computer, telecommunications and publishing industries have consistently applied the strategies spelled out in Tomita's premonitory paper and, by and large, they still do.

In fact, Tomita was able to draw on a just-completed survey of information flows and media in Japan during a thirteen-year period. For each successive year, all the different flows had been measured in terms of volume (in megabits per person), the distance covered and unit costs, whether declining or rising. The eighteen major media included were split between mass-communication and personal-communication media; whenever possible, the supply flow and the corresponding level of (information) consumption had been evaluated separately.

The main findings can be summarized under four points:

1. Since the early 1970s, the Japanese society has entered an era of information oversupply, as a result of the rapid growth of television, cinema, broadcasting, printed publications, etc., while the consumption could not keep pace; hence there was a tendency to saturation. In a subsequent study, Tomita has shown that by 1975 over 90 per cent of information provided went 'unused', a considerable jump from the 60 per cent 'wastage' reported in the earlier period.
2. In order to see the whole picture, it is necessary to analyse all information flows and their changing patterns; retrospective and parochial views are of little help.
3. While mass media displayed decreasing marginal costs, personal communications, such as telephony, postal services and early facsimile, were characterized by increasing unit costs. However, they, too, will eventually, said Tomita, come up against at least relative saturation.
4. The potency of consumer choice was stated both candidly and unequivocally: 'Formerly, we tended to think that media were selected on the merits of their functions.' ... 'The survey, however,

has revealed that information media were selected, just like any other products purchased in a free market, on the basis of a combination of cost and quantity'.

Acting on market indications

It is instructive to draw a parallel (viz. Table 6.4) between the joint American–Dutch approach, which is at best a recipe for stagnation, and the Japanese conception of marketing priorities, a conception that has contributed in no small measure to the making of the giant computer-cum-telecommunications complex of Japan. Those interested in the why and the how will profitably spend time studying and reflecting upon the upper part of the table. However, the far-sighted recommendations, which Tomita had drawn by an impeccable, stepwise inference from the survey data, deserve our admiration. They truly and fully stood the test of time, as the reader can easily verify by going through the short list in the lower part of Table 6.4: scrap telegraphy, develop data transmission, enhance telephony, move boldly towards electronic publishing and find substitutes for traditional mail services—the recipe written thirteen years ago remains yet to be fully implemented.

Two aspects call for a brief comment in order to dispel any misunderstandings. It is difficult to agree with A. D. Little's argument about the declining sectors of the economy, as against the growth sectors, said to be information intensive. Whilst fewer and fewer people work on the land, agriculture is far from backward, as is attested by rapidly rising productivity and consequently also rising output. Oil drilling and refining is surely one of the most computerized industries. Again, industrial design, engineering and manufacturing rely more and more on information systems.

When Tomita spoke of saturation, he could demonstrate the phenomenon only by reference to mass-communications media. Today, we know, for instance, that stockbrokers' offices are equipped with a terminal for every three staff, and soon the ratio is to be 1 : 2. It is doubtful whether subscribing to a long list of specialized online services, in addition to Telerate, Quotron, Reuters, Dun and Bradstreet, etc., would result in boosting the stockbroking business. The time is not far off when most office workers will have personal computers, concurrently with have easy access to the company's mainframes and minis. There is plenty of corroborative evidence to support the assertion of gradual saturation.

Our job is not yet finished. However interesting the comparison between the Japanese and the Western approaches to marketing may be, it is even more important to show that the Japanese way of assessing

Table 6.4 Contrasting two marketing philosophies and policies

A conventional recipe	A recipe for growth
In the A. D. Little study, information-intensive industries are defined as those that produce much of the information they need and then employ it in their own operations. Next, banking, insurance, retailing and a few other service industries are called growth sectors—in contrast to declining agriculture, mining, manufacturing and construction. Jumping to conclusions, the report states: 'In all cases, the growth sectors tend to have many highly information-intensive components while the declining industries have lower information content.' By and large, the model comforts the computer-telecommunications establishment and envisages only minimal changes in their *modus operandi*.	The Japanese view is that the growing oversupply of information in mass-communication media and the rising cost of information in personal communications, acting in parallel, bring about significant shifts in the structure of information flows, creating both new stresses and new opportunities. In addition to the usual competition between suppliers of identical or similar services and products, there is now also bitter fighting for market shares among the different media. Thus, all vendors find themselves under strong pressure to adopt radically new strategies calling for weeding out obsolete and declining lines of products—giving up saturated markets without temporizing and constantly thriving to reduce system unit handling costs through greater use of electronic devices.
Specific recommendations	Specific recommendations
1. Keep building on traditional strength of Dutch computer and information suppliers. 2. Stick to traditional priority markets: banking, insurance, retailing and other selected service industries. 3. Speed up innovation in specific telecommunication media. 4. Modernize the institutional and legal framework and streamline procedures.	1. Stop investing in telegraphy and eventually scrap the system altogether. 2. Focus on fast-growing markets and therefore develop data transmission facilities, enhanced telephony, facsimile. 3. Work towards replacing traditional postal services by electronic mail, facsimile, etc. 4. Move towards substituting electronic publishing for traditional publishing of newspapers, magazines, books.

Table 6.5 Assessing undeveloped market opportunities for computer systems and devices

Meeting Tomita's criteria	Type of demand	Market determinants	Marketing prerequisites
	Pent-up demand	Technology has for long been wanting to satisfy the needs for still, moving and synthesized images, electronic sound and music, interactive compound documents, realistic visual displays, etc.	The marketplace is ready for: —Travel agents and airlines electronic image selling aids —On-the-spot recording of news, data in all combinations —Electronic retraining aids —Interactive educational aids
	Derived demand	Changing systems of values bring to the fore previously unrecognized collective needs and mobilize international responsibilities. New needs are created by changing the environment.	Wanted all specifications for: —Live, multimedia encyclopaediae (e.g. of ancient cultures) —Streamlined systems for managing collective goods —Warning systems against disasters, industrial hazards
	Dormant demand	Large segments of inactive population, i.e. retired, old-age pensioners, school-leavers, handicapped, part-time workers, have for too long been overlooked by computer and information vendors.	The volume of sales is contingent upon prior adapting/redesigning information systems and electronic aids for particular market segments and on developing special, user-friendly interfaces.
	Demand for substitutes	Shifts in current buying patterns will be substantially amplified by offerings of less expensive/more sophisticated/more versatile or more convenient alternatives.	Current developments include: —Specific applications of wireless telephony, electronic mail, high-grade facsimile —Easy-to-use storage media —Cheaper distribution channels —Low-cost on-demand publishing

1. Keep away from quasi-saturated media/markets
2. Avoid concentrating on internal data flows
3. Discard technologies with rising unit costs
4. Remember: value for money sways buyers' choice

market prospects is relevant in the present-day Western environment and to indicate how this technique could be put to good use. The argument that follows is summarized and illustrated in Table 6.5.

Exciting markets yet to be developed

We begin with a recapitulation of the four original critera of commercial viability: saturation, total information flow, cost trends and buyers' preeminence. These four criteria are restated and given an operational content (see the left-hand column of Table 6.5). With the help of these signposts, we are able to break up aggregate demand into meaningful segments and subsegments, to identify the corresponding market prospects and to make a start on defining key marketing prerequisites.

What comes out strongly is the discovery—or confirmation—that vast opportunities exist in areas characterized by low penetration of computerized information systems. Vendors would be well advised to position themselves to supply those markets that have previously not been properly catered for, because the technology was not ready or because the technological solutions available were not adequate or were too costly.

The travel trade is a case in point. The airlines, tour operators and travel agents introduced electronic reservation systems a long time ago, but they still do not have at their disposal pictorial selling aids other than old-fashioned brochures and boring documentary films. This is a kind of paradox for they are in the business of selling trips to far-distant places without being able to impart to their customers even a foretaste of the real things: the beach under the moonshine, the romantic bungalow, the actual locale of a sightseeing visit. There is a ready marketplace for low-cost image systems, as there are some 300 million people in Western countries alone who travel every year.

A similar conclusion applies to the mail-order business which is fully computerized as concerns the order/reorder handling and customer/supplier billing, yet is still waiting for attractive electronic catalogues, with lively user interfaces, which would undoubtedly give a new impetus to customer sales. Likewise, leisure and cultural activities of all kinds, show business and entertainment, hobbies and collector's items offer a vast potential waiting to be tapped.

In the late 1970s, the ex-President of Senegal, Leopold Senghor, has advocated that a comprehensive live encyclopaedia of African culture, including the peoples, styles of life, languages, religious practices, music, dance, etc., be created and made accessible interactively and universally. The constant progress of new information technology will soon make this visionary project perfectly feasible. Also, as our system of values changes, it brings to the fore collective needs, e.g. preservation of cultural heritage and protection against natural and man-made hazards, which tend to assert themselves with a strength previously unknown. Clearly, the financing of such vast programmes would also have to be widespread and international. UNESCO has paid for salvaging the ancient temples of Abu Simbel in Upper Egypt and those at Borobodur in Indonesia; investing in ex-President Senghor's pan-African scheme could be justified on the same grounds.

A third type of demand and market, yet to come alive, is made up of retired people, old-age pensioners, people of independent means, but also teenagers and school-leavers, people in retraining or between jobs, and also the temporarily disabled and the permanently handicapped—in short the inactive population, who are in fact the majority and whose influence in the city grows steadily. Here is an enormous potential market, containing a dozen or two dozen subsegments, so far uninvaded by computer systems and devices—other than television sets and video cassettes.

Finally, we come to the partly unfulfilled part of the Tomita overall scheme, which was really concerned with the never-ending search for suitable substitutes for have-been media, technologies and applications. To be sure, in the intervening years, electronic printing has become common practice, telegraphy has been definitely superseded and the Japanese made considerable strides in developing facsimile techniques. Other developments are under way, some of which are listed in the appropriate box in Table 6.5, to which several additions would be in order. In either case, the market acceptance of the systems that are in the pipeline will be contingent on their vendors' ability to meet the very prerequisites enunciated by the foresighted Tomita.

6.4 IN SEARCH OF HOT NICHES

The evidence is all around: ongoing computerization of the economy and society creates fresh market opportunities, and the end of it is not yet in sight. At any one time, quite a few promising niches are waiting to be occupied, as appetite is growing especially among those who have so far had limited access to, or little use for, contemporary information technology, as we have seen in the preceding section.

The selective survey that follows offers seven suggestions on how to improve the chance of hitting the right idea at the right time, or in the right context, or, at least, of picking the right starting block. This is however not intended as a free-wheeling exercise. Towards the end of this section, we show with the help of a couple of examples how damaging it could be to have started from an assumption that, on the face of it, looked quite plausible, but whose built-in fallacy could—and should—have been detected at the inception stage.

On the other hand, too often managements of vendor companies overconcentrate on finding new markets for their line of pioneering products, yet fail to see an opportunity literally lying at their doorstep, and one that would require much less effort to turn to their advantage.

Sniffing out business opportunities

Opportunity 1

It is in the nature of things that relatively large transactions take place between suppliers of the telecommunications gear and manufacturers of computer equipment, and vice versa.This also applies, to some extent, to such alliances as exist between software houses and hardware makers, between value-added service providers and suppliers of intelligent terminals, and the like. Let us also remember that multinational companies in high technology are, by far, the biggest in-house traders. In 1985, internal sales within Digital Equipment Corp. amounted to $2 billion, as against net sales of $6.7 billion. IBM and Philips, ITT and especially the old AT&T, and several Japanese conglomerates are known to operate in very much the same way.

Suggestion 1

Medium-sized vendor companies should duplicate this trading pattern as far as possible, e.g. by negotiating swap agreements or preferential treatment accords, for instance when submitting joint bids for large public contracts. From *ad hoc* deals they could then move on to forge more permanent links between the partners.[2] In the medium term, federation may turn out to be the only practical way for the small and medium-sized vendors to achieve a sufficient volume of sales through economies of large scale, as a prerequisite for competing with Big Blue and other giants.

Opportunity 2

The border line between information systems and consumer electronics is uncertain and fluctuating, viz. enhanced telephone sets as against

---

[2] Large American and West German chemical companies have developed cross-trading to a very high degree, including reciprocal free access to otherwise secret patents in chemistry, and were thus able to expand their business considerably to the satisfaction of all partners.

intelligent terminals. This variability may be either the source of extra profits or the cause of lost market shares.

Suggestion 2

Just as consumer electronics companies attempt to enter specialized markets previously considered a preserve of makers of computer and telecommunications equipment, the latter should penetrate the marketplace with dual-purpose offerings of their own. Television receivers can be sold as video monitors for a whole range of products, e.g. electronic games, home computing, video playback, in addition to TV and CATV; the advent of digital television will soon make possible still other uses.

Whatever the area and product concerned, there are usually two problems to be reckoned with. One is moving too slowly, too late, thus allowing competition to get a head start. Second, it is essential to be fully familiar with buyers' attitudes in different markets and countries, in order to be able to make properly differentiated anticipations as to the actual reactions of this or that market segment to the presentation of multipurpose products. Whilst loading television sets with additional functions might be a worthwhile commercial target in Europe, the same strategy could backfire in the United States where the households usually have several television receivers already.

Opportunity 3

High growth rates have rewarded a number of upstart companies which had chosen to specialize in designing products closely tied to advances in some extraneous technology, e.g. medicine, navigation, engineering and creating specialized medical devices, navigation aids and systems, computer design and engineering.

Suggestion 3

Action-minded computer makers and software companies should look at junction points between two or even three scientific and engineering disciplines, whose convergence often gives birth to a new specialty, and investigate the relevant opportunities. The field is vast; here are a few ideas picked at random: bioengineering in fish breeding; electronic musical background tied to medical treatment, check-up, surgery; applying rare, freakish frequency distributions to all sorts of natural phenomena and hazards; launching a massive attack on quantitative semantics and dictionary compilation, etc. A deliberate, clever choice of this kind gives the inventive company a position of leadership, and the products attract buyers active in the two or three constituent disciplines, instead of one specialty only.

Opportunity 4

This is supplemental to the previous three points.

Suggestion 4

Established vendors would do equally well, and possibly better, by integrating born-again technologies into their planning. Both Boeing and McDonald Douglas are betting heavily on the likely comeback of streamlined, turbine-driven, propeller aircraft, loaded with electronic navigational aids and control devices. Other examples to be considered include: rehabilitation of railways through superior bulletlike trains; newest machine-tool making in West Germany; reintroduction of streetcars under computer control in some European cities; recent launch of sail coastal tankers in Japan and two American cruise sail ships built in France; revival of interest in bubble memory applications. What about redeveloping the 2,000-year-old Chinese medical practice of acupuncture with the help of computer analysis and simulation?

Opportunity 5

Our next point arises from long-standing complaints about the inadequacy, or the lack of pertinence, of hundreds of online information services. Complained George Kozmetsky,[3] the Dean of College of Business Administration, University of Texas, speaking at a White House Conference: 'The flow of published technological materials as patents, journals, and books has been primarily to satisfy the market demands of those who generate the knowledge. It has been a closed market system specially for scientists and engineers. It has not been user-oriented i.e. business. . . . Changes will and must come.'

Suggestion 5

After fifteen years of disappointing performance and in view of the demonstrable narrowness of the present-day market especially for bibliographic databases, it is increasingly obvious that the problem of public access to up-to-date information in all fields of knowledge and knowhow can be solved only by a radical redistribution of the functions and responsibilities of the several actors and agents concerned, typically vendors of computers and systems, providers of computer services, database suppliers, network operators, etc. There are, however, pitfalls to be avoided. When IBM and Merrill Lynch & Co in 1984 decided to com-

---

[3] George Kozmetsky, 'Technological transfer', in *A Look at Business in 1990* (A summary of the White House Conference on the Industrial World Ahead), US Government Printing Office, Washington, DC, 1972, p. 174.

puterize the financial services industry, they were full of hopes that, through their combined expertise, their joint subsidiary known as Imnet would leap ahead of competitors like Quotron Systems (owned by Citicorp) and Reuters. On January 1, 1987, Imnet was disbanded, as its products proved far too expensive, but for a handful of independent brokerage houses. Hence, prerequisite No. 1: the right costing and pricing structure, to start with.

Opportunity 6

The process of computerization in Europe lags behind that in the United States by a significant factor when measured by installed capacity, but only by a few years if we look at extrapolated trends in sales. All things being equal, the lower the present level of penetration in terms of supercomputers, office equipment, advanced systems, etc., the higher is likely to be the rate of growth in the several years to come. This applies also to telecommunications which are now, at long last, being expanded in Europe to cope with data traffic expected to increase at twice the US rate. This, obviously, is not the place to discuss the issue of world trade in computer equipment and services to any great length. We limit ourselves to making a further modest suggestion.

Suggestion 6

Export markets and some previously neglected market segments in the home country offer, as a general rule, attractive prospects, which however are not costless and which will not be yours for the asking. Computer and information vendors, whether based in the United States, Europe or Japan, or elsewhere, who are not in the league of multinationals, should be provided with assistance and advice, by government and industry federations, in exploring export opportunities and in drawing the balance between the extra benefits and the extra costs and efforts, not only in the short term but especially in a longer time perspective. They will often conclude that in an interdependent world they cannot afford the luxury of staying away from both global competition and global markets.

Opportunity 7: Riding on Societal Thrusts

Great inventors, ready to take great risks by swimming against the current, are generally not made of the same stuff as innovative, successful businessmen. Yet both breeds of men are endowed with that rare talent for positioning themselves to act in ways which tend to fulfill, or conform to, the deeper, often not highly visible, aspirations of their contemporaries.

Enduring concern for ecology has led in the past 20 years to the emergence of new economic activities and constraints. More recently, the universal alarm over terrorism and crime gave rise to a thriving market for all sorts of computer-based security devices and systems.

Suggestion 7

Managements of all computer and information vendor companies, together with their key designers and chief planners, should hold brainstorming sessions for thrashing out among themselves all plausible and even apparently implausible opportunities to cash in on long-term societal thrusts. Three of these are emphasized here: mobility, prevention and growing preeminence of individuals and minorities.

As people move places more and more, there is, according to a leading Swedish expert, Seth Myrby,[4] 'a very large potential market for mobile communications services waiting to be satisfied'. Indeed, demand grows fast for mobile telephones, mobile radios (in conjunction with skyrocketing sales of compact-disk players), paging devices, whilst revolutionary mobile systems for use on land, on sea and in the skies are under development.

Another relevant societal thrust not to be overlooked is: prevent rather than correct, anticipate rather than react to. As long as medical knowledge was limited, medicine has remained almost entirely curative; preventive medicine came into its own as a result of accumulation of myriads of pertinent, structured data from which the probable frequency of occurrence could be computed. The same tendency is observable in many areas: crime prevention; long-term weather forecasting for agriculture; gathering and analysis of early, complex indicators of impending economic downturns, etc. Expert systems and related techniques will undoubtedly give benefits of this type.

Conversely, the fastest growing, long-term demand is for personal communications and for intelligent terminals, particularly for personalized information retrieval. These trends are symptomatic of yet another social thrust, which is clearly in the direction of self-assertion and the growing recognition of minority rights, the first of which is of course the right to be alien, irrespective of the size of the ethnic, religious or professional group to which one belongs. Prominent among the future winners will almost certainly be those software designers, inventors of extensive pocket translators and publishers of exotic song recordings who will best succeed in capturing the 'mood' of these numerous minority groups and sects that are increasingly vocal, but also increasingly affluent.

---

[4]Seth Myrby, *Mobile Telecommunications Today and in the Future*, Swedish Telecom Radio, 1985.

The guessing game is not without risk

It may seem incongruous to invoke general societal thrusts in the context of a market assessment for new information-based technology and it is challengeable to single out contemporary tendencies to personalization, increased mobility and more systematic prevention. The simplest answer to an objection such as this is to reverse the terms of the proposition. Indeed, what is likely to be the outcome of misinterpreting a fundamental aspiration of society or seeing one where there is none?

Even before the advent of personal computers, conventional wisdom predicted that millions of people would soon be toiling at terminals in their homes. These prophetic views were given further impetus as microprocessors invaded all walks of life and business. Today, these predictions appear to have been premature at best. According to the most sanguine estimates, no more than 30,000 workers were linked full-time to their office in the United States in early 1986, and about twice that number were working at home part-time. Figures for Europe are either non-existent or ridiculously low.

When interviewed, the people concerned admit freely that they enjoy office gossiping and personal contact with colleagues. For their part, company managers acknowledge that they have been deterred by the high price of equipment, by rapidly changing technology and possibly also by their own reluctance to let loose the reins. The market is thus basically limited to freelance writers, consultants, professional programmers and perhaps a few specific categories among the handicapped. Gil Gordon, the editor of the newsletter 'Telecommuting Review' said in substance: the image of a mother holding a baby in one hand and a keyboard in the other is a myth.

We must wonder, for similar reasons, whether any massive use of videoconferencing, as some people predict, is not yet another myth. The huge amount of data-carrying capacity needed for a two-way transmission of television pictures and sound makes the current cost prohibitive for all but a handful of companies or very few very special applications—to say nothing of social resistance. Videoconferencers see the gadget as an inadequate ersatz for the real thing.

6.5 CONCLUSION AND OUTLOOK

In this brief concluding section, an attempt is made to relate the exciting, new market prospects reviewed in Chapter 6 to the main findings of the two preceding chapters. Looking through the binoculars of an astute vendor, we first focused, in Chapter 4, on how corporate buyers evaluate and indeed perceive the benefits from computing in their businesses. Then, in Chapter 5, we discussed the growing number of situations and areas in which buyers' preferences tend to prevail over the views of overconservative, or myopic, vendors, many of whom are still reluctant to face the reality of a buyers' market.

What remains to be done is to show how users' attitudes, and especially their newly found self-assertion, translate into market trends and how these market pressures culminate in new exigencies on hardware and software development, whilst at the same time creating vast new business opportunities for forward-looking vendors. A fine example of these interrelationships is provided by the current explosion in the United States of EDI, or electronic data interchange.

Electronic transactions, e.g. between auto makers and their dealers and between manufacturers and their suppliers, have been peformed for years by some large companies. Triad Systems in the 1970s built its reputation on designing custom-made systems for optimal distribution of auto parts. Reynolds and Reynolds had started by selling business forms, later on went into batch processing for the auto dealers and eventually ended up selling specialized turnkey computer systems. Until recently, however, data interchange systems amounted to no more than a small, although profitable, specialty niche.

All of a sudden, the business shot up in 1985, as shipments increased 100 per cent from the previous year. US market analysts are now confidently predicting an annual doubling up until 1990, by which time the EDI market should be worth over $1.1 billion, as against under $40 million, including telecommunications, in 1985. EDI systems are spreading rapidly, spurred by sales of personal computers, which allow even small companies to handle electronic transactions via public or dedicated networks.

A major contributory factor was provided by the rapid development of industrywide standards for electronic order forms and invoices. A Minneapolis-based food wholesaler had recently disclosed that by using EDI he was able to save $1.45 out of $1.75 on every purchase order previously handled by telephone and backed by written confirmation.

Furthermore, under the aegis of the American National Standards Institute, efforts are under way to create a generic standard for all industries that would permit, say, an auto maker to order directly from a chip maker or a software house. A similar evolution is taking place in Europe, and there is hope that the two standards could be united. Also, the concept of electronic transactions is being extended to other documents, e.g. shipping manifests, customs forms, requests for price quotations, intercompany billings and eventually electronic payments, as well. Electronic data interchanges of the future will surely benefit greatly from the emerging electronic imaging technology.

The story, though real, is a textbook illustration of how astute vendors should go about opening up new, or vastly extended, markets for their radically reshaped systems. Here is a nutshell recapitulation of the essential prerequisites, for future reference:

1. Ascertain the necessary degree of penetration of appropriate hardware, i.e. mainframes at centres and nodal points and business computers at periphery, together with adequate storage capacities.
2. Verify that all basic documents, e.g. order forms, waybills, invoices, etc., have been standardized and that these standards are acceptable to end-users.
3. Then, and then only, commission the writing of software and the adaptation, if and as required, of protocols for mainframe/microcomputer data exchange.
4. Work out the best-cost combinations and test their attractiveness to large and small users.
5. Evaluate, and review periodically, prospects for expanding the system/market mix vertically (incorporating additional transactions) and horizontally (appealing to new potential users).

Part 3

Megatrends in Technology

We are now a few years into a staggering efflorescence of information technology products made from components that are simultaneously increasing in variety and power. As the number of component types goes up the number of different products grows exponentially; on top of this, microminiaturization and technological advances in solid-state devices is creating a broadening range of power capabilities for the components. A result of this technology push is the possibility of creating a virtually complete spectrum of products for handling in any conceivable way all forms of information—numerical data, text, physical measurements, sound, graphics and images both fixed and moving, analogue and digital.

Any computer system consists, of course, of hardware and software, and must provide services that meet a set of user requirements. These three system dimensions—hardware, software and services—define a space in which regions have to be found where there are strong market development opportunities. One of the principal problems is that these regions, or niches, are fragmentary yet interrelated and dynamically changing. In each, technology is advancing, and user knowhow and expectations are evolving. In the first three chapters guidelines for determining and controlling costs were highlighted and in Chapters 4, 5 and 6 market forces were analysed, which led to the identification of some new markets that are set to explode.

Prospects for the basic underlying technology of hardware and software are set down in Chapters 7 and 8 respectively, whereas the question of how best these elements of advancing technology can be combined to pinpoint the most promising building blocks and ways of putting them together into market-successful systems is put off, together with resultant issues, until Chapter 9.

First, therefore, in Chapter 7 an attempt is made to suggest new materials that will supplement or complement doped silicon; then the likely emergence of new computer architectures is considered and the possible introduction of super-fast optical computers, required for making progress in some application areas, is discussed.

Chapter 8 deals in a novel way with the issue of bringing software performance up to that of hardware, and methods are given that can help to close the much talked-about software gap. The growing influence of the corporate buyer of computing equipment highlights a trend that may change the face of the software scene and related industries.

We take a look, too, at the impending application of the fruits of artificial intelligence research, particularly expert systems.

Proposals relating to the selective integration of hardware and software 'building blocks' to create products and services for particular market niches are set out in Chapter 9. We explore the fields of: gathering, archiving, retrieving and postprocessing the vast quantities of data nowadays required for successful management of business and our total environment; input/output devices and software that can improve the man–machine interface; high-capacity storage media; the common treatment of symbolic, image and sound data in digital form; and lastly we take a glance at potential new systems and services to be used in 'non-professional' endeavours.

The problems and issues are considered from the point of view of strategic planners and decision makers who have to be able to see the whole picture. The emphasis is, as it must be, on megatrends.

We may draw the analogy with maps. Our intention is to set down a large-scale map of the entire terrain, which brings out the relationships among whole continents and the main countries, rather than street maps, which would assist the exploration of particular, though not necessarily significant, towns. The approach to depicting trends in information technology and choosing subjects for examination is a global one, with a time horizon of about fifteen years—say the end of the century—consistent with that of Parts 1 and 2. We have not adopted a forecasting, crystal-ball gazing attitude; rather it is about what is now going on in R&D laboratories and what is commercially feasible in the timeframe.

The issues and topics addressed in relation to these evolving markets have been chosen partly subjectively, but we believe that they are the key to finding ways out of the difficulty now faced by IT suppliers, who have a bewildering variety of technologies and techniques with which to attack an increasingly diverse marketplace. Furthermore, the selected themes are topical and practical.

Chapter 7

New Exigencies on Hardware Development

Most research and development programmes seek higher speeds of operation, increasing component densities, lower energy consumption, larger overall memory capacities and better ways for human interaction with machines. Solid, and to some extent liquid, state research continues to push back the frontiers of what is realizable. These characteristics have to be traded off against each other, and against economic variables such as cost and others like serviceability, reliability, user convenience and so on. Progress in some technologies is slowing down because physical limits which cannot be overcome are now being approached asymptotically. These constraints may, however, be overcome or by-passed with innovation based on other technologies.

In Section 7.1 we shall look at the physical nature of the basic chemical materials for constructing computer components. Doped silicon is the most commonly used semiconductor for manufacturing the fundamental electrical components of computers, but other semiconducting inorganic materials are being developed. The likely contenders for supplementing, or even replacing, doped silicon are considered.

Recognizing that inorganic semiconductor technology, while not yet up against its ultimate limits, is approaching ineluctable barriers, in Section 7.4 the current work on optical computers and the glimmerings of an understanding of how macromolecular (biological) computers could come about provide the backcloth against which to assess both the present state of the technology and the developments under way.

Besides choosing better materials, two other crucially significant hardware aspects are microminiaturization and computer architecture. The gains in processor power from making circuit elements smaller and integrating more of them onto single chips have relentlessly driven computation per dollar skywards and therefore the costs down for 30 years. The same goes for information storage. This process of microminiaturization, up to the present struggles with wafer-scale technology and tentative essays at three-dimensional circuitry and memory, cannot go on for ever; Section 7.2 looks at the nature of this constraint and indirectly illustrates the need to get off the potential hook.

Promising ways of escaping this impending obstacle stem from looking again at the whys and wherefores of the original, and still going strong, von Neumann architecture for computers. Today's computers incorporate speedup features, such as pipelining, multiprocessing and hierarchical memory organization, but very few of them offer true parallel processing on a large scale. In Section 7.3 we shall consider how machines are likely to be radically changed by means of new architectures; array processors, loosely coupled multiprocessors, dataflow machines, as well as reduced instruction set computers (which may of course be von Neumann machines), all of which seem set for commercial impact, are considered.

7.1 THE CONFINES OF DOPED SILICON

Two physical properties of materials are, generally speaking, at the root of the information technology industry. With a small effort these two properties can be understood.

One, used for storing data, is that a material exhibit more than one stable state. Usually 'more than one' in this context means 'two', and such bistability is used to memorize data in the form of binary digits, called 'bits'. The data represented in this way can be numerical, textual, image, sound or other signals; thus this type of physical property can be harnessed to store any kind of data in binary form. Examples are: magnetization, transmission or reflexion of light (by paper or a metallized layer in the case of the recently developed optical disks), and voltage levels in logic arrays. As we shall see briefly in Section 7.4, non-linear optical materials hold out the prospect in the not-too-distant future of multistable devices which could work directly in decimal arithmetic and handle colour images without intermediate binary coding and processing.

The second characteristic of importance, used for processing data, is that some physical variable, e.g. electrical conductivity, be accurately controllable over a sufficiently wide operating range. Given this close control, circuits that amplify input signals, oscillate at chosen frequencies, rectify oscillating inputs or perform other useful operations can be made according to precise requirements. Semiconductors, which mimic in the solid state what old-fashioned vacuum tubes did, but with many advantages we shall come to later, give this needed degree of control over electrical conductivity. The resulting devices provide the means for setting the above-mentioned bistable (or multistable) elements in one or other of their states, switching them between states, transmitting signals between storage and other elements, and for synchronization or dynamic control of the operation of an entire digital data processor.

In the 45 years since the computer was invented such physical properties of materials have generally been realized through ferromagnetism and semiconduction. Even when light transmission/reflexion has been used it has been only peripheral and quickly transduced to electrical conductivity inside the machine. Both ferromagnetism and semiconduction arise from the behaviour of electrons in solids, which points to the origin of terms like electronic digital computer and electronic data processing.

In this context, another electronic physical property, superconductivity (discovered in 1911 by Heike Kamerlingh Onnes), has hit the headlines in early 1987. Until then only achievable in some metals and alloys at near liquid helium[1] temperatures ($<20°K$), physicists at IBM Zurich and United States, Japanese and other European centres of low-temperature research have recently succeeded in making ceramic oxide materials (typically out of yttrium, barium, and copper oxide) that superconduct at round about liquid nitrogen[2]) temperatures ($\sim 90°K$— a totally different commercial proposition.

Smaller computers resulting from high packing densities of circuit components may be achieved because resistive heating is eliminated by superconducting circuitry, and transit speeds will be faster. The technology will, however, take many years to develop, for ceramics will not be easily tamed to produce the wires and thin films required by the IT industry. Nevertheless, Bell Laboratories and others have already begun to make advances in fabrication methods. In the longer run super-fast switching can also be attempted, and maybe IBM will resuscitate its Josephson junction research.

Is common silicon too common?

Today, the most commonly used material for manufacturing electronic devices and integrated circuits is semiconducting silicon doped with impurities of, for instance, boron or phosphorus atoms at appropriate concentrations. After oxygen, silicon is the second most abundant element in the earth's crust. Although it is somewhat difficult to isolate from the variety of rocks, clays, sands and soils in which it occurs, its overall cost of production up to commercial grade silicon is relatively low. Pure silicon is a hard, metallic-looking solid with the crystal structure of diamond; its crystallization is well understood and fully controllable. Moreover, silicon possesses satisfactory semiconducting properties. Even a complete layman appreciates the fundamental distinction between conductors and non-conductors (called insulators). A conductor such as copper wire is a material that easily carries an electric current when even a small voltage is put across it. By contrast an insulator is a material that, even when a large voltage is applied across it, will not let electric current pass (e.g. ceramics or rubber).

Between these two extremes, there exist in nature intrinsic semiconductors, a kind of hybrid, which behave like insulators at low enough temperatures, but when heated jump across and become weak conduc-

---

[1] Helium boils at $4.4°K$.
[2] Nitrogen boils at $77.2°K$.

tors. In practice, they are unsuitable for making computer components because they would have to be operated at finely controlled temperatures.

Far better results are obtained by doping silicon with impurity atoms of either boron, aluminium or gallium, in which the charge carriers are positively charged holes (p-type material), or phosphorus or arsenic, giving rise to n-type material in which the charge carriers are electrons, negatively charged. The first practical utilization of doped silicon chips was in components such as memory cells, logic gates, rectifiers and amplifiers. Far more important was their usage in the entire range of computers from microprocessor to supercomputer, through minicomputers, as well as mainframes, small and large.[1] Furthermore, these silicon chips are widely used in hi-fi equipment, motor cars, advanced telephones, household appliances, aircraft, automatic cash dispensers, a wide range of sensors for monitoring and control, and a host of other pieces of equipment in everyday use. With all these advantages, it is little wonder that silicon became established as the raw material at the cornerstone of information technology and the entire computer industry. Yet this dominance of silicon has come to be challenged in key areas of the industry, because it has some inherent limitations. These have become increasingly apparent as the technology has developed.

Aristocratic gallium arsenide

Today gallium arsenide looks like the undisputed challenger to doped silicon. From fundamental research back in the 1960s, the compound has moved to the forefront of industrial laboratory research. The R&D effort with gallium arsenide is being carried out by most of the leading firms in the IT components' industry. The race is on! Among them, just to give an impression, we may cite: Rockwell International, Hughes, TRW, Texas Instruments, Westinghouse, RCA and Sandia in the United States; Hitachi, Matsushita, Mitsubishi, Oki, NEC, NTT and Sony in Japan; and in Europe, there is Plessey, Thomson-CSF, LEP (France), Siemens and Philips. It is not dificult to understand why.

First, compared with silicon, for a given performance, gallium arsenide devices consume up to three times less power and thus lessen the problem of heat dissipation.[2]

Second, switching and storage times for gallium arsenide can be achieved a hundred times faster than those with silicon. This factor alone makes gallium arsenide a key material for microwave applications including radar, satellite communications, intruder alarms, microwave ovens and direct satellite television broadcasting.

---

[1] For cost analysis of these five classes of computer see Section 2.1.
[2] This is significant in microminiaturization (see page 176).

Third, another advantage is that gallium arsenide offers better inherent protection against the effects of increases in temperature and stray radiation. We would need to go through a highly technical argument to explain why gallium arsenide is a most valuable material for solid-state laser manufacture and light-emitting devices. Most light-emitting diodes used for red display panels in pocket calculators use the light-emitting property of gallium arsenide which is a so-called direct gap semiconductor unlike silicon.

Although these properties make it an attractive new material, gallium arsenide has other characteristics that are most definitely disadvantagous, which will limit the extent to which it replaces silicon in the information technology industry. In contrast with silicon, gallium arsenide is expensive to manufacture. The abundances of gallium and arsenic in the earth's crust are minute (respectively 0.0015 and 0.0002 per cent), and gallium arsenide does not occur naturally; it has therefore to be man-made from a high-temperature chemical reaction of very pure materials, whereas silicon is extracted from the ores in which it occurs and then purified by a classical refining process.

Gallium arsenide is usually made from gallium chloride, through its reaction in the gaseous phase with arsenic and hydrogen. Gallium is an unusual metal in that it melts at 30°C—a hot room temperature—and arsenic also has its quirks, because at atmospheric pressure it sublimes, i.e. goes directly from solid to gas, at 615°C, and of course it is that most notorious poison, much used in Victorian melodramas. None of these characteristics make life particularly easy for solid-state technologists, who are trying to master ways of producing high-quality single crystals of gallium arsenide from which to fabricate electronic components with exciting properties. For example, gallium arsenide melts at 1240°C, at which temperature arsenic evaporates, and so makes crystal production difficult. There is also the problem of impurities being taken up from the crucible. On top of that, there is the difficulty of insulating gallium arsenide devices and integrated circuits, compared with those made in silicon, where it is sufficient simply to allow an oxide layer to form.

Notwithstanding these incipient technical difficulties with gallium arsenide, there is another factor affecting the putative conquest of silicon by gallium arsenide. It is simply that the superior characteristics of the latter are not needed everywhere; doped silicon chips are often more than adequate for the purposes of the design engineer and they are cheaper. It is probable therefore that gallium arsenide will topple silicon only for certain specialized components, such as very fast logic gates, high-frequency amplifiers, solid-state lasers and optronic devices. In these fields there will be no alternative to replacing silicon with something else, and gallium arsenide is being groomed to take over the crown.

Hence, in the near future we are going to have a mixed semiconductor economy, with the old drayhorse (doped silicon) continuing to provide common everyday functionality and the thoroughbred racehorse (gallium arsenide) extending its domain more and more to cope with the exacting requirements of new products at the market frontier.

We can expect, in any case, that whatever ground is lost by silicon to gallium arsenide will be recuperated in other areas like xerography, solar power convertors (where amorphous silicon will be used) and as silica for optical fibres.

Promising substitute materials

Gallium arsenide is not the only material to challenge the supremacy of silicon. Research is well under way to develop higher-performance substitutes. This entails two basic problems: that of choosing the appropriate material, and that of achieving its crystallization for large-scale, commercial production.

Although happenstance, coupled with close observation and inspired recognition of patterns in data, still plays a rôle in scientific discovery, in this particular field the alternative approach using well-established scientific theories and Mendeleyev's periodic table helps to pick up the most promising candidate materials. In the original table, elements were ordered according to the periodicity of their physical properties and grouped by the similarity of their chemical nature. Of late, industrial and academic research has quite logically concentrated on materials like gallium phosphide, indium phosphide, gallium antimonide and also on some tertiary and quaternary alloys (gallium aluminium arsenide, gallium aluminium arsenophosphide) because their elements occur in the periodic table in positions that suggest strongly that some of their relevant properties are superior to those of silicon and gallium arsenide. Some of these materials are likely to reach commercial exploitation by the early 1990s and beyond. When fully developed, they will significantly raise the level of performance of some computer components and devices.

The second major problem is how to grow high-quality crystals. Whereas for silicon there is only one element to consider, in the case of the newer materials there are two or several elements to control. In consequence, the process of doping is replaced by varying the proportions of the constituent atoms, in order to achieve the properties required for specific uses.

Crystallization via atomic engineering

Crystal growth is an accretion process, perhaps best visualized by reference to stalactites in caves or pearls in oysters. Whereas stalactites and pearls can be imperfect and yet still admired for their beauty, commercial semiconductor and optical components demand high-quality crystals.

The art of growing good single crystals of silicon, from which to make silicon chips, has become well established over the past 35 years. For gallium arsenide and other interesting semiconductors, the techniques are now becoming commercially viable, but the state of the art is some years behind that of silicon.

Each time a new material is taken, it is usually necessary to start almost from scratch to discover the best method of crystal production. Two general guidelines are that extremely pure material, of which single crystals are required, be used and the growth be controlled. The generic term for the techniques used to achieve precise growth is epitaxy from the Greek 'epi' (outer) and 'taxi' (order). There are basically two approaches. Almost exclusively, the semiconductor industry uses so-called vapour phase epitaxy for commercial-scale production; in this process, gaseous silicon hydride passes over the crystalline silicon substrate at whose surfaces the high-quality single crystal is laid down, epitaxial layer by epitaxial layer, at the rate of 0.5–1.0 microns per minute. The largest barrel furnaces, operating in parallel, produce up to 1,300 cm^2 of silicon per run.

A special category of vapour phase epitaxy is molecular beam epitaxy; it offers the following advantages: (1) use of highly pure elemental sources rather than compounds; (2) high vacuum reduces the likelihood of unwanted impurities; (3) analytical tools to monitor crystal structure quality can be used during the epitaxial growth process; (4) good growth control can be achieved enabling extremely thin layers and multilayers to be grown. Extremely small and very fast devices suitable for ultrafast switching and microwave operation can be produced in this way, as well as tunable solid-state lasers, which permit the matching of the laser wavelength to that which is optimal for transmission through optical fibres.

The other method is liquid phase epitaxy. Although it can produce extremely good quality crystals, it is not as good as vapour phase epitaxy for volume production.

7.2 LIMITS TO MICROMINIATURIZATION

Until the invention of the transistor in 1948, for which Bardeen, Brattain and Shockley won the 1956 Nobel physics prize, thermionic vacuum tubes (TVT) constituted the chief way of making the rectifiers, amplifiers and oscillators of the electronics industry. By today's norms vacuum tubes were enormous; their sizes lay in the range of 10–100 cm^3.

The transistor is the solid-state analogue of the triode TVT, in which the source, or emitter, of electrons (or holes) acts like the cathode; the drain, or collector, behaves like the anode; and the gate (in a field-effect transistor) or the base (in a bipolar junction transistor) performs the same functions as the grid.

Early transistors were small discrete devices; the surface layer was about 0.25 cm^2 in area and each device was packaged in a plastic or metal cover with leads to connect it to other devices. By 1959 technological and production problems had been overcome so that the first computer using transistors and no tubes appeared; this heralded the so-called second generation of computers.

Even before these discrete transistor computers reached the marketplace, back in the R&D laboratories of those companies engaged in advanced research an entirely new and telling step was taking place in the relentless march to miniaturization.

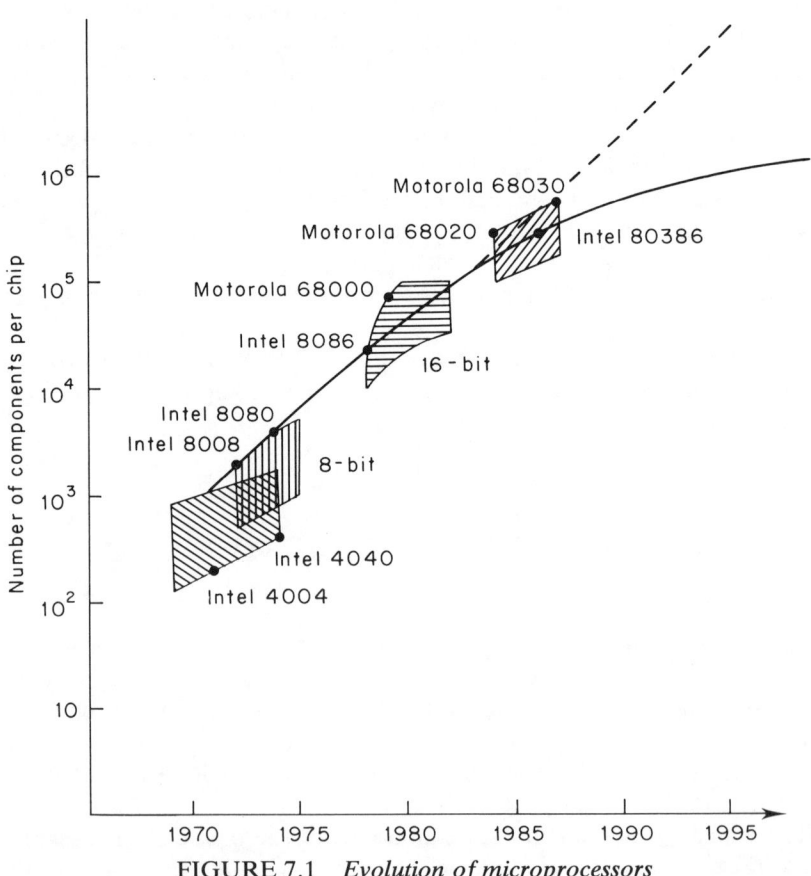

FIGURE 7.1 *Evolution of microprocessors*

It all started with an integrated circuit

In 1958 Jack Kilby of Texas Instruments and Robert Noyce at Fairchild Semiconductor were making a strong push towards the monolithic circuit, in which the resistors, capacitors and transistors and their interconnexions are fabricated in one piece of semiconducting material; in those days it was germanium or silicon. Thus the solid circuit, subsequently called the integrated circuit (IC), was achieved.

About a decade later these two pioneers (Kilby and Noyce) succeeded separately in achieving a particularly spectacular goal, that of producing the first microprocessor—an entire central processing unit of a computer including registers and essential memory as well as input/output lines—on a single chip. By 1971 the Intel 4004 and soon afterwards the 4040, 4-bit microprocessors, were in quantity production.

In 1974, 8-bit microprocessors on a chip were readily available and in 1978 16-bit ones hit the market. It has taken longer to achieve commercial production of 32-bit microprocessors but they have now appeared in 1984–5 with the arrival of Intel's 80286, National Semiconductors' 32000 series, Motorola's 68020 and Fairchild's Clipper, and already more powerful ones such as the Intel 80386 and Motorola 68030 are around.

In fact, just to show that it could be done, IBM in 1980 succeeded in putting a major part of a System 370 central processing unit on a single silicon chip of dimension 49 mm^2, but that was not of course a commercial product. The evolution of microprocessors is illustrated in Figure 7.1

Storage densities up and up

Just as these single chips have had progressively more powerful microprocessors set into their surface layers, they have also had ever-larger memory arrays implanted into them during the past 25 years. Taking dynamic random access memory (DRAM) arrays as an example, their capacity on a single chip has increased from 1 Kbit in 1970 through 64 Kbit in 1977 to 1 Mbit in 1986 with 4 and 16 Mbit chips announced in March 1987.

Not only have simple chip component densities increased dramatically but in the same period auxiliary magnetic and optical storage media (tapes and disks) have also seen astounding advances. While the devices have remained relatively large, the areas/volumes for storing one data bit have certainly become microminiature. We concentrate here on the technology and leave the applications characteristics of auxiliary (as well as main) storage devices until Section 9.3. Table 7.1 and Figure 7.2

Table 7.1 Evolution of auxiliary memory

Type		Date introduced	Recording density (Mbit/in²)	Unit capacity (Mbytes)
Floppy disks	8 in	1973		0.243
		1977	0.3	0.400
	5¼ in	1983	0.28–1.15	0.250–2.0
	3½ in	1985	0.64	1.0
Bubble		1979	0.2	0.256
		1981	0.8	1.0
		1985	1.5–2.0	4.0
½ in Magnetic tape				
	7 track	1951	0.025–0.1	5.8–23.0
	9 track	1969	0.130–1.0	23.0–180.0
	18 track	1984	12.4	200.0
Winchester	14 in	1973	2.5	70.0
		1979	4.8	570.0
		1981	11.4	1,260.0
	8 in	1978	4.0	20.0
		1982	10.0	100.0
	5¼ in	1980	10.0	16.0
		1982	12.0	40.0
Optical disks	12 in	1984	100–225	1,000–1,250
CD-ROM	4¾ in	1986	300–340	550–600

show the evolution of some of the main characteristics of this development.

Magnetic recording technology

Magnetic tape data densities increased from 200 bits/inch in the 1950s to 6,250 bits/inch in the early 1980s. This thirtyfold decrease in the size of the ferromagnetic domains for storing one bit has resulted from improvements in the technology for coating ribbons of plastic with high-quality ferromagnetic films, and placement of the read/write heads for storing and recovering the data on the tape much nearer to the recording medium in order to distinguish neighbouring bits from each other. Current state-of-the-art technology enables this head-tape gap to be about 2.5 μm, there are 19,000 flux reversals per inch (IBM 3480 cartridge) and tape speeds can reach some 16 ft/s. As a result of the increased storage density, one 560 ft reel of formatted magnetic tape with 18 tracks can store some 200 million characters, which can be read into main memory at more than 2 million bytes per second.

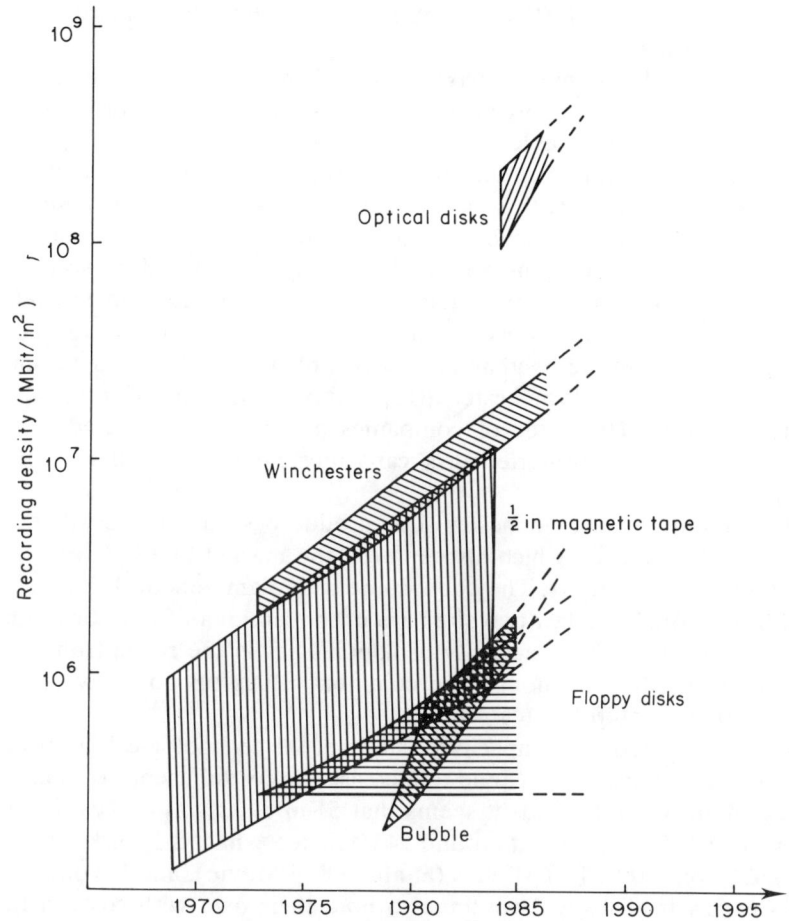

FIGURE 7.2 *Comparative evolution of recording density of different magnetic and optical storage media*

For random access auxiliary memory media, most mainframe and minicomputer installations use a mixture of fixed-head non-removable rigid disks and removable or non-removable moving-head disks. Fixed-head disks have faster access times and removable disks have the advantage that they offer almost unlimited storage for offline archiving. Microcomputers also tend to be equipped with removable diskette storage and small sealed Winchester moving-head disks for similar reasons.

Rotating disk auxiliary memory devices have developed even more dramatically than sequential memory media. Their storage volume has increased from about 1 Mbyte in the 1950s to 1,260 Mbytes per drive at the present time.

Magnetic disk technology has blossomed over the years into a bewildering array of commercial products. The principal disk drive technologies are the removable cartridge, the Winchester and the floppy.

The removable cartridge technology was the first to be introduced in the late 1950s and is still in use, mostly with 14-in diameter platters. Winchester technology, in which the head and disk assembly is sealed, is now the most popular high-capacity disk storage; it entered the scene in 1973, also with 14-in platters, but in 1978, 8-in platters came in, in 1980, 5¼-in platters were introduced and since 1983, 3½-in ones have been available. Because the head and disk assembly is sealed, the mean time between failures for Winchester disks is about twice that of removable cartridge disks. Hundreds of companies are in the Winchester disk business, where unformatted disk capacities range from 10 to 1,260 Mbytes.

The multitude of Winchester disk products is equalled by that of floppy disk products, which also entered the market in 1973 with the IBM 3740 8-in product. They now come with diameters of 8, 5¼, 3½, 3¼ and 3-in, though the last two sizes are unconventional if not downright Bohemian. The storage capacity of floppies lies in the range from 100 Kbytes to 6 Mbytes, though the common values till now have been 360, 720 and 1,440 Kbytes.

For a given required capacity of storage, the technological improvements in recording density tend to increase the cost/efficiency of smaller disks. With present trends it seems that 5¼-in disks will be best in the range of 10–50 Mbytes (at around \$45/Mbyte), whilst 8-in disks will be optimal from 50 to 150 Mbytes (at about \$25/Mbyte), and beyond 150 Mbytes, 14-in disks will continue to hold their own with costs in the region of \$10–20/Mbyte.

For the rigid disk the recording density has gone from about 2 Mbits/in^2 for the IBM 3330 in 1973 to just over 10 Mbits/in^2 for the IBM 3380 announced in 1980. Modern thin-film media have less graininess in the magnetic material coated onto the rigid disk. As a result a track density of 1,000 tracks/inch and a bit density of 25,000 bits/inch is now achievable. There is no doubt that further improvements in thin-film technology will lead very soon to commercial products with 50,000 flux reversals per inch on tracks of density 1,000 tracks/inch, giving a recording density of 50 Mbits/in^2.

Bubble memory consists of domains (or bubbles) in the surface of a chip of garnet (usually a crystal of yttrium–aluminium garnet) which are magnetized in one of two directions. Bubble memory has had a chequered history. Hailed once as the most likely form of high-capacity storage to capture large sections of the market, its implementation encountered unforeseen technical problems which, added to advances in rotating magnetic storage, caused the early enthusiasm to evaporate. Texas Instruments Inc., National Semiconductor Corp. and Rockwell International Corp. closed their bubble operations in 1981 after having invested millions of dollars. Hitachi, Fujitsu and Intel were the first to produce sample bubble memories in 1977–9. These three companies, together with Motorola, have stayed in the game, and owing to recent developments in advanced research laboratories, such as the Magnetics Technology Center at Carnegie-Mellon University, Pittsburg, where they have succeeded in integrating semiconductor devices on bubble memory chips, it seems that bubble memory is coming out of the doldrums and could once again have a bright future.

Bubble memory's most useful characteristics are that it has reasonably high recording density, it is non-volatile with a long lifetime and, being solid state, it is rugged. For these reasons it has been used in military applications but it should also have potential for pocket calculator and portable microcomputer memory.

Nevertheless, although advances in disk and bubble magnetic recording technology will continue to give succour to those companies developing it, it is clear that an asymptotic limit to recording density is rapidly being approached. Waiting in the wings and about to come to the centre of the stage are optical storage systems.

The advent of optical storage

Optical disks have been under development since the early 1970s. The main stimulus for this work has been the creation of a medium suitable for the storage and regeneration of moving and still images, with very high recording densities, and for the storage and reproduction of very high fidelity sound. For some considerable time it has been realized that this technology may have a bright future as a replacement for magnetic, random access storage for certain computing applications, notably those that require large-capacity storage.

The basis of the technology is the creation of micro-sized holes, blisters or pits in a metal surface, encapsulated for protection in a transparent plastic cover, by focusing a laser beam onto the metallic surface. Both analogue and digital recording systems have been developed. The stored information is read out by using a laser beam which is modulated either by reflection from or transmission through the holes, blisters or pits in the metallized layer.

Among the advantages of optical disk technology are its contactless readout and imperviousness to dust because the laser is distant from the disk surface, ease of mass replication, removable disks and a recording density approximately ten times that of magnetic disks. The main disadvantages are the long access times of 100–1000 ms compared with 10–25 ms for certain magnetic, rotating disk technology and at present optical disks are read-only. The practicalities are discussed in Section 9.3.

A single-sided 12 in optical disk can store more than 1,000 Mbytes of data, equivalent to some 20,000 A4-size pages stored as compressed images of some 400 Kbits/page. As in the case of magnetic disks, the tendency is to move towards smaller disks for many applications.

That commercial optical disk technology at present allows writing only once on the disk certainly eliminates it from consideration for some applications, but, on the other hand, there are others where it is considered to be an advantage. Many computer crimes occur because database records are modified; since those with criminal intent cannot change information stored in databases on write-once optical disks, a considerable security advantage is gained. Banks, police forces, insurance companies and many other organizations will therefore choose optical disks just because of this seeming defect of not being rewritable.

This being said, many companies in the business of marketing optical storage systems are carrying out intensive research and development programmes to produce erasable optical memories. Their efforts are for the most part targetted on materials which manifest either the optical bistability described in Section 7.4 in the discussion on optical computer developments, or on reversible crystalline-amorphous phase transitions, or on the magneto-optic (Kerr) effect where magnetic fields change the plane of polarization of incident laser radiation.

The principal manufacturers of optical disks and the associated technology, which are yet another example of the march to microminiaturization, are: Philips in Europe; Canon, Hitachi, Matsushita, NEC, Sanyo, Sony and Toshiba in Japan; and Hewlett-Packard Corp., Laserdata, Optical Disk Corp., RCA, Reference Technology Corp. and Storage Technology Corp. in the United States.

Why miniaturize? Where to stop?

It is natural to ask why there has been such a strong effort to miniaturize information technology components during the last 40 years. The reasons and incentives are numerous.

From the viewpoint of engineers, striving for more and more computing power in order to solve increasingly complex computational problems, vacuum tubes had many drawbacks; they were bulky, unreliable, fragile and consumed much electrical power, most of which was converted into heat. In order to be able to dissipate this heat and allow maintenance engineers access to them, the vacuum tubes had low packing density.

Engineering maintenance and repair was a full-time, intensive activity in and around computers made from TVTs. So large were early TVT computers, and so essential was continuous maintenance, that the engineers were able to walk around inside them, like a team of nurses and surgeons caring for a permanently sick patient.

A large part of the driving force towards higher densities of electronic circuits came from the military sector. The 1950s and 1960s were a nervous period for the world's major political and economic powers, the United States and Russia. It was the chilliest period of the Cold War.

The necessity of lightness and reliability for space missions and lightness coupled with complex signal processing for military vehicles and weapons maintained the strong drive to miniaturization and financed the required intense R&D effort. Civilian computer applications benefited from the spinoff. Motivated by the desire to reduce size, weight and cost of circuits, the idea was to carry out the interconnection of components simultaneously with their production—a major step forward in the fabrication of increasingly complex circuits at economic prices.

An important factor in the fabrication of ICs is the yield of good chips. An experimental relationship[1] between the yield (Y) of sound chips, the chip area (A) and the defect density (D) on the wafer is

$$Y = (1 + AD)^{-1}.$$

Thus, for a process with a given defect density, the yield of good chips can be increased by making them smaller, but to achieve the required functionality this means packing the components closer together on the chip. Also access times or switching times become shorter because the signals have smaller distances to travel. Thus, the quest for ever-smaller circuit elements and higher packing densities is both technically and economically very attractive.

Continued microminiaturization depends on many technical factors; e.g. the narrowness of the lines that can be etched into the photoresists or masks, the accuracy and the repeatability with which these lines can be made and the degree of control attainable for the implantation and diffusion of dopants.

In 1964 Gordon Moore noticed that the number of components per chip doubled each year, and postulated that this would continue, which turned out to be the case, at least until the late 1970s. The progression of the bit storage of a single chip of dynamic random access memory shown in Figure 7.3, at least up to the introduction of 64 Kbit DRAMs

---

[1] B. T. Murphy, *Proc. IEEE*, **52**, 1537–45 (1964); C. H. Stapper, *IBM J. Res. Dev.*, **20**, 228–34 (1976).

in 1977, followed Moore's hypothesis. Then progress slackened for about a decade from its former phenomenal rate, but with the early 1987 announcements of 4 Mbit and 16 Mbit prototype chips from IBM and NTT it appears to have regained its former momentum.

Such a curve has to be examined carefully for two major reasons. First, for each memory density there is a life cycle between initial laboratory prototype, first commercial production, and mass production at minimum price; the latter seems to happen at about the time when the next memory-density level becomes commercially available. Second, a different factor is the chip size, for the number of bits storable can be augmented either by decreasing the memory element size or by increasing the chip area over which a satisfactory IC can be fabricated. Recalling the above formula relating yield to chip area and defect density, to be useful such an increasing of the area must be accompanied by a corresponding decrease in the defect density. This second way of increasing the number of bits/chips is called wafer-scale technology, and has been pursued by some companies, notably Trilogy, led by Gene Amdahl, a major contributor formerly to the design of IBM's S/360, and Sinclair Research, headed by Sir Clive Sinclair.

Since, until now, some 2,000 chips can be manufactured on a typical silicon wafer, if the process were developed to the point where a whole wafer could be made reliably into a single monolithic IC, more than a thousandfold increase in the monolithic memory capacity would result without raising the component density. In 1985, however, both Trilogy and Sinclair abandoned their programmes to achieve wafer-scale technology, presumably because of insurmountable, or at least very hard, engineering problems.

In any case, what can be discerned in the curve of Figure 7.3 is that since 1977 the rise in the number of bits of DRAM per monolithic chip has slowed down; to have continued according to 'Moore's law' would have meant the appearance of 1-Mbit chips in the period 1981–3, whereas they began to arrive on the scene commercially in 1986, some three years late, when the 8-Mbit chip should already have been around.

If we set aside for the moment the lower limits to the size of individual components on an IC, set by their electrical requirements, then the drive to further miniaturization is governed by the accuracy and precision with which conductive, capacitative and resistive paths can be created in the surface of the chip and control of the regions in which dopants can be introduced into the silicon lattice. This line-drawing fineness and control of component size is dependent on the lithographic process.

The most common method of producing the lines is ultraviolet lithography (wavelength about 200 μm), which restricts the ultimate spot size to about the same value because of diffraction effects. Other possibilities that are continually being explored are X-ray lithography,

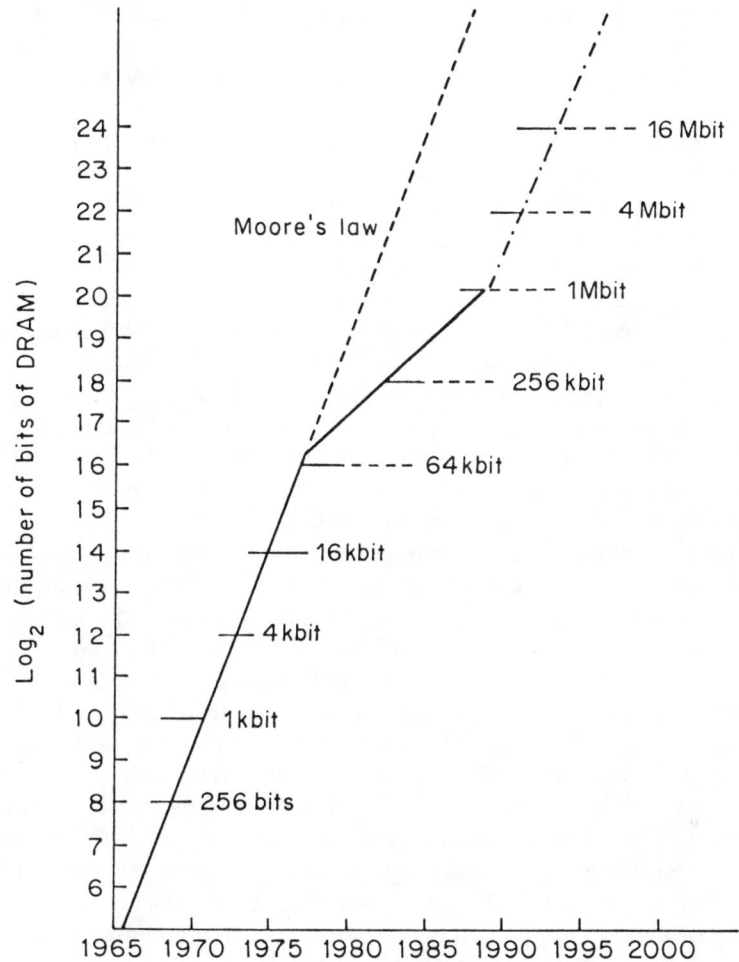

FIGURE 7.3 *'Moore's curve'*: the evolution of the number of components on a single chip, illustrated by DRAMs

with a wavelength of about 0.1 μm, and electron-beam lithography, with a spot size in the range 1–10 nm. Ion beams have also been tried.

It is natural to research into the possibilities of X-ray lithography, for the wavelength of X-rays is some three orders of magnitude less than that of ultraviolet light, which suggests much higher resolving power fixed by the diffraction limit. However, X-rays have one major disadvantage compared with visible light; they are extremely difficult to focus. Notwithstanding this, X-ray lithography is still being worked on and has indeed found some application in this field. This being said, electron-beam lithography seems to be the natural successor, or at least complement, to ultraviolet lithography.

Yet another possible technique is scanning tunnelling microscopy, which is spawning considerable R&D since the inventors (Heinrich Rohrer and Gerd Binning), along with Ernst Ruska who invented the electron microscope in the 1930s, were awarded the 1986 Nobel prize for physics. Several teams hope to turn this mechanical technique of looking at material structure at the atomic level to good purpose in drawing IC conductive paths less than 0.5 μm thick.

In order to draw the narrow lines on the reticles and masks required in the manufacture of ICs, an extreme degree of environmental control is essential. There must be practically no vibration of the beam control and wafer stepping equipment; there must be an extremely low density of dust (or any type of foreign) particles of a size above 50 per cent of the linewidth, in order to reduce the likelihood of short or broken circuits; and the temperature must be controlled so that differential expansion or contraction of parts of the equipment is negligible.

Up until the early 1980s the lithographic process was limited to 5 μm. During the current decade we are experiencing a steady development through currently available 2 and 1 μm machines towards the attainment of sub-micron lithography in the late 1980s. This progression, coupled with more ingenious design of devices and circuits, has enabled the commercial production of single chips with successively 64-, 256- and recently 1,024-Kbit DRAMS, but clearly it cannot go on for ever.

In any case there are scaling-down problems. Whilst all device parameters become more favourable as dimensions decrease, quantum mechanical tunnelling at low voltages may produce undesirable characteristics, and when logic voltage swings become comparable with electronic thermal motion ($\Delta V \sim KT/e = 0.025$ V at 300°C) the needed stability of digital circuits will be lost. This is a fundamental limit.

Perhaps the next step forward in microminiaturization will come with the making of wafer-scale ICs, or from three-dimensional ICs announced by Matsushita in 1985, or from the development of memory and processors based on organic compounds as discussed in Section 7.4.

7.3 NEW ARCHITECTURES ARE OVERDUE

The commonest digital computer architecture, around which nearly all the world's commercial machines are designed, is one in which there is one, and only one, central processing unit which controls the succession of instructions and flow of data through the machine according to instructions stored in programs. It is schematically illustrated in Figure

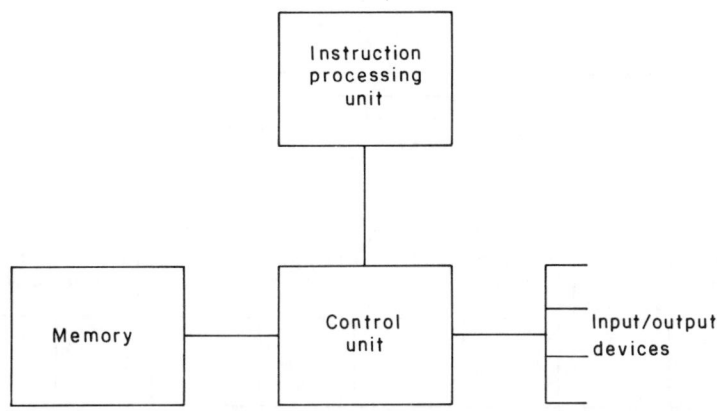

FIGURE 7.4 *Basic architecture of a von Neumann computer*

7.4, and the architecture is named after its originator, Johan von Neumann, who first propounded it in a famous paper in 1946.

An actual 'von Neumann' computer will often have a more complex architecture than that represented in Figure 7.4, but this is a question of degree rather than basic architecture. For example, no matter whether a computer is a microprocessor or a supercomputer, many of them have a communications interface to public or private telecommunications networks. This link with the 'outside world' (other computer systems) is basically no different architecturally from the input/output links shown in Figure 7.4, but it may be treated as a separate case, particularly as the interconnected systems will sometimes be 'foreign' and require standardized interfaces and protocols. Also, many machines have input/output processors that have a certain degree of autonomy but nevertheless are subservient to the unique central processor.

Another complicating factor is that when the memory is very large it is hierarchically structured along the lines shown in Figure 7.5. However, the crucial point related to the machine's architecture is that there is only one channel between the memory devices and control unit.

The principal features of the von Neumann architecture are that the instructions are executed sequentially, one at a time in rapid succession, and that program instructions and data can share the same memory locations. Simplicity and elegance give this architecture engineering advantages. It is centralized, simple to program and only one instruction is executed at a time. Each instruction is taken in the sequence given by the program being executed. Sought in memory, it is brought into the central processing unit where it is decoded and executed, which often requires finding appropriate data in memory and bringing it to the central processing unit. Once one instruction is completed the address of the next instruction is picked up in the program counter and the

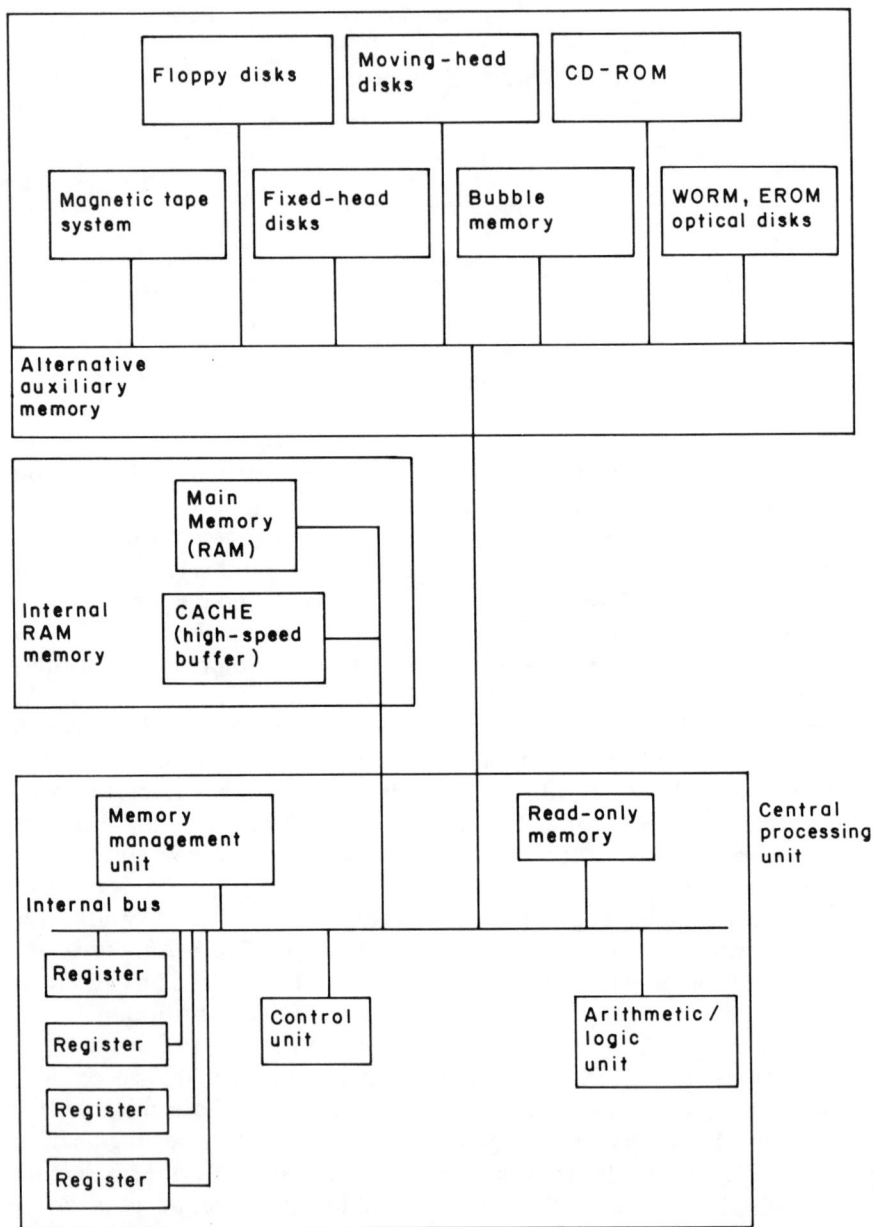

FIGURE 7.5 *Schematic diagram of memory hierarchy in a computer*

instruction execution process begins again. If the programmer has included 'branch' instructions, the result of which may depend on the truth or falsity of some arithmetic or logical condition, the machine may jump from one part of a program to another part of it. However, only one instruction is carried out at a given time. This is monoprocessing as conceived in the von Neumann architecture.

Shortcomings of the von Neumann design

The great weakness of the concept stems from the fact that the most efficient execution of a particular process (or transformation) on a data set is not necessarily a sequential algorithm. When specifying an algorithm for a computer solution to a problem, it is observed that some processes have to be completed before others can be started; such processes have to be executed sequentially and the von Neumann architecture fits the bill. However, these necessarily sequential, or ordered, processes tend to be in the minority; the majority of data processing operations in many applications could be carried out concurrently, in which case parallel processing (multiprocessing) would be more efficient. However, we must avoid going overboard in this direction, because for many applications current computers based on von Neumann's design are sufficiently rapid to solve the problems for which they are intended. (Naturally economic benefits from faster computation may be worth having, particularly when an installation is near saturation.)

Indeed, the other side of the coin is that, since different parts (e.g. processing unit, printers, disk drives, input/output channels) of a computer work at different speeds, the fastest part (the central processing unit) is often idle, waiting for some process (e.g. seeking a record on a disk and bringing it into main memory) to run to completion.

Therefore, there is not much sense in calling for multiprocessor operation at an installation where one processor can only be kept busy for a fraction of its switched-on time. The fact is, there are horses for courses; for some applications von Neumann machines give the best cost/benefit performance, and for others they are sadly lacking in computational power. We shall now examine some of the ways that have been adopted to improve computer performance, both within the von Neumann architecture and through new architectural developments.

In what follows we will examine the nature of parallelism in information processing, possible ways of classifying computer architectures to bring out their degrees of parallelism and some current implementations of underlying concepts aimed at increasing performance price ratios for a given basic technology.

Parallelism in information technology

Any given computer's central processing unit (CPU) has a theoretical maximum power (or capacity) measured in, say, millions of instructions per second (MIPS). In practice, for any given workload and configuration of memory and input/output resources, the actual throughput (also measured in MIPS) will fall somewhere below this theoretical figure. The ratio of throughput to maximum power is a number that represents, in a specific sense, the efficiency with which the workload is being put through that particular configuration. The jobs that make up the workload cannot keep the CPU busy 100 per cent of the time because the data input from peripherals (e.g. magnetic tapes, disks, terminals of various types) takes time to find and transfer through the memory hierarchy to the main memory and registers where it can be picked up by the CPU. This is dead time as far as the CPU is concerned.

One way round this problem, devised in the late 1950s, is to have an operating system that provides multiprogramming. Not to be confused with multiprocessing, most computers, except microcomputers and special systems (such as stand-alone word processors), have multiprogramming operating systems (MPOS). Even many 16-bit and most 32-bit microcomputers do.

Typically an MPOS tries to keep the CPU busy and maximize the throughput of jobs; it enables a wide variety of jobs (computation intensive, input/output intensive) to be processed in parallel by sharing a single processing unit among them in the most efficient way possible. Although we speak of parallelism, in this case only one instruction is being carried out at any one time, but at any one time in general several jobs are in the process of being executed. This kind of parallelism is achieved through software, which puts jobs into different priority queues (ordered first in/first out within them) and, whenever an active job no longer needs the CPU, starts the next, highest-priority job. It should be noted that achieving parallelism is not only a question of hardware architecture; software is also relevant and frequently the interplay between both is important.

It must be pointed out that MPOS can, if they become too complicated, defeat their own purpose and lead to inefficiencies. Indeed, by the end of the 1970s some of the major manufacturers' MPOS for large mainframes had become so complicated, through attempting to handle too wide a spectrum of jobs, that a large percentage of the CPU time was being lost as overhead in deciding which job to switch to next and allocating the necessary resources. So MPOS are no panacea for maximizing the throughput of single processors; moreover the cost of maintaining the complex software in them counteracts to some extent, and may even outweigh sometimes, their advantages, an embarrassment to their suppliers and customers alike.

Multiprogramming was devised to try to maximize the useful work done by a CPU, which otherwise under normal circumstances would be idle for a considerable fraction of its switched-on time. Now let us consider an entirely different problem. Suppose we have a CPU which is occupied 100 per cent of its switched-on time, but its throughput is still inadequate for the achievement of an objective; in other words it is simply not powerful enough. Response times are too long or there is not enough time in the day to get the results required. This is frequently the situation for large scientific calculations such as those found in meteorological forecasting, nuclear power station simulations, single crystal X-ray diffraction analysis, quantum chromodynamics calculations, etc. Another case is computer centres handling commercial aplications when near to saturation. In these circumstances we need to squeeze more processor power from somewhere. Two techniques for doing this are pipelining and multiprocessing.

Multiprocessing provides parallelism, usually at the program level. In nearly all programs, many of the operations that are carried out sequentially could be done concurrently. For example, a programming construct for which this is commonly true is the loop, in which the same sequence of instructions is executed a number of times while an index runs over a set of values; loops are often nested within loops to several levels, resulting in enormous repetition of instruction processing, and even if there is conditional branching inside, it is often possible to replace the sequential execution of n loops by the concurrent execution of a single loop by n processors. Since, in this case, at any one time it is the same instruction being carried out with different data, only one instruction stream is being applied to multiple data streams; this is called vector processing for obvious reasons and has been implemented in machines like the CRAY-1 (first delivered in 1976) and the CDC Cyber 205 (available since 1979).

Whenever a sequence of instructions in a program is data-independent they can be executed in parallel on multiple processors. Among the different possible multiprocessor architectures are processor arrays (e.g. ILLIAC IV, ICL DAP) and looser interconnections of several processors.

Pipelining takes place not at the job level (multiprogramming), nor at the program level (multiprocessing), but at the instruction level; it is a technique for overlapping the suboperations that comprise a particular computer instruction, the microcode. Strictly speaking, it can apply to broader activities carried out by a computer system than those of an operation taken from the machine's instruction set. However, the principle is the same. Suppose all computer instructions consist of n suboperations, which for the same of simplicity take the same period of time, and the computer has a sequence of instructions to be executed. When the first suboperation has been completed, the first suboperation of the next instruction to be carried out, in parallel with the second suboperation of the first instruction, provided that the hardware for decoding and executing instructions is appropriately designed and implemented. By continuing the process, at any given time n operations can be in execution concurrently and the throughput will increase by a factor of the order of n; since n might typically be 4, this represents a considerable power improvement.

Pipelining has been implemented on many commercial computers (e.g. CRAY-1, CDC Cyber 205, CDC 7600, IBM 360/195, ICL 2900) since the 1970s. It can be applied to all computer architectures, including von Neumann, and is a refinement to the design of processing units rather than an architectural innovation of the first degree.

Classifying computer architectures

It is difficult to provide a clear-cut typology of computer architectures, particularly when the interplay between hardware and software is taken into account. Various authors[1] have given classification schemes, but it is difficult to avoid quite different computers falling into the same class, or empty classes, either of which must be considered a weakness.

If we take a computer to consist of one or more stores and one or more processors and ignore input/output (including telecommunications) devices (see Figure 7.4), then Table 7.2 is a useful architectural classification, which separates uniprocessors (UP) from multiprocessors (MP) and machines capable of parallel processing (classes II to VI) from those which cannot (Class I). One evident defect of Table 7.2 is that it does not distinguish clearly between classes V and VI. The basic difference which the splitting of these two classes is intended to bring out is that of partial connectivity of strongly coupled computers (each being a processor and a store) in class V and total connectivity of weakly coupled computers through a switching network in class VI. Both are asynchronous message-passing architectures, but on theoretical grounds and from experimental systems there is reason to suppose that the class VI architecture runs into problems as the number of computers becomes large, whereas class V architectures seem to do better.

To help visualize these architectures, schematic diagrams are set out in Figure 7.6.

Reduced instruction set processors and pipelined processors can occur in any class. Dataflow machines so far realized fall into class I but could

---

[1] M. J. Flynn, 'Very high-speed computing systems', *Proc. IEEE*, **54**, 1901–9 (1966). J. E. Shore, 'Second thoughts on parallel processing', *Comput. Elect. Eng.*, **1**, 95–109 (1973).

Table 7.2 A classification scheme for computer architectures

Class[a]	Acronym[b]	Instruction stream characteristics[c]	Number of processors[c]	Data stream characteristics[c]	Examples
I	SISD (UP)	1	1	1	Classical von Neumann machines. Most commercially available computers, including pipelined scalar ones (e.g. CDC 7600)
II	SIMD (UP)	1	1	M	Pipelined vector computers (e.g. CRAY-1)
III	SIMD (MP)	1	M	M	Array processors (e.g. ICL DAP, ILLIAC IV). Specialized image processors (e.g. CLIP, UCL London)
IV	MISD (MP)	M	M	1	No known implementations. Dataflow machines (e.g. Manchester prototype) could develop in this direction. Optical computers using multiple beam splitting for a single data stream could fall into this class
V	MIMD (MP)	M	M	M	Cosmic cube. Interconnected transputers
VI	MIMD (MP)	M	M	M	Networks of computers

[a] With acknowledgements to Shore for the classification.
[b] With acknowledgements to Flynn for the concepts of single and multiple instruction and data streams leading to SISD, SIMD, MISD and MIMD. UP means uniprocessor and MP multiprocessor.
[c] 1 and M in the main body of the table refer respectively to one or many instruction streams, processors or data streams.

Uniprocessor architectures

I <u>von Neumann</u>
  <u>SISD (UP)</u>

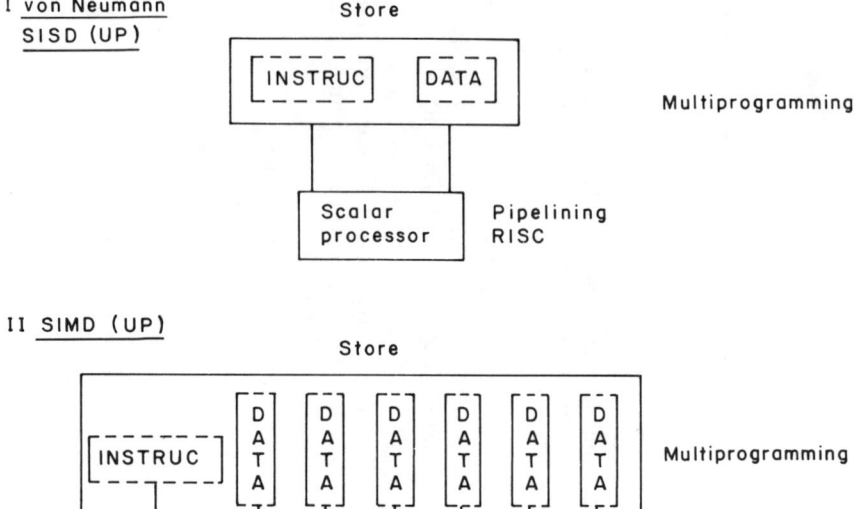

II <u>SIMD (UP)</u>

Multiprocessor architectures

III <u>SIMD (MP)</u>

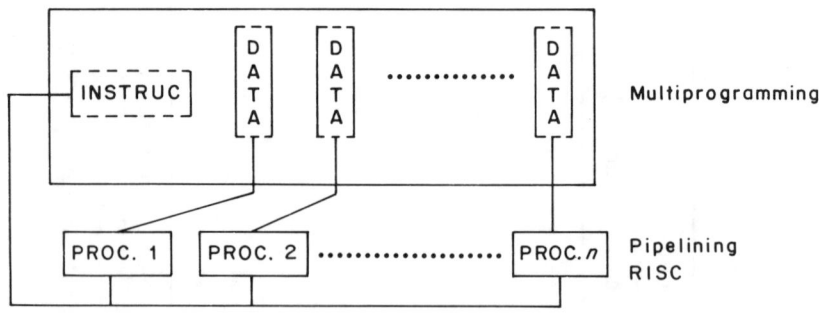

FIGURE 7.6 *Schematic diagrams giving the generic configurations of the classes of computer set out in Table 7.2 and referred to in Section 7.3*

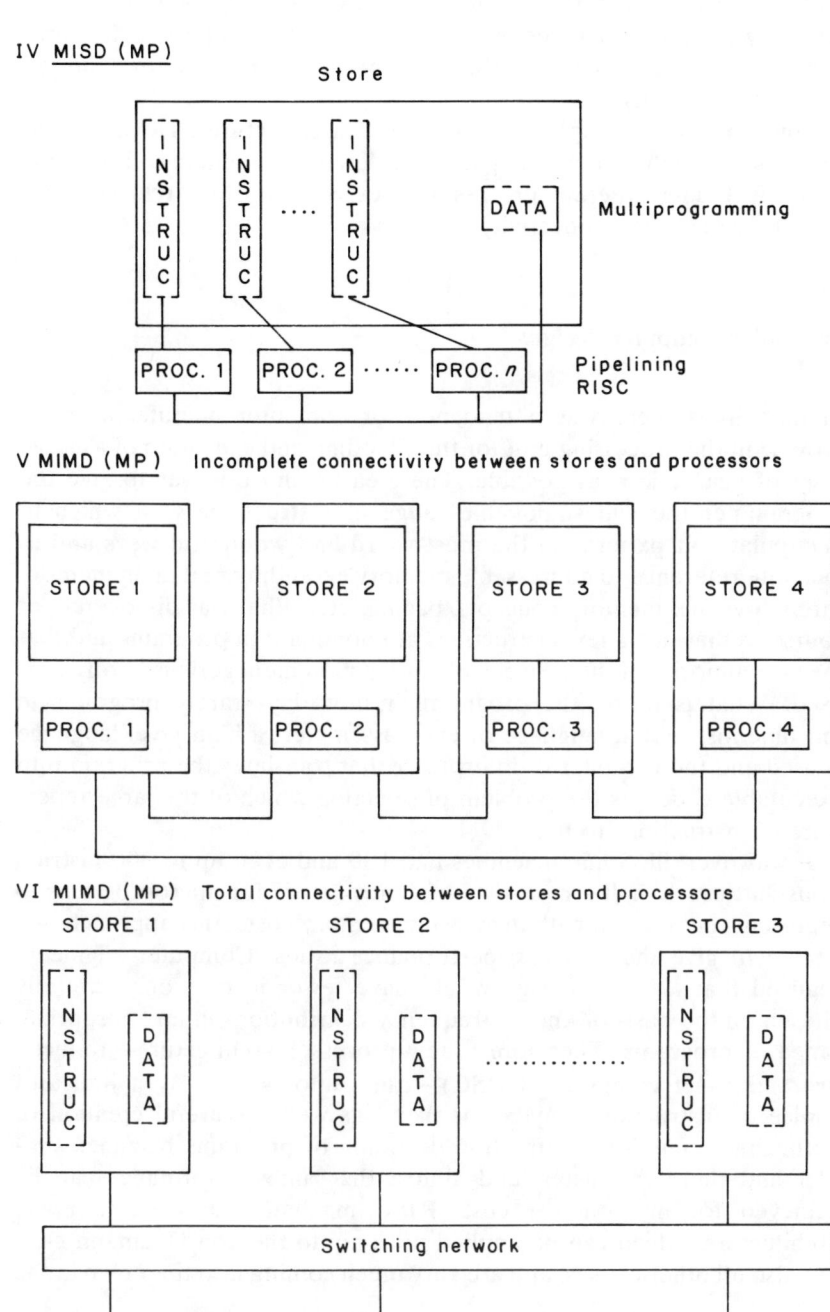

evolve towards class IV which until now is empty, and the same generally goes for machines that implement content-addressable stores (e.g. ICL CAFS, STARAN). Bit-sliced processor architectures can fall into any of the classes III to VI.

Going beyond a simple classification of architectures, Hockney and Jesshope[5] have drawn up a language for describing them in considerable detail, including different processor types, memory hierarchies, input/output devices and connectivity.

Innovative computer designs

In the 1970s there was a tendency for computer manufacturers to provide in the processing unit for the decoding and execution of as large a set of instructions as possible. The idea behind this was to give the programmer the widest possible range of instructions with which to manipulate bit patterns in the most weird and wonderful ways and to facilitate reference to addressable memory exceeding real main memory through virtual memory concepts, paging, etc. What was discovered, of course, is that just a few instructions are dominant in programs and that the vast majority of the conceivable instruction menagerie is hardly ever used. What is more, the programmer nowadays rarely programs in machine instruction language or even assembler; a high-level language is used and the compiler or interpreter that translates the program into executable code has the problem of selecting which of the large repertoire of instructions to use.

It was overkill. Some machines had 100 and even up to 300 instructions and nearly half a megabyte of control store for microprograms to represent them. Even with decreasing memory costs, this approach was unable to give the best cost/performance ratios. Computer engineers realized that a better design would have fewer instructions, carefully chosen on the basis of known frequency distributions in an appropriate range of programs. Therefore a new processor architecture—reduced instruction set computers (RISC)—came into being.[6] By a judicious choice of instructions, say 50 of them, as well as careful creation of optimizing compilers, instruction decoding of programs becomes simpler and therefore faster, and almost the same performance can be achieved for much lower cost. RISC machines represent a novel architecture, which can be applied not only to the von Neumann class but also all other classes, and are very much coming into their own in the

---

[5]R. W. Hockney and C. R. Jesshope, *Parallel Computers*, Adam Hilger Ltd, Bristol, 1981.
[6]See also Section 5.1.

1980s. Processing units of RISC machines can more easily be fabricated in silicon (or other semiconducting material) than those of the 1970s with their unnecessary complexity.

Another architectural concept beginning to make headway in the mid-1980s is that of the dataflow machine, which is radically different from the von Neumann model. We have already noted that, in almost any program, many of the steps can logically be executed in parallel; to do so physically requires only that one has more than one processing unit. However, we can go further, for merely providing more processors begs the question of how the program instructions are allocated among them in time.

The trick is to look at the problem not from the algorithm (or program instructions) point of view, but to consider it from the data side. As soon as data is ready and available to be operated on (e.g. added, compared, sent to a printer), it is so treated by any available processor. In other words, in the resultant architecture, called dataflow, instead of trying to make sure that a processor is kept busy all the time, which is what multiprogramming tries to do while the data hangs around in store until the program condescends to call it into action, the reverse takes place. As soon as data is available a processor has to jump to it in double quick time and service the data. Of course, there have to be enough processors if zero delays are to be achieved, but even if there are not, this architecture minimizes the time data is waiting for processing, when the number of processors and their speed is a constraint.

Two other machines worth mentioning for their innovative architectures are the Cosmic Cube, developed at the California Institute of Technology, and the Transputer, developed by Inmos, the IC manufacturer set up in the United Kingdom with a mixture of government and private finance. The latter is a microprocessor designed so that many of them can be put together in multiprocessing configurations.

The Cosmic Cube is an 'array' of computers interconnected in a special way, isomorphous with the edges that interconnect the vertices of a hypercube, from which equivalence it gets its mystical name. It is generic for a whole family of machines, depending on the dimensionality of the hypercube. Cosmic Cubes with four, eight and sixty-four nodal computers (corresponding respectively to two-, three- and six-dimensional hypercubes) have been built. In each case, each node is connected to n others, where n is the dimensionality and there are 2^n nodes.

Thus the six-cube has 64 identical nodal computers each with six connexions to other nodal computers. A nodal computer has a processing unit (Intel 8086/8087) and memory (128-Kbytes RAM and 8-Kbytes ROM) and communicates asynchronously with other nodes through message-passing at 2 Mbits/s. The various parameters of the Cosmic Cube design have been chosen by compromise via extensive simulation; they would normally depend on the type of application for which the machine will be used and the cost.

The Cosmic Cube architecture is that of a tightly coupled, localized array of cooperating computers, in which only nearest neighbours (in the hypercube sense) communicate through messages; there is no shared storage, nor is there a centralized control unit. Its developers believe that shared-memory, concurrent processing architectures are generally better for machines with tens of processors, but that message-passing designs like the Cosmic Cube are more likely to succeed where hundreds, or even thousands, of processors are cooperating concurrently on a problem.

Inmos' Transputer is a single-chip computer, specially designed for highly concurrent processing, and could be used in a Cosmic Cube but is not limited to such highly structured processor arrays. It has a 10-MIPS processor, 2-Kbytes RAM memory, 32-bit wide memory interface and four 10-Mbits/s input/output lines on the chip. The processor has an RISC architecture. A special language, OCCAM, specifically developed for programming parallel algorithms, has been developed. Arrays of Transputers are capable of achieving 500–1,000 MIPS. Within the ESPRIT programme of the European Community a French–British collaboration is working to create Europe's first home-grown supercomputer based on Transputers.

Here we have mentioned a few innovative architectures, but many companies and universities are carrying out, in their laboratories, R&D in this field. Cray Research Inc., International Computers Ltd, Thinking Machines Corp., Siemens, Burroughs Corp., Goodyear Aerospace, Concurrent Computer Corp. (a division of Perkin Elmer) and Floating Point Systems are some of the major contenders in this top end of the computer market, which is destined for rapid growth in the near future.

In the 1980s we have seen a renaissance of computer architecture development. Many of the fundamental ideas were thought of much earlier in the evolution of computers, but after pushing the von Neumann architecture almost to its limits throughout the 1960s and 1970s and realizing that semiconductor technology progress may be coming up against asymptotic limits, computer engineers in the late 1970s and 1980s have turned their attention to the development of these novel architectural ideas. This work will produce a blossoming of supercomputers in the 1990s; hundreds or thousands of times more powerful than current mainframe products, they will, together with the proliferation of von Neumann microcomputers, change the face of computing in many large organizations. Orthodox mainframes with processing powers in the range 2–10 MIPS seem set to be squeezed out of the middle like cream from an eclair.

7.4 COULD THE OPTICAL COMPUTER BE THE ANSWER?

At the beginning of Section 7.1 we described the two basic requirements for building computing machines, namely: memory elements for storing data and programs, and devices for carrying out arithmetical and logical operations on data. In Sections 7.1 and 7.2 we discussed materials that satisfy these requirements because they exhibit ferromagnetism and semiconduction. Ferromagnetism arises from the cooperative alignment of the spins of certain atomic systems in crystals, and semiconduction occurs when the electrons least tightly bound to atoms in crystals (of silicon, gallium arsenide, etc.) can achieve a reasonably high, yet variable, mobility when a variable electric field is applied. In other words, the two functions of data storage and processing are achieved solely through the behaviour of electrons in crystals.

The squeeze is on 2–10 MIPS mainframes

Experimental results obtained in laboratories during the last twelve years or so point to the possibility of using optical rather than electronic properties of materials to perform these two data storage and processing functions. Of course, the optical properties of materials are determined mainly by electronic structure, but the key difference is that in this instance the carriers of energy are no longer electrons but photons of the electromagnetic field. The consequences are highly significant.

In vacuum, electromagnetic waves travel at the velocity of light, which is about 186,000 miles per second, whereas in materials that transmit light, they move typically at around two-thirds of this speed. Consequently, the speeds at which information can be carried are much greater with photons than with electrons, which travel at only about 300 miles per second in a 'fast' material like gallium arsenide.

It is common knowledge that computers store information as binary digits (0 and 1), called bits. When performing logic operations, the results are either 'true' or 'false', which again requires two states. The basic circuit elements that carry out logic operations can be combined to execute simple or complex calculations, with the help of the three logic gates: OR, AND and NOT, and combinations thereof. In fact, because of necessary relationships among these three logic operations it transpires that all possible data manipulations can be achieved with just one type of logic gate—either a NAND (not AND) or a NOR gate. Thus, to construct a digital computer the minimal requirement is a bistable device from which to make two-state logic and storage elements. A superior solution by far would be n-state logic—though there would be a risk that physical devices with n stable states ($n > 2$) might be less reliable.

Some materials, e.g. indium antimonide (also composed interestingly enough from elements in the same groups of Mendeleyev's periodic table as the compound semiconductors of Section 7.1), exhibit a physical property, optical bistability, that lends credence to the idea that extremely fast optical computers will become operational in the 1990s, if not before. Predicted in 1969 and first observed in 1974, optical bistability is currently being extensively researched on both sides of the Atlantic and in Japan. Dr Alan Huang, director of the newly formed Optical Computing Department at AT&T Bell Laboratories, is confident that his team should be able to create a primitive prototype by early 1987, and a working full-scale model four years later. Advanced work is also being carried out at Heriot-Watt University in Edinburgh. However, the decisive impulse is now likely to come from SDI under whose umbrella the Optical Computing Consortium, made up of a dozen high-tech firms and universities, was set up in 1985. There is also the possibility that through the EUREKA initiative, put forward by the French Government in 1985 and gaining support from other European Community countries, a strong push towards the construction of a European optical computer will be attempted by a consortium of advanced IT companies and universities.

What is the physical basis of this new direction for computers of the future? It is really quite complicated, but we can gain a superficial impression of how optically bistable devices work without delving too deeply into the physics. Further details can be found in the article by Abraham, Seaton and Smith.[1]

At the root of the physical effect is that when electromagnetic waves of a particular wavelength are transmitted through some materials, the refractive index of the material changes with beam intensity in a non-linear way, giving rise to refractive bistability. Incidentally, a particular kind of optical bistability well known to most people, at least those who wear glasses, is illustrated by so-called photochromic lenses, which go dark when the sunlight becomes bright and revert to their normal transparency when the ambient light intensity falls again. This is termed absorptive bistability. As anyone who has worn such glasses will know, the switching speed, particularly from dark to light, can be disturbingly slow.

The discovery of non-linear refraction had to await the invention of the laser. Without the laser's coherent radiation in which all the peaks and

---

[1] E. Abraham, C. T. Seaton and S. D. Smith, *Scientific American*, **248**, No. 2, 63 (February 1983).

troughs are lined up in time and space, its observation would have been missed because of smearing-out effects resulting from the distribution of phases of different wavelets in incoherent (even monochromatic) radiation.

To make optical stores and switches, which can act as logic gates, in addition to a material showing non-linear refraction, the other requirement is an optical apparatus called a Fabry–Perot interferometer, invented in 1896 by Charles Fabry and Alfred Perot in order to measure accurately the wavelength of light from various sources. The Fabry–Perot interferometer optical switch consists of a crystal of the material with non-linear refractive index between two partially reflecting mirrors. Indium antimonide is a suitable non-linear material that works with electromagnetic radiation of about 5μm and can be generated conveniently by a carbon monoxide laser. The non-linearity of indium antimonide is between 100 and 1,000 times that of gallium arsenide. As the intensity of radiation into the interferometer from the carbon monoxide laser increases, the refractive index of the indium antimonide changes non-linearly, which causes the transmitted intensity to increase non-linearly; when the incident laser intensity falls, initially the transmitted intensity stays at the higher level and only falls to a lower level when the incident intensity falls below a certain threshold. Thus the plot of incident against transmitted radiation intensity exhibits a hysteresis loop, as illustrated in Figure 7.7(a) analogous to magnetic hysteresis used for magnetic storage of information. Such an optical device is bistable and can be used to store bits of information.

The hysteresis loop can be collapsed into the single curve of Figure 7.7(b) by suitable manipulation of the interferometer parameters. This curve is similar to the transfer characteristic of a transistor; in this form the interferometer can be utilized to make logic gates, and is called a transphasor.

In a transphasor a reference beam (analogous to the emitter–collector

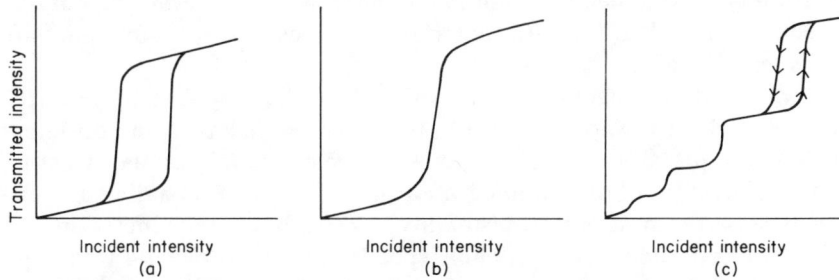

FIGURE 7.7 *A Fabry–Perot cavity filled with a crystal of optically birefringent material such as indium antimonide shows (a) hysteresis, (b) amplification and (c) multistable states. (Copyright © February 1983 by Scientific American, Inc. All rights reserved)*

current of a transistor) is modulated by a probe beam (analogous to the base–collector current). Therefore we can construct memory and logic from materials that exhibit non-linear refraction; in this way optical bistability will enable the creation of a new breed of computer.

In addition to switching speeds of the order of 1,000 times faster than current electronic logic, optical computers offer the prospect of simple parallel processing by using multibeam interferometry. One incident laser beam could be split into a number (say n) of optical paths, each of which could be passed simultaneously through different transphasors performing the operations of logic gates and arithmetic processors. Thus, n operations could be executed in parallel. Such a machine might be an example of an MISD multiprocessor in Flynn's terminology (see Section 7.3, class IV of Table 7.2).

Similarly, direct image processing through a thin-film array of optical switches seems attainable. In the longer term this could enable not only image sharpening in real time, i.e. no delays introduced through having to store images and then process them, but also pattern recognition, i.e. extraction of features from images, at very high speeds.

Yet another prospect opened up by optical computers is that of many-valued logic. We have considered single bistability of the type best illustrated by the single hysteresis loop in Figure 7.7(b). Non-linear optical materials exhibit multiple bistability, as indicated in Figure 7.7(c), and so more that two transmission states of the Fabry–Perot cavity can be obtained by varying the incident beam intensity. Therefore, we have the opportunity of building computers based not on binary logic and arithmetic, but on ternary, quaternary ... or even denary (i.e. decimal). Perhaps we shall feel more at home with machines that count in the same arithmetic system as we do.

Another advantage such optical computers will have, compared with electronic computers, will be their suitability for interworking directly through optical fibres at very high data rates, probably >1 Gbit/s. Before leaving optical computers we must stress that at present their feasibility is still being explored in the research laboratory, but the results obtained so far with materials, switches, transphasors, etc., are most encouraging.

Among the questions being explored at the moment by research teams working towards the first optical computers based on non-linear refraction, probably the crucial ones are: What should be the structure and architecture of optical integrated circuits? Which crystalline materials possess the best optical bistability? Which laser frequencies are the most appropriate? What switching speeds are achievable and what light intensities are best to use? How should optical computers be slotted into the electronic computer scene in ways that do not create interface problems? We can be almost sure that these and related questions will soon be answered and that the answers will probably lead to the dawn of a new computing age, before the end of the century.

Mimicking the human nervous system

Although optical computers promise truly dramatic increases in computational power, they will surely not be the end of the developmental pathway. It is perhaps no coincidence that carbon, the element at the basis of life, is in the same group of the periodic table as silicon and germanium, the elemental semiconductors on which the majority of computers so far constructed have been based. Both carbon and silicon (with similar electronic configurations) are capable of combining to form large molecules of long chain or complex ring compounds, but the former is much more productive in this direction.

Whereas memory and processing elements in computers are in general made from crystalline materials containing vast numbers of identical atoms, ions or molecules stacked together in regular arrays, many of the memory and processing functions of the brain and nervous system of animals seem to work at the level of a single molecule or perhaps a small number of similar molecules. Even though the organic molecules in question are much larger than the atoms, ions and molecules of common-or-garden inorganic semiconductors, since even for the smallest devices built into today's ICs, literally thousands of millions of millions of millions of atoms, ions or molecules are involved, the organic information processor offers dramatic microminiaturization possibilities. The average human brain size is about 1,400 cm^3, which is the same volume as a cube with sides of about 11.2 cm. A square chip of silicon of this dimension would have an area of some 125 cm^2, or about 208 times the area of the new 1-Mbit dynamic random access chips which came into quantity production in 1986. Therefore, two-dimensional ICs with linear dimensions comparable to those of the brain could store today of the order of 200 Mbits of data. The brain's capacity is difficult to estimate, but certainly much greater than this figure, perhaps somewhere in the region of 10^{15} bits! Thus organic macromolecules in the brain are organized to achieve much greater information density than current semiconductor technology for two principal reasons: (1) three-dimensional rather than two-dimensional structures are used and (2) the large molecules involved can take up vast numbers of configurations and interact with each other in very many, yet highly specific, ways to provide very much denser coding of information than is attainable with two-state crystalline semiconductor structures.

Although the brain is superior to present computers in its information storage density, when it comes to information transmission rates and sequential processing power it has been left a long way behind by computers ever since their beginnings in the 1940s. Examples of computer superiority are the addition of a million numbers in less than a second and the ability to react to a signal in less than a microsecond. Human beings simply do not achieve these levels of sequential data processing.

Transmission of information in biological systems takes place in the liquid phase rather than the solid. This gives rise, even at the macroscopic level, to probabilistic outcomes rather than 100 per cent predictable (predetermined) results. The brain has therefore evolved to work with fuzzy logic; it may well be that some of the more remarkable features of human information processing (such as natural language, image analysis/pattern recognition, rapid retrieval from long-term memory) result from the application of fuzzy logic. Conversely, machines operating with binary logic and deterministic algorithms may not be well adapted to solving these types of problems.

The other way in which the brain compensates for its weak sequential data processing power is through extensive use of parallel processing.

The question is: What should be the future direction for computer development? Should we try to extend the domain of research beyond classical semiconducting/ferromagnetic machines and optical computers to encompass a new species of computer based on organic macromolecules and biological systems? Or will computer R&D stay within the inorganic materials domain and efforts be launched to develop machines (hardware and software) that can interface more efficiently and effectively with human beings?

For sheer number-crunching and fast reaction to incoming signals, computers based on the same materials and principles used in existing machines, with the addition of optical computers and new architectures, will continue to satisfy the requirements and offer increasing performance. On the other hand, the development of entirely new machines using materials and procedures more akin to those operating in biological systems would seem likely to pay benefits ultimately in the field commonly known as artificial intelligence (expert systems, natural language processors, pattern recognition, etc.), where fuzzy logic may be an essential ingredient.

Two approaches to open up this new field are: (1) the simulation of neurons and synapses (where neurons interconnect) by classical systems based on traditional hardware and software (so-called perceptrons have been under investigation in the laboratory since the late 1950s, a time when major artificial intelligence breakthroughs seemed to some experts to be just around the corner) and (2) the development of new semiconducting materials based on organic compounds.

The first approach is only a simulation, and therefore its contribution is likely to increase understanding of how the brain processes information but not to the implementation of biological computers. In this respect the second approach is more promising, but it is likely that the route to computers based on organic materials and biological systems will be an extremely long and arduous one. One organic material, a polymer called polyacetylene, has already been the subject of much research. It shows electrical conductivity by reason of a special alternating arrangement of bonds between the carbon atoms in the chain that constitutes the backbone of the polymerized molecules; this gives rise to controllable conductivity when donor atoms such as sodium or acceptors such as iodine are incorporated between the chains. This is similar to doping silicon with boron or arsenic to turn it into a usable semiconductor. Japanese chemists succeeded in 1985 in making the first diode (a p–n junction), or rectifier, out of polyacetylene. To do this they have had to overcome the chief drawback of the material, namely the fact that it breaks down through oxidation in air.

This is of course only a minor step. We are a long way from controlling the electrical and optical properties of complex organic compounds found in the information processing centres and pathways of a typical mammalian nervous system and brain. However, the manufacture of semiconducting devices in polyacetylene is a start, and many other organic materials are being explored.

In fact, both these approaches acting in unison may lead to significant advances in the direction of combining the benefits of the two broadly different types of computer.

7.5 CONCLUSION AND OUTLOOK

In the foregoing sections we have considered in an elementary way a range of basic materials of interest to information technology and we have explored in a superficial way their electrical and optical properties. Moreover, we have looked at ways of making useful devices from these materials, highlighting in particular the epitaxial processes of growing single crystals, the limits to microminiaturization, new machine architecture possibilities and potential advances in optical computers and organic machines.

The main conclusions which arise from this brief survey are the following:

1. We are experiencing, since 1948, an exciting prospection of Mendeleyev's periodic table. It started with the elemental group IV semiconductors Si and Ge, and since the mid-1960s it has spread to compound III/V semiconductors such as GaAs, InP, GaP, etc. More recently ternary and quaternary alloys like GaAlAs and GaAlPAs have begun to be used in heterostructures. This search for new materials continues unabated and gives us the possibility of *tailor-made devices* for specific applications. There is as yet no end in sight to this exploration of the world of group III/V semiconductors and their challenge to the group IV progenitors.

2. In order to produce good single crystals (chips) of these materials, and the precise doping of them, the world of 'atomic engineering' has been opened up. Epitaxy, especially with molecular beams, has become a controlled process which gives us the staggering possibility, in the last few years, of building crystals practically one atomic layer at a time on high-quality crystalline substrates. This permits strained layer superlattices to be built, and multilayer crystals like neapolitan wafers enable today's solid-state technologists to tailor-make lattice spacings, and thus electron energy bands, and therefore exciting new devices.
3. In the field of microminiaturization, since the late 1970s it has not proved possible to continue to follow Moore's curve—a doubling of the number of components per chip each year. Nevertheless, considerable efforts are being made to reduce the area per circuit element by exploring a range of technologies (NMOS, CMOS, I^{2}L, etc.) and clever designs. We can, moreover, expect to push the etching process from its current 1.0–1.5 μm line widths in easy stages to 0.5 μm and then 0.25 μm, after which no further progress seems likely in increasing the component density of two-dimensional ICs.
4. Another way of increasing the number of components per chip is to increase the chip size. Despite the falterings of Trilogy and Sinclair, wafer-scale technology will almost certainly be achieved in the 1990s; it will lead to extremely powerful processors and large fast memories on single slices of semiconductor. With a powerful 32-bit microprocessor and 1-Gbit of memory on a single wafer, portable and desktop computers are likely to make mainframes go the way of dinosaurs.

    In the same vein, after wafer-scale fabrication has been mastered, R&D will lead towards the three-dimensional IC, which will also dramatically increase the power of microprocessors and the capacity of solid-state memories, and at the same time bring us nearer to systems that structurally mimic the brain more closely.
5. Optical disks, both 12 in platter videodisks and 4$\frac{3}{4}$ in (12 cm) digital audio/CD-ROM products, will penetrate the market for microcomputer storage to the detriment of magnetic storage (floppies and cassettes), though Winchesters and thin-film magnetic disks, by virtue of their shorter access times, will hold their own for certain applications.
6. On the architectural front we shall see a burgeoning of concurrent processing machines and a decrease in the number of instructions processing units will perform. In other words, multiprocessing will be combined with reduced instruction sets to provide more powerful computers. Dataflow principles will come into their own in commercial implementations. Compilers will optimally map algorithms onto

the reduced instruction sets, and new parallel algorithms and programming languages will become common tools of the 1990s.
7. It seems likely that computing systems with small numbers of processors will share memory units among the processing units through switching networks (like exchanges in the telephone network interconnecting the customer telephones), whereas systems comprised of hundreds or thousands of processors will have local memory at each processor and communications between them will consist of asynchronous messages. Many developments are anticipated in this field of concurrent processing.
8. There will be a new battleground before the turn of the century. This will be between machines based on ferromagnetism and semiconduction, using mixtures of silicon and gallium arsenide ICs, and advanced concurrent architectures, on the one hand, and optical computers, on the other. One certainty is that, before the year 2000, optical computers will be around, but they may still be too expensive for all applications except those that require so much computational speed that there is no alternative.
9. A growing field of R&D effort in the coming decade will concern organic semiconductors and the potential of carbon compounds in information technology in general. We foresee a convergence of research endeavours from diverse fields that will have for its objective a better understanding of the nature of intelligence—human and artificial. Deeper knowledge of the brain structure and the dynamics of brain processes will be sought with a view to carrying over to computers methods and techniques developed by nature through the evolutionary process. Man and computer will come that bit nearer to a valuable symbiosis, the result of which will be so much greater than the sum of the parts.

Chapter 8

Closing the Software Gap and Beyond

Every dollar currently spent on hardware is matched, and sometimes doubled, by the cost of software. Among the customers a consensus is developing that they are not getting their money's worth. As the expenditure on software keeps rising out of all proportions, so does the user dissatisfaction.

Furthermore, as computers and their applications proliferate into myriads of networks, the need for high-performance software, albeit simple and adequate, grows dramatically. Thus, the expression 'software gap', which appears in the title of this chapter, refers to inadequacy of existing software both relative to hardware and also in relation to unsatisfied user wants and expectations.

However, when the professionals in the information community talk about the need to 'close' this gap, more often than not they have in mind something more than just bridging the current hiatus between hardware and software. Perhaps the most remarkable characteristic of the digital computer is its general applicability for solving problems—or, at least, for solving problems for which a solution method can be specified as a computable algorithm. This particular constraint looks somewhat less compelling now than it was until recently. Whilst we are still very much in the dark regarding the full potentialities of artificial intelligence, the best of the few existing expert systems suggest that the problem-solving capabilities of the computer could be extended through a new software philosophy and system design.

On the other hand, claims to bridge the software gap can be overoptimistic, and, when this happens, consequential damages are usually heavy and enduring. Asking analysts and programmers to write software that would ensure fully automatic translation from Russian to English, or expecting quick progress towards speech recognition, or clamouring for high-performance distributed systems, is like reaching for the stars, at least within the next few years. Advances in these areas do not depend on programmers' skill, but they are contingent upon prior, considerable improvement in our understanding of such phenomena as human speech, human intelligence or again the laws that govern the behaviour of complex systems.

Twenty-five years of wasted effort and frustration followed the irresponsible announcement made by IBM in the early 1950s that an error-free machine translation system would be commercially available for any pair of languages within ten years. In the early 1980s a consensus emerged that priority should be given simply to developing machine aids to translation, an approach that flies in the face of the initial concept.

These are, then, some of the key issues discussed in the next five sections, dedicated to different aspects of the ongoing software revolution.

8.1 GOING IT THE GM WAY

People in Western democracies never tire of listening to the story of the underdog who wins in the end, of the poor boy who becomes a millionnaire or of an upstart company in Silicon Valley that outsmarts IBM. There is no denying that small entrepreneurs and bright innovators play an important role in the advancement of the computer business. This being said, it is only fair to credit a small number of megaprojects, launched or sponsored by very large organizations, with major breakthroughs in software conceptualization and development. To underscore this point, we have selected half-a-dozen real-life illustrations.

The history, mixed with legend, of IBM S/360, specified and announced in 1964 and first delivered (models 40 and 50) in mid-1965, still contains lessons whose validity has not diminished through aging.

OS/360: the pioneer software

Why was the S/360 such a major success? Other manufacturers had products with more advanced technology in them, faster processing speeds, more interesting memory management and more varied input/output facilities, but Big Blue won the race into the 1970s. In large measure the answer lay in IBM's understanding of the need to put emphasis on appropriate systems software. The operating system of the S/360 was designed with a specific purpose in mind: to increase serviceability through automatic fault location and reduction of service-call duration; to achieve portability of programs across the model range through compatibility of systems for memory and file management, and input/output device control, as well as of language compilers; and to provide emulation of other model ranges through microprogramming. This latter facility enabled customers to pursue easy migration of systems from other model ranges to the S/360, particularly IBM's own, but even those of other manufacturers. This was a sound strategy based on a profound understanding of the importance of the software environment of computing systems and the interdependence of software and hardware design.

The major software contribution to the success of S/360 was its operating system (OS/360), which steadily evolved from the primary control program and disk operating system (DOS), through multiprogramming with a fixed number of tasks (MFT) and multiprogramming with a variable number of tasks (MVT), to multiple virtual storage (MVS) and virtual machine facility (VM). The last-mentioned are in use today on S/370 computers and the more recent, compatible 30XX machines. From an overall market viewpoint, the disadvantage of this family of operating systems is that they tie the user to IBM hardware; they work only on IBM computers because of their intimate relation with the hardware. In essence, OS/360 was a resounding success because it met the diverse but clearly identifiable requirements of its customer base.

Turning now from operating systems to programming languages, COBOL is a fine example of a successful megaproject, which had durable impact on the software scene. COBOL, or common business-oriented language, originated in the late 1950s, championed by Commander Grace Hopper of Sperry Rand Corp. and the United States Navy. As its name suggests, it is well adapted to programming systems for the business community, e.g. accounting systems, personnel records and management information systems. Since the programming of computers for business purposes has overtaken and outdistanced their use for solving scientific and engineering problems, COBOL programming is nowadays far more common than any other. The reason it has triumphed is that, here again, clear goals were set for it, but in this case by a powerful user group—the US Navy—rather than a hardware supplier. The business community, the main beneficiary of COBOL, was only too pleased to add its support for the definition, development, standardization and use of it as a first-choice programming language.

A more recent attempt to close the software gap by means of a high-level language is ADA,[1] designed for the US Department of Defense for embedded and real-time systems, which are not handled well by languages developed earlier, like FORTRAN and COBOL. Its origins were French and British efforts and its definition and specification began in the mid-1970s. By 1975 the Department of Defense was spending more than $3 billion per year on software, using more than 400 languages and dialects, and wanted to control escalation of software costs. To do this a major investment had to be made in tools to enhance productivity, and improvements had to be achieved in the average programmer's programming methodology. Having started ADA development in 1977, an ANSI[2] standard was agreed in February

---

[1] ADA is a registered trademark of the United States Department of Defense.
[2] ANSI = American National Standards Institute.

1983. This is slow progress, but nevertheless progress, and with the backing of the US Department of Defense, as well as major efforts in Europe to provide a vital stable ADA programming environment (including financial contributions from the European Community's multiannual informatics programme), ADA is perhaps now, in the mid-1980s, on the launching pad towards a rosy future.

Front-seat drivers versus kibitzers

The giant, General Motors, is the prime mover apart from the military behind one of the largest ever megaprojects, MAP,[3] specially developed to meet user requirements yet having broader implications. After suffering heavy losses for several years the management of GM came to the conclusion that, in order to beat off Japanese competition, the company would have to acquire the ability to produce low-price cars in large quantities as well as great variety to meet individual customer's needs. In other words, integrated product design, flexible manufacturing and responsive marketing became the main goal for the company, subject naturally to adequate profits. Consequently, there would have to be a complete redeployment of computers, powered by entirely new purpose-driven software. This integrated approach to computerization has recently been dubbed JIT, or just in time technology—a sure sign that the bandwagon has begun to roll.

Since existing islands of computerization could not communicate with one another (incompatible data interchange protocols from different machine suppliers, machines 'speaking' different lingos—a modern Tower of Babel) the company earmarked several billions of dollars to overcome this complex of problems. This proved to be an effective way of achieving the required coherence, and once again lent support to the old adage—he who pays the piper (generously enough) calls the tune. Other large users became associated with the MAP initiative; among them were: Ford, Du Pont, IBM, Eastman Kodak, John Deere, McDonnell Douglas and Boeing. MAP-user groups are being set up also in Canada, Japan and in Europe, where in the United Kingdom alone 70 manufacturers are reported[4] to have joined the European MAP Users' Group. In fact by early 1986 there were no fewer than 400 companies worldwide in the MAP Users' Group.[5] MAP is a concerted effort to put into practice the OSI[6] seven-layer model architecture for data interchange of the International Standards Organization (ISO), itself an

---

[3] MAP = Manufacturing Automation Protocol. For further details see, for example, J. Bartik, *Data Communications*, December 1985, p. 147.
[4] *Computer Weekly*, 27 February 1986.
[5] *The International Herald Tribune*, 28 February 1986.
[6] OSI = Open System Interconnection.

endeavour to bring under control the growing gap between hardware and software engineering capabilities. OSI will be described briefly later on.

Another action like MAP is TOP, which is centred around office automation and whose major protagonist is the Boeing Company. It aims also to implement OSI, but, within the class of possible choices of protocols in the seven-layer OSI model, shows certain acceptable differences from MAP, resulting from its different field of application. TOP will, however, lead to systems compatible in principle with MAP because they both conform with OSI. In the standards field MAP and TOP are equally valid approaches (led by users) to the problem of driving different suppliers to put the OSI model into practice. Although not definitely committed, by early 1986, IBM, Wang and Xerox had expressed interest in TOP.

The markets at stake for MAP and TOP products will be measured in billions of dollars by 1990—hence the significance of these megaprojects aimed at overcoming software deficiencies. Making these systems compatible is the next logical step, which is already envisaged by the COS[7] endeavour.

The US Navy can justly claim to have played its part in making sense out of the software jungle. Following its considerable efforts with COBOL, since the beginning of 1983 the US Navy has been active in setting a new standard for word processing. Called Document Interchange Format (DIF), it will enable different vendors' word processors to exchange texts in such a way that they can be worked on (edited) at the receiving station.

The project to implement DIF is the Department of the Navy Office Automation and Communications System (DONOACS). Whilst there are some 200 word processing packages on microcomputers using different coding schemes, the ultimate target is to render them all capable of interworking. DONOACS focused on Datapoint, Fortune, Wang and Xerox in the first place, and now DEC, Data General and Four Phase are being put through their paces at the DIF test laboratory. Similar initiatives are ODA/ODIF[8] at IBM, MHS[9] within the Consultative Committee for International Telephony and Telegraphy (X400 Series recommendations) and MOTIS within ISO, and the Teletex Service of CCITT.

We have glanced at selected case histories quite different in their approaches, that have piloted the way towards improved software environments. By design, we did not include in that brief review several very ambitious schemes, such as the Japanese program for the so-called fifth

---

[7]COS = Corporation for Open Systems.
[8]ODA/ODIF = Office Document Architecture/Office Document Interchange Format.
[9]MHS = Message Handling System.

generation of computers, the European Community sponsored action plan ESPRIT aiming at precompetitive R&D cooperation and also various national R&D efforts, e.g. the Alvey Programme in the United Kingdom and EUREKA, proposed by France and now being pursued by several European countries. However promising, these projects have not yet reached an advanced stage and yielded conclusive evidence as to the impact they might have one day on the software scene.

The foregoing analysis of the complex field of software production leads to the conclusion that the following criteria are the key ones that determine success or failure in large-scale projects with significant and enduring impact on the software environment:

1. A precise understanding of the opportunities offered by computers to the business enterprise or government function as a whole and the definition of a global strategy for getting there is a *sine qua non* condition for success. A good example of this in practice is MAP and the background work of Dr Eliahn Goldratt, whose company, Creative Output, has produced a software development system called Optimized Production Technology.[10]
2. The driving force has to be a powerful group with money to invest, adequate staff resources and professional management; this is independent of whether the group is a supplier of the technology, a public or private user of the technology or a government that decides to intervene as part of its overall industrial, social and economic strategy.
3. A critical mass must be reached, i.e. a large market of interested partners has to be identified. Promotion of the concepts behind rationalized software product developments are important in this context. It is not enough to do something clever; a sufficient number of people have to be convinced of its usefulness and be persuaded to participate.
4. Projects should have vision; foresight of what is realistic (but not too limited) is essential if a large-scale software venture is to avoid the pitfall of being superseded or discredited before it bears fruit.
5. Attention has to be paid to the definition of appropriate standards and to the setting up of suitable procedures for implementing and verifying them. This is always a question of balance between freezing in restrictive practices too early and enabling continued development and innovation to take place. In order to keep up with the rate of advancement in information technology, the national standards bodies, the International Standards Organization and other bodies concerned with harmonization of software products are going to have to speed up their working rhythm if they are not to be rendered impotent and overtaken by events.

[10] *The Economist*, 5 April 1986, p. 85.

8.2 SOME SHORTCUTS HAVE BEEN TRIED

In contrast to multimillion dollar efforts undertaken by powerful organizations, individuals or small teams, if they are sufficiently motivated and dedicated, can achieve significant breakthroughs in software structures. In this section we shall present a few cases which show that there is always room for such initiatives. As a counterbalance, we shall later mention a few *prima facie* outstanding contributions of this type which have nevertheless failed and suggest reasons why.

The UNIX operating system can claim a place in the hall of fame for successful projects that have advanced the cause of 'software gap reduction'. Unlike OS/360, UNIX originated when one researcher, Ken Thompson at Bell Laboratories, decided in 1969–70 to write his own operating system for a Digital Equipment Corporation PDP7 because he was dissatisfied with the speed at which he was able to develop programs on the laboratory's mainframe under the MULTICS time-sharing operating system, jointly constructed by Bell Laboratories and Massachussetts Institute of Technology. As structured MULTICS was a brake on Thompson's rate of progress with his research project so he wrote his own single-user operating system, taking a selection of the most useful features of MULTICS as his starting point.

Soon after Thompson had written the early versions of UNIX in Assembler language, Dennis Ritchie, the creator of the powerful C programming language, became a collaborator, and in 1973 Thompson and Ritchie rewrote UNIX in C, incorporating at the same time functional improvements such as multiprogramming and the ability to share reentrant code. This turned out to be not just computer scientists amusing themselves but a key step in the march of UNIX towards market preeminence among operating systems, because C can be fairly quickly implemented on any computer, small or large. Thus the new version of UNIX constructed by Thompson and Ritchie was effectively portable among a wide range of computers.

Since the early 1970s, UNIX has found favour and been further developed in a number of universities; also many computer manufacturers have espoused it. Fortunately, even with so many fingers in the pie, UNIX has maintained its coherence, and with the entry of AT&T, the parent company of Bell Laboratories, into the data processing arena in the early 1980s, it looks set fair to become the dominant operating system, compatible for a wide range of computers from different manufacturers.

The first attempt at a small-scale effort to facilitate in a significant way the programming of computers can be traced back to a group of enthusiasts, particularly John Backus of IBM, who created the first high-level language, FORTRAN. Although quite a small venture compared with COBOL, even today the majority of scientists and engineers still use this language because its statements are close to mathematical expressions and therefore second nature to them. They have been able to take advantage of FORTRAN's portability, achieved via fairly comprehensive standardization, and thus exchange and share the FORTRAN programs produced. Despite some weaknesses and limitations of FORTRAN, it has survived and even triumphed in a particular sector of the computer market.

The OSI seven-layer model for data interchange is the essential framework by which computers can 'talk to each other' and 'understand each other'. The objective is simple: to render all types of computers compatible by means of standardized data communication software, structured into seven layers with carefully defined standard interfaces between the layers and functions, called protocol elements, within each layer. Today it has the appearance of a major software venture with manufacturers, standards bodies, the telecommunications administrations and users heavily engrossed in defining and implementing the layer protocols. It began in the early 1970s when a relatively small number of enthusiastic computer specialists in a few university computer centres and government research laboratories had the foresight to anticipate impending disaster for data communications if each establishment and supplier of computers were free to choose how to build its telecommunications software in the absence of well-conceived standards.

Even IBM, with its own data communications procedures, Systems Network Architecture, pays at least lip service to OSI, and all those manufacturers chasing IBM in the data processing and office automation stakes are now more or less keenly embracing it. Digital Equipment Corporation has fully espoused it.

Without the OSI foundation stone, the likelihood of economic exchange of data between computer systems, which is becoming more of a reality as the 1980s come to an end, would be negligible. Nevertheless, there is a long way to go for the implementation of all seven layers in OSI.

The foregoing three examples illustrate that small-scale endeavours can, fortunately, lead to advances that have widespread impact. These must, however, be set off against a number of failures. Although it is not our purpose to scoff at ineffective proposals, nor is the idea to take pleasure in how the mighty are fallen, the fact is that some apparently outstanding ideas have fallen on stony ground.

One such brainchild is APL, a programming language conceived, created and developed by Ken Iverson of IBM. Because of its power, programs are in general shorter in APL than in any other programming language; for numerate programmers, programs tend to be developed much quicker than in other languages. Aesthetically, at least for those with a mathematical training, it is a delightful language in which to program computers, and can be used in educational contexts to explore mathematical notions with children long before they would be normally introduced to them. Its low penetration compared with COBOL and FORTRAN is probably ascribable to the grudging and belated support by IBM itself. Iverson had an uphill struggle to persuade IBM management of the language's potential, by which time other languages with less attractive applicability had become entrenched.

Of a somewhat different nature is the history of PL/1, which was originally intended to combine the features of FORTRAN and COBOL. Despite the backing of IBM management at Hursley, United Kingdom, the project never fulfilled expectations. Clearly the goal of constructing an all-purpose programming language that would meet the needs of both the business and scientific communities, though a noble one, was certainly at that time out of reach, and may remain so for some time.

Building on more than 20 years of excellent research into the nature of the man–machine interface and the optimal design of systems based on this work, Xerox burst onto the market in the early 1980s with revolutionary new computing machines—text processors, 'mice', high-resolution laser printers, icons, bit-map screens, windowing, real multi-functionality, all interconnectable through a local area network. In short, it was the works! What every aspiring and incumbent executive and secretary wanted. To say the least, the STAR terminal, developed painstakingly from the earlier ALTOS used internally by Xerox, and combined with ETHERNET (just cable the office and attach terminals, of whatever type you need, wherever you want them and let them feast off each other at 10 Mbit/s!) and beautiful laser printer/photocopiers, gave every appearance of being the elegant answer to office automation or the computer-assisted office, if you were not too happy about repeating in offices what had been going on in factories for some years—automation.

The software effort behind these products has been enormous and much thought has gone into the parts that managed the office files and documents and looked after the man–machine interface (icons, multiple documents displayed on a high-resolution screen concurrently, the 'mouse', different character sets and type founts, etc.). Yet the market did not appear. Fortunately for future generations of office workers and home computer enthusiasts many of the brilliant concepts contained within the Xerox approach to office automations will continue life, perhaps in a less integrated way, in other vendors products. Certainly Apple Computers is bringing many of them to the marketplace.

In the light of these selected examples we may tentatively conclude that for these individualistic and spontaneous contributions to software, the following six criteria influence strongly the likelihood of success or failure. For a given initiative they need not all apply, but the more of them that do the better is the chance of a happy outcome.

1. The individual or small team which generates the idea has to have a strong conviction in order to create and maintain the necessary driving force to keep it going.
2. Certain environments are better than others for increasing the chances of success. The freedom of action, or elbow room, found in academic establishments and the best commercially run private or public research laboratories seems to be an essential ingredient for achievement of this type.
3. At some stage, usually early in the life of the project, it is necessary to obtain powerful backing, including financial support. Only with increased resources can the impetus be maintained and strengthened. The most enduring backing comes of course from market endorsement.
4. Only those ideas that contain the seed of deep understanding and insight are likely to eventually bear real fruit. In short, the initiative has to meet a real need and have the potential for meeting evolving needs.
5. The timing, or rather feeling for when the time is ripe, is crucially important for the success of small-scale initiatives.
6. On closer inspection, it turns out that the originators of these ventures are more concerned with innovation than standardization. Nevertheless, the need to harmonize appears at a later stage and is left for others to take care of.

8.3 SYSTEM SOFTWARE: THE MUSICAL SCORE

For any computer, the software consists of the programs executable by its hardware. Inside the computer's memory all information, program instructions or data appears as bits. In modern well-designed computers the machine itself has the ability to distinguish instructions from data. We must certainly do the same. In this chapter we are concerned only with sequences of executable instructions that make up programs, and not at all with data, which may share the same memory but is completely uninterpretable by the computer instruction processor and can only be operated upon (or processed) by the programs. In this context, let us remember that whereas a program can always be treated as data, the reverse is never done.

A five-layer model of the software, i.e. programs, in a computer of any type is illustrated in Figure 8.1. Microcoding, the lowest layer numbered 0, has been included for completeness; normally this layer is wholly masked from all programmers in a computer installation, and only certain programmers in computer manufacturing companies or some systems builders actually program in this layer. It has already been

LAYERS

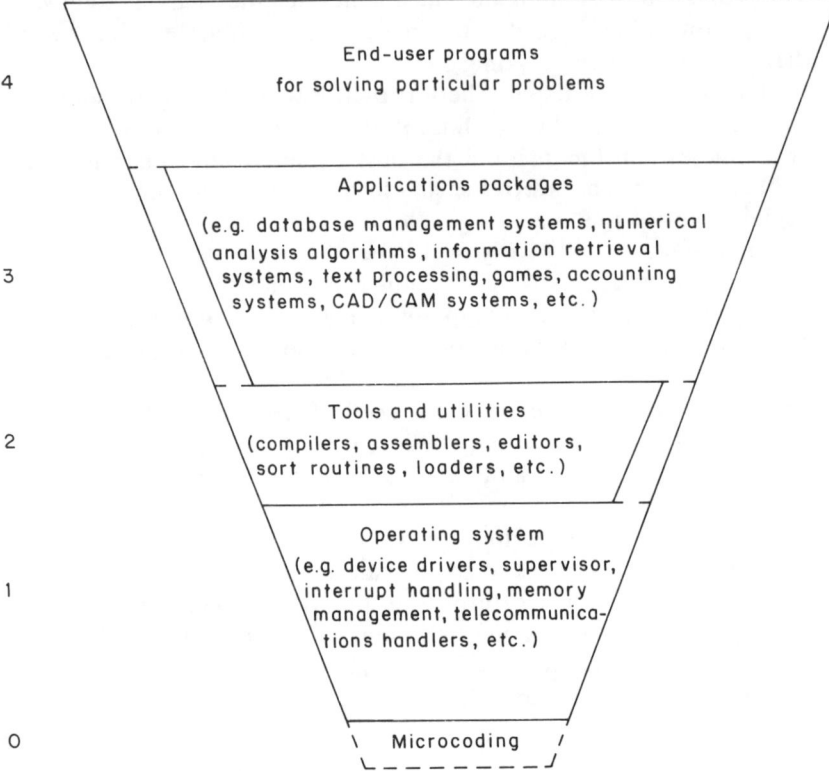

FIGURE 8.1 *The five main layers of software in a typical digital computer*

referred to in Section 7.3 and as a key aspect of IBM S/360 in Section 8.1 of this chapter. Microprograms are closest to the hardware and therefore the microorders included in them are determined by the design team. These microprograms are delivered in read-only memory with the machine.

New breed of orchestra conductors

Layer 1 comprises the operating system whose main task is to funnel concurrently a multitude of different programs through the central processing unit, even though at any one instant only one program is being carried out (assuming no genuine multiprocessing is being done). Typical functions of layer 1 software are: scheduling computing jobs, which may consist of one or more programs, through queues in priority order; managing memory utilization; linking program modules together, relocating them in the address space and loading them in executable form; submitting programs written in a particular language to the compiler for producing machine code versions; managing directories of program libraries and files; handling memory hierarchies (disks, tapes, etc.) and input/output devices (printers, keyboards, screens, telecommunications lines, exotic terminal devices, etc.); interrupt handling, detecting and correcting (or at least reporting) errors; and a host of other resource allocation and work monitoring tasks.

The message is twofold: operating systems are complicated and, in general, until recently not portable between different ranges of machines because of the way they have been developed in machine-specific assembler languages to handle particular hardware features. Examples of operating systems are MVS[11] (IBM large mainframes); VME/B[12] (ICL mainframes); CP/M[13] (many 8-bit microprocessor systems such as text processors) produced by Digital Research; MS/DOS[14] (similar hardware to CP/M) produced by Microsoft; and UNIX (now being implemented on a wide variety of computers) produced by AT&T with numerous assists from universities and others.

Whereas layer 1 software is concerned chiefly with management of the computer's throughput, layer 2 software consists mainly of tools and other prerequisites to simplify the programmer's task. Since the computer's central processing unit can execute only programs in machine language (so-called binary object programs), programs that convert or translate source programs written in high-level languages (e.g. COBOL, FORTRAN, Pascal) into machine language are required. These are called compilers (or interpreters if they carry out each statement immediately it is entered) and are among the tools to be found in layer 2. Usually a mainframe will support several high-level programming languages and so will have a compiler for each. A summary of some of the main layer 2 languages, their fields of application and relevant standards is given in Table 8.1.

Sometimes the compiler will do clever things, like optimize the efficiency of the program at run-time. Nearly always, compilers detect syntactic and semantic (though not logical) errors in programs and provide the beleaguered programmer with error messages that help to increase productivity; they also provide 'trace' facilities that enable the programmer to track through a program one instruction at a time in order to help find errors, including this time logical ones. Other facilities provided in layer 2 to programmers include routines for sorting lists of

---

[11] MVS = Multiple Virtual Storage.
[12] VME/B = Virtual Machine Environment/B.
[13] CP/M = Control Program for Microcomputers.
[14] MS/DOS = Microsoft/Disk Operating System.

Table 8.1 Comparison of usage of main third-generation programming languages according to application field

Application type	Languages	Standards
1. Business systems	COBOL	ANSI X 3.23—1974
	PL/1	ANSI X 3.53—1976
	RPG	
	Pascal	150 7185
2. Scientific/engineering problems	FORTRAN	ANSI X 3.9—1978
	Pascal	150 7185
	ALGOL	Various national standards
	APL	ISO standard in definition stage
3. Simple *ad hoc* problems	BASIC	ANSI X 3.60—1978
	FORTRAN	ANSI X 3.9—1978
	APL	ISO standard in definition stage
4. System programs	C	ANSI X 3J11—1986
5. Real-time systems	ADA	ANSI—1983
	RTL/2	BS 5904—1980
6. Artificial intelligence	LISP	ANSI TC X 3J13—1986
	PROLOG	

objects into numerical and/or alphabetical order and for carrying out other commonly required algorithms.

The generic term for layer 1 and layer 2 programs is 'system software'. Producing it is difficult and requires specialist knowledge and tight management. System programs, in order to maximize efficiency, are frequently written in assembler language, a low-level affair close to the guts of the machine, although languages such as C, with low- and high-level features, are more and more becoming used for this purpose, thereby making programs portable, or at least more so.

Two guiding ideas should be applied to the development of system software. First, it should be to the greatest extent possible independent of the hardware to avoid the need to change it when the hardware changes. Second, because networking of computers is now commonplace, this software should conform strictly with international standards for data interchange, the open system interconnection architecture being specified by ISO, the CCITT and various other bodies.

Traditionally, the major mainframe manufacturers have ignored these two concepts, each indepedendently developing operating systems of its own. Even within a single manufacturer, each range of computers has sometimes been endowed with its own distinct operating system. In this way a bewildering variety of them has come into existence, each incompatible with every other one. A veritable jungle of job control languages has resulted.

As far as customer companies are concerned this uniqueness of native operating systems progressively ties them to the computer supplier first chosen, because the cost of converting job control procedures and applications software to a new machine range would be prohibitive. Of course, the evolution of complex, incompatible operating systems cannot be entirely accredited to, or blamed on, Macchiavelian planners within the industry. Rivalry among systems software development teams has been responsible for not a little of the exotic diversity in this field. This policy of 'going it alone' will probably turn out in the 1990s to be a big mistake when millions of dollars of investment in native operating systems have to be written off quickly. Exactly the same happened with minicomputer operating systems in the 1960s and 1970s. The same has been attempted by microcomputer suppliers in the 1980s, although in the latter case a brighter future can be glimpsed.

Many microcomputers have only very primitive operating systems, but there can be seen the beginnings of a more rational approach with CP/M and MS-DOS as the most popular. These two have been produced by specialized software companies for the hardware and total system suppliers, which explains the rationalization and points the way to the future. Clearly a software company wants to sell its product to as many customers as possible, irrespective of their choice of hardware supplier. Hence, many different microcomputers have either MS-DOS or CP/M operating systems. CP/M and MS-DOS are, however, small operating systems with limited facilities, which are not at all capable of controlling the complicated mix of jobs that a mainframe computer is expected to digest with ease.

One libretto only

Recently a candidate has appeared in the form of a portable all-purpose operating system for micro, mini and mainframe computer alike. It is UNIX, developed originally by Ritchie and Thompson at Bell Laboratories as long ago as the late 1960s, as recalled from Section 8.2.

UNIX achieves its portability through being written in programming language C, which can be 'bootstrapped' onto any computer with relative ease. With this technique a C compiler is written in a subset of C and a program to compile this compiler is produced, normally in assembler for the target machine onto which the C language is being put. A subset of C is quite adequate for writing a C compiler and the task of writing a compiler in assembler is clearly simpler for the subset than it would be for the complete C language. This technique, which is like pulling oneself into the air by one's bootstraps, hence its name, enables C programs, such as those that make up the UNIX operating system, to be transported to a new machine rather quickly. UNIX is rapidly becoming the only operating system that runs on a wide variety of different computer makes and models.

Nothing in the IT business is inevitable, but it seems highly probable that in the near future UNIX will become the common software environment for running computer applications. An essential step in this march of UNIX to preeminence was the publication of the UNIX System V interface definition by AT&T in the spring of 1985. The currently evolving ANSI X3J11 standard for the C programming language is another key activity. Also, the X/OPEN Group,[15] formed by major European computer suppliers in late 1984, is another very significant contribution to this much-needed initiative to reduce the software gap. So is POSIX, the IEEE portable operating system based on UNIX.

Most large and small mainframe, as well as minicomputer, installations will eventually introduce UNIX as a portable multitask, multiuser operating system to run alongside, or under, a native operating system provided by the manufacturer of the central computer. Virtual machine facilities will enable this cohabitation of UNIX and other operating systems. Since UNIX provides the only common environment among computer installations that need to communicate and/or share applications, it will steadily become the operating system across organizations for running corporate-wide applications and between organizations for managing interbusiness information flows, e.g. customer orders, sales invoicing, electronic mail.

The native operating system will be restricted to internal data processing, such as payroll, and will gradually lose out even there to UNIX, despite the efforts of major manufacturers to keep it going to limit the customer's degree of freedom to choose the supplier on objective grounds. The irony is that no student of the upcoming battle between IBM and AT&T, when the latter was deregulated in the early 1980s, could have foreseen that one of the most potent weapons in the telecommunication giant's armoury for establishing its ascendency in the new information technology world order would be little old UNIX—a mere piece of software developed by two academic researchers well away from the glamorous hustle, bustle and hoopla of the marketing and product planning departments.

UNIX is only at its starting point, for it must take on board better communications functions and evolve to take into account the developments and breakthroughs we are likely to experience in hardware in the next fifteen years. Multiprocessor configurations, RISC machines, optical computers and dataflow machines have to be handled with equanimity by subsequent versions of UNIX. Indeed, one of the goals of the

---

[15] For details of this work see 'X/OPEN: portability guide', July 1985, and February 1987.

layer 1 software in our model is to mask the details of the hardware from the programmer and user of the computer. The operating system should present a clean sheet of paper to the programmer and computer user whose freedom would consequently be increased by several degrees.

Deciphering the script

Returning to programming languages, is there room for similar optimism? The answer is a guarded yes, but for entirely different reasons. As we have seen, the operating system's function is to present as uniform an application environment as possible, irrespective of the underlying hardware configuration. The main function of a programming language, on the other hand, is to provide the best facilities to programmers for solving problems in the external world, i.e. outside the machine. In short, whereas the operating system concentrates on minimizing difficulties associated with the machinery, programming languages focus on the provision of tools for solving problems.

According to generally accepted terminology, there have been four generations of computer programming languages starting with machine language (first) followed by assemblers (second). With third-generation languages came the first major move towards the problem domain. FORTRAN, COBOL and a host of other so-called high-level languages have been the chief tool for programming for the past 25 years. Their most notable characteristic is that, compared with machine language and assembler language, they are relatively close to natural language statements for solving problems, whereas their major weaknesses are: the lack of readability and inflexible grammars which restrict programming productivity and maintainability. A major part of this failing is attributable to the procedural, rather than descriptive, nature of these languages; the program has to specify in minutest detail exactly all of the steps to be taken with the data.

A large number of third-generation languages has been developed for a wide variety of application fields. In some fields two or more languages have competed for popularity (see Table 8.1); in others individual languages have reigned almost supreme. For each language there have usually been protagonists and antagonists; often the argument as to the merits and demerits of a particular language with respect to some problem type have been extremely heated, even acrimonious.

The evolution of the principal third-generation programming languages in the United States between 1955 and 1985 is shown in Figure 8.2, taken from a recent OECD report,[16], the source of which is an IBM study. The success of COBOL, which we have already singled out

[16]OECD, *Software: An Emerging Industry*, Paris 1985.

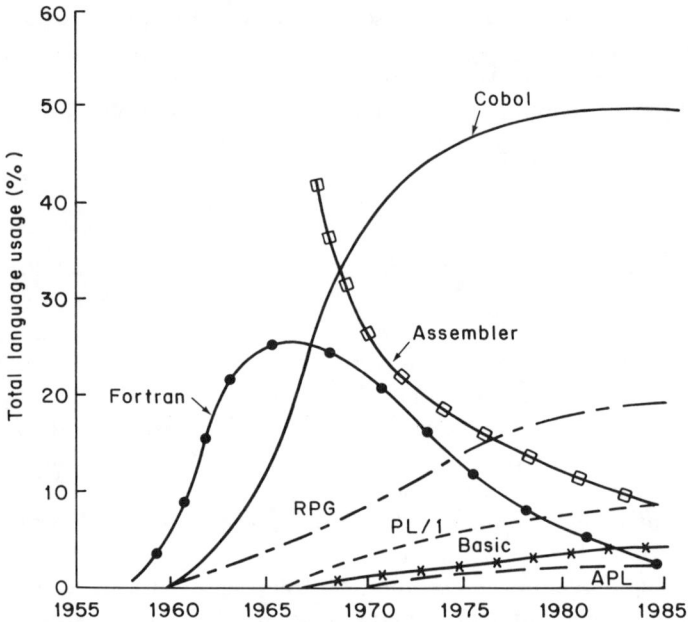

FIGURE 8.2 *Use of main programming languages in the United States. (Source: IBM) (Reproduced by permission of the Organization for Economic Cooperation and Development)*

previously, is remarkable. Even 20 years after its conception, in spite of numerous other languages appearing on the scene, 50 per cent of programs are still written in COBOL. The decline of FORTRAN can be put down to the fact that the scientific/engineering share of the programming 'market' has been continuously diminishing since the early 1960s. It can be seen that PL/1 came too late to overcome the supremacy of COBOL in the business field and that BASIC and APL, although well conceived each for its own purpose, have never really taken off in the way that COBOL and FORTRAN did in earlier times.

In considering applications software in the next section we shall come across the concepts of fourth- and fifth-generation programming languages, intimately related to making man/computer communications more natural and effective, in part through the loosening up of grammars.

8.4 EXTENDING THE MUSICAL METAPHOR

In this section we shall focus on the end-user and the layers of application software closest to the user-problem. In terms of Figure 8.1 we are considering the two highest layers of software, 3 and 4, respectively application packages and end-user programs.

Layer 3 and layer 4 software can be combined under the generic title 'application software'.

Playing for the audience

Naturally a number of key applications of computers have been identified, for each of which software packages of program modules have been developed by enterprising groups of programmers. These programming groups work in a wide variety of environments. Some of them are located within the computer manufacturers' organizations, others are in universities and yet others have created private, for profit, software houses to market such application packages. Indeed, this is a lucrative and rapidly developing field of software production. It is these application packages (e.g. database management systems like ADABAS and BASIS; test processing systems like WORD PERFECT; spreadsheet software like MULTIPLAN; statistical analysis packages like SPSS; information management and retrieval systems like MISTRAL, GOLEM, STAIRS, etc.) that constitute layer 3.

Here it is useful to distinguish three types of interface with the user:

1. *Data-driven*. Some application packages offer a direct interface to the end-user and require no use of programming languages on the part of the user, who simply inputs data as and when invited to do so by the input modules of the packages; the results are output in a form selected from a number of options. The package is transparent to the user. A common example is text processing software on a stand-alone text processor.
2. *Procedural program-driven*. At the other end of the spectrum are application packages that consist of a set of programs, sometimes called subroutines, which can be invoked by other programs written by the end-user, usually in a third-generation language such as FORTRAN or COBOL. Such packages clearly demand programming competence from the end-user. Typical examples of this type are statistical or numerical analysis packages.
3. *Description-driven*. In between the data-driven and procedural program-driven types of package is another type which requires the user to describe in a particular langage, specific to the package, the required computation; much less detail is needed than in the case when a procedural program has to be written, but more than for a purely data-driven package. The language used in this case is a fourth-generation language. The major benefit is not having to write

procedural programs. This makes the interface to the package more user-friendly, enabling the user to concentrate on problem analysis and to ignore the programming intricacies. A discrete simulation or a CAD/CAM package are examples of this third type.

Codifying the classical repertoire

Which of these three types of application package is developed in any given domain depends on the degree to which the requirement can be unequivocably established from the start. If, *a priori*, the developer of a package is satisfied that most of its functionality can be circumscribed, then, as for most text processing software, the design is frozen, and the only input from the user will be data—in this case textual and layout data. If, at the other extreme, a package addresses a general application field, all that can be done is to provide a library of programs that perform standard algorithms, which users can call into action with a minimum of fuss from their own programs.

In between these two limiting cases, if the details of a system included within an application field cannot be completely defined in advance but nevertheless the overall requirements of the application can be delineated, then the developer has to leave openings for the user to describe exactly the system for which calculations are to be carried out. This description furnished by the user, e.g. in the case of a simulation package, will probably include names of entities in the model system; parameters of the simulation, which might select particular probability distribution functions for example; the course to be followed by the simulation; and a description of the way the results are to be presented. It is this description that is written in a fourth-generation language.

We can only give here a taste of some typical application packages.

Database management systems

Database management systems (DBMS) enable the creation, updating and analysis of multiple files of structured records. Significant advantages of these packages are the cost/effective storage and retrieval of key information about the business one is engaged in. The database can be designed to contain all relevant data; it can be updated quickly to give at all times the latest 'picture' of the business; retrieval pathways to gain access can be optimized; security of the information can be arranged through passwords (and if necessary cryptography) that give access only to authorized personnel; information output can be tailored to meet the requirements of different levels of management, fail-safe back-up and recovery can be built in to overcome the setbacks of computer failure. This list gives only a flavour of the facilities offered by DBMS packages.

Moving inexorably towards the total Information Age, more and more organizations have two representations in the world: one is their physical assets and business products; the other is the aggregate of data and information which depicts the organization. This second view can be made to reflect accurately the state of the business and its probable evolution, and this can be best done using a computer in conjunction with a DBMS. Typical DBMS currently available are: SPIRES, DMS-1100, TOTAL, MRS, IDMS, INGRES, IMS, ADABAS, INQUIRE, RAPID, ALDS, CREATABASE and SYSTEM 2000. Whether the organization be a government ministry, a transnational private company, a group of hospitals, an educational establishment, a small or medium-sized enterprise, or any other, such packages can make a valuable contribution to management. In this field, in recent times, an intense debate has been going on concerning the relative merits of hierarchical, network and relational database methodologies. This controversy is still being waged, but the contribution of each of these to successful business management is now well established.

Suitable mixes of layer 3 software and hardware can create excellent business opportunities for enterprising companies in this vast domain of management information and decision support systems.

Information storage and retrieval systems

Closely related to DBMS are information storage and retrieval systems (ISRS). As in the DBMS case, the package enables the creation, updating and retrieval of information in a database comprised of files of records, but here the information is usually textual and, in the classic case, related to publications. Thus, we can imagine storing reference information to the contents of a library or to complete series of a set of journals relating to a major field of knowledge, such as chemistry, electrical engineering or biology, with a view to being able to retrieve comprehensive responses to search queries in the database.

Special features of these software packages include: setting up and managing controlled vocabularies of keywords; creating and maintaining thesauri to handle related terms and multilingual aspects; use of boolean expressions containing keywords for refining searches; selective dissemination of information based on interest profiles supplied by the user; keyword in context (KWIC) indexes; inverted files that provide retrieval pathways; and methods of treating full text. Worldwide, there are now some two thousand online databases, stored in the memories of digital computers and accessible through cheap teletype-compatible terminals (keyboards/printers, visual display units, etc.) over packet-switched data networks and the telephone network by means of ISRS packages like STAIRS (IBM), MISTRAL V (Bull), GOLEM (Siemens), STATUS (ICL), BASIS (Battelle) and several others developed by database operators.

Unambiguous categorization of application packages presents difficulties, for some files of bibliographic information contain facts (e.g. properties of compounds; time series of statistical data on trade/commerce; full-text abstracts) whereas others contain only references. In the circumstances, software for managing factual and numeric databases resembles the DBMS rather than the ISRS. Another difficulty, currently the subject of research, is the distributed database, in which input, storage and output are dispersed geographically. Also, how to handle images (moving or fixed) and sound data, such as that found in encyclopaedias and radio/television libraries, is a problem engendering a fair amount of current research in the field of ISRS. Hardware developments like content-addressable file stores (CAFS) and compact disk–read-only memory (CD-ROM) are yet another dimension to this dynamic field of development.

New market opportunities are widespread for the more advanced ISRS: we may cite electronic publishing and upgraded information services as examples of niches worth trying for.

Statistical analysis

A number of packages exist for statistical analysis of data; examples are Statistical Programs for the Social Sciences (SPSS), and Statistical Analysis System (SAS). Algorithms for analysis of variance, regression analysis, generalized data fitting, factor analysis, cluster analysis, statistical significance tests and several other statistical methods are well established; standard, validated programs for carrying them out are contained in these packages.

For most purposes they are adequate and save time; they can be used as stand-alone modules, but are usually best used by writing a main program which reads the data and calls the appropriate statistical program as a subroutine. Although many packages in this field exist they are frequently undergoing refinement, and occasionally totally new approaches, based on advances in technology or techniques, are brought into the marketplace. Thus bit-map screens, colour graphics and factor analysis allow multivariate data analysis and presentation of statistics in novel and more vivid ways. Therefore, software suppliers have a strong potential market but must keep on their toes if they are to succeed.

Numerical algorithms

Although scientists and engineers can sometimes, for the systems with which they work, devise mathematical models that have analytic solutions, more often than not, particularly when non-linearities occur, they have to resort to solving their equations numerically using digital computers. In fields as diverse as weather forecasting, nuclear fission and fusion research, crystal structure analysis using X-ray or neutron diffraction, spectrometric analysis, biological reaction mechanisms, high-energy physics and cosmological modelling, computer-aided design of engineering structures, aerospace research, and many others, the astounding power of modern computers is brought to the fingertips of the researchers through programs for solving standard mathematical problems.

The world of non-linear algebraic, transcendental, differential and integral equations, eigenvalue problems, Fourier transforms, linear programming, matrix inversions and finite element analysis may not be everyone's cup of tea, but these mathematical algorithm packages make a significant contribution to progress and profits of suppliers and users alike.

There are so many established numerical methods for solving the multitude of mathematical problems, which crop up in these different fields of endeavour, that several different packages are available, each concerned with a particular class of problems. For example, the stimulus of solving military and civilian logistics problems in the wake of World War II gave rise to the new discipline of operations research and a number of algorithms for linear programming, non-linear programming, dynamic programming, queuing theory, etc., which have led to very practical advances in stock control and resource allocation in industry. These algorithms are often brought together by computer manufacturers in a package targeted at the commercial departments of their customers.

Occasionally there can be a surprise in this field, as when a much-improved algorithm was found in the early 1980s to challenge the 40-year-old simplex method for solving linear programming problems in circumstances when the linear inequalities are ill-conditioned for finding the optimal feasible solution. However, as discussed in Section 8.5, the simplex algorithm continues to perform well in the majority of cases.

The provision of reliable, well-documented, portable packages in this number-crunching field offers market opportunities to the diligent software supplier.

Microcomputer packages

The rapid spread of microcomputers into homes and offices from the early 1980s has entrained a growth in interest in application packages for this market sector. Games led the way in home computing, but, after the initial fascination, wisdom prevailed and people began to reassert their expectation to be able to do more than play with an investment of $100–500 and more! Therefore, text processing packages, almost a necessity for office personal computers, came in to their own with many bells and whistles. Then came, following the dramatic success of Visicalc, a burst of so-called 'spreadsheet' packages, some of which introduced the concept of integrating tabular manipulation with text processing, so that complete business reports could be produced on them. More recently, the latest step forward brings database management within the reach of the humble personal computer.

Summing up, we note that application software is expensive to produce, de-bug and validate; it follows that if possible it should be regarded as an asset that is reusable. The preeminent advantage of application packages is that they constitute a bank of software investment and therefore avoid time lost in reinventing the wheel. Like good literature, good software can be accumulated; it does not wear out with usage.

Playing it solo: the risk of cacophony

Application software should be produced, as far as possible, with well-standardized third-generation languages, in order that it be portable with ease to as many machines as possible and available to programmers whose productivity is thereby enhanced.

We shall now consider layer 4 (see Figure 8.1), which contains an accumulation of end-user programs written using layer 2 tools—third-generation, or now also fourth-generation, languages. In this outermost software layer there is no such thing as a standard, or even a standard way of doing things. We are talking here about programs designed to solve problems, and not about programming languages. The closer the software is to the solution of a particular problem, the narrower the extent to which standardization can in general bring benefits. Quite the contrary, rapid adjustment to change and innovations is called for.

To be sure, in a given application field, sometimes a basic set of methods is developed for solving a considerable percentage of the problems that crop up. When this happens, and only then, these standard problem-solving methods can be frozen into a fixed piece of software. However, then it 'descends' into layer 3 and becomes an application package, possibly of one of the types discussed above. Be this as it may, it remains true that layer 4 software cannot be standardized. It is exactly this freedom of action of the application programmer in layer 4 that endows the computer with its remarkable versatility. Furthermore, of the software that exists, more of it is in layer 4 than any of the other layers.

This outermost layer of software is produced in disparate programming environments by programmers with diverse backgrounds. The information technology industry itself (including computer manufacturers, service bureaus, systems builders, software houses) is productive in this domain. This is, however, only the tip of the iceberg. Most layer 4 software is written in end-user environments in practically all sectors of the economy, including manufacturing industry, commerce, government, education and health, and the rapidly growing information industry. This latter includes publishers, database producers and service operators, and libraries; much of the audio-visual arts industry; and in today's world the financial and insurance sectors are rapidly being transformed into enormous information factories. Everywhere there are computers. In the home, in shops, in schools, in offices, in factories, in laboratories, in hospitals, in airports, in hotels, in warehouses and in many other types of location, computers are to be found of all sizes, powers, architectures and, last but not least, with multifarious end-user (layer 4) software. Associated with this vast array of computer installations is a dynamic, creative band of computer programmers producing application software in diverse programming languages and dialects.

A recent *Computer Weekly*/Datapro[17] survey of United Kingdom computer users resulted in an estimate that, in 1985, about 96 per cent of mainframe installations produce applications (layer 4) programs with in-house staff! Further statistics from this survey are shown in Figure 8.3. In-house applications programming is somewhat less common in minicomputer installations (about 82 per cent in 1985) but, as for mainframe sites, it is the commonest method of producing this outermost layer of software.

To summarize on layers of software, we need to adapt our model of Figure 8.1 in order to bring out the nature of the game, which is to produce software that allows problem-solving versatility across the widest possible range of hardware. The shape of Figure 8.1 illustrates qualitatively the volumes of software in the four layers we have discussed, leaving aside microcoding. We have noted that layers 1 and 2, which contain machine-orientated software, can be grouped together under the heading 'system software' and layers 3 and 4, holding problem-orientated software, can be taken together as application software. When however we consider the objectives of the software in terms of user requirements—the name of the game—this classical subdivision into system and application software, useful though it is, is not the most relevant for guiding us towards closing the software gap and going beyond.

The crucial subdivision seems to be, on the one hand:

Layers 2 and 3, where terra firma must be established—a fixed stable structure—through standards for tools (compilers, application packages, etc.) in order to ensure portability of software, and stability of the entire construct;

---

[17]*Computer Weekly*, 30 January 1986, p. 18.

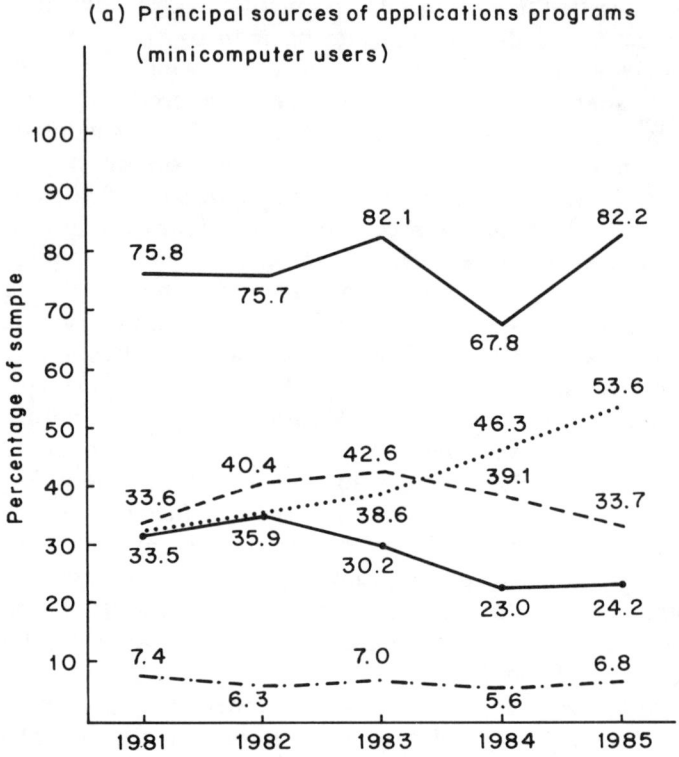

FIGURE 8.3 *Comparison of employment of different types of programming staff for applications programs in 1981–5 in (a) minicomputer and (b) mainframe installations. (Reproduced by permission of* Computer Weekly*)*

and, on the other hand:

Layer 1, where the key requirement is hardware independence so that software can run on diverse machine types (e.g. von Neumann computers from different vendors, multiprocessors, optical computers) through use of a common environment; and

Layer 4 with no standards proper to the layer, in order to permit the greatest versatility for solving new and changing problems.

That layers 2 and 3 should be standardized is slowly coming to be

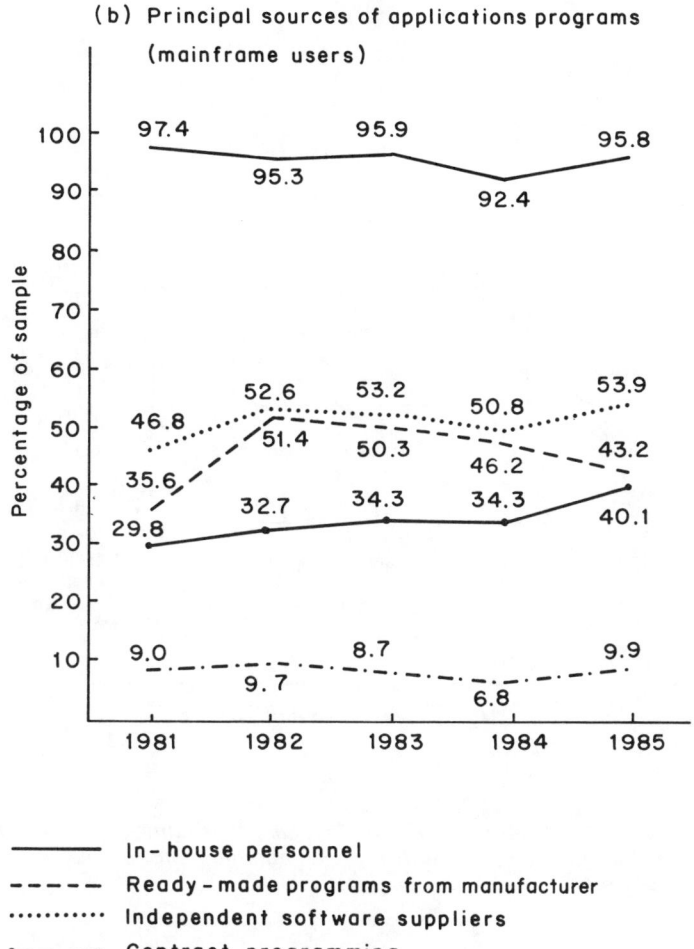

recognized. A new term, operating environment,[18] has recently been coined to extend the meaning of operating system (layer 1) to include layers 2 and 3. Operating environment refers to the entire framework in which new software is created (mainly in layer 4)—a vital concept therefore for hiking up programmer productivity and enhancing software engineering.

With this alternative perception of the layers of software and their relationships we feel it appropriate to redraw Figure 8.1 as shown in

[18]*The Economist*, 12 July 1986, p. 69.

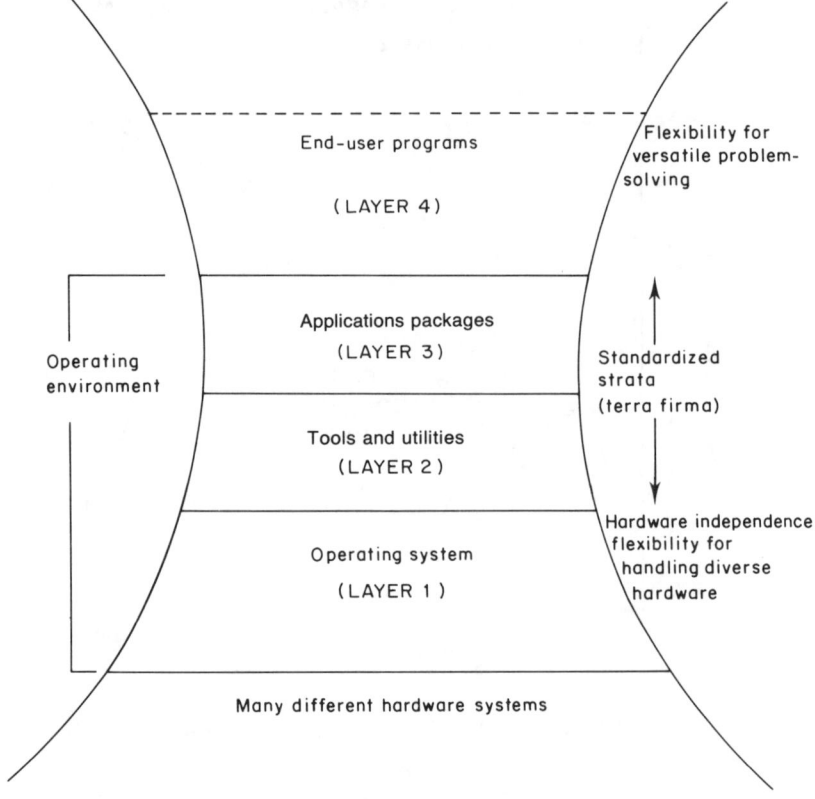

FIGURE 8.4 *A view of software layering, illustrating software that fills the gap between diverse hardware and multitudinous problems that are computer solvable*

Figure 8.4. The picture illustrates that the software structure must be pinned down (through implementation of standards) in the middle and needs to allow flexibility at both ends to achieve hardware independence and versatile problem-solving.

8.5 INTELLIGENT SOFTWARE: THE FINAL MOVEMENT?

Beyond the steadily closing software gap lies another yawning gulf, the bridging of which is currently attracting some far-sighted entrepreneurs and almost certainly will need further financial muscle. It has two aspects.

On the one hand there is a lack of knowhow for finding solutions to certain large-scale problems arising in loosely coupled complex systems, such as database and other information services distributed throughout networks. This is mainly a question of designing algorithms for resolving difficult problems.

Lack of understanding, on the other hand, limits our ability to solve a number of vexed questions in the field of artificial intelligence. Here, heuristics, i.e. rules of thumb, together with knowledge banks that represent or model limited real-world systems seem to be on the verge of breaking through this barrier.

The trouble until now has been that all too often software has been produced too soon, before understanding of the requirement at hand or knowhow for achieving it have been established with reasonable certainty. It is small wonder that systems developed in this way do not give even partial satisfaction, but the software and its methods of production should not be made the scapegoat.

Algorithms: turning the handle and complexity

The ideal situation in which computers can be applied occurs when the required results can be specified in the form of mathematical equations whose solution can be achieved algorithmically in an acceptable time period by 'turning the handle'. Examples come from all walks of life. Scientific and engineering as well as statistical and economic problems often boil down to solving clearly defined sets of algebraic or transcendental equations. Numerical analysis and discrete arithmetic have become highly polished tools with which to solve this type of problem and the resultant generalized solutions embedded in stable software environments (application packages) for the benefit of generations of users.

When things become a little less deterministic, e.g. payroll packages, the definitive solution that is to be frozen into software must be sought with more diligence. This might seem strange in view of the apparent simplicity of the arithmetic, but requirements to adapt to changing taxation and social benefit structures and legislation mean that the calculation is not completely defined for all time. However, the variability in this example is not serious enough to create a gap between the promise and the reality of the computer solution.

In contrast to these malleable situations, where turning the handle is sufficient, there is a class of problems that admits no golden route to success, for their solutions demand too much computational power owing to their complexity. The question becomes: how efficient is a particular algorithm? A satisfactory measure of efficiency, irrespective of the computer used, is the number of operations (instructions), or time, to reach a solution as a function of the size or number of variables to be considered.

A digression on problem complexity and efficient algorithms

Mathematical problems come in many shapes and sizes: shape refers to the form or generalized expression of the problem statement and solution; size is a question of the number of data, parameters or variables. For any problem shape, in general there is a wide, perhaps infinite, range of sizes. Some problem shapes turn out to be simple for the derivation of computer solutions, in the sense that no matter how big their size, within reason (say a few thousand unknowns or a few million potential solutions to choose from) a moderately powerful computer will execute an algorithm to find the solution with an acceptable time delay.

For example, solving a set of n simultaneous linear equations using the direct method of Gaussian elimination on a serial computer takes of the order of n^3 operations. Thus, if for the sake of illustration one operation corresponds to one machine instruction, on a 1 MIPS von Neumann computer rough estimates of the times required to solve respectively 2, 10, 100 and 1,000 simultaneous linear equations are 8 microseconds, 1 millisecond, 1 second and 16 minutes 40 seconds. It is clear that quite large problems of this type (or shape) can be solved quickly with not especially powerful machines. This type of problem can be considered to be simple, because we have found an algorithm for its solution within a reasonable time on an ordinary computer.

It is worth noting, in connection with computer architectures discussed in Section 7.3, that (using an iterative algorithm due to Carl Gauss and Ludwig Seidel) an array processor, because of its parallelism, can solve this problem in a time which increases only linearly with the problem size; therefore a thousand equations could be solved in about 1 millisecond instead of the $16\frac{2}{3}$ minutes required by the serial processor referred to above!

A practical measure of the efficiency of an algorithm is the number of operations it requires (F, say) as a function of the problem size (n, say). If, for a particular algorithm, $F(n)$ is a polynomial, solutions can be found in a time that increases polynomially with the problem size, and the algorithm is said to be efficient. On the other hand, if $F(n)$ increases exponentially (e.g. 2^n or n^n or $n!$) it will, for some large enough value of n, eventually be greater than any polynomial function of n. Such exponential-time algorithms are said to be inefficient, and are generally of no use for obtaining solutions to real problems which frequently have tens, if not thousands, of variables. To give some idea of the futility of

Table 8.2 Illustration of the rate of growth of some common polynomial and exponential functions. If the 'problem size' is greater than about 20 variables, the futility of using exponential-time algorithms is readily seen: already 20! is of the order of one million million million. Even the fastest computers today are of no use when confronted with executing this number of instructions

Size of problem input

Measure of number of operations or time to find solution to problem $F(n)$

n	n^2	n^3	2^n	n^n	$n!$
1	1	1	2	1	1
2	4	8	4	4	2
3	9	27	8	27	6
4	16	64	16	256	24
5	25	125	32	3,125	120
10	100	1,000	1,024	1×10^{10}	3,628,800
20	400	8,000	1,048,576	1.048576×10^{26}	2.432902×10^{18}
50	2,500	125,000	1.12590×10^{15}	8.881784×10^{84}	3.041410×10^{64}
100	10,000	1,000,000	1.267651×10^{30}	1×10^{200}	9.332621×10^{157}

using exponential-time algorithms, Table 8.2 shows how some polynomial and exponential functions increase with n. From the table we can see that if, for a particular algorithm, $F(n)$ were the factorial function $(n!)$, for $n = 20$ only, a von Neumann machine of 1,000 MIPS would take of the order of 76 years to find the solution, assuming it could continue working for that time without irreparable breakdown!

We can say that problems for which polynomial-time algorithms are not known are complex problems; they are called NP (for non-polynomial) problems if it is not proved that polynomial algorithms do not exist and NP-complete if it is proved that they do not exist.

For NP problems, such as the shortest itinerary taking in n cities, much mathematical research is directed either towards finding polynomial algorithms or proving that they are NP-complete, in which case alternative methods such as heuristics, approximate solutions, probabilistic algorithms or iterative algorithms are investigated. In these substitute or makeshift methods complexity is traded off against uncertainty in the solution, which may, therefore, be non-optimal but good enough for the purpose.

In the foregoing we have considered only time as a criterion for the efficiency of algorithms. It should also be remembered that space, or the amount of storage required to find optimal or suboptimal solutions, is also important when evaluating the total cost of an algorithmic computation.

In summary, therefore, problems for which algorithms exist fall into three classes:

1. Those where the algorithms happily involve a number of operations which increases only as a polynomial function (linear, quadratic, cubic, etc.) of the problem size;
2. Those, fortunately esoteric and uncommon, for which only algorithms with numbers of operations that increase exponentially with the problem size exist, and finally;
3. A tantalizing group for which only algorithms that grow exponentially with problem size are known, but for which undiscovered polynomially increasing algorithms may exist.

Far from being theoretical, a number of significant problems in industry, commerce and government fall into the third class and, as such, solution methods are of practical importance to suppliers (and users) of computers.

Examples are: what is the shortest (i.e. cheapest) itinerary including N cities for a travelling salesman, delivery vehicle or tourist? Or, how should a factory's resources be allocated to jobs in order to optimize throughput (and idle time), and hence maximize profit? Again, a company which makes a number of products from a set of raw materials of different and fluctuating prices wishes to know which ingredients should be used in each product, taking into account constraints on their quality or performance, in order to maximize profits.

Many such problems, applicable to a wide range of industrial and commercial situations, can be solved by linear programming, using the simplex algorithm developed by George Dantzig in the late 1940s. Although this algorithm does not increase polynomially with problem size, it has proved itself able to find optimal solutions to practical problems with thousands of variables, even on moderately powerful computers, and is an example of the fruits of mathematical research, whereby seemingly intractable problems are brought within the bounds of computability. The message is that computer manufacturers and software houses should keep in touch with university research teams and be ready to pounce whenever a new star algorithm is discovered so as to encapsulate it into layer 3 software.

As one further illustration of the significance of efficient algorithms, let us consider cryptography. For national security, confidentiality of personal information to protect the individual citizen from snoopers, as well as for the safeguarding of industrial and intellectual property, encryption will be a growth area in the coming years. Public key cryptography puts to good use the complexity inherent in factoring composite numbers—a problem in the third class. In a public key cryptography system each participant has two keys, one known to everybody (public) and the other secret, known only to the participant. To send a protected message, the sender uses the recipient's public key to encrypt the clear text of the message, which can be de-crypted only with the secret key, known solely by the recipient. The method works because finding the inverse of the function chosen to encrypt the message is a complex problem for which only algorithms taking an inordinately long time on even the most powerful computers exist at the moment.

However, it is not certain that an efficient algorithm does not exist. If it does, and can be found, new approaches to ensuring security must be sought. Once again, to capture a significant share of the encryption market, vendors are advised to follow closely developments in this field.

Complex problems, for which polynomial algorithms have not yet been established, occur also in network analysis, switching theory and resource allocation. For this reason some of the current efforts to develop distributed database management systems and computer workload sharing may be, if not premature, at least dependent on advances at the leading edge of complexity theory.

The real value of the findings in this field is the recognition of the fact that, even for finite, well-defined problems, it is not always simply a question of turning the handle. Seeking more efficient algorithms for solving difficult problems in complex situations and looking for alternative strategies, rather than specific algorithms, are indeed expedient and potentially profitable endeavours.

How artificial is artificial intelligence?

Remarkably, some programs perform better at decision-taking than their authors. This does not mean, of course, that computers executing such programs are more intelligent than, or even as intelligent as, any human being. After all, without the human creator of the program the machine would be incapable of any computation. Computers are not self-motivated, but their ability to outperform humans in complex tasks tends to suggest that a goal worth aiming for is a better synergy between computers and humans, so that the strengths of each can complement the other and make up for weaknesses.

A typical case of this apparently intelligent behaviour is a good chess-playing program. Here, the programmer can arrange for the depth of the analysis to be great, as well as the ways of evaluating the positions to be subtle. Whereas the programmer's memory and logical thinking capacity and speed may well be inadequate when faced with so many options, the program, once de-bugged, has no difficulty.

Examination of all possible moves is akin to the pure algorithmic approach. Evaluation of each position is, however, not *a priori* evident; this requires built-in expertise to work out strategies—a difficult puzzle. Master chess players can still beat the best chess programs. How? It could be through brilliant qualitative strategies or it could be rapid semi-quantitative assessment. If they could be encapsulated in heuristics and polynomial algorithms, programs could be written to defeat even the world champion, Gary Kasparov.

Whereas speed of computation was originally the single most useful feature of computers, these recent developments, in which probabilistic decision-taking is incorporated, represent an additional leap forward in the field of application of machines in the service of man. As well as being faster than human calculators, computers with 'intelligent' software may help improve our judgement.

Decision-taking programs, trained by human input, have already been produced for pattern recognition; only a few examples taken from the almost infinite set of each type of pattern are sufficient to 'train' for, or enable, the recognition of all patterns in the family. Such algorithm-training techniques have been used in fields as diverse as speech recognition, mass spectrometric analysis (Joshua Lederberg, 1964), optical character and handwriting recognition, as well as image processing of a more general nature.

Even more ambitious than human training of the parameters in these decision-taking algorithms are attempts to construct self-adaptive programs which learn as they go along about the problem space they are designed to explore. Examples have already been demonstrated in robotics and game-playing.

Today we are almost certainly on the verge of an explosive growth in the use of expert systems[19] and other fruits of knowledge engineering, based on principles of heuristics and evolving methods for representing knowledge in the form of facts and relationships in computer storage. Some expert systems and related tools used in practice are set out in Table 8.3. Many of these appear to be about to take off as commercially exploited products.

The ability to structure data in memory, as and when it is captured, so that it can be retrieved and processed, is an essential prerequisite for expert systems to do real work and pay for themselves. Moreover, symbolic, pictorial and acoustic data types have to be handled. We are experiencing rapid progress in this area at the moment. Also, programs for working with sharp and fuzzy logical relationships between the information sets representing the objects and entities stored in the knowledge base are being developed in high-level languages (e.g. LISP, PROLOG mentioned in Section 8.3, and SMALLTALK) and suitable application layer environments (fourth-generation languages, referred to in Section 8.4), such as INTERLISP and KEE, are under construction.

Three main approaches to the implementation of expert systems can be expected, according to the levels of staff commitment an organization is able to make. First, if qualified knowledge engineers are justifiable in the company and can be afforded, a specialized department is worth setting up, recruiting staff from such centres of excellence as Stanford, Pittsburgh and MIT in the United States, Grenoble in France and Edinburgh in the United Kingdom. A second option is to use existing programming and analysis departments, providing them with, for between $2 and 100 thousand, software environments and tool kits to facilitate the process of building knowledge bases and logical machines. A third way is to pay a specialized consulting firm to do the entire job under contract.

In other words these systems can be set up from scratch by engineers qualified in the field (options 1 and 3) writing layer 4 software using a mixture of layer 2 programming languages (e.g. LISP, PROLOG, OPS, SMALLTALK) and layer 3 standard modules. Or they can be made almost entirely from layer 3 tools by people without research experience in artificial intelligence.

Layer 3 software packages include: Automatic Reasoning Tool (Inference Corporation, Los Angeles), Knowledge Engineering Environment (Intellicorp, Palo Alto) and S.1 (Teknowledge, Palo Alto).

---

[19]See Chapter 5, page 129 *et seq*.

Table 8.3 Some expert systems which have been successfully applied in limited domains

System name	Date	Developer	Knowledge branch	Objectives
MYCIN	Mid 1970s	Stanford University	Medicine	To help physicians to diagnose and treat meningitis and bacterial infections in the blood
DENDRAL	1964–5	Lederberg, Feigenbaum and Buchanan: Stanford University	Chemistry/mass spectrometry	Identification of molecular and structural formulae of chemical compounds from their mass spectra
MACSYMA	1968 onwards	Engleman, Martin and Moses: MIT	Mathematics	To help provide analytic solutions to tough algebraic and transcendental equations
HEARSAY	Late 1960s	Carnegie–Mellon University, Pittsburgh	Speech recognition	Understanding of connected human speech via heuristics
INTERNIST/ CADUCEA	1974	Pople and Myers: University of Pittsburgh	Internal medicine	Assistance with analysis of difficult clinical problems
PROSPECTOR	Late 1970s	Stanford Research Institute	Geological prospection	To help geologists assess ore deposit potential
DESIGNET	Mid 1980s	Bolt, Beranek and Newman	Network design	Design of networks with good reconfigurability and economics
NET/ADVISOR	1985	Avant–Garde and MIT	Network fault analysis	Identification of faults in networks and recommendation of solutions
REACT	1986	AT&T	Network analysis and control	Similar to NET/ADVISOR

Since development and use of expert systems require the management of large quantities of data of various types in dynamic ways, specialized hardware (multifunction workstations and powerful processors) is called for. Good man–machine interfaces with bit-map screens, windowing, icons, pointers such as mice, and colour graphics and image handling capability are therefore needed. Some of the key manufacturers of this equipment are Symbolics Inc., Hewlett-Packard, Sun Microsystems, Digital Equipment Corp., Texas Instruments, Xerox, Tektronix and AT&T. As business in this sector seems set to boom, we suppose that IBM has something up its sleeve, but the giant appears to be watching the game so far, waiting to join in when the stakes are higher. Some market estimates talk of $10 billion in 1990 and of the order of $50 billion by 1995!

One field where expert systems are breaking out of the ivory tower with a vengeance into the real commercial world is that of networking. Right through from design, to fault analysis, traffic routing and control, and to maintenance and repair of networks, expert systems are entering with a bang. They seem certain to save money for network operators and improve service to the customers.

DESIGNET, an example from Bolt, Beranek and Newman, runs on Symbolics workstations and its powerhouse is software written in Zeta LISP, an object-oriented language like SMALLTALK. NET/ADVISOR, developed by Avant-Garde Computing Inc. in conjunction with M.I.T. for trouble-shooting in network management, comprises a LISP package for automatic data collection to keep the network model and database updated in real time and a PROLOG processor for the rules that enable rapid identification of snags and recommended solutions to be presented to the network operational staff. One day soon NET/ADVISOR may become reliable and proficient enough to reconfigure directly, without human expert intervention, the network to overcome faults that do not require actual maintenance and repair by human engineers.

A number of similar expert systems (e.g. REACT, real-time expert analysis and control tool, and NEMESYS, network management expert system) are under development and soon to become intrinsic parts of network operations, in AT&T.

Brilliant opportunities promised by expert systems pervade the network operation domain in the late 1980s. Resultant dramatic advances in the management of these complex systems can be expected to usher in the age of highly reliable worldwide communication services based on both public and private switched networks (PSDN, ISDN). Telephony will no longer be alone in its ubiquity; it will be joined by information services handling all forms of data. Expert systems, together with other products which provide reasoning support to the over-burdened human, will have played a significant rôle.

Moreover, we anticipate that expert systems will spill over into other spheres, especially the information services that sit in the seventh and highest layer of the OSI model. Not only will the transmission of bits in frames and packets be guaranteed; the pathways into the complex of stored data in order to find exactly the information required will be supported by expert systems.

In order to improve access to information by this route natural language processing, another major domain of artificial intelligence, is expected to play a rôle. To start with it will probably be used to handle symbolic, keyed-in language, but eventually—probably not much before the end of the century—speech recognition systems may provide the interface between man and information stored in computer networks. Semantic and syntactic analysis alone are necessary but not sufficient for computers to 'converse' with humans or translate between natural languages. Understanding what lies behind the words is also required. Whether this most human of all facilities can be transferred to computer software remains to be seen. Many of the problems in the field of translation are known to be NP-complete (see page 232 for an explanation of this term). Current practice in translation is to isolate the NP problems for special research attention and produce software modules for carrying out those parts of the overall process where polynomial-time algorithms are known.

The message to be derived from this brief visit to the frontiers of information processing can be summed up in the following terms. Methods for finding approximate solutions to hard problems seem likely to flourish in the run-up to the twenty-first century. This will be the fruit of some 40 years of research in artificial intelligence.

In well-defined though complex and ill-understood domains, especially medicine, physical science, complex systems' management (e.g. network inventory control) and finance and economics we can expect to see the growing application of expert systems, built on knowledge engineering environments, logic programming languages and advanced data management facilities.

To avoid duplication of scarce intellectual resources, suppliers of computer systems should watch closely the results of the research conducted in AI centres of excellence with a view to selecting marketable products.

8.6 CONCLUSION AND OUTLOOK

Despite the shortness of this chapter's survey, we believe that some useful conclusions are discernible, which lead naturally to recommenddations of interest to strategists in hardware manufacturers and software producers. We have considered the complete software spectrum from microcode buried deep down in the processing unit of the hardware, through operating systems, tools and utilities such as compilers, applications packages, to end-user programs, embedded in the environment provided by these lower layers of software, for specific solutions to problems.

Throughout we have tried to keep uppermost in mind that the computer's *raison d'être* is the cost/effective solution of problems in the world of science, engineering, commerce, education and government. Software, just like hardware, is only a means to an end. With this in mind, we proffer the following impressions, inferences and guidelines for steering a course towards the Promised Land:

1. In the process of finding computer solutions to problems, two gaps immediately become apparent. Different in kind, both contribute to the shortfall between the promise and the reality of computing. One gap is that of finding efficient algorithms to solve complex, and sometimes barely comprehended, problems; it is a true flaw in our knowledge and understanding. The second is what we have called the software gap, which arises because software engineering falls well short of the level of sophistication achieved in hardware engineering.
2. In the short term, we should try to close the software gap through implementation of standards in programming languages and application packages so that full benefits can be reaped from the considerable investment in software in all layers.
3. Although many tears would be spilt throughout the software departments of computer manufacturers, it is high time that a hardware-independent multitasking operating system became universally accepted and implemented throughout the industry, at least for all machines of more than 200 kips and 20 Mbytes of online memory. The front-runner for this accolade is UNIX V with appropriate communication-facility upgrading as developed at the University of Berkeley. This operating system will need, in any case, to evolve to take account of technology developments, and should do so in a way that allows continuing compatibility of existing software.
4. All seven layers of the ISO OSI model architecture for data interchange should be incorporated into the telecommunications modules of UNIX as a matter of urgency.
5. By adopting the previous three recommendations (2, 3 and 4), portability of programs would be eased, which should discourage reinvention of the wheel, provide a framework for software engineering to catch up its hardware brother and make the closing of the software gap a real possibility.

6. National and international standards bodies need to speed up their working rhythms in order to accelerate the specification of unique standards, and the customers must insist that suppliers of IT products and services implement these standards internationally.
7. Since software houses are more likely than hardware manufacturers to construct hardware-independent software, if only to increase the market potential of their products, there is an opportunity for this sector to expand with benefits to the computer user.
8. Software production is likely to remain a labour-intensive activity in the timescale of this book; its disproportionately high costs in comparison with hardware will remain, but, if due attention is paid to standards, software engineering and maximum use of packages, they will not diverge out of sight, which would otherwise happen.
9. Both megaprojects with massive financial backing and small-scale initiatives can succeed in the software business, but they thrive in different circumstances. Gigantic projects such as MAP, initiated by General Motors; TOP, the brainchild of Boeing; and several being master-minded by the US Armed Forces are illustrations of a new awareness of the defects caused by the software gap and a strong determination to put matters right. We are witnessing the development of purpose-driven software environments.
10. Having a brilliant idea is not enough to guarantee a happy ending in the IT business. The field is strewn with the decaying remains of ventures that started life with outstanding prospects. The reason for failure can often be traced to a mismatch between the product and evolving market requirements. Come what may, small-scale projects do eventually need powerful support, especially financial injections, if they are to break through to success.
11. Megaprojects are strongly influencing the software scene in the 1980s. There is a shift away from the supplier-driven ventures towards those led and controlled by large corporate customers or the military—the user side of the market. Software developments are at the heart of it.
12. The knowledge and understanding gap is a much wider gulf than the software one. Bridging it will require much painstaking effort over many years. A start has been made with commercially applicable expert systems and the beginnings of knowledge engineering. Among the many topics currently being researched in the field of artificial intelligence, pattern recognition, complexity theory, combinatorial and probabilistic optimization, heuristics and natural language analysis (both spoken and symbolic) seem set to bear fruit before the end of the century. Large markets for software products based on these techniques will appear for those companies bold enough to embark on this route towards greater synergy between man and machine.

Chapter 9

Signposting Rejuvenated and Novel Systems

In Chapter 7 we have glimpsed the underlying physical phenomena that have given rise to the IT industry and driven it to ever more impressive achievements over the last fifteen or so years, and put forward arguments that a base camp has been established from which to launch a second IT revolution. New materials and technologies are about to make a major impact on machine performance; despite microminiaturization approaching asymptotic limits in inorganic semiconductors, ways forward are opening up through optronics and novel architectures.

In parallel with these hardware advances, though lagging behind them in scientific understanding and engineering knowhow, we have seen in Chapter 8 signs that software is leaving its infancy as a result of a better understanding of how to structure and produce it. For processing all forms of information, for enabling efficient data interchange between computers via networks or exchange of media and for making man–machine interaction more effective and fruitful, software is beginning to show its colours.

The issues we have selected for this final chapter may come as a surprise to some readers who have for too long been exposed to stereotyped clichés and worn-out images such as paperless society, manless factory, costless communications in the long run, and so on.

In our considered opinion computerization of the economy and of society cannot go much further unless we master the problem of gathering and inputting the ever-growing masses of data, which before the end of the century threaten to become several orders of magnitude greater than now. Input has always been the most acute and costly aspect of computing, and as remuneration of labour continues to increase and the volume and variety of information to be handled continues to grow exponentially, the critical issue is how to find ways of replacing human effort by machines (Section 9.1).

Assuming the input volume problem can be solved, then clearly the classical issue of the man–machine interface is put into a different perspective. Once freed from the tediousness of dealing with masses of data, the interplay between man and machine can be improved, especially in the direction of better synergy between human and machine intelligence. These, then, are some of the themes we address in Section 9.2.

Much activity recently going on in storage technology has changed the outlook beyond recognition compared with ten years ago. Cheap mass storage has been a major breakthrough arising from advances in both magnetic and optical devices. Substitution between storage, processing and network capacity, together with notable advances in data compression and decompression, have enabled better ways to be found of capturing, archiving and treating the vast quantities of data referred to above, as well as of representing the information in a more easily consumable form. The great strides being made in this field are considered in Section 9.3.

Finally, in Section 9.4 we attempt to look at some new services that these new systems could provide, particularly for the non-work side of life, opening up completely new vistas. Here we prefer to concentrate on the ways the various ingredients could be put together for the creation of a range of societal and personalized services, so far neglected, except perhaps for the example of education.

9.1 AUTOMATING DATA GATHERING AND INPUT

Much has been written about the data explosion. How big the total data inventory is and its annual growth rate is difficult to estimate, but we may set the scene with some back-of-the-envelope calculations.

Some 9,000 daily newspapers are published around the world; assuming that each edition contains about 300,000 characters from whichever alphabet is appropriate, this means that nearly 2.7 billion characters are captured daily, requiring maybe 150,000 man-hours for input alone. This excludes the need to incorporate images that increase the impact of the news and advertising, which contributes to circulation and financial equilibrium of the publisher.

There are some 2,000 commercially accessible online databases currently in production. Some contain references, others facts, yet others comprise numerical data and some have mixtures of these data types. Most include only linguistic symbols and numbers. Probably about 280 million characters are added daily to them, corresponding to approximately 15,000 man-hours of daily input activity. None of this includes, of course, internal databases built and used for organizations' own purposes.

Worldwide, about 270 billion pieces of mail are handled each year, or 740 million per day on average. Some of these items contain thousands, or more, of symbolic characters, as well as black/white, greyscale or coloured images. Many of them are not of lasting value and can be destroyed almost immediately (e.g. mail shots, general publicity, etc.), another large group needs to be kept at least until a reply has been sent and still a significant quantity of these items requires to be filed for future reference.

Throughout the world there are perhaps 8,300 television stations. Assuming that on average each transmits programmes for 5 hours daily, and 10 per cent is original material, new images equivalent to some 200 trillion bits are being accumulated on video tape and disk every single day that goes by.

A typical family in the information-rich, developed countries may have something like 1,000 irreplaceable (and therefore precious) photographs, 100 long-playing records of music, the same number of cassette tapes, 100 books and a regular throughput of one daily newspaper and three weekly journals. Digitized, this represents an archive of round about 30 billion bits and an annual turnover of, say, 3.5 billion bits of information for each family.

Today's complex society with its welfare schemes, taxation conditions, health recording, credit ratings, criminal records and other information-intensive snapshots and life histories of each individual calls for a massive and growing data gathering exercise. From birth, through school, jobs, hospitals, to death and beyond, each one of us accumulates relentlessly an autobiographical tome of considerable proportions. The geographical dispersion of this personal information, together with the fact that it is stored on incompatible media, makes it difficult to update, validate and manage; the picture is practically impossible to bring into focus.

Remote-sensing satellites, even those restricted to civilian purposes (e.g. geological/geographical surveying, meteorology, etc.), collect in the region of 3.5 billion bytes per day. No labour is used in the process, save that needed to operate and maintain the earth stations which receive the data. If the military use of such satellites were included, the data volumes would certainly be two, and probably three, orders of magnitude higher!

It is estimated that the proton–antiproton collider for carrying out high-energy physics experiments at CERN,[1] Geneva, collects about 15 trillion bits of data per annum to be stored on magnetic or optical media for subsequent detailed analysis (i.e. approximately 7.8 billion bytes per working day!). This is after much of the raw data has been thrown away as a result of real-time filtering during experiments.

The foregoing quantitative estimates, which amount to about 93 trillion bytes per day, are just a small random sample of figures intended to give a feeling for the phenomenal rate at which data is now generated. They are summarized in Table 9.1. Even in the domains mentioned, such as publishing and scientific experimentation, only a part of the

---

[1] CERN = Centre Européen pour le Recherche Nucléaire.

Table 9.1 Estimation of data generation rates in 1986 for a representative set of applications

Type of data generation	Data capture rate (bytes/day)	Main input type (K = keyboarding, A = automated)
Newspapers	2.7×10^9	K
Remote sensing: civil	3.5×10^9	A
military	1.0×10^{12}	A
Online databases	2.8×10^8	K + A
Mail	7.4×10^{11}	K + A
Laboratory science and engineering	6.2×10^{11}	A
Television programmes	2.0×10^{13}	A
Family collections[a]	5.6×10^{13}	A
	1.5×10^{13}	K[b]
Personal information[c]	1.8×10^{11}	K
Total keyboarded	1.6×10^{13}	16.8%
Total auto-collected	7.8×10^{13}	83.2%
Grand total	9.3×10^{13}	

[a] The figures for family collections include a multiplier representing 1 per cent of the world's families, given in the *Encyclopaedia Britannica 1986 Yearbook* as 823.9 million.
[b] Half of this figure has been included in the total to cover published magazines, as newspapers are already encompassed in the first row.
[c] The world population factor given in the *Encyclopaedia Britannica 1986 Yearbook* as 4.858 billion is incorporated into this estimate.

picture has been uncovered. This has been hinted at in the case of online databases, where we know that internal data collections exceed in volume by a considerable margin those offered as an online information services to paying or privileged customers. For example, we can cite a recent estimate[2] of some 20,000 'buried' machine-readable governmental databases in the United States alone.

In similar vein, whereas we have cited newspapers, the publishing industry also produces thousands of magazines for all ages and interests, as well as growing numbers of learned journals for specialists. When considered as digitized documents, these other publications represent much greater volumes of data because of their extensive use of colour images and graphics. Corporate electronic publishing is an additional major growth area.

Likewise, scientific experiments and remote-sensing applications go

[2] United Nations Centre on Transnational Corporations report entitled 'Transborder data flows: access to the international database market', 18 August 1982.

far beyond those briefly mentioned above. At least eight high-energy physics (HEP) laboratories other than CERN are busy collecting data on the same scale, and medical, agricultural and engineering research establishments within universities and industry, as well as those administered nationally and internationally, are accumulating data at even greater rates than the HEP community.

Remote sensing usually conjures up ideas of orbiting satellites like INMARSAT, METEOSAT, LANDSAT, SPOT, etc., but it can also include non-space methods and techniques. Since the 1960s man has become steadily more conscious of his potential and real capacity to damage the environment through the wanton application of destructive technology, driven by unthinking short-term economic policies. By its nature, monitoring the environment on a regional or global scale necessitates the remote measurement of significant variables (e.g. atmospheric and water pollutant levels). Whilst satellites play a rôle, data communications networks on the earth's surface, with their rapidly increasing transmission capacities, also provide the means.

Moreover, we have not commented upon data gathered in banking, customs and trade paperwork, legal information and government statistics (censuses, etc.), to mention just four other key data-rich fields.

Also, the figures give only the static picture of data capture. The rate of growth of the volume of data collected each year almost certainly lies in the range 5–10 per cent per annum, which leads to a doubling of this business every seven to fifteen years. By the mid-1990s, conservatively we may suppose that twice as much data will be collected as today!

Have mercy on keyboard workers

Despite the small sample considered, if the data were all collected manually through keyboards, it would take more than 5.1 billion man-hours per day to capture. Fortunately most of it (about 85 per cent), notably the remotely sensed and scientific experimental data, as well as image data in publishing and television, is obtained automatically by means of a wide variety of transducers (e.g. cameras, flying-spot scanners, scientific instruments to which analogue-to-digital convertors may be attached) for digitizing the sample measurements. Thanks to these tools the human effort required to get hold of these data is an order of magnitude smaller than that demanded by keyboards and similar devices.

Nevertheless, from our small sample, the other 15 per cent of the estimated daily data diet (about 16.0 trillion bytes), if it were mainly input by human keyboarding, would take more than 800 million man-hours of work, equivalent to more than the entire economically active population of the United States, assuming the high figure of 6 hours of typing per day per person. Moreover, these work estimates do not include the severe difficulty of classifying and indexing the data input for subsequent retrieval purposes.

Admittedly these are very rough estimates, but they do give a strong indication of the magnitude of the data-gathering and input problem, and they may serve to point out some future directions for the appliction of information technology. In particular, they show clearly the strengths of automatic as opposed to manual data collection, and the mis-match between symbolic data and image or sound data with respect to volumes.

Thus, the sources of data we have chosen to mention account for only a small percentage of the aggregate daily increment, but for our purposes that does not matter; rather it emphasizes the data problem we are confronted with today.

Not all of the manually prepared data estimated in Table 9.1 is in fact entered via keyboards; indeed, much of it is not put into computers at all, but only handwritten as in the case of personal mail. This, however, does not alter the conclusion that there is not great room for expansion in this method of capture owing to the limited human resources trained in the necessary keyboarding skills. Worse than being hardly more than drudgery, this method of symbolic data capture can be a waste of time, for it is often simply a duplication of effort. The text, or other data, is first written down on paper, sometimes on tailor-made forms, or dictated onto tape by the author or originator, and then input by the typist to a machine, where it is digitized and stored for future processing.

In fact, to be fair to typists, they frequently do more than simply reproduce the originator's work: for example, noise is removed from the initial version through intelligent interpretation of hieroglyphics and incoherent mumblings; correction of grammar and spelling, as well as improvement in presentation and layout are done; and typists generally speed up, though only marginally, the rate of input compared with the original. Be that as it may, information technology is coming to the rescue in nearly all these aspects of cleaning the raw data generated by human beings, and must soon be called into play in a major way if this particular bottleneck is to be eliminated.

Spelling checkers, mark-up languages, forms-handling software, image scanners, vectorization of raster images, optical character recognition in limited situations, document composition and page layout packages capable of looking after multiple founts and colour are already available. Definition and implementation of standards by systems suppliers are urgently required in order to maximize the effectiveness of these technical developments.

Waiting in the wings to further enhance efficient input of human-generated data are some advanced technologies such as handwriting interpreters, grammar checkers, speech recognition and machine-assisted translation software. Since these are not yet completely mastered we expect them to be applied in a stepwise approach, so that where recognition of the data is not achieved the original signal is digitized and processed thereafter without identification of the intended symbols. Even if only, say, 50 per cent of the pattern is recognized this will still be an improvement on the past, and increasing memory sizes (e.g. 1-Mbit chips, 1-Mbyte RAMs, 1-Gbit digital optical disks) at decreasing cost per bit will provide economic viability of products.

A massive upsurge in the demand for improved data capture is anticipated not only in the fields of electronic publishing (including corporate publishing of manuals, publicity materials, house magazines, etc.), database production (with a growing component of image and sound) and straightforward electronic mail and messaging, both inter- and intraorganizational, but also in the domestic environment with the penetration of ever more powerful home computers.

This upgrading of human input methods will be accompanied by a dramatic growth in automatic data gathering on a global scale. From Table 9.1 we have already seen that this other class of data dwarfs the former in volume of bits collected, mainly because it is chiefly image data with a fair sprinkling of physical variable measurements (e.g. temperature, pressure, wind velocity, sea height, concentration of chemical species, energy and momentum of particles, reflectance, absorptivity, conductivity, etc.—the list is very long indeed).

The audio-visual civilization

The saying 'a picture is worth a thousand words' is if anything a gross understatement, for a typical A4 page image, with data compression, uses up as many bits as would some 10,000 words. Whilst a picture is more easily interpreted by people than a text, there is a cost in extra electronic storage requirements, which is one of the reasons why the data processing world has taken longer to get round to handling images than character-set symbols. Similarly, one minute of speech digitized at the CCITT recommended 64 Kbit/s rate corresponds to 3.84 million bits (i.e. 480 Kbytes or about 80,000 printed words), also greedy for storage. With recent and current technological advances the time is now ripe for computers to make the transition to the audio-visual world. In Table 9.2 are set out rough estimates of the partitioning of the total data inventory among voice, symbolic, image (fixed and moving) and other physical parameters, on the one hand, and between human and automated input, on the other.

The lion's share of the image and sound data is currently stored in

Table 9.2 Estimated daily input of data (1986) measured in bytes by types of data and capture method (input)

Capture method \ Data Type	Voice	Symbolic	Image		Non-visible, non-voice, physical parameters	Total	Total (neglecting voice)
			Fixed	Moving			
Human input	2.079×10^{14} (92.9%) (100%)	1.560×10^{13} (7.0%) (99.7%)	1.78×10^{11} (0.08%) (0.60%)	—	—	2.237×10^{14} (100%) (74.1%)	1.578×10^{13} (16.8%)
Automated input	—	5.180×10^{10} (0.07%) (0.33%)	2.946×10^{13} (37.7%) (99.4%)	1.992×10^{13} (25.5%) (100%)	2.871×10^{13} (36.7%) (100%)	7.814×10^{13} (100%) (25.9%)	7.814×10^{13} (83.2%)
Total	2.079×10^{14} (68.9%) (100%)	1.565×10^{13} (5.2%) (100%)	2.964×10^{13} (9.8%) (100%)	1.992×10^{13} (6.6%) (100%)	2.871×10^{13} (9.5%) (100%)	3.018×10^{14}	9.392×10^{13}

In each cell of this matrix the first percentage figure is the row percentage, giving the share of the data type collected with that input mode, and the second is the column percentage, giving the share of the input mode for that data type.

analogue form on video and audio tape and disk, but in the course of the next few years a growing volume of this information-rich data can be digitized, thereby offering a wider range of processing possibilities, especially filtering, retrieval and synthesis of new information products and services, including integration of symbols, images and sound.

High-resolution flying-spot scanners will be able to capture fixed images at rates progressively in excess of 10 per minute; immediate filtering using compression techniques (e.g. Huffmann or READ coding, vectorization, character recognition and edge detection for picking out selectable objects) will reduce storage and transmission requirements, as well as facilitate further processing. Moving images gathered from cameras will be digitized and compressed in similar ways; voice and music will be digitized and stored with increasing precision for high-fidelity playback.

Already bar-code scanners are used in some of the more go-ahead supermarket chains; advantages like automatic inventory control, fewer errors in customers' bills by elimination of keyboarding and speed of goods handling at the checkout will attract more users to this data capture method. When linked with electronic funds transfer in the next few years the data generated in everyday shopping transactions will no longer cause an input jam, though the crucial issue will be one of making the various applications software (e.g. bank accounting systems, different shops' sales records and inventory systems, etc.) interwork properly through strict implementation of standards (see Chapter 8).

CAD/CAM and flexible computer integrated manufacturing (CIM) systems will also require advanced data collection front-ends and will contribute to the image data inventory in a big way.

Reasonably rapid piecewise transformation of the public switched telephone network into integrated services digital networks (ISDN) from 1988 onwards, together with the construction of transnational broadband networks (TBB) using mixtures of optical fibres, coaxial cables, microwave links and satellites, will eventually provide the means for transmitting and switching kilobit and megabit data streams and will provide the infrastructure for these new integrated audio-visual information services.

A 64-Kbit/s ISDN bearer circuit can carry 230.4 Mbit/h, enough to download all sorts of interesting information (e.g. specially profiled newsletters, encyclopaedia extracts, short educational films, etc.) to the inquiring consumer with his or her personal computer fitted with hard disk and/or CD-ROM. Since telephony may take precedence during the day, such services could take place at night. In any case the basic local loop between the subscriber and the local digital exchange of this revolutionary new network, the ISDN, is specified to provide two 64-Kbit/s circuits for digital voice plus 16 Kbit/s for transmission of digital data, giving a total capacity of 144 Kbit/s and therefore the possibility of simultaneous digital voice and data at any time of the day or night. Initially, to be sure, only islands of ISDN will exist with sparse broadband trunks to interconnect them on a national basis, but by the mid-1990s or shortly thereafter this high-capacity digital network will probably have penetrated on a global scale most of the industrialized regions and other centres of population.

The applications for automated data gathering both in the laboratory and in the rest of the biosphere are almost boundless, and the ISDN and TBB seem set to provide the principal centralization and distribution mechanisms for transporting data and the results of its analysis to where they are needed. There will remain competition, however, from traditional postal and courier services (particularly delivery of CD-ROM) in certain niche markets, e.g. where the information is less evanescent.

Remotely sensed data acquired via satellites is the late twentieth century offspring of aerial photo-reconnaissance used especially in war, but also for peaceful purposes such as cartography, urban planning, agriculture, forestry and archeology. Since satellites in geostationary orbit have become also a mainstay of international telecommunications, the marriage between the two types of satellite for monitoring a whole gamut of events all over the earth's surface, on land and sea as well as in the atmosphere, in populous and inaccessible regions, is a natural one.

In addition to those applications already mentioned we are witnessing a growth in satellite data collection for meteorology, environmental science, reaction to natural and man-made (e.g. the Tchernobyl nuclear incident) catastrophes and shipping movements.

As noted previously, remote sensing is not restricted to satellite data collection. Transducers and networks on the earth's surface can also be used for automatic pollution monitoring, surveillance of unattended buildings or equipment, and measuring domestic service usage (e.g. electricity, water, fuel and, of course, already the telephone). With the increase in crime in recent years, and in labour costs, more remote data gathering of these and related types is sure to arrive soon on the scene.

Since the advent of computers the collection of scientific data in research laboratories has benefited from analogue-to-digital conversion (ADC), storage on magnetic tape or disk and subsequent analysis. There is absolutely nothing new in recording scientific data in this way. In the past, however, owing to limited sampling rates and precision of ADCs and insufficient memory densities, the techniques have been mainly limited to spectrometry and X-ray diffractometry with relatively long experimental times. Faster logic and bigger storage capacities on ICs and backup memory now offer superior collection, filtering and analysis of data; also image data from electron micrographs can be treated more comprehensively.

It is appropriate here, as a counterbalance to avoid going overboard as regards digitization of data, to recognize the existence and importance of analogue data. Despite the ubiquity of the digital computer, the central character if not hero of this book, and the daily hoo-hah concerning the latest development in its relentless march forward, at the macroscopic level we do live in an analogue world. Analogue data storage and processing are sometimes more efficacious than their digital big brothers.

It is clear that these developments will be judged by the marketplace. Taken together they, and trends towards integrated data gathering and preanalysis, will create a golden opportunity for existing suppliers of hardware, software and systems to give new impetus to their business, provided that they identify the niche markets and shape their development programmes and financial plans with the right mixture of courage and common sense. As with previous explosive waves of innovation, some new ventures can be expected to succeed dramatically on the audio-visual data processing scene.

9.2 IMPROVING MAN/SYSTEM INTERACTION

We have glanced at the spectacular growth rate of data that can be usefully handled by computers, especially the high proportion of audio-visual information, and the need for automated collection and input, if we are to cope adequately with it. Nevertheless, computers are (or should be) applied for the benefit of mankind, and because of this the input, as well of course as the output, of data/information between man and computer will always be of primordial importance. In this section we shall be concerned with the qualitative aspects of the interaction between man and machine.

Until quite recently, by far the commonest way for people to work with computers was through a visual display unit, comprised of a keyboard close in layout to that of a typewriter for input, and a cathode-ray tube screen, generally of 24 lines of 80 characters for output. Well-equipped users had slave printers, usually noisy, slow and of low quality, to produce permanent records of the output received on the screen. Less-fortunate users had only the printer/keyboard combination, giving slower output speed than the dispensed-with screen, but at least meeting the requirement of hard copy.

This situation is beginning to change rapidly in the mid 1980s. Stimulated by office automation developments, the explosive growth of personal computer markets, and the drawing together of automated manufacturing, design and business information systems, vendors are now putting on the market more advanced input/output devices such as graphic displays, digitizing tablets and laser printers. Advanced electronic and electromechanical, not to mention optical, technology is starting to breakthrough in a dramatic way in the area of the man/machine interface.

This new-wave blossoming of the IT industry at the interface between the user and the machinery, as is usual at times of fast evolution in its early phase, can be seen as very many independent innovations. So many and so seemingly unrelated are these newly-developed products that not only is the vendor frequently uncertain about his market placement, but also the potential user is confused and therefore hesitant to take the plunge to procurement. Because of this, rationalization is required in the next phase, so that the IT customer can see the wood, and not just the trees. It seems likely that the driving force to get rationalization will come from a basic need to interconnect all, or at least as many as possible, of the information services and systems provided through the man–machine interface. This does not imply, however, that all users at every interface will have access to all services and systems, which would be a ludicrously expensive solution, at least with foreseeable technology. What is required is that any given user can access those necessary services through one single terminal that presents a simple convenient interface.

Input technologies are mushrooming

Keyboards based on the typewriter layout are still the usual devices for putting data into computing machinery, whether directly or indirectly. Standard keyboard layouts define the relative positions of 44–48 graphics character keys, which with the shift key give twice the number of typable symbols; with some difficulty this arrangement has allowed the languages based on the Latin alphabet, including diacritical marks, to be handled. The allocation of characters to the keys on the standard layout varies, as is well known, from country to country, which creates problems in multilingual environments.

In contrast to simple typewriters, computer terminals need keys for generating control characters (for telecommunications, format effectors, presentation control functions, etc.) and sometimes other graphics characters (for creating images with colour, for example). The same goes for most word processors, microcomputers and videotex editing terminals. It is not unusual to find keyboards on the market with well in excess of 80 keys on them. It is perhaps interesting to compare this with a typical 88-key concert grand piano, designed for virtuosi. Small wonder that except for professional typists, most people show a strong resistance to using these complicated keyboards.

In a nutshell, the problem of keyboard design is that of finding a convenient intermediate machine that enables the mapping of the very large set of required graphics and control characters onto the ten digits with which we are blessed, in the most efficient way possible. Although much keyboard standardization has been achieved, there is as yet no universally accepted way of doing this, even for Latin-based alphabets, let alone Greek, Arabic, Japanese, Chinese, Indian and others.

To give some measure of the problem of the size of the set of characters to be keyed, the character repertoire recommended for the international Teletex service offered by the telecommunications administrations contains 309 graphics and 14 control characters—a total of 323 symbols that may be entered through a keyboard. If the Videotex service is also considered the total number of characters rises to 448! This represents a considerable difficulty in designing and standardizing keyboard layouts, and incidentally complicates processor and memory arrangements because at least 9 bits are needed to represent so many symbols, whereas most machines are built around the philosophy of the 8-bit byte.

A novel approach for text processing, which makes use of variable-length bit codes, is the Velotype butterfly-shaped keyboard developed in the Netherlands. It takes account of the orthographic structure of a language to let one key represent a group of characters commonly found together, such as 'str', 'the' and 'ent' in English. By this mechanism the number of keys has been reduced to a more satisfactory 37, these being laid out conveniently for typing by having initial consonants or prefixes on the left, vowels in the middle and final consonants or suffixes on the right. Typing becomes rather like playing chords and stops on an organ, but with the simplification of fewer keys and extremely elementary compositions. Also, hand movements are minimized. Being microcomputer-controlled, the Velotype machine is provided with software to handle the orthographic structures of different languages.

Whereas professional typists with conventional keyboards can achieve 60–80 words per minute, with proper training operators of Velotype machines can easily attain 200 words a minute. Perhaps the Velotype, after a considerable amount of research over the past 25 years, is getting close to the optimum. However, of course it is still a keyboard with all of the complexity of operation that that entails for people who have not been, and have no inclination to be, trained in the use of such devices. What about alternatives?

First, we note that speed is not everything; other significant criteria for input devices are diversity of information types handled, convenience of use and cost. Thus, although handwriting is generally slower than keyboarding by an expert, it is easier for the majority of us and, with the added possibility of freehand drawing, opens up new vistas for getting information into computers through tablet-type devices. We are now seeing the emergence of a host of new input devices for the man–machine interface, which apply technology to make the user's task simpler. Pointing systems, in which objects (e.g. icons, graphic shapes, commands, standard texts, etc.) are stored in memory and presented to the user in menus for selection by means of a 'mouse', a light pen or a touch-sensitive, or even eye-controlled, screen are coming onto the market with adequate support software at affordable prices. Also, voice input systems seem likely in the next few years to burst onto the scene and flourish for a much wider range of applications than they have been able to satisfy in the past, even though continuous speech recognition of a generalized type is probably some time away.

Tablets are most useful for capturing and digitizing freehand, sparse or irregular graphics, such as signatures, sketches or handwritten marginal comments. Their data input rate is well-matched to that at which human beings think and generate data themselves. Because of this, they are eminently suited not only to real-time manual input by non-specialists in keyboarding techniques but also to situations in which human preprocessing of existing graphical information results in major advantages. Too many vendors do not seem to realize that human ability to extract patterns, or indeed essential features of any type, from complex graphical data can often result in large savings of processor time and storage; sometimes such intelligent intervention on the part of the user is the only realistic way of getting hold of the required data for subsequent treatment. In these circumstances tablets constitute a significant step forward in man–machine interface design. Many examples of their use can be found in the field of analysis of graphical output from scientific instruments, cartography, engineering draughtsmanship, as well as, of course, signature capture and validation.

Where the objects to be handled can be to a large extent defined in advance, whether they be graphical shapes, pieces of text, operations on data or whatever, then storing the objects, providing a menu and giving the user a pointing mechanism makes a very effective, efficient and user-friendly interface. This type of input device technology is now spreading like wildfire among microcomputer suppliers.

The mouse, which the user rolls over any convenient flat surface to move the cursor around the screen or to draw on the screen and which has one or two control buttons on it, was made famous by Xerox with its STAR workstation and afterwards with more success by Apple with its Lisa and Macintosh machines, and subsequently by many other makers of workstations. The mouse has, at least for the moment, gained the ascendency over the other varieties of this type of pointer technology. Its widespread adoption by manufacturers in the last couple of years seems certain to ensure its place at the forefront of input technologies for many years to come, especially as the mixing of text with graphics and digital (as well as analogue) video, using colour and greyscale monochrome monitors, gathers pace. The revolution is under way;

computer applications abound where it is useful, if not necessary, to mix text, graphics, fixed and moving images; the mighty mouse in conjunction with bit-mapped screens, menus and software-defined objects are at the heart of it.

It is worth noting in this context that even for texts alone this pointer technology is invaluable because of the demand for so many founts, typefaces and colour. Keyboards are in general too cumbersome to cope. Shapes and sizes of characters, their spacings and line spacings can all be treated as attributes of text blocks and selected by means of the mouse and a menu, or menus.

Of course a pointer, whether it be a mouse or any other, is heavily dependent on large amounts of cheap memory for bit-map representations of objects and software, and the availability of bit-map screens, as well as cheap processor power. The dramatic developments of computer power and memory also serve to enhance the capability of the humble keyboard, which is where we started this exploration of input devices. For instance, if characters keyed in are generated from bit-maps stored in re-writable RAM rather than ROM, multiple character repertoires can be assigned to a keyboard, one at a time of course. The repertoire can be considered to be an attribute of the keyboard, selectable either by a key on the latter or from a displayed menu with, say, a mouse—an interesting combination of pointer and keyboard.

What has just been described is a soft keyboard. At the push of a button the operator can decide what character set (Latin, Greek, Russian, Chinese, Japanese, Arabic, mathematical, chemical, etc.) he or she wishes to work with. There remains, however, the problem of labelling the keys.[3] One solution is to display the keyboard layout at the bottom of the bit-map screen. This is not ideal because of the difficulty of making the right correspondence between the display and the keyboard. Another possibility, which seems not yet to have been implemented, would be to put liquid-crystal displays in the keytops. Though more ambitious because of technological development costs and the lifetime of LCDs, it would be a more elegant and effective solution. Some innovative company will probably do it in the near future, and such truly soft keyboards could then become commonplace.

From babblings to speech

The idea of being able to speak to a computer has existed for a long time. It would be a perfect way of putting human-generated data into a

---

[3] Key labelling is of course not a problem for the touch typist, but it most certainly is for the majority, who are lesser mortals, in this respect at least.

machine, particularly in situations where the hands and eyes are otherwise occupied, such as quality control on the production line, goods handling in warehouses and perhaps text editing by non-typing managers. While systems capable of interpreting continuous speech irrespective of the speaker are still in the realms of science fiction, recent developments have led to useful commercial products of more limited applicability; moreover, continuing research in universities as well as industrial laboratories, notably Texas Instruments, IBM, DEC, Intel, Voice Systems International and PA Technology in the United Kingdom, seem likely to make this dream come true, at least for a number of situations, by the end of this century.

The goal of speech-driven production of printed texts is particularly interesting as its achievement would lead to a major bypassing of all forms of manual input—keyboarding, pointers and tablets. IBM has already produced an experimental system that quickly and accurately recognizes English sentences composed from a 5,000-word business correspondence vocabulary, with a 95 per cent success rate for spoken word recognition. It is speaker-independent and trains itself by listening to a standard text. Some measure of the complexity of such a system, and of the implied cost, can be inferred from the fact that it runs on hardware comprised of a dedicated IBM 4341 and three Floating Point Systems array processors with an IBM PC for inputting and communication!

A firm specializing in speech recognition technology is Kurzweil AI, which planned to bring out its Voicewriter product in 1986; this, though speaker-dependent, is intended to convert connected speech to text with a vocabulary of some 10,000 words.

The three principal obstacles to be overcome before this technology can really flourish are: coping with the huge variety of voice characteristics (accents, talking speeds, frequency patterns, etc.) for a given language; handling a large enough vocabularly; and packaging the components on single chips and boards which can be mass-produced in order to get the price down to the same level as that of alternative technologies. The first and last of these are quite strongly interdependent since, if the price came down to the level where every user could afford his or her own (a bit like the telephone), there would not be such a big incentive to completely crack the first problem. Conversely, while the price stays high, removing the first obstacle is of paramount importance. Only by doing so can the machines be shared among many users, thereby justifying the expenditure.

The basic methods for solving these problems are established, at least in principle, and therefore there is every likelihood that we shall see progress in the next few years. Conversion of analogue voice to a digitized representation in real time has been done for years. In order to conserve bandwidth, and more significantly in the speech recognition context to save storage requirements, the trick will be in the design of efficient data compression methods. Here, linear predictive coding offers the solution, and current state of the art produces 2 Kbits per second of speech. For voice messaging, either by itself or as an additional feature for commenting on stored texts, where machine recognition of word content is not required, this digitization technique is all that is required and will allow some 10 hours of continuous speech to be stored on a 10 MB Winchester disk, or 8 seconds per block on a CD-ROM. Of course, the quality of the produced voice at 2 Kbit/s is not high fidelity, but it is adequate for the purpose.

When something more than simple regurgitation of the digitized voice for human interpretation is required, like recognition of the spoken words in order to print them out or to act upon them in a meaningful way, the problems become much more difficult. We enter the world of pattern recognition. During the last 30 years tremendous strides forward have been taken in this field as part of the general drive towards so-called artificial intelligence. Notwithstanding this progress, word recognition from continuous speech presents particularly awkward knots to unravel. The general idea is to store a set of bit patterns that represent each of the basic sounds from which continuous speech is built up and to compare the incoming bit stream with the members of this set, in each case selecting the element that best fits according to some carefully chosen criteria. Easier said than done!

First, what do we mean by 'in each case' in the last sentence? In other words, how would the bit stream be sliced up into individual sounds, bearing in mind for the general case different talking speeds and accents, etc.? Second, what should be the sounds stored in the reference set? In order to diminish the uncertainty in the pattern-matching process, the latter set has to be chosen in such a way that, with an appropriate goodness-of-fit criterion, clear discrimination between its members can be achieved. A variety of advanced mathematical techniques are employed for recognizing the sounds and sorting out timescale variability caused by different talking speeds. Moreover, the representations of the basic sound set are created by training the system with one or more speakers, and isolated utterances or continuous speech. This necessitates making the sound or sounds a few times and telling the system what it is.

With so many numerical techniques, all of them computation intensive, speech recognition, especially continuous speech, requires powerful processing facilities. No wonder IBM, as mentioned above, have thrown so much hardware at the problem!

A start has nevertheless been made along this road towards the attainment of perhaps the most natural of all interfaces between man and computer—conversation. Texas Instruments, Intel, Voice Systems International, Sperry, Ceratech, NEC and Kurzweil AI all have commercial products (chips, boards, integrated systems, workstations), which provide limited solutions in this domain. Some deal with small vocabularies of about 30 words sufficient to drive cursors and input numbers; others handle intermediate vocabularies of some 100–200 words more tailored for giving enough commands to run a complete application in, say, a factory or warehouse; yet others which can recognize a few thousand words are beginning to appear on the market for more word-intensive applications. Some of these products demand very precise speech; others are more forgiving. Prices range from about $300 for a bread-and-butter chip to $10,000 and upwards for a complete working system capable of a specific, though restricted, set of functions. The recognition success rate naturally affects the price, but all of them give at least 95 per cent and many of them are reputed to achieve better than 99 per cent.

One of the principal themes of IT in the mid 1980s is the convergence of computing and communications. There are some 500 million telephones in the world and an estimated 15 million personal computers in homes and businesses. Voice input/output[4] would seem a natural technology for bringing this vast IT resource into even stronger synergy.

Other forms of input device aimed at making the man–machine interface simpler, such as optical bar-code readers and magnetic strip readers for credit cards, have already made some impact on the everyday transactions of the hypothetical 'man in the street', and these types of input/output device are set to make an even bigger mark as we approach the 1990s.

9.3 NEW STORAGE TECHNOLOGY IMPACTS

Some pundits have been predicting the demise of paper as the main information support; the 'paperless office', the 'electronic filing cabinet' and the 'electronic encyclopaedia' have entered our vocabulary as new catchwords, indicative of the way many self-appointed gurus see our inevitable movement towards the 'information society'—yet another watchword. The likely evolution is, we believe, by no means predetermined.

In order to clarify the several issues involved, it may be useful, first, to examine the rapidly changing hierarchy of storage media; second, to

---

[4] Voice output technology is much easier to achieve by machines than input. Voice synthesizers are well established and, provided enough is paid, mimic the human voice with remarkable accuracy. DEC has shown particular interest in this technology for text-to-speech applications with its DECTalk product.

review the recent and current development of competing display technologies; yet always to consider the mutual interdependence between output presentation and storage requirements.

Floppy paper resists hard disks

Quite obviously, the threat to paper comes, in the first place, from high-density magnetic and optical storage, a subject already discussed briefly in Chapter 7 in connection with the basic architecture and operation of the computer. Three of the main advantages of magnetic (or optical) data storage are, compared with paper, smaller physical space requirements, the use of data compression techniques and the ability to process the data directly through computers. Set against these, the convenience of paper stems from its readability without special equipment and the ease with which it can be carried about, although in this last respect floppy disk and CD-ROM present no particular difficulties; paper is traditionally much loved as a medium for storing information.

Table 9.3 sets out the alternative number of pages that can be stored on the principal alternative media, depending on whether only coded characters in the form of 8-bit bytes are present, or whether graphics or image data are required as well. In the latter case, if the picture contains mainly linear elements (graphics) compression can be achieved of the order of 80:1 by vectorizing; otherwise Huffman or READ[5] coding of raster images can lead to reduction of about 8:1 in storage needs.

Graphics terminals have mainly constructed pictures by vectorizing, in which the 'drawing' is represented by line segments in one of 4, 8 or 16 directions, i.e. vectors. The coordinates of the origin of each vector, its length, and its direction referred to screen (x,y) coordinates (or points of the compass) are sufficient to trace even complex graphics such as those found in engineering drawings.

Vectorizing saves memory space compared with the other main method for storing non-symbolic data which is pixelization, or the digitization, on a two-dimensional matrix, of picture elements by scanning the image with a raster; this is the method commonly used for imaging with cathode ray tubes (e.g. oscilloscopes, TVs, . . .) and storing the matrix of digital values, commonly called pixels. Instead of storing all the pixels, various data compression algorithms have been developed. Modified Huffman coding is a one-dimensional technique (used for so-called group 3 facsimile[6] transmission) in which different

---

[5] READ = Relative Element Address Designate.
[6] See CCITT Red Book Vol. VII-3 Recommendations T4 and T5, Geneva, 1985.

run lengths of black or white pixels are represented by bit patterns (code words), whose lengths are chosen, to be roughly inversely proportional to their frequency of occurrence in a typical set of page images. This obviously saves memory, and, in the case of transmission, time and telecommunication bills.

READ coding is a method of compressing images, adapted to their two-dimensional nature, and is also used for group 4 facsimile transmission. Although the algorithm is in fact complicated, broadly speaking, each line in the raster scan is compared with the previous one, and only changing data are coded. In order that error detection and correction doesn't become too complex and expensive, after a certain number of lines the data compression process is re-started with a complete new line of pixels. This READ coding is applied also to moving images, such as videoconferencing, which, thanks to these clever compression algorithms, swallows only 2 Mbit/s; the same technique will be used similarly for videophony, together with slow raster-scanning over 64 Kbit/s bearer circuits in the ISDN.

Indeed, the innate resilience to errors of well-engineered digital storage and transmission systems, coupled with strong detection and correction algorithms for when errors do creep in, using these compression/decompression techniques is likely to lead to far more audio-video data being stored per byte of memory and transmitted per unit of bandwidth than has been conceived until recently. Even videoconferencing at 64 Kbit/s and telephony at 8 kbit/s seem not to be out of reach.

On a terminological point, vectorized pictures are usually called graphics, whereas raster-scanned matrix representations (with or without compression) are called images.

From Table 9.3, we can see that a single-sided, single-density floppy disk can hold (approximately) 120 pages of coded characters, or 10 pages of graphics, or only two pages of raster images, with a seek time of about 30 milliseconds and transfer rate into main memory of some 1 Mbyte/s. By contrast a similar size CD-ROM is a gigantic store and can hold (about) 180 thousand pages of coded characters, or 4,000 page images, but with slow access times and transfer rates of, respectively, half a second to a second and 150 Kbytes/s.

The figures in the rightmost column assume that the whole page (ISO A4 size) has to be digitized and that the horizontal and vertical resolution ranges from 100 to 300 picture elements (pixels) per inch with typical data compression coding schemes. The number of A4 page images that can be stored on these alternatives to paper comes down, of course, if half-tone (for pictures, highlighting) or colour is required.

As storage capacity increases, the problem of access time becomes ominous. Beyond the memory types set out in Table 9.3 some manufacturers (e.g. Philips, Pioneer, Sony, Thorn EMI) are developing juke-box

Table 9.3 Approximate page capacities and access characteristics of the principal semiconductor, magnetic and optical storage media (1986)

Memory type	Capacity (bytes)	Access time (ms)	Transfer rate (MB/s)	MTBF (h)	Approximate equivalent number of pages		
					Character-coded	Vectorized (graphics)	Raster (image)
Main—RAM	64K–1M	0.0005	4.0	—	20–520	2–70	0.5–30
Magnetic floppy disks	360K–1.44M	30	1.0	25,000	120–720	10–100	2–40
Magnetic hard disks (for microcomputers)	10M–50M	15–35	0.5–3.0	40,000–80,000	4,000–20,000	500–2,500	80–400
Magnetic tape ½ in	20M–180M	0–300,000	0.5–2.0	25,000	6,000–90,000	600–12,000	150–4,800
CD-ROM	550M–625M	500–1,000	0.15	80,000	180,000–320,000	18,000–40,000	4,000–16,000
Digital optical disk (WORM, DRAW)	1.25G–2.5G	100–500	0.7–2.5	80,000	400,000–1,250,000	40,000–175,000	10,000–60,000

style machines with many digital optical disks or cassettes in them, presumably to cater for major libraries' applications and archiving requirements of governments, public utilities and large multinational companies. Products of this type under development go up to 1 terabit (10^{12} bits), i.e. say 250 million A4 pages of coded characters or 1 million A4 pages in image format! The designers hope to achieve access times of not more than 10 seconds.

Most business personal computers delivered in 1986 had 256/512 KB RAM and typically 360/720 KB diskette drives, 10/20 MB Winchester drives and 16-bit processors. This represents a significant advance in computer power on the desktop in a very short time.

As recently as 1982 the typical configuration had only 16/64 KB RAM, a 360 KB floppy disk, no hard disk and an 8-bit processor. At that time 55 per cent of the market in Western Europe had 64 KB RAM or less.[7]

Breakthroughs galore!

Great though the advance has been in the four years 1982–6, the next four years to the end of the decade promise to be equally exhilarating because certain thresholds will be passed. The business microcomputer will commonly have 1 MB or more of RAM and a 32-bit processor of about 4 MIPS, giving it the power of a minicomputer of recent times or a mainframe of the 1970s! In addition to the already available 1.44 KB floppy drive and 50 MB Winchester, it can be equipped with a 600 MB CD-ROM[8] drive for some $500–1,000 extra. A high-quality laser printer giving 300/400 pixels/inch (10–15 pages/minute), a high-resolution colour display (1,024 ×1,024 pixels), with its own frame-store, a pointer as well as a keyboard and a telecommunications port will complete the hardware configuration, the whole for about $5,000 (at 1985 prices).

These frontiers currently being broken through with commercial products and services:

1. 512 KB RAM for holding programs and data to handle bit-mapped high-resolution colour images, for storing digital sound or for multi-programming;
2. From 16-bit processors (e.g. Intel 8086, Motorola MC 68000) running at 6–8 MHz (i.e. 6–8 machine cycles per microsecond) to

[7] *The Telematica Service*, 1984 Edition, Logica.
[8] CD-ROM = Compact Disk–Read-Only Memory.

full 32-bit processors clocked at 16–20 MHz (e.g. Intel 80386, Motorola 68020, National Semiconductor 32032, Fairchild Clipper);
3. Backup memories greater than 50 MB on hard disks for local active files and the phenomenal 600 MB CD-ROM for archives, including mixed and compound documents;
4. High-resolution colour displays (1,024 × 1,024 pixels) and laser page printers (300/400 pixels/in) at affordable prices;
5. Digital circuits for transmitting data at 64 Kbit/s and beyond, instead of only up to 9.6 Kbit/s;
6. Implementation, at an accelerating pace, of the higher layers of the open system interconnexion architecture for data interchange leading to universal, compatible electronic mail and messaging services, as well as online access to information and document delivery services; and
7. A range of new software packages for driving the man–machine interface in a more effective way, enabling the mixing of symbolic, sound, graphic and image data, as well as the use of computational power to be harnessed through the application of AI products such as expert systems, natural language processors and pattern recognizers.

Underlying the foregoing innovations, the key development is the availability of greater data capacity, at acceptable prices, throughout the hierarchy of storage technologies from central to mass memory, which in turn have a dramatic impact on output devices like printers and screens.

Thus, high-quality page printers require 128–512 KB for storing compressed A4 page images in black and white if they are to satisfy the high standards set by the publishing industry and its customers. Colour and greyscale images boost this demand by a factor of eight or more, at least an order of magnitude. As a yardstick, photographic images have a resolution an order of magnitude better still, so the production of brochures and other glossy literature by fully electronic means offers a challenging target for microcomputer systems builders aiming at new publishing markets in the 1990s. Such paper-based products are, however, unlikely to succumb to all-electronic information products in our timeframe.

Another main impact of mega-RAM, nothing to do with the war on paper, is the opportunity it gives for running multitasking operating systems like UNIX in the office microcomputer. Word processing, spreadsheet manipulation, database management and retrieval, electronic mail and messaging and many other applications can be run in parallel by many users working through cheap keyboard/screen workstations, with of course implications for office organization and management.

Even in those limited areas where paper can be ousted as a storage medium, bigger memories are being applied to driving colour displays, where framestores of 512 KB (and above) offer real advantages in resolution and image-change speed for the CAD/CAM community, publishers and the education/training market.

Similarly, high-capacity optical disks and thin-film magnetic disks are opening up new vistas for microcomputer system suppliers to the office, library and home electronics markets. These high-volume storage media, in conjunction with greater transmission capacity through both local, metropolitan and wide area networks, may well, during the next decade, cause some of today's fusty paper archives to disappear. For example, electronic filing systems for the office and home seem likely to herald the cleaning up of these locations and greater efficiency of information handling in them. Nevertheless, for a multitude of situations, paper will remain a preferred support for information storage and usage because of its favourable characteristics of readability, portability and modifiability.

The CD-ROM, developed from digital audio disks for the home, has a relatively high pre-mastering and mastering cost of from $10,000 to $50,000 at present, but this can be spread over the very many copies that can be produced at, say, $20–200 according to the value of the information stored. In 1986 CD-ROM drives were interfaced to personal computers for between $500 and $1,000, but it is likely that this will come down to $200–400 by 1988. Moreover, whilst commercial optical storage has until now laboured under the disadvantage for many purposes of being either read-only (OROM[9], CD-ROM) or write-once/read-many (WORM), because of the irreversibility of the recording process, this situation is about to change.

With several companies, notably Eastman Kodak (Verbatim), Sony, Matsushita, Hitachi, Optical Storage International (Philips' and Control Data's joint venture) and Optimem (subsidiary of Xerox), striving to transform R&D prototypes of erasable optical stores into commercial products, their entry into the market as head-on competitors for the latest magnetic technology promises a fierce battle.

Flat screens and laser images

Three principal complements to the memory developments just reviewed are needed, and are indeed evolving in parallel, i.e. better output (or presentation) hardware; improved, easy to understand and use, software; and relevant information products and services, based upon carefully packaged data, facts, images and sounds tailored to the requirements of specific user populations.

---

[9]OROM = *O*ptical *R*ead-*O*nly *M*emory.

Leaving aside sound reproduction from digital storage which is a highly developed technology, the main presentation devices at the man–machine interface are screens, printers and plotters. Screens give, in general, poorer resolution than printers (even matrix printers) and plotters.

A 14-inch cathode-ray tube (CRT) display has almost the same dimensions as an A4 page, although the aspect ratios are usually 90° rotated. Thus even with $1,024 \times 760$ pixels such a screen gives only about 90 pixels/in, compared with typically 150 pixels/in for a matrix printer and 200–400 pixels/in for a laser page printer. Using larger screens of course reduces the resolution. Many CRT displays supplied with PCs give considerably fewer picture elements; for example, 640×200 pixels is usual for IBM monitors and 512×342 for the Apple Macintosh display. Only expensive machines, such as those for CAD/CAM or for digitizing documents in the publishing industry, have been equipped with displays providing 1,024 pixels in both dimensions. As we approach the 1990s, however, the humble PC will be sold with better displays, colour of course, as a result of technological advance and decreasing unit costs. As for erasable optical memories, a number of technologies are competing in the race for electronic display devices that meet higher performance requirements, are attractive and ergonomic, inexpensive and of a convenient size and weight.

The CRT has held sway in this domain until now because its technology is well established and robust, having been developed for the two-dimensional presentation of analogue inputs (e.g. television, oscilloscopes, etc.) some 40 years ago, and, because of volume production, it is cheap. Its big disadvantage is its bulk and weight. The race to replace this technology with one that will enable the large, portable, elegant television on the drawing room wall to become a reality, at a price most consumers can afford, is being extremely hard-fought in the R&D laboratories of almost every major and many small consumer electronics firms.

Displacement of the classical CRT from its overwhelming dominance of the market for visual display computer terminals is imminent. The challenge is coming from several technologies: gas discharge; solid-state electroluminescence, liquid crystal phase change and vacuum fluorescence (like CRT but with new 'thin' geometries).

All, except the liquid crystal devices (LCD), emit light as a result of electrons being excited and then relaxing to a lower energy level either in gaseous or solid materials. The wavelength of the light emitted depends on the energy level difference, and the light intensity for a given input energy dissipated varies considerably according to the physical processes and the materials involved. This gives much room for R&D, and gives rise intuitively to the hope that major breakthroughs can yet be produced.

LCDs use ambient light incident on the liquid crystalline material, reflecting, transmitting or absorbing it according to which of the liquid crystalline phases are present. The phase changes in different parts of the material are brought about by electrical input through a two-dimensional matrix. Compared with light-emitting devices very little electrical power is consumed in LCDs, which explains their use in digital wristwatches, portable computer displays and other products where electrical energy is at a premium.

For flat screen displays with high resolution and colour the most promising technology to rival CRTs appears to be the gas discharge panel, but electroluminescent devices cannot be dismissed as contenders for the marketplace of the 1990s.

We began this section by considering whether or not paper is likely to be largely superseded as an information support in the foreseeable future, as some forecasters have suggested. At the outset we contended that it seems unlikely. The trends in rival storage and display technologies having been sketched out, we return briefly to technological trends driving the use of paper as an output medium for computers.

There are two basic classes of printer: impact and non-impact. Within the impact class the three commonest types are daisywheel, barrel and dot matrix, of which the latter is by far the most significant in terms of sales. Although daisywheel printers produce typewriter quality output, they are hamstrung nowadays by being slow (30–45 characters/second, (cps)) and cumbersome to use when multiple alphabets or typefaces are involved, and are therefore on the way out. Barrel printers are dinosaurs confined to the longest-established mainframe computer rooms.

Dot matrix printers, on the other hand, are having an exciting period of expansion in performance and sales in the office automation area. More than 75 per cent of office printers in Western Europe in 1985 were of this type, with speeds in the range of 60 cps for letter quality to 400 cps for drafts. They come with 9-, 12-, 18- and 24-pin heads, can store large character repertoires in ROM and produce graphics through software, for prices in the range $700–3,500 with some very good products under $1,500. Most products offer colour as an option.

The main question is: will these devices be able to hold at bay the attack from the non-impact class, particularly the laser page printer? Whilst it is likely that other non-impact types—thermal and ink-jet—will find niche markets, the rising star is the laser printer, despite the present lack of colour. Machines with speeds of 4 to 6 pages/minute cost in 1986 about $5,000; laser printers running at 40 pages/minute cost in the region of $20,000–25,000.

In general the quality of these printers is excellent, and they produce documents with characters, graphics and images mixed together. Most PCs cannot drive such a printer at more than about 10 pages/minute, which at a resolution of 300 lines/in represents a data rate of about

165 Kbit/s. Indeed, in most office environments this speed, equivalent to a maximum of some 4,800 pages/working day, is likely to be more than adequate. The robustness of the print engine, which may in some cases limit the usage to some 3,000 pages/day if maintenance and refurbishment problems are to be avoided, is also a constraint. A crucial factor in choosing a laser printer is the controller, i.e. its memory and processing power, and the amount of software available for handling mixed characters, graphics and images, as well as its efficiency at data compression/decompression.

Dozens of companies are developing and manufacturing memories, screen display devices, printers and plotters in the United States, Japan and other Pacific basin countries, as well as Western Europe. Hundreds more are building systems out of them for the general and specialized markets. Competition is intense, but it is a dynamic consumer market, evolving all the time according to new technological advances and changing, expanding demand. This should enable a significant number of the competitors to carve out long-term profit-making businesses.

In conclusion, more memory on a chip is leading to vastly improved output onto both screens and paper. It is rarely enough to see information on a screen; when it is in final form people want it on paper. Moreover paper can store more information, at higher resolution than screens. It is unlikely, therefore, that paper can be replaced by chip memory; on the contrary its dominance is strengthened.

As regards optical disk(ette)s the situation is more complicated. One way of looking at CD-ROM is that it is a straight substitute for paper; books, reports, any volume with mixed symbolic, graphics, image information could be stored and distributed on it. However, it cannot be read directly by humans, the data on it cannot be modified (scribbled on) and it costs more than paper in practice, if not in theory, because the unit size is so vast. There is a high probability that most information stored on CD-ROM will therefore finish up on paper anyway, because screens are so limiting. In the same way that microfiche/microfilm have not dented paper's supremacy, CD-ROM will probably not do so either, even though the coming of the microcomputer may be a useful, though not determinant, ally.

9.4 FLORESCENT SOCIETAL AND PERSONAL IT SERVICES

Whether or not we like E. Schumacher's exuberant ideas in support of his message that 'small is beautiful', we can hardly dispute his observation that less than 5 per cent of human endeavour is spent at work of one kind or another. A similar calculation shows that on the average only about 20 per cent of an individual's wakeful time is dedicated to working. What about applying information technology at long last to the other 80 per cent of our lifetime, generally given to all sorts of non-remunerated pursuits?

Whilst it is true that some companies, notably Tandy, Sinclair, several Japanese suppliers and, most recently, Amstrad, have in the recent past made pioneering initiatives to penetrate the household market, the majority has ignored non-work applications. Another group of IT or electronics companies have been active and successful in the market for home entertainment centres: hi-fi sets, radios, televisions, videotape recorders and so on.

Until the small personal computer came along, computer vendors had sold directly to the customers through specialized salesmen, customer and systems engineers. No shops retailing the product existed and so no independent feedback was available to the manufacturers. In contrast, audio and video equipment for the home has always been retailed.

These two separate selling channels have contributed largely to keeping the two types of IT product (computers and audio/video players) apart. The main reasons for these different supply chains are the relative unit costs (until recently much higher for computers) and the reliability of the two sorts of product. Retailers are naturally hesitant to take on expensive, and therefore low turnover, items, which frequently require specialist maintenance and repair services. However, the advent of $100–1,000 home computers in the 1980s is radically changing the situation, and more interaction, and even interpenetration, of these previously separate product lines seems inevitable as the 1990s approach.

Information technology for the collective good

Applications of information technology in the home, or away from home, or indeed anywhere outside the workplace,[10] are not easily categorized. Too often, the issue has been approached from the one-sided viewpoint of stereotyped societal needs, e.g. education, training, health care and the like. This is, surely, only one part of the story, possibly the smaller part. The more promising alternative is by way of more diversified services, greater ease of combinations, more flexible applications and, above all, personalized use of these tools, products and systems.

---

[10] Workplace is here used in the traditional sense: office, factory, laboratory, etc. In any case, it is still largely true that the self-employed working at home do not as yet make much use of IT.

For instance, watching one-way television with its set programmes for several hours every day is likely in a matter of a single decade to be looked upon as an anachronism and replaced by à la carte entertainment, including digital three-dimensional television to a limited extent, plus flashback facilities, disconnect and replay, sandwiched-in file or encyclopaedia searching, file merging on the spot, person-to-person communication/interrogation, etc.—all that at will—plus many other niceties we have difficulty imagining today.

In his retirement, Sir Harold Wilson, former British Prime Minister, when asked in the early 1980s what he felt to be his greatest achievement during his eight years of premiership, replied: the creation of the Open University. Tongue in cheek or not, there can be little doubt that he is proud of this initiative to bring tertiary-level education to the masses, via the ubiquitous television set, and with good reason.

The education/training problem which recently has preoccupied developed nations is even worse in the underdeveloped countries. Furthermore, most people can expect to have three, four or even more distinct careers during a lifetime, each one requiring different knowledge, *savoir faire* and the accumulation of new experiences. Yet the teaching profession in most countries is already stretched to its limits; there are too few qualified teachers, especially in the newest technological subjects; all teachers are overworked and possibly underpaid, and they, too, require retraining. In-house training by employers is one thing but it is well to remember that many potential customers for education unfortunately do not have a place of work in these days of rampant unemployment.

Just about the only solution to these problems would appear to lie in self-education and self-training, through the application of IT in new ways. Sir Harold Wilson's Open University is but one small, though highly significant, step in the right direction.

Two of the goals of such self-training, or computer-aided instruction (CAI), must be that of reducing unemployment, at least for those who find it an unbearable indignity, and that of liberating people to create a new renaissance similar to that created by Gutenberg's printing press into the Europe of the fifteenth century. Based on the use of spare broadcasting capacity and the common television, the Open University is limited by both the medium and the machine. How much better it would be if more interactivity between teacher or machine and student were possible. Not all students want to proceed at the same pace.

The manipulation of text, sound, moving and fixed images with high resolution and colour are essential for education. Documentary course materials could be electronically deliverable, and many other information services allied to the educational television programmes ought to be available to the students in their homes. For example, the *Encyclopaedia Britannica*—graphics, coloured images, as well as the text—

could be offered as an electronic information service to end-users, equipped with appropriate microcomputer and output devices (colour screens, printers), at a small fraction of the price of $1,500+ for the set of volumes. Indeed, one company, Grolier, in January 1986 started to offer a 20 volume, 9 million word encyclopaedia on CD-ROM for about $900.[11] These prices are expected to come down drastically by the end of this decade.

Not all education and training can of course be done in this way. Learning is often much more effective between pupil and human teacher face to face, and learning how to learn is incomparably better taught in this way than with computerized artefacts. However, there are many situations in which CAI is perfectly adequate.

The tools (e.g. home computers, backup memories, input/output devices, software, etc.) for doing this are now at hand and their prices, too, will come down soon to levels at which large numbers of users are reportedly prepared to take the plunge. Even though education budgets are being squeezed till the pips squeak, schools, colleges and universities, to which the growing army of go-it-aloners who will educate and train themselves at home can be added, will guarantee a big upsurge in this market sector as we move into the 1990s.

A second potentially major IT applications field is health care. The age distributions of the populations of Western European countries in particular, of Japan and, to a lesser extent those of North America are steadily and rapidly shifting towards higher ages. This will increase the strain on health services: although elderly people are healthier than their forebears were—a trend we hope will continue—man still has no way of preventing illness and senescence in the long run.

Since it will not be possible to raise the number of hospital beds and the numbers of doctors and other medical or paramedical staff to cater for the growth in the number of people in the age bracket 60–90, these senior citizens will need to receive as much preventive medicine as possible. Significantly for the computer industry, a market is likely therefore to come into being for health monitoring systems in the home, capable of being operated by all but the worst invalid cases, who should anyway be catered for in hospitals and nursing homes.

These monitoring systems—electronic house nurses—will be equipped to collect specific patient data, measure key parameters (e.g. temperature, blood pressure, blood and urine analyses, etc.) and transmit them to the nearest doctor or medical centre which will then be able to spot any apparent deterioration in the patient's condition. Expert systems are likely to have a rôle to play in the 1990s in this context.

---

[11]$700 for the drive, which could be used for reading other CD-ROMs and should not therefore be charged wholly to the encyclopaedic information service, and $199 for the disk with the information on it.

Keeping a continual electronic eye in this way on the elderly in their homes may be a more efficient way of carrying out geriatric medicine, and if done properly could impact positively the psychology of these patients, who often feel lonely, neglected and even unwanted. Of course, use of such products as health monitoring systems is not restricted to the elderly. They would be of value to any age group.

The linking together of groups of individuals with common interest through networks of personal computers will provide the basis for a third applications field; system vendors are advised to focus their hard and soft products on facilitating electronic information exchange within such groups.

New relatively powerful home computers (say 3–5 MIPS) with 16-bit or 32-bit buses linked to high-capacity (64, 128, 144 Kbit/s) digital networks will be able to render person-to-person and group communications easier than ever before. Despite its enormous value, telephony's weaknesses hitherto have been that it handles only verbal messages and it has non-existent, or unreliable, or too limited information storage. In other words, both the communicating parties, in general, have to be present simultaneously; inconvenient if it happens to be 4.00 a.m. for one of them.

The convergence of computer and communications technologies resulting from the irresistably ascendant digital technology will bring about growth of asynchronous personal messaging, without the unacceptably long delays of the postal services. Perhaps surprisingly this technology will thus have a very human side to it, enabling easier socializing on a wider scale, mitigating the distances that separate family and friends in modern high-mobility societies and bringing us closer to what may be termed 'the global village'.

Like-minded individuals will be able to interact within both formal and informal distributed groups bound by common social or cultural interests. In turn, improved information/communication channels can be expected to modify the political climate and mechanisms of government at the international, national, regional and local levels. Referenda, opinion polls and demographic surveys, being easier to organize, will probably become commoner.

Expansive individual expression

Having briefly scanned how IT in the 1990s is set to broaden and deepen traditional societal functions, we turn to ways in which the same technological advances will enable the individual to grow intellectually and creatively. So far most PCs have been applied to doing old things in new ways; e.g. games, text preparation and spreadsheet manipulation have been done non-electronically from time immemorial. However, computers should not be regarded solely as a replacement technology; on the contrary, in the hands of the average individual they should permit exploration of new endeavours, formerly only available to a privileged few.

In this context market growth opportunities may well lie in entertainment and creative pursuits like computer art and music. Moving images and sound stored in digital form on tape or disk, attached via standardized interfaces to the bus of a home computer, can be built up, managed and manipulated; such libraries of audio and video programmes will allow new personalized products and services to grow out of this nexus of technologies.

Archived public audio-visual materials could, for example, be furnished so that individuals could make up their own montages and do reasonably comprehensive research of informational material of timely interest to them. The combination of television, compact disk and computer in the home clearly has considerable potential for market development of new products and services. It is not even in its infancy yet; present-day machines are very limited in their functionality and programmability. CD-Interactive is a move in this direction.

Within this century it seems likely that every second household in developed countries will be attracted inexorably to having a home information/communication/entertainment (ICE) centre. The word ICE-box may take on a new meaning. Keeping up with the Jones' will not be the only reason for having one; the accelerated pace of development will mean the rest of the world will not be far behind in wanting this particular status symbol. A very large market is, therefore, in prospect provided problems of software and standards are solved.

Aside from such à la carte entertainment, through networking and powerful home computer set-ups, the coffee-table version of the erstwhile mainframe, individual cultural growth may be another valuable source of sales. Computer art, the exploration of shape and texture, in colour, in four-dimensional space–time, is a field hardly touched upon yet and musical composition with the aid of a computer could well attract increasing numbers of people with more leisure time. The essence of this new blossoming of personalized IT will be increased freedom of choice and opportunity for cultural development.

Just as the 1960–70s craze for do-it-yourself (DIY) craft activities sprang out of new-found wealth and leisure, and enabled office workers to find satisfaction in practical manual work to improve their homes, in the 1990s similar driving forces—leisure and more disposable cash—are likely to push IT into the DIY arena, this time offering not the down-to-earthness of the former but the chance for personal cultural achievement and awareness.

Photography has been a popular hobby from the start, for people like to record the world about them and their most momentous experiences, but the promise has exceeded the reality because of the cumbersome developing, printing and storing of the pictures. With digital recording of fixed and moving images from cameras, as well as sounds, people will be able to set up personal/family audio-visual archives in the home and have simpler access to them compared with that offered by previous technology.

All hobbies have a strong information component; much of the attraction is to become quite an expert in a field other than one's profession, and this requires the hobbyist to continually seek new information on a worldwide canvas. This is equally true of the action-orientated and the collecting hobbies; ornithologists, basket-weavers, aeroplane modellers, origami practitioners and embroiderers, for example, as well as stamp, coin, porcelain and other collectors could all become specialized markets for new information technology products and services. The audio-visual explosion of the 1990s is capable of stimulating and broadening hobbyism.

Another sector of this personalized DP market stems from the new business opportunities afforded the individual who owns a PC and wishes to become an entrepreneur in the information industry: a broker, a database producer, a consultant, a specialized publisher, etc. This type of home computer user has been steadily growing in Western Europe and North America throughout the 1980s; the rapid ebbing and flowing of the tide of fortune for many high-technology companies and their employees will cause more and more professionals to set up a second line of business, based at home, as a cushion to soften the blow of sudden unemployment.

A more mundane application outside the professional workplace is home economics. Much talked about, experience to date shows that home computers will be used for this purpose only with reluctance. Nevertheless there will almost certainly be a growing number of software package sales for budget management, diary keeping, address lists, cooking recipes, local transport timetables and a host of other requirements related to running an efficient home. Most householders seem to be happy with time-honoured methods, quaint and scrappy though they be; however, having bought a machine to satisfy some other need, they can use it to tackle home economics problems.

A miscellany of other applications of computers outside the workplace is waiting to be tapped. The choice of areas outlined so far in this section is personal and arbitrary, except that we do think they are serious contenders for large new markets.

From the miscellany, to give its flavour and food for thought, consider teleshopping, especially for bargains and discounts. Inelegant the word may be, but the activity it represents is set to grow by leaps and bounds. Allied to videotex services offered by the PTTs and RPOAs,[12] to electronic funds transfer (EFT) and to the fact that too much energy (in the form of motor fuel) and time is wasted shopping and looking for parking spaces in inner cities, many are going to prefer to purchase goods by electronic consultation of what is on offer (prices, etc.) and electronic ordering. Goods can be delivered to the home and paid for by EFT.

Other randomly chosen examples could be machine translation services and home-help robots. The microprocessor's entry into the motor car is also likely to develop considerably and extend to public transport vehicles (buses, trains, aeroplanes), particularly with the advent of cellular radio services.

In discussing the foregoing applications we have not distinguished hardware from software from network requirements, but it is clear that different applications will require different elements of each. A basic core of hardware and software is common to all, but on top of that each system will have its particular needs in both departments and will require easy access to flexible (multiple) networks.

The big questions are: will we be any better off? Assuming the needs for this all-pervading network of machines, will the domestic and business customers agree and know how to make use of it? The key to answering these questions resides in three fundamental prerequisites: standards, software and simplicity—the three Ss—without which the information society would not be sustainable. This last conclusion re-emphasizes indeed some of our previous findings and further substantiates the recommendations made to this effect in other parts of this book.

9.5 CONCLUSION AND OUTLOOK

In late 1986, Frost and Sullivan, a market research organization active in the United States, as well as in Europe, has released a set of estimates, which add an extra dimension to the rapid evolution in input/output devices and storage techniques, discussed in Chapter 9. The world market for microprocessor hardware should grow to over $7 billion in 1990, from approximately $4.5 billion in 1985, or at 9 per cent per annum cumulatively. During the same period, however, the market for 'add-on equipment' is expected to expand to $8.5 billion from a mere $3 billion, which is equivalent to a growth rate of 23 per cent per annum.

---

[12] RPOAs = *Recognized Private Operating Agencies*.

In view of the heterogeneous nature of the many different technologies involved and the increasing number of their possible combinations, the figures cited are obviously subject to wide margins of error. It remains nevertheless that demand for peripherals, for interface equipment and for storage devices will soon surpass the demand for microprocessor hardware and will keep expanding at least twice as fast and sustain the momentum well into the 1990s. This is fully substantiated by our own findings, summarized below.

1. A rising flood of data is being gathered daily from a wide variety of sources; it presents a veritable puzzle of immense complexity, but at the same time represents a marvellous opportunity to the astute vendor. The tools are at hand, or will soon be, that will usher in an era of richer and better information for everyone and perhaps greater control over the environment. Image and sound data will dominate systems from the late 1980s onwards. Systems devoted only to text and numbers will rapidly come to be regarded as old-fashioned and outmoded.
2. We can expect to see a dramatic growth in the automatic gathering of physical data by remote sensing, both through satellites and terrestrial networks. Global monitoring of events in the biosphere, identification of resources, security of premises, networked demographic surveys, customs and trade monitoring and control, as well as service usage measurements, seem likely to lead the way.
3. Automatic collection of human-generated data, using handwriting tablets, voice input and digitizing scanners, ought to enter steadily into use over the next decade in order to overcome the input bottleneck, which is particularly costly in the publishing and database industries as well as office administration. Accumulation of data will continue at increasing rates from medical, agricultural, engineering and basic science research laboratories.
4. Application of IT in the workplace is only the tip of the iceberg; a major market growth outside this is awaiting development in the alliance of computers and audio-visual information, and will lead to societal and personal benefits. On the collective front, education, health care and group communications constitute an as-yet undeveloped market, beckoning vendors of hardware, software and systems.
5. The individual will look increasingly to IT products and services to provide absorbing personalized entertainment, to support and widen the horizons of hobbies and to enable freedom to participate in the graphic arts, music and literature. Our culture will be fuelled to a significant and growing extent in this way.
6. Advances are being achieved in the hardware and software at the man–machine interface; a combination of keyboards, pointers and,

in the longer term, speech recognition devices is rapidly leading to a new mix of products which will strengthen the interaction between man and computers.
7. High-density, random-access, back-up memory, capable of storing locally practically all information needs, is now coming online for the personal computer. This is a watershed in the history of computers and presages their application as an everyday tool in the work and leisure spaces of the individual. It will surely have a direct impact on the network service mix and the way networks are used.
8. Thin-film magnetic technology and optical technology will vie with each other for supremacy in some applications, but for many others will complement each other. The much shorter access times and greater transfer rates of the former will have to be weighed carefully against somewhat higher densities and greater reliability (no head crashes) of the latter.
9. In the late 1980s a confluence of memory technology developments will no doubt lead to the passage of thresholds, significant for applications of computers, namely: DRAM with 10 $Mbit/in^2$, thin-film magnetic disks with 50 $Mbit/in^2$ and optical disks with 100 $Mbit/in^2$ (WORM) to 350 $Mbit/in^2$ (CD-ROM). We await with impatience the arrival, probably in the mid-1990s, of three-dimensional memories to produce the next quantum leap; meanwhile ways of taking maximum advantage from the current splash of large memories have to be worked out and diligently exploited.
10. This technology wave of the 1980s is really the sum of a number of independent innovations all coming to a peak at about the same time. Its momentum is irrepressible, but for those companies, large and small, thrilled to be in the thick of it, the main issue is whether the wave will break through to new and profitable pastures in the 1990s or whether it will dissipate itself on the beaches of office desks, laboratory benches, factory floors, classrooms and even coffee tables, occupied by disinterested or bemused potential customers.

General Conclusion

Barring an improbable accident of history, 1990–9 will be the years of the great divide in the computerization of society. To future historians and analysts the forthcoming decade may appear more as a curtain raiser, a preliminary to a second information revolution, in the course of which the level of computer penetration will have been pushed, by new vendor strategies, pertinent and more amicable to the user, to perhaps 40–50 per cent of the population in the industrial nations, from the present 5–10 per cent.

Other key findings include the following.

WATERSHED LINES IN TECHNOLOGY

Ongoing technological developments mark a break, in one way or another, with current information technology applications. The major trends have already emerged. Their potentialities are being assessed. More specifically:

1. By 1990 we shall know with precision the ultimate bounds to miniaturization of electronic components and figure out the limits to the development of computer systems based on current materials, concepts, designs.
2. By trial and error, we shall have also identified the limiting parameters of industry-relevant applications of artificial intelligence and determined their ideal scope.
3. At this point, it is appropriate to enter a caveat, not about whether software engineering will become an industry in its own right, as is commonly expected, but about how long it will take and, moreover, how it will impact upon the cost of software, whether packaged or custom-made, in relation to hardware.
4. By the end of this decade, we shall be able to start making learned guesses about future markets for higher orders of performance machines, using different materials and/or based on entirely new technologies, inasmuch as the pre-1990 lines of product will have left a large slice of demand wanting.

5. Resistance-free, heat-free superconductive circuits could lead to still smaller and faster computers in the near future, thus giving a boost to electronic technology. However, in the somewhat longer-run, electronics will be increasingly challenged by photonics, announcing the advent of laser computers. By 1990, or shortly afterwards, today's laboratory research in this area will have resulted in life-size prototypes, ready for testing and commercial assessment.
6. Also, the outcome of the current emulation between magnetic technology and optical technology will have been determined, particularly as regards their impact on the storage function and I/O techniques, and consequently also on the crucial problem of man–machine–system interaction.
7. Finally, by 1990 the spin-offs from the vast R&D effort going into remote sensing, real-time control, new materials, within the framework of SDI (the star wars programme) will have become available for civilian applications, e.g. computers.
8. No vendor can afford to ignore the megatrends in computer system technology or dismiss lightly the new vistas being opened up. However, when it comes to positioning/repositioning himself for action, he should remember the red faces of those early enthusiasts who used to profess that anything that is technically feasible will, sooner or later, come to pass.
9. Using a more up-to-date terminology, the warning is clear: technological leapfrogging alone will not do the trick. Important additional ingredients will have to go into the pudding.

CONFLICTING MARKET POINTERS RECONCILED

The signals we get from the marketplace these days amount to a mixed bag of exciting prospects, together with some dire syndromes. However, when these messages have been properly analysed and sorted out, we begin to discern significant lines of convergence. The cheerful symptoms are listed first.

1. In keeping with the contemporary 'audio-visual' style of life, potential demand for versatile electronic imaging is virtually limitless, although it has been held in check by technical inadequacies and prohibitive costs. As these impedimenta are being effectively eliminated, the market for all sorts of vision systems is about to explode, and by 1992 it should be worth as much as the present IBM's total sales.

2. Supercomputers and the suddenly revitalized business of EDI (electronic data interchange) are among the few risk-free, steady-growth markets, on which it is safe to bet in the medium term. On the other hand, the present emulation between high-capacity optical disks and thin-film magnetic disks, or that between programmable PCs and smart terminals, come close to a game in which ultimate winners take all and only crumbs are left for the losers.
3. The big prize, however, is the till-now non-user market, made up of over 90 per cent of the population in the Western countries. The so far limited inroads into this unmapped territory by a few pioneering vendors augur a larger-scale penetration in the coming years, and the movement is probably unstoppable. A customer-friendly and truly pertinent segmentation of the untapped and/or undeveloped markets is an absolute prerequisite.
4. Enough discretionary purchasing power is now concentrated in the hands of persons of independent means, rich widows, employees in between two jobs, the retired, the handicapped, etc., to provide vendors with an incentive to design/redesign information systems and aids, tailored to the specific needs of these much neglected categories.
5. In view of the fact that only 5 per cent of human endeavour is spent on productive work, there have been so far surprisingly few successful applications of computing to education, health care, leisure, travel, creativity and other unremunerated pursuits. Overcoming user reluctance will, however, require radically new product policies and a different marketing approach, holding up the ultimate promise of personalized services.
6. The rising tide of physical and man-generated data makes it imperative to find ways of massively automating their capture, de-pollution, storage and redistribution. This necessity, lest we all be drowned in a sea of information, can of course be turned into a blessing for the suppliers of the many diverse facilities yet to be invented, mass-produced and implemented, together with proper monitoring equipment and services.

In order to arrive at a balanced picture, it is now necessary to set off these positive prospects against several rather derogatory marketplace signals, and especially the following:

1. One after the other, world markets for mainframes, for minicomputers, home computers, business PCs, portables, for word processors, office workstations, databases, etc., after a period of buoyant demand, have subsequently shown unmistakable signs of slowdown, damped growth, even saturation.

2. For a while, the computer industry could take some comfort from the meteoric success of the new breed of specialized vendors catering for narrow market segments. For many of these newcomers, however, the fireworks began petering out when the big boys, headed in fact by Big Blue, moved in force into these momentarily juicy niches.
3. The relatively recent tendencies to product diversification, narrower specialization and differentiation did contribute to the widening of the market, by attracting additional categories of users. However, they also siphoned off part of the demand for older or standard products and systems.
4. Thus, while overall spending on computer equipment is still rising, albeit at a slower pace—as is also average expenditure on new information technology by the corporate buyer—vendors' net earnings have generally taken the plunge, owing to (much) lower-than-anticipated sales.
5. In particular, American and European vendors, no longer immune to business fluctuations, are further challenged by buyers' growing dominance of the marketplace. Moreover, they are afflicted with skyrocketing R&D expenditure, an often prohibitive financial burden, and rapidly rising costs of software. Their competitiveness is seriously eroded and for many of them it may already be irretrievably lost.
6. Could Japan supplant the United States as the world leader in informatics? Boasting current sales superior to those of Digital Equipment, is Fujitsu poised to become a match for IBM? Could the Far East swamp the world not just with memory chips and PC clones, but a great many staple computer products? As Asian imports are making further advances into the American and European markets, there is something ominous about these questions, which only a few science-fiction writers dared to ask five short years ago.
7. Paraphrasing the psalmist, the fear of Japan could well be the beginning of wisdom. In that sense, the warning signals which the marketplace is sending around could indeed provide decisive stimulus to American manufacturers and provoke at least some of them into revising their business outlook, overhauling their operation base and reorienting their plans.

FORK IN THE ROAD

As they prepare to enter the 1990s, computer vendors, particularly in the United States, must eventually confront the fundamental issue of business strategy. Their choice boils down to two alternatives: either keep muddling through as best they can in the hope of a (problematic) reversal of fortunes or position themselves for riding the new wave, thus spearheading the second information revolution in the (fair) hope of reaping early rewards. Let us concentrate on the second proposition.

1. Defining a radically new strategy and then implementing it implies harder work for company executives and involves taking calculated risks; but that, after all, is what modern managers have been trained for. A far greater difficulty is to secure acceptance, by all concerned, of the required changes in attitudes and approach, as developing new business opportunities must now receive precedence over development of new products/systems/services.
2. The relevant new set of priorities, i.e. user feedback, demand driven technologies, product policies based on comparative cost analysis, emphasis on undeveloped markets, mark an almost complete inversion of the prevailing business philosophy of most vendors who tend to privilege intrinsic technological brilliance, clever design and quantitative performance of systems, and put a premium on captive customers, domestic clientele and well-established markets.
3. The best resolutions would, however, remain ineffectual unless and until the gains from computerization accruing to each and every customer become a major concern of the vendor, and incidently also his strongest selling point. Manufacturers and designers will have to reconcile themselves to consumer sovereignty and accept the latter's scale of values, including his (occasionally odd-looking) preferences for simpler procedures rather than excessive sophistication; for PC clones as consumer items rather than durables; for limited, modular integration; for only partly distributed networks and the like.
4. As the new strategy requires heavy investment, constant high-level attention must be given to costing and cost control. Equity financing should be the rule. Productivity targets should be set and enforced. Spending on in-house R&D must be seriously curtailed through cooperative ventures and through more frequent purchases of patents (as the Japanese do).
5. Vendors who opt for the new strategy should logically support timely international standardization, not only because it contributes to the widening of the market but also because it introduces a measure of stability into the marketplace. This particular aspect has often been overlooked, although it plays an important rôle in such matters as control over product life cycles, scheduling the introduction of new lines of product, harmonizing conflicting business targets, e.g. increased market shares or immediate higher profits.
6. Whatever the vendor's main line of business—computer systems, factory automation, vision systems, software, new office

technology—there is of course no guarantee that the new set of policies will meet with a 100 per cent, or even a 75 per cent, success. In the real world, as experienced managements know all too well, allowance must always be made for environmental uncertainty and for human error.

7. The strategic master plan must therefore be well structured yet modular, both short and medium term, and supplemented with a complete financial blueprint; it must provide for contingency planning and include built-in mechanisms for regular monitoring and quick feedback to the top executives of the vendor company.

8. There remains the tricky question of transition from current to new strategy. Two unhappy precedents may perhaps be recalled. US mainframe manufacturers, without a single exception, have failed to capitalize in time on the technology that produced the minicomputer, a highly profitable venture throughout most of the 1970s. Yet, the successful makers of the minis have in turn failed to move in time into the microprocessor market, thus missing forever a golden opportunity. The lesson is clear: for most US and European vendors, the time to start making active preparations for a change in strategy, though only a partial one, is now.

Index

Acceleration principle, 48–54
Acorn Computer (UK), 63, 66–68, 78
ADA, 47, 204–205, 214
ADABAS (Database Management System), 219
Advanced Microdevices, 73
Akers, John F., 53, 65–66
Alcatel Thomson (France), 70, 72
ALGOL (programming language, 214
Algorithms, 202, 220, 222–223, 229, 234, 259
   efficiency of, 229, 230, 232–233, 239
   polynomial and NP, 230–234, 238
   simplex, 223, 333
Alphabets and character codes, 252–253
Alvey Program (UK), 73–74, 207
Amdahl, 25, 56, 70, 71
Amdahl, Gene, xii, 70, 71, 178
American Association for Computing Machinery, 104
American National Standards Institute, 159
Amortization, xix, 45
Amstrad (UK), 65, 78, 267
Analysis
   cost, 29–33, 57, 280
   cost–benefit, 85, 89, 90
   input–output, 90–96
   statistical (packages), 219, 222
   systems, xvi–xvii
Antitrust law, legislation, 73
APL (programming language), 209, 214–218
Apple Computer
   competing with IBM, 63–68
   imaging systems, 140
   Lisa, 64, 120, 254
   Macintosh, 64, 210, 254, 265
   personal computers (PCs), 63–68
   staff reductions, 76

Applications, 83, 88, 98–100
   artificial intelligence, 229–238, 277
   electronic imaging, 140–146
   expert systems, 129, 236–238
   operational research, 96
   PC business, 83
   programs and programming, 130, 225–227
   software packages, 124–125, 212, 219–224, 228–239
Appropriation for R&D, 69–72
Apricot Computers (UK), 68
Artificial intelligence (AI), xvii, 73, 128, 162, 197–199, 202–203, 214, 229–238, 240, 257, 263, 276
Ashton Tate, 68, 127, 128
Assembler (programming language), 208, 213–214, 217
Atari, 63–68
AT&T
   artificial intelligence (AI), 236–237
   Bell Laboratories, 47, 79, 194, 208–209
   competing with IBM, 47, 68, 216
   divestiture, 75, 82
   EDS connection, 82
   in-house trading, 153
   level of indebtedness, 78
   Olivetti connection, 68, 82, 133
   patent licensing, 79
   Philips connection, 82
   productivity, 75–77
   quality control, 81
   R&D policy and spending, 70, 72
   staff reductions, 75–76
   UNIX, 47, 208–209, 213, 216
Atomic engineering, 71, 168–169, 200
Audio-visual
   archives/libraries, 259–262, 272
   civilization, 247–251, 272

Audio-visual (*cont.*)
  data and integrated information services, 249–250
  processing, 115, 251
  technology markets, 271–273
Automation
  benefit from, xiv–xv, 93–96
  data capture by, 242–251, 278
  factory, 56, 57, 73, 81, 84, 88, 90–96, 101–105, 108, 124–125, 134–135, 280
  office, 56, 81, 101–105, 124–125, 134–135, 206, 210
Automatizable industries, 94–96
Avant-Garde Computing, 236–237

Backus, John, 208
Bardeen, John, 169
BASIC (Programming language), 214, 218
Batch processing, 121, 141, 159
Benefit(s)
  from automation, xiv–xv, 93–96
  from computerization, computing, xx, 86–90, 100–105, 159
  from (new) technology, 93–96
  intangible, 89–90
  tangible, 89–90, 105
  value-added, 90
Binning, Gerd, 180
Biological computers, 198–199
Biological systems, 197–199
Bistability, 193–194
Boeing Corporation, 73, 112, 155, 205–206, 240
Bolt, Beranek and Newman, 236–237
Brady, Michael, 141
Brainstorming, 32, 157
British Telecom, 82, 119
Bubble memory, 155, 172–175, 182
Budgeting, 69–71
Bull (France), 70, 72, 77, 221
Bundespost (Germany), 82, 115–118
Burroughs
  Burroughs-Sperry merger (Unisys), 72–73
  cooperative R&D, 73
  innovative architecture, 192
  level of indebtedness, 78
  mainframes, 54
  operating systems, 46
  productivity, 75–77
  R&D policy and spending, 70
  staff reductions, 75–76

Business
  cycles, xx, 34, 43, 47–54, 78–79
  indicators, 31, 157
  PCs, 260–262, 278
  prospects, surveys, 34
  strategy, xii–xvi, 279–81
  user(s), 105, 106–107
Buyer(s)
  corporate, 29, 84, 90, 142, 161, 279
  market, xx, 84, 109–133, 134, 159–160
  potential, 134

C (programming language), 208, 214–215, 216
CAD/CAM (computer-aided design and computer-aided manufacturing, 73, 86–87, 110–111, 140–146, 223, 249, 263, 264
CAFS (content-addressable file store), 190, 222
CAI (computer-aided instruction), 268–271
California Institute of Technology, 191
Cambridge ring (British LAN), 126
Canion, Rod, 67
Canon (Japan), 21, 176
Capital stock, 48–54
Capitalization, 77–78, 81
Carnegie Group, 129
Carnegie–Mellon University, 105, 126, 175, 235
CAS (Chemical Abstract Service), 113
CCITT (Consultative Committee for International Telephony and Telegraphy), 115–116, 206, 214, 247
CD-ROM (Compact Disk/Read-Only Memory), 113, 182, 222, 249–250, 257, 259–264, 267, 269, 275
Cellular radio, 273
Centralization, 122–125
Ceratech, 257–258
CERN (Centre Européen pour la Recherche Nucléaire), 243, 245
CGE (Compagnie Générale d'Électricité, France), 72
Character recognition, 246, 249

Choice
  customer, 83–84, 121
  rational, 94, 111, 130
CII (Honeywell–Bull–CII, France), 37, 70, 72
Circuit packing densities, 169–180
Circuitry, 55, 71, 110–112, 135–137
Closed shop, 121
Closed user group, 112
COBOL (programming language), 204, 206, 209–210, 213–214, 217–219
Commodore, 63–68
Communication(s)
  computer-to-computer, 119
  data, 40, 138–139, 245
  personal, 147, 157, 271
  satellite, 139
Compaq, 63–67
Compatibility, 39, 203–205, 208
Competition
  foreign, 31
  future, 133
  global, 156–157
  imperfect, 31
Competitiveness, 279–281
Compilers, compilation, 110, 190, 200–201, 203, 213, 215
Complexity (syndrome, theory), 84, 109–111, 229–234, 240
Components, 71, 81, 110, 161, 176, 200, 256, 276
  market for, 135–137
  miniaturization of, 170, 179, 277
Compound interest curve, 8–13, 23, 25, 32
Computer(s)
  architecture, ix, 42, 47, 74, 161, 180–192
  art, 271, 272, 275
  computer-to-computer communication, 119
  communications convergence, 258, 270
  design, 40, 109, 111, 190–192
  graphics, 140–141, 143
  industry, ix–x, 31–34, 37, 53–54, 57, 83–85, 109
  music, 271, 274
  optical (laser), 161, 193–196, 201, 216, 277
  performance and throughput of, 184–186
  power, ix, 35, 55, 109
  stores and retailing, 128, 268–269

Computer-aided instruction (CAI), 268–270
Computer Sciences Corporation, 78
Computer Vision, Inc., 70, 78, 143
Computerization, 83–84, 86, 95, 131, 146, 152, 156, 241, 277
  benefit from, xx, 84–90, 100–105, 159, 280
  indicator, 95
Computerland, 64–65
Computing
  expenditure on, 104
  gain from, 84, 86–90, 141
  games, 234–235
  power, ix, 109, 229–234
  resources deployment, xvi, 109, 121–126, 132, 205
Concurrent Computer Corporation, 192
Concurrent processing, 185, 192, 201
Consumer electronics, xiii, 71, 135–138, 153–154
Control
  cost, 280–281
  of inventory, 78–79, 90, 238, 249
  quality, 75, 81, 88, 90, 124–125, 143, 256
  real-time, 277
  systems, 74
Control Data Corporation (CDC), 31
  cooperative R&D, 73
  integrated information systems, 115
  level of indebtedness, 78
  mainframes, 43, 54
  operating systems, 46
  optical storage, 264
  peripherals, 54
  productivity, 77
  staff reductions, 76
  supercomputers, 42, 56, 185–187
Convergent Technologies, 120
Convex Computer, 42, 110
Corporation for Open Systems (COS), 206
Cosmic cube, 187, 191–192
Cost(s)
  analysis of, 29–33, 57, 281
  benefit analysis, 85, 89, 90
  capital, 94–96
  computer time, 86
  control of, 281–282
  conversion, 45, 215
  differential, 23–25, 29–33
  diversification, 89

Cost(s) (cont.)
  efficiency, 28, 34, 112–113, 122, 220, 239
  expert systems, 129
  financial, 75–79, 80–81
  fixed, 107
  hardware, 30, 57–61
  input, 104
  maintenance, 104
  operating, 35
  PC clones, 64–67
  performance, 12–14, 23–25, 37
  processing, 12, 13, 28–30, 35–37, 113
  projections, 16–19
  R&D, ix, 57–58, 71–74, 80–81, 279–280
  saving, 13, 75–82
  software, 47, 57–61, 80, 202, 276, 279
  spread, 24–25
  storage, 12, 13, 21, 28, 113
  switching, 26–29, 40–41, 60–61, 72, 119–120
  telecommunications, 26–33
  transmission, 26–27, 40–41, 60–61
  trends, patterns, xix, 11–15, 23–25, 29, 151
  unit, 18, 26–27, 34, 102, 147, 150, 264–265
  variable, 106–107, 130
CP/M (operating system), 213, 215
Cray Research, 56, 192
  supercomputers, 42, 56, 185–187
Crayette (Minisupercomputer), 42
Creative Output, Inc., 207
Cross-licensing, 79–80
Cryptography, 220, 233
Crystal growth, 165–169, 200
Cullinet, 126, 131
Custom-made software, xvii, 47, 106, 109, 126–131
Cycle(s)
  amplitude of, 52
  business, xx, 34, 43, 47–54, 78–79
  computer industry and, 51–54
  duration of, 48–51
  earnings, 48–49, 56, 279
  life, xvii, 43–46, 54–55, 279
  product, 34, 43–47

Dantzig, George, 233
Dassault-Systèmes (France), 86
Data
  automatic processing, 246–247, 248
  automation of capture, 242–251, 254–255, 274, 278
  classification indexing of, 245–246
  comparison of types, 245–247
  data communication, 40, 138–139, 245, 249–250
    communications standards, 209, 249–250
    compression, 242, 247, 257, 262, 267
    explosion, 242, 274
    filtering, 249, 250
    interchange (protocols), 205–206, 209, 239, 241, 262
    inventory growth rate, 242–245
    networks, 74, 119, 249–250
    remotely sensed by satellite, 243, 245, 250
  environmental, 245
  high-speed (networks), 196, 249–250
  image and sound, 235, 245, 247
  manual collection of, 245–246, 248–255
  mixing of, 247–248, 254, 263, 267–268
  unloading of, 113
Data General, xiii, 76, 78, 206
Database(s), 99, 102, 104–105, 242, 244, 247, 278
  bibliographic, 155–156, 222
  distributed, 122–125, 222, 233
  image and sound, 222
  management, 131, 212, 219–222, 224, 263
  online interrogation of, 46, 113, 321
  relational, 131, 221
  underutilization of, 104–105
Dataflow machines, computers, 186–191, 200–201, 216
Datapoint, 206
DBMS (Database Management Systems), 129, 131, 212, 219–222, 224, 233, 263
Decentralization, 37, 121–126
Decision-support system(s), 90, 99–100, 143, 221
Decline in costs, 19–22, 23–29, 32–33
Decreasing returns, xx, 85–86, 100–107
Deere, John, 205
Defense Advanced Research Projects Agency, 123
Demand
  derived, 150–152

discontinuities in, 40–41, 55, 104
driven technologies, 280–281
elastic and inelastic, 41, 104–105, 142
for electronic imaging, 150–152, 278
for LANs, 126
for MIPS, 103
for substitutes, 150–152
replacement, 48–54
Deployment of computing resources, xvi, 109, 121–126, 132, 205
Depreciation, 48, 69, 104
Design
computer, 40, 109, 111, 190–192
network, 74, 236–237
product, 86–87
semiconductor, 32–33
system, 106, 111, 132, 210
Desktop computer(s), 55, 121–123, 124–125, 127
DIALOG, 46
Diebold Group, Inc., 29, 78
Diebold, John, 104
Differentiation of products, 34–42, 279
Digital cartography, 142, 250
Digital Equipment Corporation (DEC), xiii, 113, 208, 209
 artificial intelligence, 237
 competing with IBM, 39, 67, 79, 237, 279
 cooperative R&D, 72–73
 in-house trading, 153
 input/output technology, 237
 integrated systems, 126, 132, 206
 LANs, 126
 level of indebtedness, 78
 mainframes and minicomputers, 39, 112
 marketing, 107, 153
 product strategy, 39
 productivity, 76–77
 R&D policy and spending, 70–73
 RISC technology, 111
 speech recognition, 256–258
Digital Research, 68, 213
Digital switch, switching, 72, 112
Digital television, 154
Diminishing returns, xx, 85–86, 100–107
Discontinuities in demand, 40–41, 55, 104
Disk(s)

drive technology, 21–22, 65–66, 172–176
 floppy, 22, 75, 81, 172–175, 182, 259–262
 optical, vii, 22, 172–176, 258–266, 279
 thin-film magnetic, 264, 279
 Winchester, 22, 172–174, 257
Display
 competitive technologies, 259, 264–267
 image, 139–141, 251, 253–255, 262, 263, 265–268
 screen resolution of, 111, 263, 264–265
Distributed, local intelligence, 113
Distributed processing, 35–37, 122
Distributed systems, xvii, 37, 122–126, 132
Diversification (e.g. of product), 34, 55, 82, 89, 279
Document
 digitization, 253–255, 258–263, 265
 electronic delivery, 262
 interchange format (DIF), 206, 262
 multimedia, 258–263, 264–268
Do-It-Yourself (DIY) computing, 272–273
DONOACS, 206
DRAM (dynamic random access memory), 80, 171–173, 177–180, 262–264, 275
Du Pont Nemours, 205
Duchin, Faye, 91
Dumping (practices), 31, 81
Dun and Bradstreet, 148
Durables, 48–51, 281

Early warning systems, 142, 150–152
Earnings cycles, 48–49, 56, 280
Eastman Kodak, 140, 205, 264
Economies of scale, 124–125, 153
Education and training, 263, 268, 274
Educational television, 78, 268–269
Ein-Dor, Phillip, 35–39, 40, 56
Electrical conductivity, 164–165, 198
Electronic Data Systems, 78, 96
Electronic encyclopaedia, 258, 269, 270
Electronic filing cabinet, 258, 264
Electronic funds transfer (EFT), 249, 273
Electronic games, xii, 154, 223, 272

Electronic imaging, xviii, 139–146, 150–152, 278
Electronic International Corporation, 134–136
Electronic mail and messaging, 98–99, 114–116, 149–151, 216, 247, 263, 264
Electronic publishing, printing, 143, 148–152, 222, 247, 263, 265
Electronic transactions, 159–160, 271
Electronics
  consumer, xiii, 71, 135–138, 153–154
  defense, US, 74, 135–137
    industry, ix–x, 135–139
    patents, 75, 79, 80
  global market(s) for, 32, 134–139, 143
  medical and space, 135–137, 142
  world trade in, 134–139
Encyclopaedia Britannica, 244, 270
End-user, 123, 126, 132, 134, 218–228
Engineering
  applications, 128
  parameters, 111
  quality, 81
  software, xix, 73–74, 239–240, 277
  trade-off, 111–114
Entrepreneurship, 89, 105
Envelope curve, 19–20
Eosat Corporation, 142
Epitaxy (processes), 169, 200
Equatorial Communications, 113
Equity financing, 77–78, 281–282
Ericsson (Sweden), 70, 72, 82
Error detection and correction, 259–261
ESPRIT (R&D program), 74, 192, 207
Ethernet (LAN), 124–126, 210
EUREKA (R&D program), 74, 194, 207
Eurodata Foundation, 28–30
Euronet/DIANE (network), 73, 74
European Community, 73, 74, 99, 192, 205, 207
Expert systems, 99, 129, 157, 162, 198, 202, 235–238, 262
  applications of, 129, 236–238
  commercial, 235–236
  cost of, 129
  for network management, 237
  health, 270–271
  implementation of, 235–236
  market for, 129–130, 237–238
Exponential function, curve, 8–16, 23–33, 230–234, 241
Extrapolation, xv, 26–30, 62, 88, 156

Fabry, Charles, 195
Fabry–Perot interferometer, 195–196
Facsimile, xiii, 32, 99, 115, 147–152
Factory automation, 56, 57, 73, 81, 84, 88, 90–96, 101–105, 108, 124–125, 134–135, 281
Factory of the future, 95–96
Fail-safe computers (back-up), 55, 220
Fairchild Semiconductor, 73, 76, 171
Federal Aviation Administration, 111
Federal Communications Commission, 61
Fifth-generation computers, 206–207
Financial costs, 75–79
Flexible manufacturing, 73, 87, 88, 90, 107–108, 205, 249
Floating Point Systems, 192, 256
Floppy disk(s), 22, 75, 81, 172–175, 182, 259–262
Fluctuations, 34–55, 278–279
Flynn's terminology for computer architectures, 186–189, 196
Ford Motor Corporation, 96, 205
FORTRAN (Programming language), 204, 208–210, 217–219
Four Phase, 206
Frequency distributions, 10, 111, 154, 220
Fujitsu (Japan)
  bubble memory, 175, 279
  infringement of patents, 79
  productivity, 77
  semiconductors, xiii, 20
  supercomputers, 56
  telecommunications, 72
Fundamental and applied research, 71–74

Gain(s)
  from computerization, 84–90, 91, 100–105, 280
  from computing, 84, 86–90, 141
  intangible, 85
  productivity, 51, 88, 103
Gallium, arsenide, 42, 166–168
Gateway, 122
Gauss, Carl, 230

GEC (UK), 77–78
General Electric, 73, 143
General Motors, 95–96, 203–206, 240
Goldratt, Eliahn, 207
GOLEM (information retrieval system), 46, 221
Gompertz curve, 9–10, 60
Goodyear Aerospace, 192
Gordon, Gil, 158
Government funding, procurement, 71–74
Graph, graphing, 3, 4–11
Graphics
  computer, 140–144, 254–255, 258–263, 265–268
  resolution, 33, 64, 258–262, 265–268
  software, 131
Grolier, 270
Grosch's law, 35–39, 40, 55–56
Growth
  environment, 31, 57
  industry, 51, 54
  prospects for PCs, 63–68
  sectors, 56, 84, 159, 238–240, 274–276, 278–279

Hammer, Michael, 120
Hardware
  cost, 30, 57–61
  development, 163–201
  sales, 63
Harvard University, x–xi, 61
Health care information technology, 269–270, 274
Heat dissipation, 166–167
Herriot–Watt University, 194
Heuristics, 229, 232–233, 234, 235, 240
Hewlett–Packard, xiii, 78
  mainframes, 38
  marketing, 107
  optical disks, 176
  R&D policy and spending, 70, 73
  RISC technology, 110
  staff reductions, 76
Hitachi (Japan)
  bubble memory, 175
  infringement of patents, 79
  Olivetti connection, 133
  optical disks, 176
  R&D policy and spending, 166
  semiconductors, xiii, 20

supercomputers, 42, 56
telecommunications, 72
Hobbies and information technology, 271–272, 274–275
Home computers, computing, 55, 83, 120–121, 223, 271, 272, 279
Honeywell, 31, 54, 73
  level of indebtedness, 77–78
  mainframes, 54
  operating systems, 46
Hopper, Grace, 204
Huang, Alan, 194
Huffmann coding, 249
Hughes Aircraft, 96, 166

IBM
  automatic translation, 202–203
  business cycles, 52–53
  CAD/CAM, 86–87
  competing with Apple, 63–68
  competing with AT&T, 47, 68, 216
  cooperative R&D, 73
  decline, 25, 33, 53–54, 64–67, 79
  disk and disk drive technology, 21, 172
  dominance of market, xii, 11, 16, 25, 45, 54–56, 63
  earnings cycles, 48–49, 56
  IBM/plug compatible, 70
  imaging systems, 140, 144
  in-house trading, 153
  integrated circuit, 171
  integrated systems, 115, 132–133, 188
  inventory turnover, 78–79
  investment per employee, 82
  investment in plant, 53, 81
  LANs, 126
  level of indebtedness, 78–79
  mainframes, 22, 37–39, 45–46, 54–56, 71, 186, 203–204, 212–213
  marketing, 31–32, 107, 153
  4-megabit chip, 18–19
  Merrill Lynch connection, 155–156
  operating systems (OS), 46–47, 67, 131, 204, 213
  patents, 79–80
  PCs and clones, 25, 33, 57, 63–68, 279
  pioneering software, 203–204, 206, 208, 210
  pricing strategy, 22–23, 33, 54, 80

IBM (*cont.*)
  product cycles, 34, 45–46, 54
  product strategy, 38–39, 54–55, 63, 65–67
  productivity, 76–77
  R&D policy and spending, 63, 70–71
  rental policy, 45
  RISC technology, 111
  ROLM connection, 56, 82, 133
  SBS connection, 133
  speech recognition, 256–258
  standards, 67, 133, 209
  System Network Architecture, 209
  workforce, 75
ICE (Information, Communication, Entertainment) box, 271
ICL (UK), 37, 186, 192, 213, 221
  CAFS (content addressable file store), 190
  mainframes and parallel processor, 185–187, 213
  operating systems (OS), 213
Icon(s), 143, 210, 237, 254–255
ICOT (Institute for New Generation Computer Technology, Japan), 73
ILLIAC IV, 185–187
Image(s)
  digital recording of, 273
  digitization of, 259–263
    compression, 249
      display, 139–141, 251, 253–255, 262–264, 264–266
      processing, xviii, 115, 139–146, 186, 234
        resolution, 140–141, 262–264
    photographic, 263–264
    raster, 246, 259–265
    synthetic, 141, 150
Imaging, electronic, xviii, 139–146, 150–152, 277
IMNET (network), 155–156
Increasing returns, 85–86, 100–105
Indebtedness, 77–79, 82
Indicator(s)
  business, 31, 157
  of computerization, 95
  of performance, 100
  productivity, 76–77
Indium antimonide, 194–195
Inference Corporation, 129, 235
Information
  flows, 147–151, 216
  media, 146–152
  online, 46, 104–105

  pollution, de-pollution, 104, 278
  products and services, 237, 249, 252, 268–274, 275–276
  retrieval, 46, 98–99, 157, 219–222
  revolution, 276–281
  selective dissemination of, 221
  storage density of, 171–180, 197–199
  storage and retrieval of, 220–222
  supermarkets, 46
  technologies, xiv, xix–xxi, 68, 83–85, 88, 89, 91, 96, 98, 100, 151–152, 220–222, 242, 264, 277–282
  visual, 141
Information Industry Association, x
Infringement of patent(s), 79–80
Inmos (UK), xviii, 191–192
Innovation, 43–45, 192, 251, 263–264, 276
  labour saving, 89–90
  rate of, 43, 45
Input–output analysis, 90–96
Input–output technologies, 111, 162, 210–211, 222–223, 251–258, 264–267, 277
  flat displays, 264–267
  graphics, 251, 254–255
  icons and menus, 143, 210, 237, 254–255
  keyboards, 65–66, 158, 213, 244, 246, 251, 252–253, 255, 262, 264
  laser printers, 140, 210, 251, 262, 262, 264–266
  LCDs (liquid crystal displays), 255, 266
  magnetic/optical, 259–265
  markets and cost trends, 266–267
  mouse, mice (pointers), 64, 129, 143, 210, 237, 254–255
  multilingual aspects, 253, 255
  pointers, 254–255, 256–258, 262
  printers, 55, 99, 124–125, 213, 251, 263–267
  R&D on displays, 263, 265–267
  user features, 266–267
  software aspects, 266–267
  tablets, 251, 253–254, 256, 275–276
  voice, 254, 255–258, 275–276
Instruction decoding, 190
Intangible benefit(s), gain(s), 85, 89–90
Integrated circuit(s) (ICs), 55, 81, 171′–172, 196

3-dimensional, 180
history of, 171–172
packing densities of, 171–175, 177–180
VLSI (very large-scale ICs), 73, 79–80
yield of, 177
Integrated system(s), 83, 114–121, 258
Integrated workstation(s), 114–115, 120
Integration
concept of, xviii, 112, 114–121
limited, 120, 280
multifunction, 114–121
multimedia, 114–121
multipurpose, 114–121
Intel
bubble memory, 175
LANs, 126
microprocessors, 66–67, 171, 191, 262
semiconductors, xiii, 20
speech recognition, 256–258
UNIX, 47
Intellicorp, 129–130, 235
Interface, interfacing, xxi, 73–74, 111, 115, 122–126, 150, 210, 219–220, 237
Interferometry (multibeam), 196
Intergraph, 70, 131, 143
Interworking, 119, 123–125, 206, 252
Inventory, 31, 42, 48, 57, 81, 83
control of, 78–79, 90, 238, 249
Investment
gross, net, 50–52
in software, 224, 239
planning of, 85
return on, 41, 87, 97
ISDN (Integrated Services Digital Network), 114–120, 237, 249–250, 259–260
ISO (International Standards Organization), 205–207, 214, 238, 239
ITT, 70, 72, 126, 153
Iverson, Ken, 209

KAYAK (French LAN), 126
Kaypro, 65–66
Kelly, Philip T. F., 119
Keyboards, 65–66, 158, 213, 244, 246, 251, 252–253, 255, 262, 264

Kilby, Jack, 171
King, John Leslie, 104
Knowledge
based systems, 73–74, 235–237
bases, databases, 229, 235
engineering, 235–237, 238, 240
Kurzweil AI, 256–258

Labour
productivity of, 97–98, 102–103, 105–106
saving innovations, 89–90
saving on, 87–89
Landsat (network), 142, 245
LANs (Local area networks), xvii, 96, 124–126, 210
Laser
computer, 161, 193–196, 201, 216, 278
printer, 140, 210, 251, 262, 263
solid-state, 167, 169
technology, 54, 276–277
Laserdata, 176
Layoff(s), 75–76, 81, 83, 90, 101
Leading Edge Computer Products, 64–65
Lederberg, Joshua, 234
Leontief, Wassily, 90–91, 96, 107–108
Leontief model, 90–96, 107–108
LEP (France), 166
Licence and licensing, 58, 79–80, 128, 130
Life cycle, xvii, 43–46, 54–55, 280
Light emitting diodes, 166–167
Light transmission/refection, 164–165
Linear programming, 223, 233
Liquid crystal display (LCD), 255, 266
LISP (programming language), 214, 235, 237
LISP Machines, 237
Lithography, 178–180
Logarithms, xxi, 3–11
Logic
binary, 193–196
fuzzy, 198, 235
gates, 166–168, 193–194, 196
multistate, 194–196
programming, 235–238
Logistic function, 9–10, 60
Lotus Development, 68, 127, 128
Lumpiness, 34, 39–42

Machine translation, xvii, 202–203, 247, 274

Magnetic Technology Center
   (Carnegie-Mellon University), 175
Magnetic disk, 172–174, 250, 278
   floppy, 22, 75, 81, 172–175, 182,
      259–261
   recording densities, 172–174
   Winchester, 22, 172–174, 257
Magnetic tape, 172–174, 182, 250
Magnetization, 164–167, 193
Mailbox services, 114–116
Mainframes, 22, 36–46, 54–55, 71,
      101, 180–192, 218
   market for, 37–39, 80, 278
   micro/mainframe link, 119
   sales of, 45–46, 62–63, 78–79
   software for, 127–131, 211–228
Maintenance, 104, 124–125, 128, 217
Management information system(s),
      98–99, 204
Man/machine interface, xxi, 111, 162,
      210, 218, 237, 241, 251–255, 257,
      262, 264–267, 274–275
Man/system interaction, 241, 251–258
Man/machine synergy, 218, 234,
      240–241
MAP (Manufacturing Automation
      Protocol), 205–207, 240
Market(s)
   buyers', xx, 84, 109–133, 134,
      159–160
   captive, 45
   educational, 78, 269–270
   electronic imaging, 139–146
   export, 72, 136–138, 156
   global, for electronics, 84, 134–139,
      156–157
   for software, 127–131
   market, audio-visual technology,
      271–273
   circuitry, 135–137
   components, 135–137
   EDI (electronic data interchange),
      159–160
   electronics, 32, 84, 134–139,
      156–157
   expert systems, 129–130, 237–238
   factory automation, 134–138
   home computers, 279
   input–output technologies,
      266–268, 274–275
   mainframes, 37–39, 80, 278
   medical electronics, 135–137
   microcomputers, 37–39, 274
   minicomputers, 37–39, 279
   model for software, 130–131
   niches, 82, 152–158, 162, 251
   office automation, 134–138
   PCs, 25, 62–63
   prospects, 83, 134–160
   segment, segmentation, xviii,
      134–160, 279–282
   share(s), 134, 148–149, 280
   software, 127–131
   supercomputers, 42, 56, 278
   telecommunications, 135–139, 156
   PC shares, 63–68
   sellers', xx, 132
   underdeveloped, undeveloped,
      279–282
   widening of, 55, 278–281
Marketing, xix, 84, 107–108, 129,
      148–151, 279
Marketplace, 84, 278–282
Martin Marietta Corporation, 128
Materials
   bistable and multistable, 164
   optical, 164, 193, 195–196
   physical properties of, 164–165,
      193–194
   semiconducting, xvi, 163–169
   substitute, 168–169, 198–199
   substitute for silicon, 166–169
Matsushita (Japan), 166, 176, 180, 264
McClellan, Stephen T., xii–xiii, 44, 77,
      78, 155
McDonnell Douglas, 205
MCI Communications, 75
Medical electronics, 135–137, 142,
      270–271
Memory, 166, 181
   bubble, 155, 172–175, 182
   disks, 172–176
   dynamic random access (DRAM),
      80, 171–173, 177–180,
      260–264, 275
   hierarchy, 181–183, 213, 263–264
   main, 22, 181–183
   tape, 171–173
Mendeleyev's periodic table, xvi, 168,
      194, 199
Merrill Lynch, 155–156
Message handling systems (MHS), 115,
      206
Microcode, microprogramming, 110,
      185, 190, 211–212, 225, 239
Microcomputer(s), 36–39, 63–68, 101,
      121–123, 215
   characteristics of, 252, 263–265

market, 37–39, 274–275
  sales, 62–63, 124–125
  software, 68, 215, 223–224
Microminiaturization, 161, 169–180, 197, 200, 279–282
Micron Technology, 20
Microprocessor(s), 38–39, 55–56, 63, 67, 110–111, 170, 281
Microsoft, 67–68, 127, 128, 213
Microwave radio system, 112, 249–250
Milne, Frank, 130–131
Minicomputer(s), 36–39, 55, 101, 121–123, 279, 282
  market(s), 37–39, 279
  sales, 62–63
MIPS (millions of operations/second), 12–13, 22, 35–36, 43, 103, 184, 271
MIPS Computer Systems, 110
MIS (management information system), 98, 221
MISTRAL (information retrieval system), 221
MIT (Massachusetts Institute of Technology), 102, 120, 126, 141, 208, 235–237
MITA (Japan), 21
Mitsubishi (Japan), 166
Mix
  product, 75, 76
  revenue, 63
  system/market, 160
Mobile radio, 139, 157
Model, modelling, xix, 8, 9, 12–16, 29–31, 48–54, 60, 85, 96, 99–100, 102, 121, 149, 222
  constant-sum, 62–63
  Leontief, 90–96
  market for software, 130–131
Moore, Gordon, 177
Moore curve, 177–179, 200
Motorola
  bubble memory, 175
  microprocessors, 171, 262
  R&D policy and spending, 70, 73
  semiconductors, xii, xiii, 20, 67
  UNIX, 47
Mouse/mice (pointers), 64, 129, 143, 210, 237, 254–255
MS/DOS (Operating system), 68, 213–215
MULTICS, 208
Multifunction integration, 114–121

Multifunction workstation, 99, 210, 237, 263–264
Multinationals, 107, 128, 156
Multiplexing, 40
Multiprocessing, 183–185, 196, 200–201, 216
Multiprogramming, 184–185, 204
Multi-user systems, 33, 124–125
Myrby, Seth, 157

NASA (National Aeronautics and Space Administration), 22
National Advanced Systems, 25
National Semiconductor, xii, xiii, 20, 47, 67, 73, 171, 175, 263
Natural language processing, 198, 238, 263
Natural scale, 5–8
NCR, 31, 54, 77, 78
NEC (Nippon Electric Corporation, Japan)
  optical disk, 176
  patents, 80
  R&D policy and spending, 166
  semiconductors, xii, xiii, 20
  speech recognition, 257–258
  supercomputers, 56
  telecommunications, 72, 112
Network(s), 26, 29, 33, 115–116, 237
  broadband, 115, 119, 249–250
  circuit-switched, 124–125
  data, 74, 119, 245, 249–250
  dedicated, 119, 159
  design, 74, 236–237
  internal and by-pass, 81, 112
  local area (LANs) xvii, 96, 124–126, 210, 263
  packet-switched, 124–125, 133, 221, 237
  public, 112, 114, 159, 237, 249
  teletext, 113
New York University, 90–91, 94
Nixdorf (Germany), 77, 107, 132
Northern Telecom (Canada), 70, 72
Noyce, Robert, 171
NTIS (National Technical Information), 113
NTT (Nippon Telegraph and Telephone, Japan), 18–19, 82, 166
Numerical algorithms, 222–223

Obsolescence, ix, xiv, 43–47, 70, 149
OCCAM (special language), 192
ODA/ODIF (office document

architecture/office document
interchange format), 206
OECD (Organization for Economic
Co-operation and Development),
12–13, 38, 58–59, 217–218
Office automation, 56, 81, 101–105,
124–125, 134–135, 206, 210
  imaging systems for, 140
  market for, 134–138, 263–265
  new technology and, 85, 94, 96–100,
    105, 108, 281
OKI (Japan, 166
Olivetti (Italy), 64, 68, 77, 82, 107, 133
Online interrogation of databases, 46,
    104–105, 113, 221–222, 242,
    263–264
Open System Interconnection (OSI),
    115, 133, 205–207, 209, 214, 239
Open University, 269
Operating environment, 225, 228
Operating systems (OS), 47–48, 204,
    212–213, 214–215, 216–217, 228,
    264–265
  CP/M, 213, 215
  microcomputer, 68, 215
  MS/DOS, 213, 215
  multiprogramming, 264–265
  portability of, 215–216
  proprietary, 66–67, 213–214
  UNIX, 208, 215–217, 239, 264
Operational research, 96, 131, 223
Optical bistability, 194–196
Optical (laser) computers, 161,
    193–196, 201, 216, 278
Optical Computing Consortium, 194
Optical disk(s), CD-ROM, ix, 22,
    172–176, 258–265, 267, 278
Optical Disk Corporation, 176
Optical fibres, ix, 44, 73, 168–169, 196
Optical integrated circuits (ICs), 196
Optical Storage International, 265
Optical Storage R&D, 176, 195
Optical switches, 195–196
Optical technology, 172–198, 264–265,
    278
Optimem, 264
Optronics, xiii, 33, 167, 241
Order of magnitude, 4–6, 26, 43, 102,
    241
Organic materials, 180, 196–199, 201
OSI (Open System Interconnection),
    115, 133, 205–207, 209, 214, 239
Overhead(s), 53, 57, 75–79, 106–107,
    110, 119

Oversupply, 83, 147–148
Oxford University, 141

PA Technology (UK), 256
PABX (Private Automatic Branch
    Exchange), 116–120, 124–125
Paper
  demand for, 94
  office without, 241, 259
  versus electronic media, 258–265
Parallelism, parallel processing, vii, 73,
    115, 141, 183–189, 196, 198, 230
Parallel programming, 192
PASCAL (Programming language),
    213–214
Patent, patenting, 58, 71, 75, 79, 80,
    153, 155, 280
  electronics, 75, 79, 80
  infringement of, 79–80
  rights, 79–80
Pattern recognition, 143, 196, 198, 234,
    240, 257, 264
Penetration (level), 95, 151, 156, 160,
    247, 277, 279
Peripherals, 54, 55, 81, 115, 276
Perot, Alfred, 195
Personal computer (PC), 25, 63–68, 86,
    110, 112–113, 148, 158, 251, 262,
    281
  evolution of, 260–263
  growth prospects for, 63–68
  IBM clones, 25, 33, 63–68, 280
  market for, 62–63, 279
  market shares, 63–68
  noncompatible, 64–67
  sales of, 62–68, 79, 132, 159
  software, 127–128
Philips (Netherlands)
  AT&T connection, 82
  in-house trading, 153
  optical disks, 176, 260, 263
  R&D policy and spending, 70, 72,
    166
  semiconductors, xiii
  telecommunications, 72, 73 82
Photocopiers, photocopying, 21, 96,
    104
Photography, 263–264, 273
Pioneer, 260
Pipelining, 185–189
Pixel(s), 140, 259–262, 265
Plan, planning, xxi, 31, 62, 84–85, 90,
    99–100, 107, 124–125, 131, 155,
    166, 280–282

Plessey (UK), 72
PL/I (Programming language), 210, 214, 218
Polyacetylene, 198–199
Polysilicon, 81
Portable computers, 55, 63, 279
Portable software, xvii, 203, 208, 215–216, 223–225, 239
Preprocessing, 113, 122–125, 254
Pricing, 23, 31, 64
Prime computer, 42
Printer(s), 55, 99, 124–125, 213, 260–263, 265–268
   laser, 140, 210, 263, 265–268
Processing
   audio, 115
   batch, 121, 141, 159
   cost, 12, 13, 28–30, 35–37, 113
   distributed, 35–37, 122
   image, xviii, 115, 139–146, 186, 234
   parallel, ix, 73, 115, 141, 183–189, 196, 198, 230
   text, 55, 68, 99, 115, 219, 223–224
   vision, 140–141
Processor arrays, 185, 191–192, 230, 256
Procurement, 69, 73–74
Product(s)
   cycle, 34, 43–47
   differentiation, 34–42, 280
   Digital Equipment strategy, 39
   diversification, 34, 55, 82, 89, 280
   IBM strategy, 37–39
   strategy, xii, 35, 37–39, 56
Productivity
   concept of, 96–100, 108, 148, 281
   gains, 51, 88, 103
   index, 97
   indicators, 76–77, 281
   labour, 97–98, 102–103, 105, 106
   programmer, 213, 217
Programming by end-user, 218–219, 224, 226–227
Programming languages, 204–205, 214, 217
   ALGOL, 214
   APL, 209, 214–218
   Assembler, 208–214, 217–218
   BASIC, 214, 217–218
   C, 208, 214–215, 216
   COBOL, 204, 206, 209–210, 213–214, 217–219
   comparative use of, 217–218
   FORTRAN, 204, 208–210, 217–219
   fourth generation of, 220, 224, 235
   generations of, 217–218, 220
   high-level, 213–214, 217, 235
   job control, 215
   LISP, 214, 235, 237
   object-oriented, 237
   Pascal, 213–214
   PL/I, 210, 214, 218
   procedural, 219–220
   PROLOG, 214, 235–237
   real-time, 204
   SMALLTALK, 235, 237
   standards, 214, 224, 239
PROLOG (programming language), 214, 235–237
Prospects
   growth for PCs, 63–68
   market prospects, 83, 134–160, 150–160
Protocol(s) 124–125, 133, 160
   data interchange, 124–125, 205–206, 209, 239
   DIF, 206
   MAP, 205–207, 240
   MHS, 206
   ODA/ODIF, 206
   TOP, 206, 240
Prototyping, xxi, 128
PSDN (Packet-switched data networks), 124–125, 133, 221, 237
PTTs (Post, Telephone and Telegraph Administrations), 28

Quality control, 75, 81, 88, 90, 124–125, 143, 256
Quotron Systems, 148, 155–156

RACE (R&D program in telecommunications), 74
Radio Shack, 64–65
RAM (Random Access Memory), 16–20, 44, 80, 171–173, 182, 247, 260–263, 264, 276
Ratio chart, 11–13
Rational choice, 94, 111, 130
RCA (Radio Corporation of America), 54, 166, 175
R&D
   appropriation(s) for, 69–72
   cooperative, pre-commercial, 57, 73–74, 207
   cost of, ix, 57–58, 71–74, 80–81, 280
   duplication, 71–72
   electronic imaging, 141

R&D (cont.)
  failures, 71–72
  policy and spending, xx, 63, 69–74, 279–280
  in telecommunications, 72, 74
Reference Technology Corporation, 176
Refraction, non-linear, 194–196
Remington Rand, 54
Remote sensing, 133, 135–137, 142–146, 243–245, 250, 275, 278
Remote-sensing satellites, 142–146, 243–245, 274
Replacement demand, 48–54
Reprography, 96
Resolution
  display, 111, 262, 264–267
  graphics, 33, 64, 258–260, 263–264, 264–267
  image, 140–141, 264–266
Retrieval of information, 46, 98–99, 157, 219–222
Return on investment, 41, 87, 91–94, 97
Returns to scale, 101–102, 106
Reuters (UK), 148
Reynolds and Reynolds, 159
Ricoh (Japan), 21
RISC (reduced-instruction-set computer), xvii, 109–111, 120, 186–192, 200–201, 216–217
Ritchie, Dennis, 208
Robot, robotics, robotization, 73, 87, 107–108, 137, 143, 235, 274
Rockwell International Corporation, 73, 112, 166, 175
Rohrer, Heinrich, 180
ROLM, 56, 72, 82, 107
Royalties, 68, 79–80
Ruska, Ernst, 180

Sales
  of mainframes, 45, 46, 62–63, 78–79
  of microcomputers, 62–63
  of minicomputers, 62–63
  of PCs, 62–68, 79, 132, 159
  of semiconductors, 74
  of vision systems, 142–146
  per employee, 76–77
  volume of, 48–54, 150, 153
Sandia, 166
Sanyo (Japan), 176
Satellite(s),
  communications, 139, 250
  remote-sensing, 142–146, 243–245, 275
Saturation, 9, 146, 147–150, 279
Saving(s)
  on costs, 13, 75–82
  on personnel, 75, 87–89
Scale
  economies of, 124–125, 153
  logarithmic, 3–33
  natural, 5–11
  returns to, 101–102, 106
  values, 280
Scanning tunnelling microscopy, 186
Schlumberger, xiii, 107
Schumacher, E., 267
Scientific Computer Systems, 42
SDC (Systems Development Corporation) 46
SDI (Space Defense Initiative, US) 74, 277
Segment, segmentation of market, xviii, 134–160, 279–282
Seidel, Ludwig, 230
Sellers' market, xx, 132
Semiconductor(s)
  design of, 32–33
  intrinsic, 165, 197
  Japan's industry, xiii, 16–20, 32–33, 73
  market for, 135–137
  n-type and p-type, 165–166
  organic, 197–199, 201
  penetration of, 95
  sales of, 74
  US industry, xii–xiii, 16–20, 32–33, 70–71, 73
Sensors, 115, 140, 166
Service bureau, 112–113, 224–225
Shockley, William, 169
Siemens (Germany), 82
  GOLEM (information retrieval system), 46, 221
  innovative architecture, 192
  mainframes, 37
  R&D policy and spending, 166
  telecommunications, 72
Silicon
  amorphous and crystalline, 168–169
  doped, xvi, 161, 164–167
  wafers, 71, 178
SIMPLEX (algorithm), 223, 233
Simulation, 92, 96, 99, 102, 140, 142, 155, 220
Sinclair, Clive, 78, 178

Sinclair Research, 68, 78, 178, 200, 268
Software
　applications, 124–125, 219–224, 235–237
　case histories, 203–211
　cost of, 47, 57–61, 80, 202, 277, 280
　custom-made, xvii, 47, 106, 109, 126–131
　intelligent, 228–238
　investment in, 224, 239
　mainframe, 127–131, 211–228
　market for, 127–131, 135–138
　market model for, 130–131
　microcomputer, 68, 215, 223–224
　PC, 127–128
　portable, xvii, 203, 208, 223–224, 225, 239
　purpose-driven, 203–207
　small-scale/high impact, 208–210
　software engineering, xix, 73–74, 227, 239–240, 276
　　environment, 203–204, 215–217, 229, 235, 240
　　gap, xii, xvii, xx, 161, 202–240
　　industry, 32, 127–131, 225–227
　　packages, 46–47, 68, 126–131, 235–237
　　production, 207, 210
　　structure, 211–215, 225–228
　　tools, 212–215
Solow, Robert, 102
Sony (Japan), 140, 166, 176, 262, 265
Specialization strategy, 34, 68, 82, 133, 279
Speech recognition, 234, 238, 247, 254, 255–258, 275
　costs involved, 256–258
　vocabulary size, 256–258
Sperry
　Burroughs–Sperry merger (Unisys), 31, 72–73
　COBOL (programming language), 204
　level of indebtedness, 78
　mainframes, 46, 54
　operating systems (OS), 46
　R&D policy and spending, 70, 72
　voice recognition, 257–258
Spot Image (France, 142
Spreadsheets, 219, 223–224, 264, 272
STAIRS (information retrieval system), 46, 221
Stand-alone systems, xvii, 29, 33, 98, 104, 114–115, 121, 124–125, 219, 222
Standards, 214, 239
　conformance with, 214
　generic for all industries, 159–160
　IBM and, 67
　international, 240, 281
　protocol, 124–125, 160
Standardization, 207, 209–210, 224, 240, 253, 281
STAR terminal, 210, 254
Statistical analysis packages, 219, 222
Storage
　CD-ROM, 258–265, 270–272
　floppy disk, 172–175, 259–261
　high-density magnetic and optical, 171–176, 262, 265, 276
　juke-box, 262
　magnetic tape, 171, 259–265
　optical, 171–173, 165–176, 259–265
　optical versus magnetic, 275
　RAM, 177–180, 262–263, 264
　storage access time and transfer rate, 262–264, 276
　capacity, 39, 112–113, 119, 160, 250, 263
　cost, 12, 13, 21, 28, 113
　density, 171–180, 197–199
　hierarchy, 111, 181–183, 213, 258–265
　media, 21–22, 62, 162, 171–176, 182, 243, 258–265
　Winchester disk, 172–174, 257
　WORM optical, 265, 276
Storage Technology Corporation, 77–78, 176
Strategy, xii–xxi, 162, 277–282
　business, 280–282
　change in, 277–282
　Digital Equipment product, 39
　IBM product, 37–39
　product, xii, 35, 37–39, 56
　specialization, 34, 68, 82, 133, 280
Subsidy, 73–74
Substitute materials, 168–169, 198–199
Substitution, xviii, 4, 33, 59, 101, 242
Sun Microsystems, 237
Supercomputers, 36–37, 56, 83, 156, 192
　market for, 42, 56, 278
　mini, 42

Superconductivity, 164–165, 278
Superminicomputers, 55
Switching
  cost of, 26–29, 40–41, 60–61, 72, 119–120
  digital, 112
  speeds, 194, 196
Symbolics, Inc., 237
System(s)
  complexity of, 229–234
  decision support, 90, 99–100, 143, 221
  distributed, xvii, 37, 122, 126, 132
  expert, 99, 129, 157, 162, 198, 202, 235–238, 263–264
  information, 80, 219–222, 279
  integrated, 83, 114–121, 258
  knowledge-based, 73–74, 235–237
  microcomputer operating, 68, 215
  open, 66–67, 209–210
  operating (OS), 47–48, 204, 212–213, 214–215, 216–217, 228, 263
  proprietary operating, 66–67, 214
  stand-alone, xvii, 29, 33, 98, 104, 114–115, 121, 124–125, 219, 222
  systems analysis, xvi–xvii
    design, 106, 111, 132
    software, 203, 211–212, 214–215, 225
  telecommunications, 138–139, 250
  turnkey, 112, 159
  vision, 141–146, 277, 280

Tandon, 65–66
Tandy, 63–67, 268
Technology
  benefit from (new), 93–96
  choice of, 90–96
  computer, 72, 171–180, 278
  demand-driven, 280–282
  information, xiv, xix–xxi, 68, 83–85, 88, 89, 91, 96, 98, 100, 151–152, 164, 276–281
  new office, 85, 94, 96–100, 105, 108, 281
  optical, 172–198, 264, 278
  RISC, 109–111, 180, 186–192, 200–201, 216
  semiconductor, 73–74, 164–169
Teknowledge, 129, 235
Tektronix, 237

Telecommunications
  costs and tariffs, 26–33
  market, 135–139, 156
  R&D in, 72, 74
  systems, 138–139, 250
Telemetry, 133, 135–137
Telerate, 158
Teleshopping, 274
Teletex Service, 206
Teletext, 113
Terminals, 112, 148, 158, 221, 252, 266
  integrated voice-data, 120
  intelligent, smart, 33, 153–154, 157, 279
  multifunctional, 116
Texas Instruments (TI)
  artificial intelligence, 237
  bubble memory, 175
  imaging systems, xviii
  integrated circuits (ICs), 171
  patent licensing, 79–80
  PCs, 63–64, 67
  R&D policy and spending, 166
  semiconductors, xii, xiii, 20, 75
  speech recognition, 256–258
Text processor, processing, 55, 68, 99, 115, 219, 223–224
Thesauri, 221
Thinking Machines Corporation, 192
Thomson, Ken, 208
Thomson CSF (France), 166
Thorn-EMI, 260
Tomita, Tetsuro, 147–152
TOP (Technical Office Protocol), 206, 240
Toshiba (Japan), xiii, 20–21, 176
Trade-off, xvii, 109, 111–114, 127, 129, 132
  technical/economic, xix, 84, 114, 122
  system design, 111, 232
Transmission
  cost, 26–28, 40–41, 60–61
  standards, 120
Transnational broadband networks, 249–250
Transphasor, 195–196
Transputer, 191–192
Trend(s)
  cost, xix, 11–15, 23–25, 29, 151
  market, 128, 158–159
Triad Systems, 159
Trilogy Systems, 71, 72, 178, 200

TRW, 73, 128, 166
Turnkey system(s), 112, 159

UNESCO, 152
Unisys (Burroughs-Sperry), 72-73
Univac, 31, 46, 54
University of California, 110
University of Texas, 155
UNIX
  development, 124-125, 208-209
  operating system, 47, 208-209, 213, 215-217, 239, 263
Upgrade, upgrading, 43-44, 47, 55, 85, 97, 104, 199
US Department of Defense, 204
US Navy, 204, 206
User(s)
  business, 105, 106-107
  closed groups, 112
  corporate, 66, 83
  end-user, 123, 126, 132, 134, 218-228
  feedback, 280
  needs and requirements, 107, 114, 126, 132, 133, 205
User-friendly interface, 252-258

Value-added services, 102, 112
Vector processing, 185-187
Vectorizing, 246, 249, 259-262
Verbatim, 265
Victor Technology, 64
Videoconference, videoconferencing, 158, 259
Videotex, xii, 83, 120, 252-253, 273
Virtual memory, storage, 190, 204
Vision
  aids, 141-146
  processing, 140-141
  systems, 141-146, 278, 281
VLSI (very large-scale integration, integrated circuits) 73, 79-80
Voice
  as I/O technology, 255-258, 274-275
  characteristics, 255-256

data integration, 120, 250
digitization, 256-258
recognition, xvii, 255-258
Voice Systems International, 256-258
Von Neumann, Johan, ix, 180
Von Neumann architecture, ix, 163, 180-183, 187, 190-191, 226, 232

Wafer scale technology, 178, 180, 200
Wang Laboratories, xiii
  imaging systems, 140
  integrated systems, 115, 126, 132, 206
  level of indebtedness, 77-78
  marketing, 107
  PCs, 67
  productivity, 77
  staff reductions, 76
  Wang-Net, 126
Wear and tear, 43-44
Weber, Ron, 130-131
Wilson, Harold, 268
Winchester disk, 22, 172-174, 257, 263
Word processing (processor), 96, 98-100, 115-116, 129, 131, 219, 263, 278
Workforce, 75-76, 101-103, 104
Workstation, 96, 98, 120, 124-125, 254, 258, 279
  integrated (office), 114-115, 120, 254
  multifunction, 99, 210, 237, 264

Xerox, xiii
  artificial intelligence (AI), 237
  Ethernet, 124-126, 210
  imaging systems, 140
  integrated systems, 126, 132, 206, 210, 237, 254
  level of indebtedness, 77-78
  office automation, 120, 206, 210, 254
  product strategy, 21, 38, 206
  PCs, 63
  R&D policy and spending, 70, 71, 210, 265
  text processors, 210
X/OPEN, 216